Stand!

Race and Ethnicity

Contending Ideas and Opinions

Academic Editor
Barbara Mori

California Polytechnic State University, San Luis Obispo

coursewise
publishing
inc.

Bellevue • Boulder • Dubuque • Madison • St. Paul

Our mission at **Coursewise** is to help students make connections—linking theory to practice and the classroom to the outside world. Learners are motivated to synthesize ideas when course materials are placed in a context they recognize. By providing gateways to contemporary and enduring issues, **Coursewise** publications will expand students' awareness of and context for the course subject.

For more information on **Coursewise,** visit us at our web site: http://www.coursewise.com

To order an examination copy, contact Houghton Mifflin Sixth Floor Media: 800–565–6247 (voice); 800–565–6236 (fax).

Coursewise Publishing Editorial Staff

Thomas Doran, ceo/publisher: Environmental Science/Geography/Journalism/Marketing/Speech
Edgar Laube, publisher: Geography/Political Science/Psychology/Sociology
Linda Meehan Avenarius, publisher: **Courselinks**™
Sue Pulvermacher-Alt, publisher: Education/Health/Gender Studies
Victoria Putman, publisher: Anthropology/Philosophy/Religion
Tom Romaniak, publisher: Business/Criminal Justice/Economics
Kathleen Schmitt, publishing assistant
Gail Hodge, executive producer

Coursewise Production Staff

Lori A. Blosch, permissions coordinator
Mary Monner, production coordinator
Victoria Putman, production manager

Note: Readings in this book appear exactly as they were published. Thus, inconsistencies in style and usage among the different readings are likely.

Cover photo: Ian Lawrence/1998/nonstock

Interior design and cover design by Jeff Storm

Library of Congress Catalog Card Number: 99-067986

ISBN 0-395-97379-1

Printed in the United States of America by Coursewise Publishing, Inc.
7 North Pinckney Street, Suite 346, Madison, WI 53703

10 9 8 7 6 5 4 3 2 1

Edgar Laube
Coursewise Publishing

As a middle-aged Caucasian male, I've never been forced to confront some of the challenges that members of minority groups face. I've never been "profiled" by police as worthy of suspicion due to my skin color, my neighborhood has never been redlined by companies that insure houses, and my English (my first language) is as clear as . . . Bill Murray's. Accordingly, I do not suffer, either personally or institutionally, from some of the hazards or indifference that mainstream society can accord minority groups.

But it wasn't always so. Thirty years ago, many in my generation turned against mainstream values and acted out their opposition in a variety of ways. The acting out might have been protesting the war in Vietnam or becoming a Buddhist. We "new" people embraced a huge range of thought and action. However, in the eyes of many, we all had one thing in common: we were "different." And regardless of what you wore or what you said, your hair was the thing that symbolized the differentness.

My hair was long for a few years, which allowed total strangers to stereotype me and treat me accordingly. The sheriff in a small mountain town in Colorado used to shine his squad car's searchlight into my house windows at night. A state trooper in New Jersey stopped my van for no reason and spent an hour searching it for drugs. And an off-duty posse volunteer picked me up hitchhiking, then pulled a gun from under the seat and told me how people like me were ruining the United States. Then he made me get out in the middle of nowhere (noooo problem). And there were the landlords who wouldn't rent to people with long hair, the employers who wouldn't hire them, and the restaurants who wouldn't serve them. It felt like a war, although I never spent a night in jail or got seriously hurt.

Having experienced the power of negative stereotyping and seen the kind of fear and anger that total strangers can harbor toward others, I tend to listen to complaints of racism and bias and assume that they're true. And I tend to hear charges of reverse racism, such as the complaints about affirmative action, and think they're bogus. People who have never experienced discrimination just have no clue about how powerful it is. And, yes, that's my bias.

And so I commend you on taking this course, and I hope that you make an honest effort to think about these issues and inform yourself. Barbara Mori has chosen a wonderful set of issues that look at these problems in real life. I think you'll be able to relate. Along the way, check out the rich resources at the **Courselinks**™ site for Race and Ethnicity (http://www.courselinks.com). And don't hesitate to let Barbara and me know what you think. Good luck!

from the Academic Editor

Barbara Mori
California Polytechnic State University, San Luis Obispo

Barbara Mori is a professor of sociology in the Social Sciences Department at California Polytechnic State University in San Luis Obispo. She received her Ph.D. in sociology from the University of Hawaii–Manoa. She has received grants and fellowships from the Japan Foundation and California State University programs.

Professor Mori's other books include Americans Studying the Tea Ceremony: The Internationalizing of a Japanese Traditional Art *(Edwin Mellon Press, 1991) and a chapter in* Re-Imaging Japanese Women *(edited by Anne Imamura, University of California Press, 1996). Her manuscript on Japanese studying the tea ceremony is currently being considered for publication. She has also published several articles on the tea ceremony and traditional arts in Japan.*

Professor Mori spent many years teaching English as a second language in Korea, Japan, and China. She spent two years learning the tea ceremony in Kyoto and also studied calligraphy in Japan and China for several years.

Professor Mori teaches courses in global race relations, American minorities, the sociology of gender, social theory, and Japanese and Chinese culture.

The study of race and ethnicity began with the application of the scientific method to the study of human beings. The questions that were raised about human beings were the same as those raised about the physical world: What do they consist of, and how do they work? To study something, you need to define it. Then you need to collect examples so you know the range of items under the definition. This is the beginning of taxonomy. Researchers observe and make lists.

The easiest phenomena to observe are the physical aspects of being human. This is especially true when the researcher does not know the languages spoken. So early researchers collected information on the physical characteristics of human beings. They looked for characteristics that could be observed in both living and dead members of different groups, such as head shapes and sizes, bone lengths, hair types, skin colors, brain capacities, and eye and nose shapes. They made lists that enumerated similarities and differences, just as was done in chemistry and biology.

Scientists are often asked to explain the reasons behind observations before they have a chance to test any theories. Thus, ideologies about the meaning and cause of particular human physical characteristics sprang up readily, without much in the way of real investigation. These ideologies followed the religious, philosophical, social, and political thinking of the times. We rarely ask why hydrogen is different from oxygen, but we do ask why some people are different from others. Thus, the study of race, the physical characteristics of human beings, was begun. Differences, rather than similarities, needed to be explained to people who took their society as the norm for human behavior (ethnocentrism).

When race proved to be insufficient to answer many of the questions concerning similarities and differences, another aspect of human beings came under scrutiny—group behavior. Why do you do this, and why do you do it this way? Explaining human behavior became the goal in all the diverse areas of human society. Culture, and later, culture of specific groups (ethnicity) became the focus of attention. However, as groups came to have further contact with one another, the isolation that produced and enabled the development of various specific cultural practices lessened, and people began borrowing from one another and also trying to get others to adopt their particular practices. Cultural defusion and maintenance are now concerns for many groups.

Human physical and cultural diversity has existed for a long time, but the approach to understanding and explaining this diversity changed as the scientific method became the preferred way of explaining the world. We study human diversity because it is part of the world in which we live, and to understand ourselves, we compare ourselves with others. We might ask, "Why are we similar?" but those things that we know rarely need explanation. So our approach focuses on explaining diversity rather than similarity.

Why study race and ethnicity? As the poet once said, "No man is an island. No man stands alone." We all live on this planet together, and at this point in time, there is no place else to go. Human beings are social animals who cannot develop normally without relationships to one another. This is true in the family, the community, the nation, and the world. We live and work with people of different backgrounds, and our attitude toward difference affects our successes. We can view differences as enrichments or as problems to be overcome. When we encounter someone who is different, we choose to respond in one of three ways: We can be friendly and curious, hostile, or indifferent. The talents, skills, philosophies, and knowledge that individuals from various ethnic, religious, social, and political perspectives bring to their interactions with others can produce innovation and creativity. But if the environments are hostile and if differences are viewed as impediments, misunderstanding and conflict result.

Education helps us learn about the different approaches to life that various groups under diverse conditions developed. These different approaches can help us to make our own decisions and create a prosperous, supportive, and enjoyable society. In the United States, this is what Americans have declared to be their purpose: to create a society where individuals are free to develop their talents, abilities, and interests in the pursuit of happiness. The U.S. Constitution and Bill of Rights purport to be neutral documents that proclaim a specific role for government, clear protections for individuals from group pressure and coercion, and a basic respect for the people, who are to govern and make decisions for themselves.

"We, the people" includes men and women, rich and poor, old and young, cautious and adventurous, wise and foolish, short and tall, optimists and pessimists—all who are citizens. (This is an important distinction. Nothing is promised to anyone who is not a citizen.) U.S. history demonstrates the expansion of coverage from an elite few to a more inclusive general populace and the elimination of exclusion based on race, gender, income, and educational level. Americans believe that their form of government and society is a model for others, and they actively encourage the adoption of their principles outside U.S. borders. Americans' ability to live up to their own values is tested. Sometimes, they succeed, and sometimes, they fail.

Diversity is part of the American past. Diverse languages, cultures, and values have long been a part of American history, even if that history is sometimes selectively told. Diversity is also part of the American future. Although Americans may come to share many of their practices and ideas, they are not becoming homogeneous. They relish their uniqueness, as well as rely on their similarities. *Stand! Race and Ethnicity* presents some of the issues that confront American society as it struggles with American diversity.

I would like to thank Ed Laube, of **Coursewise Publishing,** for his support and commitment to this project. His patience and gentle prodding were appreciated and enabled the completion of this book.

I dedicate this book to my son, Christopher Yoshitake, who struggles to live in a world that is enriched but also complicated by diversity. *Kodomo no tame ni* [for the sake of the children] is a Japanese phrase used to understand the approach to their hardships taken by Japanese who came to settle in the United States in the twentieth century. This is also one of the reasons I was willing to take on this project: For the sake of the children, our future.

WiseGuide Introduction

Question Authority

Critical Thinking and Bumper Stickers

The bumper sticker said: Question Authority. This is a simple directive that goes straight to the heart of critical thinking. The issue is not whether the authority is right or wrong; it's the questioning process that's important. Questioning helps you develop awareness and a clearer sense of what you think. That's critical thinking.

Critical thinking is a new label for an old approach to learning—that of challenging all ideas, hypotheses, and assumptions. In the physical and life sciences, systematic questioning and testing methods (known as the scientific method) help verify information, and objectivity is the benchmark on which all knowledge is pursued. In the social sciences, however, where the goal is to study people and their behavior, things get fuzzy. It's one thing for the chemistry experiment to work out as predicted, or for the petri dish to yield a certain result. It's quite another matter, however, in the social sciences, where the subject is ourselves. Objectivity is harder to achieve.

Although you'll hear critical thinking defined in many different ways, it really boils down to analyzing the ideas and messages that you receive. What are you being asked to think or believe? Does it make sense, objectively? Using the same facts and considerations, could you reasonably come up with a different conclusion? And, why does this matter in the first place? As the bumper sticker urged, question authority. Authority can be a textbook, a politician, a boss, a big sister, or an ad on television. Whatever the message, learning to question it appropriately is a habit that will serve you well for a lifetime. And in the meantime, thinking critically will certainly help you be course wise.

Getting Connected

This reader is a tool for connected learning. This means that the readings and other learning aids explained here will help you to link classroom theory to real-world issues. They will help you to think critically and to make long-lasting learning connections. Feedback from both instructors and students has helped us to develop some suggestions on how you can wisely use this connected learning tool.

WiseGuide Pedagogy

A wise reader is better able to be a critical reader. Therefore, we want to help you get wise about the articles in this reader. Each section of a *Stand!* reader has three tools to help you: the WiseGuide Intro, the WiseGuide Wrap-Up, and the Frame the Debate review form.

WiseGuide Intro

In the WiseGuide Intro, the Academic Editor gives you an overview of the issue covered in that section and explains why particular articles were selected and what's important about them. You'll also find questions designed to stimulate critical thinking. Wise students will keep these questions in mind as they read the articles for each issue. When you finish reading the articles for an issue, check your understanding. Can you answer the questions? If not, go back and reread the articles. The Academic Editor has written sample responses for many of the questions, and you'll find these online at the **Courselinks**™ site for this book. More about **Courselinks** in a minute. . . .

WiseGuide Wrap-Up

Be course wise and develop a thorough understanding of the topics covered in this course. The WiseGuide Wrap-Up at the end of each issue will help you do just that with concluding comments or summary points that repeat what's most important to understand from the articles you just read.

In addition, we try to get you wired up by providing a list of select Internet resources—what we call R.E.A.L. web sites because they're **R**elevant, **E**nhanced, **A**pproved, and **L**inked. The information at R.E.A.L. sites will enhance your understanding of a topic. (Remember to start at http://www.courselinks.com so that if any of these sites have changed, you'll have the latest link.)

Frame the Debate Review Form

At the end of the book is the Frame the Debate review form. Your instructor may ask you to complete this form as an assignment or for extra credit. If nothing else, consider doing it on your own to help you critically think about the readings for each issue.

Prompts at the end of each article encourage you to complete this review form. Feel free to copy the form and use it as needed.

The Courselinks™ Site

http://www.courselinks.com

The **Courselinks** site for your course area is a wonderful world of integrated web resources designed to help you with your course work. This is where the readings in this book and the key topics of your course are linked to an exciting array of online learning tools. Here you will find carefully selected readings, web links, quizzes, worksheets, and more, tailored to your course and approved as connected learning tools. The ever-changing, always interesting **Courselinks** site features a number of carefully integrated resources designed to help you be course wise. These include:

- **R.E.A.L. Sites**   At the core of a **Courselinks** site is the list of R.E.A.L. sites. This is a select group of web sites for studying, not surfing. Like the readings in this book, these sites have been selected, reviewed, and approved by the Academic Editor. The R.E.A.L. sites are arranged by topic and are annotated with short descriptions and key words to make them easier for you to use for reference or research. With R.E.A.L. sites, you're studying approved resources within seconds—and not wasting precious time surfing unproven sites.

- **Editor's Choice**   Here you'll find updates on news related to your course, with links to the actual online sources. This is also where we'll tell you about changes to the site and about online events.

- **Course Overview**   This is a general description of the typical course in this area of study. While your instructor will provide specific course objectives, this overview helps you place the course in a generic context and offers you an additional reference point.

- **Take a Stand!** Register your opinion about the issues presented in your *Stand!* reader online. You can see what students and faculty members across the country are thinking about the controversial issues presented in your text. Then add your own vote.

- **www.orksheet** Focus your trip to a R.E.A.L. site with the www.orksheet. Each of the 10 to 15 questions will prompt you to take in the best that site has to offer. Use this tool for self-study, or if required, email it to your instructor.

- **Course Quiz** The questions on this self-scoring quiz are related to articles in the reader, information at R.E.A.L. sites, and other course topics, and will help you pinpoint areas you need to study. Only you will know your score— it's an easy, risk-free way to keep pace!

- **Topic Key** The online Topic Key is a listing of the main topics in your course, and it correlates with the Topic Key that appears in this reader. This handy reference tool also links directly to those R.E.A.L. sites that are especially appropriate to each topic, bringing you integrated online resources within seconds!

- **Message Center** Share your ideas with fellow students and instructors, in your class or in classes around the world, by using the Message Center. There are links to both a real-time chat room and a message forum, which are accessible all day, every day. Watch for scheduled CourseChat events throughout the semester.

- **Student Lounge** Drop by the Student Lounge, a virtual "hangout" with links to professional associations in your course area, online article review forms, and site feedback forms. Take a look around and give us your feedback. We're open to remodeling the Lounge per your suggestions.

Building Better Stand! Readers

Please tell us what you think of this *Stand!* volume so we can improve the next one. Here's how you can help:

1. Visit our **Coursewise** site at: http://www.coursewise.com
2. Click on *Stand!* Then select the Building Better *Stand!* Readers Form for your book.
3. Forms and instructions for submission are available online.

Tell us what you think—did the readings and online materials help you make some learning connections? Were some materials more helpful than others? Thanks in advance for helping us build better *Stand!* readers.

Student Internships

If you enjoy evaluating these articles or would like to help us evaluate the **Courselinks** site for this course, check out the **Coursewise** Student Internship Program. For more information, visit: http://www.coursewise.com/intern.html

Contents

At **Coursewise,** we're publishing connected learning tools. That means that the book you are holding is only a part of this publication. You'll also want to harness the integrated resources that **Coursewise** has developed at the fun and highly useful **Courselinks**™ web site for *Stand! Race and Ethnicity.* Visit http://www.coursewise.com.

section 3

Should English Be Our Official Language?

In Reading 5, Geoffrey Nunberg explores the connection between English language usage and American political values and practices. In Reading 6, Eric Hobsbawm explores the relationship between language and culture as a new definition of the nation.

section 4

Does Ethnic Humor Improve Group Relations?

In Reading 7, A. Michael Johnson explores the issue of taking offense at jokes. His research shows that joke-tellers are more focused on the intent to amuse than are their listeners. Audience members are less aware of this intent and are more likely to see the joke as an expression of the teller's attitudes. In Reading 8, David Segal argues that risqué humor has social value in that it can defuse tensions. He also believes that laughing at a stereotype can serve to undermine it. Reading 9 from *The New Republic* offers etiquette guidelines for telling jokes.

section 5

Should Hate Be a Crime?

In Reading 10, James B. Jacobs expresses concern about the issue of prosecuting individuals on the basis of motive, which allows for a person's beliefs to become the focus of the prosecution. Jacobs feels that court cases will come to focus on areas that are protected by the First Amendment, rather than on the actions of the defendant. In Reading 11, John Kleinig similarly opposes the enactment of hate crime legislation and expresses concern about the impact of such laws on society. Kleinig discusses arguments that Ohio public defender Susan Gellman made at a Symposium on Penalty Enhancement for Hate Crimes at Arizona State University.

and social position. In Reading 18, Reuven Feuerstein and Alex Kozulin focus on issues of cognitive assessment. They find I.Q. testing as presented by Charles Murray and Richard Herrnstein to be deficient due to a static definition of intelligence, a rejection of change, and the limited scope of the I.Q. test. In Reading 19, Charles Murray and Richard Herrnstein argue that "the best and indeed the only answer to the problem of group differences is an energetic and uncompromising recommitment to individualism."

section 9

Is Race a Meaningful Concept in Understanding Human Behavior?

Claude Levi-Strauss has been an important voice in pointing out the significance of race and culture, and the relative contributions of these concepts to an understanding of human societies. In Reading 20, he focuses on the contributions of our biology and our cultures to a realization of what it is to be human. Jonathan Marks continues the discussion in Reading 21. He raises important questions about how we attribute explanations for human behavior to biology or the social environment.

section 10

Is Participation in Sports the Best Avenue to Minority Success and Acceptance?

In Reading 22, Gerald R. Gems presents a concise history of Black and Native American football players. He explores the impact of sports participation on the changing identity of individuals and the use of sports as a means to enter the wider society. In Reading 23, Robert M. Sellers and Gabriel P. Kuperminc look at Black college students in sports programs and express concern with the degree to which an emphasis on sports has skewed the goals of the Black community.

section 11

Does Teaching Mathematics or Science in Traditional Ways Discriminate Against Minorities?

In Reading 24, Dirk J. Struik looks at the history of the teaching of mathematics and points out a Eurocentric bias that leads us to ignore, devalue, or distort contributions from outside Western culture. Craig E. Nelson focuses in Reading 25 on improving the teaching of math and science with methods that do not include a middle-class bias.

section 12

What Is American Identity?

In Reading 26, Jerry Adler discusses the emergence of class identity as a new factor in the definition of what it is to be an American. He also explores the importance of economic and lifestyle issues. In Reading 27, Robert Bellah focuses on the relationship between culture and institutions, and looks at the role that educational institutions and the media play in creating a dominant culture.

Topic Key

This Topic Key is an important tool for learning. It will help you integrate this reader into your course studies. Listed below, in alphabetical order, are important topics covered in this volume. Below each topic you'll find the reading numbers and titles, and R.E.A.L. web site addresses, relating to that topic. Note that the Topic Key might not include every topic your instructor chooses to emphasize. If you don't find the topic you're looking for in the Topic Key, check the index or the online topic key at the **Courselinks**™ site.

Acculturation
1   Ten Myths about Affirmative Action
2   Color Code
3   Two Languages Are Better Than One
4   Bilingualism and Education
5   Lingo Jingo: English Only and the New Nativism
15 From Yellow Peril through Model Minority to Renewed Yellow Peril
16 Asian Americans in the Public Service: Success, Diversity, and Discrimination
22 The Construction, Negotiation, and Transformation of Racial Identity in American Football: A Study of Native and African Americans
23 Goal Discrepancy in African American Male Student-Athletes' Unrealistic Expectations for Careers in Professional Sports
25 Student Diversity Requires Different Approaches to College Teaching, Even in Math and Science
26 Sweet Land of Liberties
27 Is There a Common American Culture?

People for the American Way
http://www.pfaw.org/

Center for the American Founding
http://www.founding.org/

National Clearinghouse for Bilingual Education
http://www.ncbe.gwu.edu/

Review of Data on Asian Americans
http://www.pafb.af.mil/deomi/asir.htm

Affirmative Action
1   Ten Myths about Affirmative Action
2   Color Code
16 Asian Americans in the Public Service: Success, Diversity, and Discrimination
17 Measuring Intelligence: Bell, Book, and Scandal
18 "The Bell Curve": Getting the Facts Straight
19 Race, Genes and I.Q.—An Apologia: The Case for Conservative Multiculturalism
20 Race, History and Culture
21 Science and Race
23 Goal Discrepancy in African American Male Student-Athletes' Unrealistic Expectations for Careers in Professional Sports

Americans United for Affirmative Action
http://www.auaa.org/

The Feminist Majority Foundation Online
http://www.feminist.org/

American Civil Rights Institute
http://www.acri.org/

Anti-Semitism
1   Ten Myths about Affirmative Action
2   Color Code
6   Language, Culture, and National Identity
10 Should Hate Be a Crime?
11 Penalty Enhancement for Hate Crimes
21 Science and Race

Anti-Defamation League
http://www.adl.org/

Southern Poverty Law Center
http://www.splcenter.org/

The Nizkor Project
http://www.nizkor.org/

Assimilation
1   Ten Myths about Affirmative Action
2   Color Code
3   Two Languages Are Better Than One
4   Bilingualism and Education
5   Lingo Jingo: English Only and the New Nativism
6   Language, Culture, and National Identity
7   The "Only Joking" Defense: Attribution Bias or Impression Management?
8   Excuuuse Me: The Case for Offensive Humor
9   Tell Me Another One
15 From Yellow Peril through Model Minority to Renewed Yellow Peril
16 Asian Americans in the Public Service: Success, Diversity, and Discrimination
22 The Construction, Negotiation, and Transformation of Racial Identity in American Football: A Study of Native and African Americans
23 Goal Discrepancy in African American Male Student-Athletes' Unrealistic Expectations for Careers in Professional Sports
26 Sweet Land of Liberties
27 Is There a Common American Culture?

National Association for Bilingual Education
http://www.nabe.org/

Chinese American Identity
http://www.owlnet.rice.edu/~jenlin/HIST310/main.html

National Association for the Advancement of Colored People
http://www.naacp.org/

Citizenship
2   Color Code
5   Lingo Jingo: English Only and the New Nativism
6   Language, Culture, and National Identity
15 From Yellow Peril through Model Minority to Renewed Yellow Peril
27 Is There a Common American Culture?

American Civil Liberties Union
http://www.aclu.org/

People for the American Way
http://www.pfaw.org/

Center for the American Founding
http://www.founding.org/

Class
3   Two Languages Are Better Than One
4   Bilingualism and Education
15 From Yellow Peril through Model Minority to Renewed Yellow Peril
16 Asian Americans in the Public Service: Success, Diversity, and Discrimination
17 Measuring Intelligence: Bell, Book, and Scandal
18 "The Bell Curve": Getting the Facts Straight
25 Student Diversity Requires Different Approaches to College Teaching, Even in Math and Science
26 Sweet Land of Liberties
27 Is There a Common American Culture?

Chinese American Identity
http://www.owlnet.rice.edu/~jenlin/HIST310/main.html

Center for the American Founding
http://www.founding.org/

Courts
1   Ten Myths about Affirmative Action
2   Color Code
10 Should Hate Be a Crime?
11 Penalty Enhancement for Hate Crimes
27 Is There a Common American Culture?

Tolerance

Xenophobia

section 1 | Is Affirmative Action Fair?

Take a Closer Look

1. Are affirmative action programs the same as quotas?

2. Are affirmative action programs necessary?

3. Do affirmative action programs provide equal opportunities?

4. Do affirmative action programs stigmatize minorities?

5. Should affirmative action programs be continued?

WiseGuide Intro

Is affirmative action a milestone or a millstone? Current debates are focused on whether affirmative action policies are necessary and should be continued. One concern is that affirmative action is not a uniform set of policies and laws. Its policies and programs are diverse, as is their application. Which particular policies are under discussion should be clearly indicated in debates about the efficacy of affirmative action.

The affirmative action policy or practice most frequently opposed is the use of quotas. Quotas are specifically forbidden in the Civil Rights Act of 1964, and few affirmative action policies would be considered quota policies. Quotas have different uses. In the past, racially discriminating practices used quotas to exclude rather than to include. We have become sensitive to practices of exclusion and see them as unfair. Practices of inclusion can be mistaken in their intent.

Another important point in the affirmative action debate is the concern for equity. The United States prides itself on offering equal opportunity. The initial definition of who was considered a U.S. citizen was limited to a small percentage of the population and was based on race, gender, wealth, education, and age. Over time, this definition has clearly expanded. Today, every American should be treated equally under the law and is entitled to the education, health-care, and Social Security benefits that government provides through taxation of all. Yet, not everyone is treated equitably, and equal outcomes are not guaranteed.

How do we define equity, and how do we know when equity is occurring? Statistical disparity is one way of knowing whether equity is operating. If the opportunities are, in fact, available to all, then we should expect to see diversity in any social or occupational group that reflects the diversity in the total population. If this is not the case, then we know that something is directing members of one group away from or toward a particular occupation or practice. Statistics can tell us if this is occurring, but not necessarily why or what to do about it.

The sports concepts of "fair play according to the rules," "a level playing field," and "running a race" all apply to affirmative action. The concept of "fair play according to the rules" assumes that the rules themselves are fair and impartial, which is not always the case, as the "Jim Crow laws" of the past illustrate. However, to change the situation, you must change the rules. This focuses energy on discussions of the rules and process, rather than on the situation.

The concept of "a level playing field" assumes that only the effort of the individual or the team will make a difference in the outcome. How do we know that the social, economic, or political playing field is level? If the playing field is not level, how do we level it? This is where affirmative action comes in. Finally, how do we know when the playing field has become level? In other words, when are affirmative action policies no longer necessary to keep the playing field level? Some people cite the gains of individuals to indicate that U.S. society has achieved a level playing field. Others cite differences in income, wealth, health care, standard of living, education, employment, and treatment of individuals to indicate that more needs to be done.

The concept of running a race also applies to affirmative action. Do the runners begin the race with a fair start, or have some runners been given an advantage? Are some runners burdened by disadvantages like extra weights, poor training, or poor nutrition? Are other runners unfairly advantaged by having a head start in the race due to the successes of their fathers? What can we do to overcome unfair past practices and empower newer runners in the race? Do these policies take into account unsportsmanlike practices that have enabled some to get to the head of the field? While there is a concern for equity in society, there is no consensus on what it looks like, how to get there, or when it is achieved.

Scott Plous thinks that the case against affirmative action rests on myth and misunderstanding. In Reading 1, he discusses and refutes ten myths he identifies as skewing the discussion on affirmative action. He says that research indicates that the public is specifically against quotas, set-asides, and "reverse discrimination," but not necessarily opposed to other forms of affirmative action. According to Plous, "Unless preexisting inequities are corrected or otherwise taken into account, color-blind policies do not correct racial injustice—they reinforce it."

In Reading 2, Paul Craig Roberts and Lawrence M. Stratton Jr. list all the reasons for opposing affirmative action and cite specific cases where they feel that affirmative action has been unfair to certain individuals. They believe that the U.S. Constitution and laws are color-blind. They assert that racial discrimination is costly to those who practice it and that, therefore, self-interest will assure that fair policies and affirmative action are unnecessary, especially in the use of quotas. The reading focuses on the Equal Employment Opportunity Commission and the way in which it sought to eliminate differences.

Issue 1: Is affirmative action fair?

Ten Myths about Affirmative Action

Scott Plous

Scott Plous is Associate Professor of Psychology at Wesleyan University. He earned his Ph.D. in social psychology from Stanford University and has been the recipient of two research awards from SPSSI: the 1984 Gordon Allport Intergroup Relations Prize and the 1993 Otto Klineberg Intercultural and International Relations Award. Dr. Plous is author of The Psychology of Judgment and Decision Making *as well as numerous articles on prejudice and discrimination, international conflict, and ethical issues concerning the use of animals and the environment. He edited a JSI issue (Vol. 49, No. 1) entitled "The Role of Animals in Human Society" and has served as a member of the journal's editorial board.*

The case against affirmative action rests heavily on myth and misunderstanding. In this paper I discuss ten of the most common myths concerning affirmative action, and I present public opinion poll data suggesting that support for affirmative action is greater than typically assumed.

During the past year, affirmative action has been debated more intensely than at any other time in its 30-year history. Many supporters view affirmative action as a milestone, many opponents see it as a millstone, and many others regard it as both or neither—as a necessary, but imperfect, remedy for an intractable social disease. My own view is that the case against affirmative action is weak, resting, as it does so heavily, on myth and misunderstanding. Here are some of the most popular myths about affirmative action, along with a brief commentary on each one.

Myth 1: The only way to create a color-blind society is to adopt color-blind policies. Although this assertion sounds intuitively plausible, the reality is that color-blind policies often put racial minorities at a disadvantage. For instance, all else being equal, color-blind seniority systems tend to protect White workers against job layoffs, because senior employees are usually White (Ezorsky, 1991). Likewise, color-blind college admissions favor White students because of their earlier educational advantages. Unless preexisting inequities are corrected or otherwise taken into account, color-blind policies do not correct racial injustice—they reinforce it.

Myth 2: Affirmative action has not succeeded in increasing female and minority representation. Several studies have documented important gains in racial and gender equality as a direct result of affirmative action (see Murrell & Jones, this issue, for an overview). For example, according to a recent report from the Labor Department, affirmative action has helped 5 million minority members and 6 million White and minority women move up in the workforce ("Reverse Discrimination," 1995). Likewise, a study sponsored by the Office of Federal Contract Compliance Programs showed that between 1974 and 1980 federal contractors (who were required to adopt affirmative action goals) added Black and female officials and managers at twice the rate of noncontractors (Citizens' Commission, 1984). There have also been a number of well-publicized cases in which large companies (e.g., AT&T, IBM, Sears Roebuck) increased minority employment as a result of adopting affirmative action policies.

Myth 3: Affirmative action may have been necessary 30 years ago, but the playing field is fairly level today. Despite the progress that has been made, the playing field is far from level. Women continue to earn 72 cents for every male dollar. Black people continue to have twice the unemployment rate of White people, half the median family income, and half the proportion who attend four years or more of college (see Fig. 1). In fact, without affirmative action the percentage of Black students on many campuses would drop below 2%. This would effectively choke off Black access to higher education and severely restrict progress toward racial equality.

Myth 4: The public doesn't support affirmative action anymore. This myth is based largely on public opinion polls that offer an all-or-none choice between affirmative action as it currently exists and no affirmative action whatsoever. When intermediate choices are added, surveys show that most people want to maintain some form of affirmative action (see Table 1). For example, a recent *Time*/CNN poll found that 80% of the public felt "affirmative action programs for minorities and women should

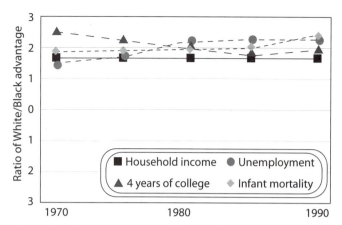

Figure 1. Common standard of living indices. Despite Black gains in median family income and the number of students attending college during the past 25 years, the ratio of White-to-Black advantage has remained virtually unchanged with respect to several common standard-of-living indices (based on data from the U.S. Bureau of the Census, 1984, 1994).

be continued at some level" (Roper Center, 1995a). What the public opposes are quotas, set-asides, and "reverse discrimination." For instance, when the same poll asked people whether they favored programs "requiring businesses to hire a specific number or quota of minorities and women," 63% opposed such a plan. As these results

suggest, most members of the public oppose extreme forms of affirmative action that violate notions of procedural justice—they do *not* oppose affirmative action itself.

Myth 5: A large percentage of White workers will lose out if affirmative action is continued. Government statistics do not support this myth. According to the Commerce Department, there are fewer than 2 million unemployed Black civilians and more than 100 million employed White civilians (U.S. Bureau of the Census, 1994). Thus, even if every unemployed Black worker were to displace a White worker, less than 2% of Whites would be affected. Furthermore, affirmative action pertains only to job-qualified applicants, so the actual percentage of affected whites would be a fraction of 1%. The main sources of job loss among White workers have to do with factory relocations and labor contracting outside the United States, computerization and automation, and corporate downsizing (Ivins, 1995).

Myth 6: If Jewish people and Asian Americans can rapidly advance economically, African Americans should be able to do the same. This comparison ignores the unique history of discrimination against Black people in America. As historian Roger Wilkins has pointed out, Blacks have a 375-year history on this continent: 245 involving slavery, 100 involving legalized discrimination, and only 30 involv-

Table 1	**Survey Results Suggesting That the Public Wants to Reform Rather Than Eliminate Affirmative Action**				
Item		**Source**	**Date**	**n**	**Responses in %**
In your view, should federal affirmative action programs that give preferences to women and minorities be continued as they are, be continued but reformed to prevent reverse discrimination, or should they be ended?		NBC News/ *Wall Street Journal*	8/95	1005	Kept as are: 13 Kept but reformed: 57 Ended: 26 Not sure: 4
What is your view of affirmative action today—it is fundamentally flawed and needs to be eliminated, it is good in principle but needs to be reformed, or, it is basically fine the way it is?		Gallup	7/95	1208	Needs to be eliminated: 22 Needs to be reformed: 61 Fine the way it is: 9 Don't know: 9
What do you think the federal government should do with its affirmative action programs . . . eliminate all of them, eliminate many of them, keep many of them, or keep all of them?		Gallup	7/95	801	Eliminate all: 11 Eliminate/keep many: 67 Keep all: 10 Don't know: 11
If you had to choose, would you rather see the federal government's affirmative action programs mended—that is, changed in certain ways—or ended altogether?		*Time*/CNN	7/95	1000	Mended: 65 Ended: 24 Kept as is (volunt.): 1 Not sure: 10
What about affirmative action programs that set quotas . . . Do you favor affirmative action programs with quotas, or do you favor affirmative action programs only without quotas, or do you oppose all affirmative action programs?		Associated Press	7/95	1006	Favor with quotas: 16 Favor without quotas: 47 Oppose all: 28 Don't know: 9

From Roper Center for Public Opinion—POLL database (Question: VSYANKP.95007.Q21 and VSYANK.95007.Q18A [electronic database]. Storrs. © Roper Starch Worldwide.

Note: All questions taken from the Roper Center (1995b).

ing anything else (Wilkins, 1995). Jews and Asians, on the other hand, have *immigrated* to North America—often as doctors, lawyers, professors, entrepreneurs, and so forth. Moreover, European Jews are able to function as part of the White majority. To expect Blacks to show the same upward mobility as Jews and Asians is to deny the historical and social reality that Black people face.

Myth 7: You can't cure discrimination with discrimination. The problem with this myth is that it uses the same word—*discrimination*— to describe two very different things. Job discrimination is grounded in prejudice and exclusion, whereas affirmative action is an effort to overcome prejudicial treatment through inclusion. The most effective way to cure society of exclusionary practices is to make special efforts at inclusion, which is exactly what affirmative action does. The logic of affirmative action is no different than the logic of treating a nutritional deficiency with vitamin supplements. For a healthy person, high doses of vitamin supplements may be unnecessary or even harmful, but for a person whose system is out of balance, supplements are an efficient way to restore the body's balance.

Myth 8: Affirmative action tends to undermine the self-esteem of women and racial minorities. Although affirmative action may have this effect in some cases (Heilman, Simon, & Repper, 1987; Steele, 1990), interview studies and public opinion surveys suggest that such reactions are rare (Taylor, 1994). For instance, a recent Gallup poll asked employed Blacks and employed White women whether they had ever felt others questioned their abilities because of affirmative action (Roper Center, 1995c). Nearly 90% of respondents said no (which is understandable—after all, White men, who have traditionally benefited from preferential hiring, do not feel hampered by self-doubt or a loss in self-esteem). Indeed, in many cases affirmative action may actually *raise* the self-esteem of women and minorities by providing them with employment and opportunities for advancement. There is also evidence that affirmative action policies increase job satisfaction and organizational commitment among beneficiaries (Graves & Powell, 1994).

Myth 9: Affirmative action is nothing more than an attempt at social engineering by liberal Democrats. In truth, affirmative action programs have spanned seven different presidential administrations—four Republican and three Democratic. Although the originating document of affirmative action was President Johnson's Executive Order 11246, the policy was significantly expanded in 1969 by President Nixon and then Secretary of Labor George Schultz. President Bush also enthusiastically signed the Civil Rights Act of 1991, which formally endorsed the

principle of affirmative action. Thus, despite the current split along party lines, affirmative action has traditionally enjoyed the support of Republicans as well as Democrats.

Myth 10: Support for affirmative action means support for preferential selection procedures that favor unqualified candidates over qualified candidates. Actually, most supporters of affirmative action oppose this type of preferential selection. Preferential selection procedures can be ordered along the following continuum:

1. *Selection among equally qualified candidates.* The mildest form of affirmative action selection occurs when a female or minority candidate is chosen from a pool of equally qualified applicants (e.g., students with identical college entrance scores). Survey research suggests that three-quarters of the public does not see this type of affirmative action as discriminatory (Roper Center, 1995d).

2. *Selection among comparable candidates.* A somewhat stronger form occurs when female or minority candidates are roughly comparable to other candidates (e.g., their college entrance scores are lower, but not by a significant amount). The logic here is similar to the logic of selecting among equally qualified candidates; all that is needed is an understanding that, for example, predictions based on an SAT score of 620 are virtually indistinguishable from predictions based on an SAT score of 630.

3. *Selection among unequal candidates.* A still stronger form of affirmative action occurs when qualified female or minority candidates are chosen over candidates whose records are better by a substantial amount.

4. *Selection among qualified and unqualified candidates.* The strongest form of preferential selection occurs when unqualified female or minority members are chosen over other candidates who are qualified. Although affirmative action is sometimes mistakenly equated with this form of preferential treatment, federal regulations explicit prohibit affirmative action programs in which unqualified or unneeded employees are hired (Bureau of National Affairs, 1979).

Even though these selection procedures occasionally blend into one another (due in part to the difficulty of comparing incommensurable records), a few general observations can be made. First, of the four different procedures, the selection of women and minority members among equal or roughly comparable candidates has the greatest public support, adheres most closely to popular conceptions of procedural justice, and reduces the changes that affirmative action beneficiaries will be perceived as unqualified or undeserving (Kravitz & Platania, 1993; Nacoste, 1985; Turner & Pratkanis, 1994). Second, the selection of women and minority members among unequal candidates—used routinely in college admissions—has deeply divided the nation (with the strongest opposition coming from White males and conservative voters). And finally, the selection of unqualified candidates is not permitted under federal affirmative action guidelines and should not be equated with legal forms of affirmative action. By distinguishing among these four different selection procedures, it becomes clear that opposition to stronger selection procedures need not imply opposition to milder ones. What is needed, I would argue, is less of an effort to caricature affirmative action and more of an effort to discuss which of its many forms are beneficial.

References

Bureau of National Affairs. (1979). *Uniform guidelines on employee selection procedures.* Washington, DC: Author.

Citizens' Commission on Civil Rights. (1984, June). *Affirmative action to open the doors of job opportunity.* Washington, DC: Author.

Ezorsky, G. (1991) *Racism and justice: The case for affirmative action.* Ithaca, NY: Cornell University Press.

Graves, L. M., & Powell, G. N. (1994). Effects of sex-based preferential selection and discrimination on job attitudes. *Human Relations, 47,* 133–157.

Heilman, M. E., Simon, M. C., & Repper, D. P. (1987). Intentionally favored, unintentionally harmed? Impact of sex-based preferential selection on self-perceptions and self-evaluations. *Journal of Applied Psychology, 72,* 62–68.

Ivins, M. (1995, February 23). Affirmative action is more than black-and-white issue. *Philadelphia Daily News,* p. 28.

Kravitz, D. A., & Platania, J. (1993). Attitudes and beliefs about affirmative action: Effects of target and of respondent sex and ethnicity. *Journal of Personality and Social Psychology, 78,* 928–938.

Nacoste, R. W. (1985). Selection procedure and responses to affirmative action: The case of favorable treatment. *Law and Human Behavior, 9,* 225–242.

Reverse discrimination of whites is rare, labor study reports. (1995, March 31). *New York Times,* p. A23.

Roper Center for Public Opinion—POLL Database (Question IDs: USYANKP.95007.Q21 and USYANKP.95007.Q18A). [Electronic database]. (1995a). Storrs, CT: Roper Center for Public Opinion [Producer and Distributor].

Roper Center for Public Opinion—POLL Database (Question IDs: USNBCWSJ.080495.R20C, USGALLUP.95JL20.R24, USGALLUP.95JUL7.R27, and USYANKP.072195.R24B). [Electronic database]. (1995b). Storrs, CT: Roper Center for Public Opinion [Producer and Distributor].

Roper Center for Public Opinion—POLL Database (Question ID: USGALLUP.95MRW1.R31). [Electronic database]. (1995c). Storrs, CT: Roper Center for Public Opinion [Producer and Distributor].

Roper Center for Public Opinion—POLL Database (Question ID: USGALLUP.95MRW1.R32). [Electronic database]. (1995d). Storrs, CT: Roper Center for Public Opinion [Producer and Distributor].

Steele, S. (1990). *The content of our character: A new vision of race in America.* New York: St. Martin's Press.

Taylor, M. C. (1994). Impact of affirmative action on beneficiary groups: Evidence from the 1990 General Social Survey. *Basic and Applied Social Psychology, 15,* 143–178.

Turner, M. E., & Pratkanis, A. R. (1994). Affirmative action as help: A review of recipient reactions to preferential selection and affirmative action. *Basic and Applied Social Psychology, 15,* 43–69.

U.S. Bureau of the Census. (1984). *Statistical abstract of the United States: 1984* (104th ed.). Washington, DC: U.S. Government Printing Office.

U.S. Bureau of the Census. (1994). *Statistical abstract of the United States: 1994* (114th ed.). Washington, DC: U.S. Government Printing Office.

Wilkins, R. (1995, May). Racism has its privileges: The case for affirmative action. *The Nation,* pp. 409–410, 412, 414–416.

Form at end of book

Issue 1: Is affirmative action fair?

Color Code

Bureaucrats and judges have turned the 1964 Civil Rights Act on its head, creating a system of preferences based on race and sex. Can we restore equality before the law?

Paul Craig Roberts and Lawrence M. Stratton Jr.

Mr. Roberts is John M. Olin Fellow and Mr. Stratton is a research fellow of the Institute for Political Economy. This article is adapted from their book, which is forthcoming from Regnery.

Forty years after *Brown* v. *Board of Education,* the civil-rights movement has strayed far from the color-blind principles of Martin Luther King Jr. Public outrage over preferential treatment for "protected minorities" has taken the place of guilt over segregation. Americans who supported desegregation and equal rights are astonished to find themselves governed by quotas, which were prohibited by the Civil Rights Act of 1964.

In California momentum is building for a 1996 initiative, modeled on the 1964 Civil Rights Act, that would amend the state's constitution to prohibit the use of quotas by state institutions. Polls indicate that the initiative's objective of ending affirmative action is enormously popular, even in traditionally liberal bastions such as Berkeley and San Francisco. Citizens in other states are organizing to place similar measures on the ballot. The prospects for such measures are bright: surveys find that some 80 per cent of Americans oppose affirmative action in employment and education.

The hostility to race and gender preferments reflects a general sense that reverse discrimination violates fundamental norms of justice and fair play. Thomas Wood, a co-drafter of the California initiative and executive director of the California Association of Scholars, says he has been denied a teaching job because he is a white male: "I was once told by a member of a search committee at a university, 'You'd walk into this job if you were the right gender.' " Glynn Custred, a California State University anthropology professor, says he decided to join Wood in drafting the initiative because he was concerned about the destructive impact racial quotas were having on higher education, where "diversity" overshadows academic merit.

The California initiative has drawn support from across the political spectrum. Charles Geshekter, a teacher of African history at Chico State University and a supporter of the initiative, wrote in the August 14 *Chico Enterprise Record:* "As a liberal Democrat, I despise those who advocate preferential treatment based on genitalia or skin color. Having taught university classes on the history of European racism toward Africa for 25 years, I am appalled to watch sexist and racist demands for equality of outcomes erode the principle of affirmative equality of opportunity." University of California Regent Ward Connerly, a black businessman who supports the initiative, lamented in the August 10 *Sacramento Bee* that "we have institutionalized this preferential treatment."

The Pervasiveness of Preferences

Opposition to quotas was initially unfocused, because their impact was not widely felt. The public was aware of a few celebrated cases, but they seemed to be the exception rather than the rule. This is no longer the case. Preferential treatment based on race and sex pervades private and public employment, university admissions and hiring, and the allocation of government contracts, broadcast licenses, and research grants. Consider a few examples:

- A 1989 survey by *Fortune* magazine found that only 14 per cent of Fortune 500 companies hired employees based on talent and merit alone; 18 per cent admitted that they had racial quotas, while 54 per cent used the euphemism "goals."

- A Defense Department memo cited on the November 18 broadcast of ABC's *20/20* declares, "In the future, special permission will be required for the promotion of all white men without disabilities."

- The Federal Aviation Administration officially recognizes the Council of African American Employees, the National Asian Pacific American Association, the Gay, Lesbian, or Bisexual Employees group, and the Native American/Alaska Native Coalition, granting them access to bulletin boards, photocopiers, electronic mail, voice mail, and rooms in government buildings for meetings on government time. By contrast, the Coalition of Federal White Aviation Employees has been seeking recognition from the FAA since 1992 without success; FAA employees are even forbidden to read the group's literature.

- In the 1994 case *Hopwood* v. *State of Texas,* U.S. District Court Judge Sam Sparks found that the constitutional rights of four white law-school applicants had been violated by quota policies at the University of Texas. However, he awarded them each only $1 in damages and refused to order them admitted ahead of protected minorities with substantially lower scores.

A case that came before the U.S. Supreme Court in January shows even more clearly how preferential policies have warped basic concepts of fairness. Randy Pech, owner of Adarand Constructors, lost in the bidding for a guard-rail construction project in Colorado's San Juan National Forest because of his skin color. Pech put in the lowest bid. However, the prime contractor was eligible for a bounty of $10,000 in taxpayers' money from the U.S. Department of Transportation for hiring minority-owned subcontractors, and the bounty was greater than the difference in the bids submitted by Pech and his competitor, a Hispanic-owned firm.

Pech filed a discrimination lawsuit. When it reached the Supreme Court, U.S. Solicitor General Drew S. Days III argued that Pech had no standing to sue, even though the U.S. Government had paid the prime contractor $10,000 to discriminate against him. Whatever the technical merits of the solicitor general's argument, it reveals the system of racial preferments that today passes for civil rights. "Protected minorities" have standing to sue without any requirement of showing that they themselves have ever suffered from an act of discrimination. Today's college-aged protected minorities have never suffered from legal discrimination, yet U.S. policy assumes they are victims and provides remedies in the form of preferments. In contrast, victims of reverse discrimination have no remedy and no legal standing.

The political repercussions of this double standard are by no means restricted to California. In November's congressional elections, white males deserted the Democratic Party in droves, voting Republican by a margin of 63 per cent to 37 per cent. The *Wall Street Journal* has identified "angry white males" as an important new political group.

But more is at stake than the plight of white males and the relative fortunes of political parties. At issue is equality before the law and the democratic process itself. As freedom of conscience, goodwill, and persuasion are supplanted by regulatory and judicial coercion, privilege reappears in open defiance of Justice John Marshall Harlan's dictum: "There is no caste here. Our Constitution is color-blind."

Color-blindness was the guiding principle of the 1964 Civil Rights Act. The basic act was full of language prohibiting quotas, and various amendments to it defined discrimination as an intentional act, insulated professionally developed employment tests from attack for disproportionately screening out racial minorities, and restricted the Equal Employment Opportunity Commission (EEOC) from issuing any substantive interpretive regulations. Senator Hubert H. Humphrey (D., Minn.), the chief sponsor of the act, confidently declared that if anyone could find "any language which provides that an employer will have to hire on the basis of percentage or quota related to color, race, religion, or national origin, I will start eating the pages one after another, because it is not in there." In less than a decade, federal bureaucrats and judges had cast aside Congress's rejection of preferential treatment for minorities and stuffed the pages of the 1964 Civil Rights Act down Hubert Humphrey's throat.

Two Models of Discrimination

The Civil Rights Act of 1964 undertook to put millions of employer decisions through a government filter. Such a massive intrusion into private life had not previously occurred in a free society. Congress assumed that the EEOC, the agency created by the act to run the filter, would be like the state Fair Employment Practice (FEP) commissions that had been created in some Northern states after World War II.

Civil-rights activists regarded these commissions, many of which had more power than the EEOC, as ineffective. As University of Chicago economist Gary Becker observed, however, there was an explanation for the paucity of enforcement actions by the FEP commissions: discrimination doesn't pay. In his 1957 book, *The Economics of Discrimination,* Becker showed that racial discrimination is costly to those who practice it and therefore sets in motion forces that inexorably reduce it. Meritorious employees who are underpaid and underutilized because of their race will move to firms where they get paid according to their contributions. An employer who hires a less qualified white because of prejudice against blacks will disadvantage himself in competition against those who hire the best employees they can find.

Indeed, scholars who studied the cases handled by FEP commissions found that the complainant's problem was usually job qualifications, not his race. Sociologist Leon Mayhew, who studied employment-discrimination complaints filed with the Massachusetts FEP commission from 1946 to 1962, found that most complaints were based on "mere suspicion" and usually resulted in a finding that the employer had not discriminated. He pointed out that most complainants were poor and lacked job skills. Thus, ordinary, profit-oriented business decisions "regularly produce experiences that could be interpreted as discrimination." This phenomenon "permits Negroes to blame discrimination for their troubles. Hence, some complaints represent a projection of one's own deficiencies onto the outside world."

This argument did not appeal to those who wanted to achieve racial integration through government policy. Activists such as Rutgers law professor Alfred W. Blumrosen, who as the EEOC's first compliance chief became the de facto head of the commission in its formative years, rejected the complaint-based, "retail" model of FEP enforcement and envisioned a "wholesale" model attacking the entrenched legacy of discrimination. In 1965 Blumrosen wrote in the *Rutgers Law Review* that FEP commissions focused too much on individual acts of discrimination and "did not remedy the broader social problems" by reducing the disparity between black and white unemployment. Seeking to redefine discrimination in terms of statistical disparity, he dismissed other explanations of economic differences between blacks and whites, such as education and illegitimacy, as harmful "attempt[s] to shift focus." Blumrosen disdained the Civil Rights Act's definition of discrimination as an intentional act, preferring a definition that Congress had rejected. In his 1971 book, *Black Employment and the Law,* he wrote:

If discrimination is narrowly defined, for example, by requiring an evil intent to injure minorities, then it will be difficult to find that it exists. If it does not exist, then the plight of racial and ethnic minorities must be attributable to some more generalized failures in society, in the fields of basic education, housing, family relations, and the like. The search for efforts to improve the condition of minorities must then focus in these general and difficult areas, and the answers can come only gradually as basic institutions, attitudes, customs, and practices are changed. We thus would have before us generations of time before the effects of subjugation of minorities are dissipated.

But if discrimination is broadly defined, as, for example, by including all conduct which adversely affects minority group employment opportunities . . . then the prospects for rapid improvement in minority employment opportunities are greatly increased. Industrial relations systems are flexible; they are in control of defined individuals and institutions; they can be altered either by negotiation or by law. If discrimination exists within these institutions, the solution lies within our immediate grasp. It is not embedded in the complications of fundamental sociology but can be sharply influenced by intelligent, effective, and aggressive legal action.

This is the optimistic view of the racial problem in our nation. This view finds discrimination at every turn where minorities are adversely affected by institutional decisions, which are subject to legal regulation. In this view, we are in control of our own history. The destruction of our society over the race question is not inevitable.

Blumrosen's Agenda

Blumrosen figured that a redefinition of discrimination to include anything that yielded statistical disparities between blacks and whites would force employers to give preferential treatment to blacks in pursuit of proportional representation, so as to avoid liability in class-action suits. He set out to "liberally construe" Title VII of the Civil Rights Act, which prohibited discrimination in employment, in order to advance "the needs of the minorities for whom the statute had been adopted." By promoting quotas, he could "maximize the effect of the statute on employment discrimination without going back to the Congress for more substantive legislation."

Blumrosen's EEOC colleagues kidded him that he was working on a textbook entitled *Blumrosen on Loopholes.* He took pride in his reputation for "free and easy ways with statutory construction." He later praised the agency for being like "the proverbial bumble bee" that flies "in defiance of the laws governing its operation." Blumrosen's strategy was based on his bet that "most of the problems confronting the EEOC could be solved by creative interpretation of Title VII which would be upheld by the courts, partly out of deference to the administrators." History has proved Blumrosen right.

As inside-the-Beltway lore expresses it, "Personnel is policy." Blumrosen had a free hand because Franklin Delano Roosevelt Jr., the EEOC's first chairman, spent most of his time yachting. Staffers jokingly changed the lyrics of the song "Anchors Aweigh" and sang "Franklin's Away" during his frequent absences. Roosevelt resigned before a year was out, and his successors stayed little longer. The EEOC had four chairmen in its first five years, which enhanced Blumrosen's power.

The White House Conference on Equal Employment Opportunity in August 1965 indicated what was to come. Speaker after speaker described "deeply rooted patterns of discrimination" and "under-representation" of minorities that the EEOC should counter in order to promote "equal employment opportunity." The conference report stressed on its first page that the "conferees were eager to move beyond the letter of the law to a sympathetic discussion of those affirmative actions required to make the legal requirement of equal opportunity an operating reality." Another telling line said that "it is not enough to obey the technical letter of the law; we must go a step beyond in order to assure equal employment opportunity." One panel concluded that "it is possible that the letter of the law can be obeyed to the fullest extent *without* eliminating discrimination in hiring and promotion. For the legislative intent of Title VII to be met, the law will have to be obeyed in spirit as well as in letter."

The report noted that many panelists shared Blumrosen's suspicion that if the EEOC limited its activities to responding to complaints of discrimination, the agency would never "reach the extent of discriminatory patterns." Blumrosen inserted a paragraph into the report suggesting that the agency should initiate proceedings against employers even in the absence of complaints of discrimination. Underutilizers of minority workers could be identified by using "employer reports of the racial composition of the work force as a sociological 'radar net' to determine the existence of patterns of discrimination."

Blumrosen succeeded in setting up a national reporting system of racial employment statistics despite the Civil Rights Act's specific prohibition of such data collection. An amendment introduced by Senator Everett Dirksen (R., Ill.), said employers did not have to report statistics to the EEOC if they were already reporting them to local or state FEP commissions. Blumrosen later admitted that the requirement he imposed on employers to report the racial composition of their work forces was based on "a reading of the statute contrary to the plain meaning." But what was a mere statute?

Columbia University law professor Michael Sovern predicted that the EEOC would be called on the carpet for exceeding its authority. In a study for the Twentieth Century Fund, *Legal Restraints on Racial Discrimination,* he wrote that Title VII "cannot possibly be stretched to permit the Commission to insist on the filing of reports" and predicted that Blumrosen would "encounter resistance." But no resistance materialized. As Hugh Davis Graham observed in *The Civil Rights Era,* "In 1965 Congress was distracted by debates over voting rights and Vietnam and Watts and inflation and scores of other issues more pressing than agency records."

After Blumrosen got his way in forcing employers to submit reports, the agency developed the confidence to dispense with other statutory restrictions on its mission. The EEOC saw the reporting requirement as a "calling card" that "gives credibility to an otherwise weak statute."

Blumrosen knew that "with the aid of a computer," the EEOC could now get "lists of employers who, prima facie, may be underutilizing minority-group persons" and eventually force them to engage in preferential hiring of blacks.

In mid 1965 Blumrosen sent EEOC investigators to Newport News, Virginia, to solicit discrimination complaints against the Newport News Shipbuilding & Dry Dock Company, one of the world's largest shipyards, employing 22,000 workers. Knocking on doors in black neighborhoods, the investigators found 41 complainants, later narrowed down to 4. Blumrosen then successfully pressured the company, which received 75 per cent of its business from Navy contracts, to promote 3,890 of its 5,000 black workers, designate 100 blacks as supervisors, and adopt a quota system in which the ratio of black to white apprentices in a given year would match the region's ratio of blacks to whites. One shipyard worker told *Barron's* that the EEOC had done its worst to "set black against white, labor against management, and disconcert everybody."

Armed with the national reporting system's racial data and the victory at Newport News, Blumrosen and his colleagues decided to build a body of case law under Title VII to impose minority-preference schemes on employers across the country. The barrier to this strategy was Title VII itself. An internal EEOC legal memorandum concluded: "Under the literal language of Title VII, the only actions required by a covered employer are to post notices, and not to discriminate subsequent to July 2, 1965. By the explicit terms of Section 703(j), an employer is not required to redress an imbalance in his work force which is the result of past discrimination." Fearing a storm over quotas like the one that had occurred during the congressional debates on the Civil Rights Act, the EEOC ruled out trying to amend the Act itself. The memorandum instead urged the agency to rewrite the statute on its own and influence the courts to embrace the EEOC's "affirmative theory of nondiscrimination," under which compliance with Title VII requires that "Negroes are recruited, hired, transferred, and promoted in line with their ability and numbers."

The Assault on Employment Tests

To implement the "affirmative theory of nondiscrimination," the EEOC decided to assault employment tests that failed blacks at a higher rate than whites. Commissioner Samuel Jackson told members of the NAACP that the EEOC had decided to interpret Title VII as banning not only racial discrimination per se but also employment practices "which prove to have a demonstrable racial effect." EEOC lawyers formed an alliance with civil-rights attorneys at the NAACP and began a litigation drive to re-define discrimination in terms of statistical effects.

Summer riots and Vietnam protests helped activists target employment tests. The Kerner Commission's report on civil disorders described employment tests as "artificial barriers to employment and promotion." The Kerner Commission blamed these "artificial barriers" and the "explosive mixture which has been accumulating in our cities" on racism and concluded, "Our nation is moving toward two societies, one black, one white—separate and unequal."

The EEOC's chief psychologist, William H. Enneis, attacked "irrelevant and unreasonable standards for job applicants and upgrading of employees, [which] pose seri-ous threats to our social and economic system. The results will be denial of employment to qualified and trainable minorities and women." Enneis said the EEOC would not "stand idle in the face of this challenge. The cult of creden-tialism is one of our targets," to be fought "in whatever form it occurs."

The EEOC issued guidelines in 1966 and 1970 de-signed to abrogate the pro-testing amendment to the Civil Rights Act introduced by Senator John Tower (R., Tex.) by defining the phrase "professionally developed ability tests" as tests that either passed blacks and whites at an equal rate or met complex "validation" requirements for "fair-ness" and "utility." Under the validation requirements that Enneis designed, employers had to prove that the tests measured skills they needed. The objective was to make tests so difficult to defend in court that employers would simply abandon them and hire by racial quota. Enneis tes-tified before Congress in 1974 that he knew of only three or four test-validation studies that satisfied his guidelines. As a 1971 *Harvard Law Review* survey of developments in employment law deduced, the EEOC guidelines "appear designed to scare employers away from any objective stan-dards which have a differential impact on minority groups, because, applied strictly, the testing requirements are impossible for many employers to follow." As a result, the guidelines "encourage many employers to use a quota system of hiring." An EEOC staffer told the *Harvard Law Review* that "the anti-preferential-hiring provisions [of Title VII] are a big zero, a nothing, a nullity. They don't mean anything at all to us."

The EEOC's attack on tests gutted not only Senator Tower's amendment but also the statutory definition of discrimination as an intentional act. The commission was well aware that it was treading on legal thin ice. A history of the EEOC during the Johnson Administration, pre-pared by the EEOC for the Johnson Library under the di-rection of Vice Chairman Luther Holcomb, detailed the EEOC's strategy of redefining discrimination and sug-gested that it was on a collision course with the text and legislative intent of Title VII. The history said the EEOC had rejected the "traditional meaning" of discrimination as "one of intent in the state of mind of the actor" in favor of a "constructive proof of discrimination" that would "disregard intent as crucial to the finding of an unlawful employment practice" and forbid employment criteria that have a "demonstrable racial effect without clear and convincing business motive."

Noting that this redefinition would conflict with Senator Dirksen's insertion of the word "intentional" into the statute, the history said "courts cannot assume as a matter of statutory construction that Congress meant to accomplish an empty act by the amendment" defining dis-crimination as intentional. The history predicted that "the Commission and the courts will be in disagreement as to the basis on which they find an unlawful employment practice" and concluded that "eventually this will call for the reconsideration of the amendment by Congress or the reconsideration of its interpretation by the Commission."

As things turned out neither the EEOC nor Congress had to reconsider the meaning of discrimination, because the courts also ignored the law. In the 1971 case *Griggs* v. *Duke Power,* the Supreme Court accepted the EEOC's rewrite of the Civil Rights Act. The opinion was written by Chief Justice Warren Burger, President Richard Nixon's first appointee to the Supreme Court. Coveting the fame of his predecessor, Earl Warren, Chief Justice Burger told his clerks that he wanted to "confuse his detractors in the press" by writing some "liberal opinions."

Blumrosen Wins His Bet

When Burger declared that "the administrative interpre-tation of the Act by the enforcing agency is entitled to great deference," Professor Blumrosen won his bet that the EEOC's "creative interpretation of Title VII would be upheld by the courts, partly out of deference to the administrators." Burger got the acclaim he coveted. Blumrosen cheered the Chief Justice's opinion as a "sensi-tive, liberal interpretation of Title VII" that "has the imprimatur of permanence."

In *Griggs* the Court ignored clear statutory language and unambiguous legislative history. In fact, *Griggs* paral-leled a 1964 Illinois case, *Myart* v. *Motorola,* that had trou-bled many of the legislators who approved the Civil Rights Act. *Myart* struck down Motorola Corporation's use of an employment test that blacks failed at a higher rate than whites. The EEOC's history for the Johnson Library noted that "many members of Congress were concerned about this issue because the court order against Motorola was handed down during the debates. The record establishes that the use of professionally developed ability tests would not be considered discriminatory." Nevertheless, the Supreme Court ruled that Duke Power Company was discriminating against blacks by requiring employees seeking promotions to have a high-school diploma or a passing grade on intelligence and mechanical-comprehension tests.

The Supreme Court agreed with the lower courts that Duke Power had not adopted the requirement with any intention to discriminate against blacks. Burger admitted that the company's policy of financing two-thirds of the cost of adult high-school education for its employees suggested good intent. But the lack of a racist motive did not make any difference to the Chief Justice. He decreed that the "absence of discriminatory intent does not redeem employment procedures or testing mechanisms that operate as 'built-in headwinds' for minority groups." Burger was mistaken when he wrote, "Congress directed the thrust of the Act to the *consequences* of employment practices, not simply the motivation." It was precisely this misinterpretation of the statute that the Dirksen Amendment was crafted to prevent.

Burger viewed the promotion requirements as "built-in-headwinds" against blacks because blacks were less likely than whites to have completed high school or to do well on aptitude tests. He cited 1960 census statistics showing that 34 per cent of white males in North Carolina had completed high school, compared to 12 per cent of black males, and EEOC findings that 58 per cent of whites passed the tests used by Duke Power, compared to 6 per cent of blacks. Blaming these disparities on segregation, Burger said that "under the Act, practices, procedures, or tests neutral on their face, and even neutral in terms of intent, cannot be maintained if they operate to 'freeze' the status quo of prior discriminatory employment practices." Burger destroyed job testing when he declared, "The Act proscribes not only overt discrimination but also practices that are fair in form, but discriminatory in operation."

Burger's casuistry was to be given a name. In the 1976 book *Employment Discrimination Law*, EEOC District Counsel Barbara Lindemann Schlei and co-author Paul Grossman called the new emphasis on consequences "disparate impact" analysis. One year later, the Supreme Court used the phrase for the first time in the case *International Brotherhood of Teamsters* v. *United States*, which dealt with burdens of proof in Title VII cases attacking union seniority systems. "Proof of discriminatory motive," the Court said, "is not required under a disparate-impact theory." Henceforth, any requirement that had a disparate impact on the races, regardless of intent or the

reasonableness of the requirement, constituted discrimination. In employment and promotions, unequals had to be treated as equals. The same was soon to follow in university admissions testing. Race-based privileges had found their way into law.

In *Griggs* Chief Justice Burger said employers could escape prima facie Title VII liability only if test requirements are "demonstrably a reasonable measure of job performance." Pulling a phrase out of thin air, Burger said "the touchstone is business necessity. If an employment practice which operates to exclude Negroes cannot be shown to be related to job performance, the practice is prohibited." Burger invented a statutory hook for his ruling by asserting, falsely, that "Congress has placed on the employer the burden of showing that any given requirement must have a manifest relationship to the employment in question." It was precisely this heavy-handed intrusion into job requirements that the Tower Amendment was designed to prevent.

Burger's deference to the EEOC meant that the agency would become the national arbiter of job tests. Following *Griggs*, the agency immediately issued manuals warning employers that unless they "voluntarily" increased their minority statistics, they risked costly liability. Ultimately, it became prohibitively expensive to use job tests unless they were race-normed so that blacks could qualify with lower scores.

The Impact of Disparate Impact

In a subsequent case interpreting *Griggs*, Justice Harry Blackmun expressed his concern that the EEOC's guidelines would lead to hiring based on race rather than merit. He warned that "a too-rigid application of the EEOC guidelines will leave the employer little choice, save an impossibly expensive and complex validation study, but to engage in a subjective quota system of employment selection. This, of course, is far from the intent of Title VII."

By then it was too late. *Griggs* had killed four birds with one stone: Senator Tower's amendment on tests, Senator Dirksen's amendment on intent, Senator Humphrey's guarantee that the Civil Rights Act could not be used to induce quotas, and the amendment introduced by Representative Emanuel Celler (D., N.Y.) prohibiting the EEOC from issuing substantive regulatory interpretations of Title VII. The EEOC wanted quotas, and thanks to *Griggs* it would get them. "At the EEOC we believe in numbers," Chairman Clifford Alexander declared in 1968. In pursuit of its goal, the agency assumed powers it did not have. In 1972 Blumrosen boasted in the

Michigan Law Review that the EEOC's power to issue guidelines "does not flow from any congressional grant of authority."

When Burger created what would come to be known as disparate-impact analysis he did not realize its quota implications. He thought he was just attacking "credentialism." As the holder of a law degree from an obscure night school in St. Paul, Minnesota, Burger may have been thinking of himself when he wrote that "history is filled with examples of men and women who rendered highly effective performance without the conventional badges of accomplishment in terms of certificates, diplomas, or degrees." Surrounded by Court colleagues and clerks with prestigious Ivy League degrees, Burger might have tasted credential discrimination. He thought that the Court could take away the "headwind" of credentialism that blew against blacks without creating a position for minorities.

Yet before *Griggs,* any employer who was so inclined could take the measure of prospective employees and make bets on people with obscure backgrounds who may not have had the best chances in life. After *Griggs,* no employer could risk hiring a white male from William Mitchell Law School in St. Paul over a black from Harvard. *Griggs* made race a critical factor in employment decisions. High-school diplomas, arrest records, wage garnishments, dishonorable military discharges, and grade-point averages all became forbidden considerations in hiring decisions, because they are criteria that could have a disparate impact on blacks. Farmers have even been sued for asking prospective farm hands whether they could use a hoe, on the grounds that blacks have a greater propensity to back problems. Perfectly sensible height and weight requirements for prison guards and police officers have also been struck down for having a disparate impact on women.

The EEOC strategy that led to *Griggs* was not created in a vacuum. Civil-rights activists needed a new cause, and preferences that would enable blacks to attain equality of result became the new goal. In January 1965, *Playboy* asked Martin Luther King Jr., "Do you feel it's fair to request a multibillion-dollar program of preferential treatment for the Negro, or for any other minority group?" King replied, "I do indeed." In 1969, the U.S. Court of Appeals for the Fifth Circuit, the same court that had initiated school busing in the name of "racial balance," cast aside the prohibition of quotas in Section 703(j) of the Civil Rights Act by upholding a court order that every other person admitted to a Louisiana labor union must be black. Responding to the argument that this order clearly violated Section 703(j), the three-judge panel simply wrote, "We disagree."

President Johnson was the most prominent proponent of the shift away from the color-blind ideal. At his commencement speech at Howard University on June 4, 1965, Johnson said the disappearance of legal segregation was not enough:

You do not take a person who, for years, has been hobbled by chains and liberate him, bring him up to the starting line of a race, and then say, "You are free to compete with all the others," and still justly believe that you have been completely fair.

Thus it is not enough just to open the gates of opportunity. All our citizens must have the ability to walk through those gates.

This is the next and the more profound stage of the battle for civil rights. We seek not just freedom but opportunity. We seek not just legal equity but human ability, not just equality as a right and a theory but equality as a fact and equality as a result.

To back up his speech with action, Johnson issued Executive Order 11246, which put the phrase "affirmative action" into common parlance. The order required all Federal Government contractors and subcontractors to "take affirmative action to ensure that applicants are employed, and that employees are treated during employment, without regard to their race, creed, color, or national origin."

Johnson's equality-of-results rhetoric and his metaphor of helping a hobbled runner have provided the main emotional justification for "affirmative action," but the quotas that now web federal contractors under Executive Order 11246 were not implemented by his Administration. Facing strong opposition from the Department of Defense, labor unions, members of Congress, and Comptroller General Elmer Staats, Johnson's labor secretary, Willard Wirtz, dropped his plans to impose quotas on federal construction projects in Philadelphia.

That task fell to George P. Shultz, Richard Nixon's labor secretary. Just as Burger considered *Griggs* a blow against credentialism, Shultz, a labor economist from the University of Chicago, saw the Philadelphia Plan as a way of making an end run around the Davis-Bacon Act, which inflated the cost of federal construction contracts by setting wages at "prevailing union levels." Davis-Bacon meant non-union contractors and laborers (many of whom were black) could not get government contract work. Sensitive to charges that he was hostile to civil rights, Nixon wrote in his memoirs that he accepted Shultz's proposal to revive the Philadelphia Plan in order to demonstrate to blacks "that we *do* care."

On June 27, 1969, Assistant Secretary of Labor Arthur A. Fletcher, a black former businessman who had been a professional football player, announced the Philadelphia Plan in the City of Brotherly Love. He said that while "visible, measurable goals to correct obvious imbalances are essential," the plan did not involve "rigid quotas." The *Congressional Quarterly* disagreed with Fletcher's scholastic distinction, calling the Philadelphia Plan a "nonnegotiable quota system."

Under the plan, the Labor Department's Office of Federal Contract Compliance (OFCC) would assess conditions in the five-county Philadelphia area and set a target percentage of minorities to be employed in several construction trades, with the aim of attaining a racially proportionate work force. Potential federal contractors would have to submit complex plans detailing goals and timetables for hiring blacks within each trade to satisfy the OFCC's "utilization" targets. Arthur Fletcher said the Philadelphia Plan "put economic flesh and bones on Dr. King's dream."

In 1971 the U.S. Court of Appeals for the Third Circuit accepted the Nixon Administration's argument that "goals and timetables" were not quotas and that, even if they were, the Civil Rights Act's ban on quotas applied to Title VII remedies, not to executive orders. The Supreme Court avoided the controversial quota issue by refusing to review the case. Although the appeals court's ruling had no force outside the Third Circuit, the Nixon Administration interpreted the Supreme Court's lack of interest as a green light. As Laurence H. Silberman, who was undersecretary of labor at the time, later wrote, the Nixon Administration went on to spread Philadelphia Plans "across the country like Johnny Appleseed." The Labor Department quickly issued Order #4, which required all federal contractors to meet "goals and timetables" to "correct any identifiable deficiencies" of minorities in their work forces. The carrot of government contracts and the stick of disparate-impact liability under *Griggs* quickly established quotas. For many corporate managers, hiring by the numbers was the only protection against discrimination lawsuits and the loss of lucrative government contracts. Contractors hired minorities to guard against the sin of "underutilization," and racial proportionality became a precondition of government largesse. Arthur Fletcher estimated that the new quota regime covered "from one-third to one-half of all U.S. workers."

The Section 703(j) prohibition of quotas in the Civil Rights Act remained in the law but meant nothing. Reverse discrimination was in. When the liberal William O. Douglas, the only remaining member of the *Brown* Court, tried to get his Supreme Court colleagues to review the case of a white who was refused admission to the Arizona bar to make room for blacks with lower bar-exam scores, he argued that "racial discrimination against a white was as unconstitutional as racial discrimination against a black." Douglas failed to persuade his fellow Justices. He reports in his autobiography that Thurgood Marshall replied: "You guys have been practicing discrimination for years. Now it is our turn."

The Spread of Quotas

Although the phrase "federal contractor" conjures up images of workers in hard hats busy with construction projects or weapons systems, colleges and universities are also federal contractors, receiving federal funds through research grants and financial aid to students. Following the Labor Department's lead, Nixon's Department of Health, Education, and Welfare soon required similar "goals and timetables" for faculty hiring. Before long the practice had spread to student admissions as well.

In 1974 Douglas tried to get the Court to address quotas in this area. Marco DeFunis challenged the University of Washington Law School's 20 per cent quota for blacks. The school had rejected DeFunis though his GPA and test scores surpassed those of 36 of the 37 admitted blacks. Using his powers as a Circuit Justice, Douglas stayed the Washington Supreme Court's ruling against DeFunis and ordered his admission.

By the time DeFunis's case came before the Supreme Court, however, he was about to receive his degree. This let the Court avoid the quota issue by declaring the case moot. Douglas dissented on the mootness ruling and addressed the case's merits. He viewed *DeFunis* just as he had *Brown:* "There is no superior person by constitutional standards. A DeFunis who is white is entitled to no advantage by reason of that fact; nor is he subject to any disability, no matter what his race or color. Whatever his race, he had a constitutional right to have his application considered on its individual merits in a racially neutral manner."

But time had passed Douglas by. In Douglas's mind, discrimination was still connected with merit. DeFunis's scores showed that he met a higher objective standard than those admitted in his place. But by this time any standard that had disparate impact was ipso facto discriminatory. In the eyes of Douglas's colleagues, DeFunis was simply a beneficiary of a discriminatory standard. Douglas, who had supported the *Griggs* decision, obviously did not comprehend its implications.

The quota issue re-emerged in 1978, when Allan Bakke, a white male refused admission to the University of California Medical School, challenged the school's policy of reserving 16 per cent of its slots for minorities. Each of the accepted minorities had academic credentials inferior to Bakke's. In a 156-page opinion with 167 footnotes, the

Justices reached the schizophrenic conclusion that Bakke should be admitted, but that certain skin colors could nevertheless be considered grounds for college admissions if the goal was to enhance "educational diversity."

A year later the Supreme Court ruled that companies could "voluntarily" impose quotas on themselves to avoid liability. Pressured by OFCC affirmative-action requirements and the need to forestall Title VII liability under *Griggs,* Kaiser Aluminum, like many other companies, had entered into a quota agreement with its union, the United Steelworkers of America, in 1974. The agreement stipulated that "not less than one minority employee will enter" apprentice and craft training programs "for every nonminority employee" until the percentage of minority craft workers approximated the percentage of minorities in the regions surrounding each Kaiser plant. Two seniority lists were drawn up, one white and one black, and training openings were filled alternately from the two lists.

Brian Weber, a 32-year-old white blue-collar worker who had ten years' seniority as an unskilled lab technician at Kaiser Aluminum's plant in Gramercy, Louisiana, applied for a training-program slot but was denied in favor of two blacks with less seniority. After his union denied his grievance, Weber wrote the local EEOC office requesting a copy of the 1964 Civil Rights Act. When the Civil Rights Act arrived in the mail, Weber read it through and found that it said "exactly what I thought. Everyone should be treated the same, regardless of race or sex." Encouraged by the statute's words, he filed a class-action suit representing his plant's white workers and won before district and appellate courts.

During Supreme Court oral arguments in *United Steelworkers* v. *Weber* Justice Potter Stewart quipped that the Justices had to determine whether employers may "discriminate against some white people." Justice William Brennan's answer, for a 5 to 2 majority, was an emphatic "yes." Brennan said the meaning of the 1964 Civil Rights Act could not be found in its statutory language but resided in its spirit, which Brennan had divined. He asserted that the Act's clear statutory language and the Dirksen, Tower, and Celler amendments conveyed a meaning that was the opposite of what Congress had really intended. A literal reading of Title VII, he said, would "bring about an end completely at variance with the purpose of the statute." In enacting the Civil Rights Act, Brennan continued, "Congress's primary concern" was with the plight of the Negro in our economy. Anything that helped minorities was broadly consistent with this purpose. This included racial quotas, as long as they were voluntarily adopted by companies and not required by the Federal Government under Title VII. Brennan denied that

Kaiser's plan would lead to quotas: "The plan is a temporary measure; it is not intended to maintain racial balance, but simply to eliminate a manifest racial imbalance."

Burger Has Second Thoughts

Chief Justice Burger had created disparate-impact analysis in his *Griggs* opinion without realizing its quota implications. Now that quotas were upon him, he found himself joining in dissent with Justice William Rehnquist. Brennan's *Weber* opinion, they said, was "Orwellian." In *Griggs,* the Court had declared that "discriminatory preference for any group, minority or majority, is precisely and only what Congress has proscribed." But eight years had passed, and the Civil Rights Act had been fully reconstructed. Burger and Rehnquist's alarm showed in their dissenting language: "By a tour de force reminiscent not of jurists such as Hale, Holmes, and Hughes, but of escape artists such as Houdini, the Court eludes clear statutory language, uncontradicted legislative history, and uniform precedent in concluding that employers are, after all, permitted to consider race in making employment decisions." The Court "introduces into Title VII a tolerance for the very evil that the law was intended to eradicate," Rehnquist said. Moreover, Brennan's reading of Section 703(j) was "outlandish" in the light of Title VII's other "flat prohibitions" against racial discrimination and is "totally belied by the Act's legislative history." Rehnquist cited a congressional interpretative memorandum clearly stating that "Title VII *does not permit* the ordering of racial quotas in businesses or unions and does not permit interferences with seniority rights of employees or union members." But Burger had set the stage for *Weber* with *Griggs,* and it was the pot calling the kettle black when he accused Brennan of amending the Civil Rights Act "to do precisely what both its sponsors and its opponents agreed the statute was not intended to do."

Having ruled in *Weber* that reverse discrimination was "benign discrimination," the Supreme Court upheld other quota schemes in subsequent cases. In the 1980 case *Fullilove* v. *Klutznick,* the Court said a federal spending program setting aside 10 per cent of public-works money for minority businesses violated neither the Constitution's guarantee of equal protection of the laws nor the 1964 Civil Rights Act.

In the 1987 case *Johnson* v. *Transportation Agency, Santa Clara County,* the issue was the maleness rather than the whiteness of white males. The Court ruled that job discrimination against a white male in favor of a woman with lower performance ratings was perfectly legal under Title VII, even though the county's transportation agency had no record of prior discrimination remedies. Rehnquist, Byron White, and Antonin Scalia didn't like the decision. Scalia said, "We effectively replace the goal of a discrimination-free society with the quite incompatible goal of proportionate representation by race and by sex in the workplace." He noted that civil rights had become a cynical numbers game played by politicians, lobbyists, corporate executives, lawyers, and government bureaucrats.

In 1989 there was a brief retrenchment when the Supreme Court, with its Reagan appointees, confronted the quota implications of *Griggs* and the decisions that had followed it. In *Wards Cove* v. *Atonio,* the Court ruled that statistical disparities were insufficient to establish a prima facie case of discrimination. In this case, the racial minorities who made up a majority of the unskilled work force at two Alaskan salmon canneries brought a discrimination lawsuit based on the fact that whites held a majority of skilled office positions. The suit claimed that this constituted underutilization of preferred minorities in office positions and was evidence of racial discrimination. The majority opinion, written by Justice White, rejected the discrimination claim. White noted that

any employer who had a segment of his work force that was— for some reason—racially imbalanced, could be hauled into court and forced to engage in the expensive and time-consuming task of defending the "business necessity" of the methods used to select the other members of his work force. The only practicable option for many employers will be to adopt racial quotas, ensuring that no portion of his work force deviates in racial composition from the other portions thereof; this is a result that Congress expressly rejected in drafting Title VII.

A week after *Wards Cove,* the Court ruled in *Martin* v. *Wilks* that victims of reverse discrimination due to consent decrees that imposed quotas had the right to challenge the decrees in court. The Court noted that victims of reverse discrimination found their rights affected by lawsuits to which they were not parties. Citing a long-standing legal tradition, the majority held that "a person cannot be deprived of his legal rights in a proceeding to which he is not a party."

These rulings caused an uproar among civil-rights activists, who charged that the new Reagan Court was racist. The illegal privileges that had evolved in the 18 years since *Griggs* was decided had become a squatter's right, and Congress and the Bush Administration were bullied into enacting the new inequality into law. The 1991 Civil Rights Act in effect repealed the 1964 Act by legalizing racial preferences as the core of civil-rights law. The new Act was designed to overturn the *Wards Cove* and *Wilks* rulings and to codify the disparate-impact standard of *Griggs.*

The statute also slammed shut the courthouse doors on white male victims of reverse discrimination. If statistical disparities or racial imbalance is proof of discrimination, white males adversely affected by quotas can have no standing in court. To give them standing would necessarily imperil the quota remedies for racial imbalance. You cannot simultaneously declare that anything short of proportional racial representation is discrimination and recognize the adverse impact of the "remedy" on white males. Under the 1991 Civil Rights Act, white males have no grounds for discrimination lawsuits until they are statistically underrepresented in management and line positions. They have no claims to be statistically represented as hirees, trainees, and promotees until preferred minorities are proportionately represented in management and line positions. Indeed, under Brennan's interpretation of the Civil Rights Act, which says that anything that helps preferred minorities is broadly consistent with the law, the disparate-impact standard could one day be ruled inapplicable to whites.

The 1991 Civil Rights Act added the threat of compensatory and punitive damages to the pressure for quotas. In "Understanding the 1991 Civil Rights Act," an article in *The Practical Lawyer,* Irving M. Geslewitz recommended that corporations apply cost-benefit analysis to determine whether "they are safer in hiring and promoting by numbers reflecting the percentages in the surrounding community than in risking disparate-impact lawsuits they are likely to lose." To counter charges of "hostile work environments," company lawyers want to be able to tell juries that their clients have many minority and women employees at all levels.

The day after the Civil Rights Act of 1991 became law, a *New York Times* article, "Affirmative Action Plans Are Part of Business Life," observed that quota policies are as "familiar to American businesses as tally sheets and bottom lines." A 1991 *Business Week* article entitled "Race in the Workplace: Is Affirmative Action Working?" reported that affirmative action is "deeply ingrained in American corporate culture. . . . The machinery hums along, nearly automatically, at the largest U.S. corporations. They have turned affirmative action into a smoothly running assembly line, with phalanxes of lawyers and affirmative-action managers."

The 1964 Civil Rights Act, which undertook to eliminate race and sex from private employment decisions, has instead been used to make race and sex the determining factors. Reverse discrimination is now a fact of life. Indeed, in strictly legal terms, the situation for white males today is worse than the situation for blacks under *Plessy* v. *Ferguson*'s separate-but-equal doctrine. In practice, blacks suffered unequal treatment under *Plessy*, but the decision officially required equal treatment. Under today's civil-rights regime, by contrast, whites can be legally discriminated against in university admissions, employment, and the allocation of government contracts.

In his famous dissent from *Plessy*, Justice John Marshall Harlan worried that the Louisiana law requiring racial segregation on public transportation would allow class distinctions to enter the legal system, since blacks and whites were economically as well as racially distinct. Harlan was certain that he wanted no status-based distinctions in the law. Our Constitution, he said "is color-blind, and neither knows nor tolerates classes among citizens. In respect of civil rights, all citizens are equal before the law. The humblest is the peer of the most powerful." Today, civil-rights activists reject Harlan's color-blind views. Privilege before the law has replaced equality before the law.

Form at end of book

WiseGuide Wrap-Up

Two forms of discrimination can be identified. One form—for example, being told that you cannot eat at a particular restaurant—has clear intent and is easy to identify. Less obvious is "institutionalized discrimination," a form of discrimination that permeates the written and unwritten rules of society. We are not always aware of institutionalized discrimination until we look at outcomes. Some of these practices, like seniority or height and weight requirements, seem impartial or related to the occupation. A closer look, however, may reveal that these ways of operating can lead to disparities of treatment along race, ethnic, and gender lines, and may actually have little to do with the job. However, they do serve to keep certain people in positions of privilege and power. The intent is not evident, but outcomes show a uniformity of population and an exclusion of talent. Preferential policies are not always seen as actually being discriminatory.

White men who have traditionally benefited from past policies are not hampered by a loss of self-esteem or feel that their talents are any less valued just because they did not compete against minorities or women to get their positions. In fact, they may believe that their achievements recognize an innate, unquestionable superiority. When Harvard admitted men only, few men felt that their admission was undeserved because women were not allowed to apply. Few rich people feel that their possessions are undeserved, even if their wealth is inherited. Are veterans less deserving than others if they take advantage of the policies that enable them to get government jobs, loans, scholarships, and university placements? Are these policies a form of affirmative action? If so, why are they more acceptable than other forms?

Can you think of a situation in which you have been unfairly treated? What happened, and what did you do about it? Almost everyone can remember such a situation in detail and has strong feelings about it. Can you think of a situation in which you were especially privileged—when you received something you did not deserve or when you were honored for something you didn't achieve? What did you do about it? Did you point out the mistake and correct it? How did you feel about it? Now, can you think of a situation when you treated someone else unfairly? When someone pointed it out to you, what did you do about it? Can you remember every detail? How did you feel about it? Why aren't we as conscious of our infringement on the rights of others as when the situation is reversed?

Most people want a "color-blind" society in which individuals can develop their talents and pursue happiness in any way they choose. However, individuals who run into difficulties often find that it is their group membership that prevents them from achieving the "American Dream."

R.E.A.L. Sites

This list provides a print preview of typical **Coursewise** R.E.A.L. sites. (There are over 100 such sites at the **Courselinks**™ site.) The danger in printing URLs is that web sites can change overnight. As we went to press, these sites were functional using the URLs provided. If you come across one that isn't, please let us know via email to: webmaster@coursewise.com. Use your Passport to access the most current list of R.E.A.L. sites at the **Courselinks** site.

Site name: Americans United for Affirmative Action

URL: http://www.auaa.org/

Why is it R.E.A.L.? Co-founded by Martin Luther King III, Americans United for Affirmative Action is a nongovernmental organization dedicated to defending affirmative action programs. Its web site has articles on the issues surrounding affirmative action, ongoing follow-ups of government bills and court cases, a time line of affirmative action legislation and events, and a civil rights library. It also has links to other sites with affirmative action information.

Key terms: affirmative action, civil rights

Site name: The Feminist Majority Foundation Online

URL: http://www.feminist.org/

Why is it R.E.A.L.? The Feminist Majority, a nongovernmental organization, devotes a page on its web site to affirmative action issues. This page has news stories that deal with racism, sexism, and gay rights in higher education, technology, and broadcasting from 1996 to the present.

Key terms: racism, sexism, gay rights

....

Site name: American Civil Rights Institute

URL: http://www.acri.org/

Why is it R.E.A.L.? The American Civil Rights Institute, a nongovernmental organization based in Sacramento, California, supports Ward Connerly's position on affirmative action. Its purpose is to educate the public about race and gender preferences and to monitor the implementation of California's Proposition 209.

Key terms: civil rights, preferences, set-asides, quotas

....

section 2 | Is Bilingual Education Failing America's Schoolchildren?

Take a Closer Look

1. Are bilingual education programs effective in teaching students English?

2. Are bilingual education programs successful in teaching or maintaining the student's native language?

3. Are bilingual education programs expensive to operate and maintain? Are they worth the cost?

4. Do bilingual education programs retard acceptance into American society?

5. Does participation in bilingual education programs stigmatize students?

WiseGuide Intro

Is bilingualism strictly the knowledge and use of two languages? The emotion generated by the debates this topic engenders suggests that something more is going on. While expressing concern for the social and cultural adjustment of immigrants, those who argue against bilingual education seem to be more interested in eliminating the native language than in teaching English. Their suggestions rarely call for increased spending to assist immigrants or to improve or expand school programs.

The attitude toward the native language is important. Positive outcomes are more likely when bilingualism is not a stigmatized trait but rather a symbol of elite status. Research indicates that, all things being equal, higher degrees of bilingualism are associated with higher levels of cognitive attainment. This is particularly true when the second language is enrichment to the native language.

The Internet and the increasingly interconnected world of business indicate that English is becoming a worldwide form of communication, which means that acquiring English is beneficial to everyone. However, other languages do not necessarily have to be sacrificed to attain this. Multilingual abilities are a definite advantage.

In Reading 3, Wayne P. Thomas and Virginia P. Collier look briefly at other societies with bilingual populations. They discuss the teaching methods in the classroom and list successful strategies. They conclude, "Students who graduate with monolingual perspectives will not be prepared to contribute to their societies, for cross-cultural contact is at an all-time high in human history as population mobility continues throughout the world."

In Reading 4, Kenji Hakuta and Eugene E. Garcia look at the problems associated with bilingualism. They note that the U.S. immigrant population has changed substantially over the course of the century and that this is a factor in the approach to bilingual education. They refute the notion that bilingualism is a mental burden and discuss the problems of social context regarding language acquisition. From their perspective, bilingualism is an asset that should be fostered rather than a problem to be solved.

Issue 2: Is bilingual education failing America's schoolchildren?

Two Languages Are Better Than One

Dual language programs help native and nonnative speakers of English speak two languages proficiently—and they do so in cost-effective ways that lead to high academic achievement for all students.

Wayne P. Thomas and Virginia P. Collier

Wayne P. Thomas is Professor of Research and Evaluation Methods, and Virginia P. Collier is Professor of Bilingual/Multicultural/ESL Education, Graduate School of Education, George Mason University. The authors are researchers with the Center for Research on Education, Diversity, and Excellence (CREDE), funded by the Office of Educational Research and Improvement, U.S. Department of Education.

Among the underachieving youth in U.S. schools, students with no proficiency in English must overcome enormous equity gaps, school achievements tests in English show. Over the past three decades, schools have developed a wide range of programs to serve these English learners. After much experimentation, U.S. schools now have clear achievement data that point to the most powerful models of effective schooling for English learners. What is astounding is that these same programs are also dynamic models for school reform for all students.

Imagine how the 21st century will look. Our world will surely be in constant change, for we are facing this pattern now. The predictions of the near future also depict an interconnected world, with global travel and instant international communications. Right now, many U.S. businesses seek employees proficient in both English and another language. Students who graduate with monocultural perspectives will not be prepared to contribute to their societies, for cross-cultural contact is at an all-time high in human history as population mobility continues throughout the world (Cummins in Ovando and Collier, in press). Thus, majority and minority language students together must prepare for a constantly changing world.

Tapping the Power of Linguistic Diversity

For more than three decades, as we have struggled to develop effective models for schooling English learners, we have mostly considered the choices available to us from a deficit perspective. That is, we have often viewed English learners as a "problem" for our schools (oh, no—they don't know English), and so we "remediate" by sending them to a specialist to be "fixed." In the remedial program, English learners receive less access to the standard grade-level curriculum. The achievement and equity gap increases as native English speakers forge ahead while English learners make less progress. Thus, underachieving groups continue to underachieve in the next generation. Unfortunately, the two most common types of U.S. school services provided for English learners—English as a Second Language (ESL) pullout and transitional bilingual education—are remedial in nature. Participating students and teachers suffer often from the social consequences of this perception.

But when the focus of any special school program is on academic enrichment for all students, the school community perceives that program positively, and students become academically successful and deeply engaged in the learning process. Thus, enrichment programs for English learners are extremely effective when they are intellectually challenging and use students' linguistic and cultural experiences as a resource for interdisciplinary, discovery learning (Chiang 1994, Ovando and Collier in press, Thomas and Collier 1997). Further, educators who use the enrichment models that were initially developed for English learners are beginning to see the power of these models for *all* students.

A History of Bilingual Enrichment

These innovative enrichment models are called by varying names—*dual language, bilingual immersion, two-way bilingual,* and *developmental bilingual education.* We recommend these models as forms of mainstream education through two languages that will benefit all students. Let's examine the history of their development and some basic characteristics of these models.

Initially, the first two 20th-century experiences with bilingual education in the United States and Canada in the early 1960s came about as a result of parental pressure. Both of these experiments were enrichment models. In Canada, English-speaking parents who wanted their children to develop deep proficiency in both French and English initiated what became known as immersion education. Immersion is a commitment to bilingual schooling throughout grades K–12 in which students are instructed 90 percent of the school day during kindergarten and grade 1 in the *minority* language chosen for the program, and 10 percent of the day in the majority language (English). The hands-on nature of academic work in the early grades is a natural vehicle for proficiency development of the minority language.

Immersion programs emphasize the less dominant language more than English in the first years, because the minority language is less supported by the broader society, and academic uses of the language are less easily acquired outside school. Gradually, with each subsequent grade, the program provides more instruction in the majority language until children learn the curriculum equally through both languages by grade 4 or 5. By grade 6, students have generally developed deep academic proficiency in both languages, and they can work on math, science, social students, and language arts at or above grade level in *either* language. From the 1960s to the 1990s, immersion bilingual schooling has grown immensely popular in Canada and has achieved high rates of success with majority and minority students, students of middle- and low-income families, as well as students with learning disabilities (Cummins and Swain 1986, Genesee 1987).

About the same time that the first immersion program started in Canada, Cubans arriving in Miami, Florida, initiated the first U.S. experiment with two-way bilingual education in 1963. The term *two-way* refers to two language groups acquiring the curriculum through each other's languages: *one-way* bilingual education refers to one language group receiving schooling through two languages (Stern 1963). Intent on overthrowing Fidel Castro and returning to their country, the Cuban arrivals established private bilingual schools to develop their children's English and maintain their Spanish. The public schools, losing significant enrollment, chose to develop bilingual classes to attract students back. As English-speaking parents enrolled their children in the classes, two-way, integrated bilingual schooling emerged as a new program model in the United States. These classes provided a half day of the grade-level curriculum in Spanish and a half day in English, now known as the *50-50* model of two way.

Over time, these two experiments have expanded to many states in the United States as school communities recognize the benefits for all students. The immersion model, originally developed in Canada for majority language speakers, has become known as the *90-10* two-way model in the United States because during the first two years both language groups receive 90 percent of the instruction through the *minority* language.

Students As Peer Language Models

Key to the success of all two-way programs is the fact that both language groups stay together throughout the school day, serving as peer tutors for each other. Peer models stimulate natural language acquisition for both groups because they keep the level of interaction cognitively complex (Panfil 1995). Research has consistently demonstrated that academic achievement is very high for all groups of participants compared to control groups who receive schooling only through English. This holds true for students of low socioeconomic status, as well as African-American students and language-minority students, with those in the 90-10 model achieving even higher than those in the 50-50 model (Lindholm 1990, Lindholm and Aclan 1991, Thomas and Collier 1997).

The Role of Careful Planning

What are other essential characteristics of this school reform? An important principle is clear curricular separation of the two languages of instruction. To maintain a continuous cognitive challenge, teachers do not repeat or translate lessons in the second language, but reinforce concepts taught in one language across the two languages in a spiraling curriculum. Teachers alternate the language of instruction by theme or subject area, by time of day, by day of the week, or by the week. If two teachers are teaming, each teacher represents one language. When two teachers share and exchange two classes, this is a cost-effective, mainstream model that adds no additional teachers to a school system's budget. In contrast, ESL pullout is the most costly of all program models for English learners because extra ESL resource teachers must be added to the mainstream staff (Crawford 1997).

Successful two-way bilingual education includes

- a minimum of six years of bilingual instruction;

- focus on the core academic curriculum rather than on a watered-down version;

- quality language arts instruction in both languages;

- separation of the two languages for instruction;

- use of the non-English language for at least 50 percent of the instructional time and as much as 90 percent in the early grades;

- an additive bilingual environment that has full support of school administrators;

- a balanced ratio of students who speak each language (for example, 50:50 or 60:40, preferably not to go below 70:30);

- promotion of positive interdependence among peers and between teachers and students;

- high-quality instructional personnel; and

- active parent-school partnerships (Lindholm 1990).

Demographics influence the feasibility of two-way programs, because the students in each language group serve as peer teachers for each other. A natural choice for many U.S. schools is a Spanish-English two-way program, because Spanish speakers are most often the largest language group. In the 204 two-way bilingual schools identified in the United States in a 1997 survey, other languages of instruction in addition to Spanish include, in order of frequency, Korean, French, Cantonese, Navajo, Japanese, Arabic, Portuguese, Russian, and Mandarin Chinese (Montone et al. 1997).

Closing the Equity Gap through Bilingual Enrichment

What makes these programs work? To answer this question, let's look at the students who are initially the lowest achievers on tests in English. Most school policymakers commonly assume that students need only a couple of years to learn a second language. But while these students make dramatic progress in English development in the first two years, English language learners are competing with a moving target, the native English speaker, when tested in English.

The average native English speaker typically gains 10 months of academic growth in one 10-month school year in English development because first language acquisition is a natural work in progress throughout the school

U.S. schools now have clear achievement data that point to the most powerful models of effective schooling for English learners. What is astounding is that these same programs are also dynamic models for school reform for all students.

years, not completed until young adulthood. Although some score higher and some lower, on average they also make a year's progress in a year's time in mathematics, science, and social studies. Thus students not yet proficient in English initially score three or more years below grade level on the tests in English because they cannot yet demonstrate in their second language all that they actually know. These students must outgain the native speaker by making one and one-half years progress on the academic tests in their second language for each of six successive school years (a total of nine years progress in six years) to reach the typical performance level of the constantly advancing native English speaker.

When students do academic work in their primary language for more than two to three years (the typical support time in a transitional bilingual program), they are able to demonstrate with each succeeding year that they are making more gains than the native English speaker—and closing the gap in achievement as measured by tests in English across the curriculum. After five to six years of enrichment bilingual schooling, former English learners (now proficient in English) are able to demonstrate their deep knowledge on the academic tests in English across the curriculum, as well as in their native language, achieving on or above grade level (Thomas and Collier 1997).

Bridging the Gap to a Better Tomorrow

Why is such progress for English learners important for our schools? Language-minority students are predicted to account for about 40 percent of the school-age population by the 2030s (Berliner and Biddle 1995). It is in our pragmatic self-interest to ensure their success as young adults, for they will be key to a robust economy to pay retirement and medical benefits for today's working adults. We must close the equity gap by providing enrichment schooling for all. For native English speakers as well as language-minority students, the enrichment bilingual classes appear to provide a constant stimulus and intellectual challenge similar to that of a gifted and talented class. The research evidence is overwhelmingly clear that *proficient* bilinguals outperform monolinguals on school tests (Collier 1995). Crossing cultural, social class, and language boundaries, students in a bilingual class develop multiple ways of solving human problems and approach ecological and social science issues from a cross-national perspective. These learners acquire deep academic proficiency in two languages, which becomes a valuable resource in adult professional life. And they learn to value each other's knowledge and life experiences—leading to meaningful respect and collaboration that lasts a lifetime.

References

Berliner, D. C., and B. J. Biddle. (1995). *The Manufactured Crisis: Myths, Fraud, and the Attack on America's Public Schools.* Reading, Mass.: Addison-Wesley.

Chiang, R. A. (1994). "Recognizing Strengths and Needs of All Bilingual Learners: A Bilingual/Multicultural Perspective." *NABE News* 17, 4: 11, 22–23.

Collier, V. P. (1995). *Promoting Academic Success for ESL Students: Understanding Second Language Acquisition for School.* Elizabeth: New Jersey Teachers of English to Speakers of Other Languages-Bilingual Educators.

Crawford, J. (1997). *Best Evidence: Research Foundations of the Bilingual Education Act.* Washington, D.C.: National Clearinghouse for Bilingual Education.

Cummins, J., and M. Swain. (1986). *Bilingualism in Education.* New York: Longman.

Genesee, F. (1987). *Learning Through Two Languages: Studies of Immersion and Bilingual Education.* Cambridge, Mass.: Newbury House.

Lindholm, K. J. (1990). "Bilingual Immersion Education: Criteria for Program Development." In *Bilingual Education: Issues and Strategies,* edited by A. M. Padilla, H. H. Fairchild, and C. M. Valadez. Newbury Park, Calif.: Sage.

Lindholm, K. J., and Z. Aclan. (1991). "Bilingual Proficiency as a Bridge to Academic Achievement: Results from Bilingual/Immersion Programs." *Journal of Education* 173: 99–113.

Montone, C., Christian, D., and A. Whitcher. (1997). *Directory of Two-way Bilingual Programs in the United States.* Rev. ed. Washington, D.C.: Center for Applied Linguistics.

Ovando, C. J., and V. P. Collier. (in press). *Bilingual and ESL Classrooms: Teaching in Multicultural Contexts.* 2nd ed. New York: McGraw-Hill (available in Nov. 1997).

Panfil, K. (1995). "Learning from One Another: A Collaborative Study of a Two-way Bilingual Program by Insiders with Multiple Perspectives." *Dissertation Abstracts International* 56–10A, 3859. (University Microfilms No. AAI96-06004).

Stern, H. H., ed. (1963). *Foreign Languages in Primary Education: The Teaching of Foreign or Second Languages to Younger Children.* Hamburg, Germany: International Studies in Education, UNESCO Institute for Education.

Thomas, W. P., and V. P. Collier. (1997). *School Effectiveness for Language Minority Students.* Washington, D.C.: National Clearinghouse for Bilingual Education.

Form at end of book

Issue 2: Is bilingual education failing America's schoolchildren?

Bilingualism and Education

Kenji Hakuta and Eugene E. Garcia

University of California, Santa Cruz

Abstract

The concept of bilingualism as applied to individual children and to educational programs is discussed, and the history of research on bilingual children and bilingual education programs in the United States is reviewed. Bilingualism has been defined predominantly in linguistic dimensions despite the fact that bilingualism is correlated with a number of nonlinguistic social parameters. The linguistic handle has served policymakers well in focusing on an educationally vulnerable population of students, but the handle is inadequate as the single focus of educational intervention. Future research will have to be directed toward a multifaceted vision of bilingualism as a phenomenon embedded in society.

Bilingualism is a term that has been used to describe an attribute of individual children as well as social institutions. At both levels, the topic has been dominated by controversy. On the individual level, debate has centered on the possible costs and benefits of bilingualism in young children. On the societal level, fiery argument can be witnessed in the United States about the wisdom of bilingual education and the official support of languages other than English in public institutions. Particularly in the latter case, emotions run hot because of the symbolism contained in language and its correlation with ethnic group membership.

The controversy surrounding bilingualism is magnified by a sense of urgency generated by the changing demographic picture. In the United States, there are over 30 million individuals for whom English is not the primary language of the home. Of those, 2.5 million are children in the school age range, with this number expected to double by the year 2000. There are now many states in which the linguistic-minority school population is approaching 25% or more (Arizona, California, Colorado, Florida, New Mexico, New York, and Texas), and in many large urban school districts throughout the United States, 50% of the students may come from non-English-speaking homes.

Whether the debate is over the merits of bilingualism in individuals or institutions, there is considerable confusion over a basic definitional issue. The problem can be succinctly stated as follows: Is bilingualism strictly the knowledge and usage of two linguistic systems, or does it involve the social dimensions encompassed by the languages? Oscillation between these linguistic and social perspectives on bilingualism has frequently led to misconceptions about the development of bilingual children as well as misunderstanding in educational initiatives to serve linguistic-minority populations.

As a case in point, consider the linguistic and social complexities contained in the following statement about school experiences by a ninth-grade Mexican-born boy who had immigrated from Mexico six months earlier:

There is so much discrimination and hate. Even from other kids from Mexico who have been here longer. They don't treat us like brothers. They hate even more. It makes them feel more like natives. They want to be American. They don't want to speak Spanish to us, they already know English and how to act. If they're with us, other people will treat them more like wetbacks, so they try to avoid us. (Olsen, 1988, p. 36)

Bilingualism, thought of simply as a bivariate function of linguistic proficiency in two languages, underrepresents the intricacies of the social settings. The history of research on bilingual children contains many false inferences about the effects of bilingualism based on a miscalculation of the complexity of the phenomenon. Similarly, current research to evaluate bilingual education programs takes an extremely narrow definition of bilingualism, that is, as the usage of two languages in instruction.

The importance of language in helping us understand the phenomenon is obvious. Nevertheless, language's accessibility to scientists must not be confused with its role in either the cause of problems or solutions to them. Wage distribution can be useful in telling us about the structure of racial discrimination, but changing wage distribution may not help solve the root causes of the problem. In a similar way, looking at language, we realize, only helps to facilitate the identification of problems and potential solutions, but additional steps are needed to provide adequate education to linguistic-minority students.

In this article we argue that although language provides an important empirical handle on the problems associated with bilingualism, one must be careful not to overattribute the causes of those problems to linguistic parameters. We provide brief overviews of the knowledge of bilingual children and bilingual education programs that has been gained through reliance on narrow linguistic definitions, bearing in mind its heuristic value. We then offer future directions for research.

The Bilingual Child

In the calculus of mental energy, what are the costs of bilingualism? Early research on the effects of bilingualism on immigrant children, conducted primarily at the turn of the century, painted a bleak picture. As Thompson (1952) wrote in summarizing this body of literature, "There can be no doubt that the child reared in a bilingual environment is handicapped in his language growth. One can debate the issue as to whether speech facility in two languages is worth the consequent retardation in the common language of the realm" (p. 367).

Much of this early work on bilingualism in children can be interpreted within the context of the social history surrounding the debate over the changing nature of immigration in the early 1900s. The basic data to be explained were bilingual children's poor performances on various standardized tests of intelligence. From the empiricist point of view, the bilingualism of the children was thought to be a mental burden that caused lower levels of intelligence. This viewpoint was offered as an alternative to the hereditarian position, argued forcefully by prominent nativists such as Carl Brigham, Lewis Terman, and Florence Goodenough, that the new immigrants were simply from inferior genetic stock (Hakuta, 1986). Subscribers to the latter viewpoint sounded the social alarm that "these immigrants are beaten men from beaten races, representing the worse failures in the struggle for existence. . . . Europe is allowing its slums and its most stagnant reservoirs of degraded peasantry to be drained off upon our soil" (Francis Walker, quoted in Ayres, 1909, p. 103).

What is interesting about this early literature is its definition of bilingualism. The bilingual children included in these studies were not chosen on the basis of their linguistic abilities in the two languages. Rather, societal level criteria having to do with immigrant status were used,

such as having a foreign last name (see Diaz, 1983). It is not clear whether the "bilingual" children in these studies were at all bilingual in their home language and English. Yet, on the basis of such studies using social rather than linguistic criteria, conclusions were drawn as to the effects of linguistic variables on intelligence. The point here is that language is a salient characteristic of children from immigrant and minority backgrounds that provides an opportune dumping ground for developmental problems that may or may not be related to language.

Research in the last few decades, fortunately, has developed considerable sophistication in understanding second-language acquisition and the nature of bilingualism. What has emerged is a relatively consistent set of answers to some fundamental questions about the linguistic and cognitive development of bilingual children. These answers argue against the early view—still held to be fact by some laypersons and educators—that bilingualism could be harmful to the child's mental development and that the native language should be eliminated as quickly as possible if these effects are to be avoided.

Indeed, more recent studies suggest that all other things being equal, higher degrees of bilingualism are associated with higher levels of cognitive attainment (Diaz, 1983). Measures have included cognitive flexibility, metalinguistic awareness, concept formation, and creativity. These findings are based primarily on research with children in additive bilingual settings, that is, in settings where the second language is added as an enrichment to the native language and not at the expense of the native language. Causal relationships have been difficult to establish, but in general, positive outcomes have been noted, particularly in situations where bilingualism is not a socially stigmatized trait but rather a symbol of membership in a social elite.

Second-Language Acquisition

An important theoretical justification for the early view about the compensatory relationship between the two languages can be found in behaviorist accounts of language acquisition. If first-language acquisition consists of the establishment of stimulus-response connections between objects and words and the formation of generalizations made on the basis of the frequency patterns of words into sentences, then second-language acquisition must encounter interference from the old set of connections to the extent that they are different. The two languages were seen, in this empiricist account, as two sets of stimuli competing for a limited number of connections. This provided justification for the advice given to immigrant parents to try and use English at home so as not to confuse the children.

This empiricist account of language acquisition was strongly rejected in the late 1950s and 1960s on both theoretical (Chomsky, 1957) and empirical grounds (Brown & Bellugi, 1964). As with most revolutionary changes in the empirical disciplines, the nature of the questions about language acquisition changed in a qualitative manner. The new metaphor for the acquisition of language was the unfolding of innate capacities, and the goal of research became to delineate the exact nature of the unfolding process. If language acquisition was not the forging of connections between the stimuli of the outside world, then one would no longer have to see the learning of a second language as involving a "dog-eat-dog," competition with the first language. To borrow James Fallows's (1986) recent metaphor, having two languages is more like having two children than like having two wives.

There is considerable research support for this more recent view. For example, in the process of second-language acquisition, the native language does not interfere in any significant way with the development of the second language. Second-language acquisition and first-language acquisition are apparently guided by common principles across languages and are part of the human cognitive system (McLaughlin, 1987). From this structural point of view, the learning of a second language is not hampered by the first. Furthermore, the rate of acquisition of a second language is highly related to the proficiency level in the native language, which suggests that the two capacities share and build upon a common underlying base rather than competing for limited resources (Cummins, 1984).

Language Proficiency

Just as recent work in intelligence has moved away from regarding it as a single unitary construct (Sternberg, 1985), recent work on the notion of "language proficiency" has revealed a rich and multifaceted concept (Cummins, 1984; C. E. Snow, 1987). Research has extended the notion of language ability beyond grammatical skills to the use of language in various contexts, and more sophisticated notions are developing regarding language acquisition.

For example, C. E. Snow has identified at least two different dimensions of language proficiency in bilingual children. One dimension involves the use of language in face-to-face communicative settings (contextualized language skills), and the other dimension encompasses language use relatively removed from contextual support (decontextualized language skills). Contextualized and decontextualized language skills are independent, such that facility in interpersonal language use may not imply the ability to use the language in academic situations.

The diversification of language proficiency into different task domains complicates the task of understanding bilingual ability. The measurement of bilingualism has always been complex, and the maintenance of bilingualism in communities has been regarded by sociolinguists as best understood with respect to situational and functional constraints imposed in language use (Fishman, Cooper, & Ma, 1966). What is important is that language ability does not develop or atrophy across the board, that is, across the various domains of applications.

Social Context of Language Usage

Research on the use of the two languages in bilingual children (Zentella, 1981) suggests that they are adept at shifting from one language to the other depending on the conversational situation (a process known as code-switching) and that this behavior is not the result of the confusion of the two languages. Rather, bilinguals code-switch with each other to take advantage of the richness of the communicative situation, and from the viewpoint of ethnographers, one function of such code alternation is to establish and regulate the social boundaries of the two worlds (Gumperz, 1982). Such studies are important because they remind the student of child language that bilingualism (and language use in general) is a social phenomenon that takes place between two or more parties and that questions of language use are really questions about social context, not about linguistic structure.

Conclusions about Bilingual Children

The research evidence suggests that second-language acquisition involves a process that, rather than interacting structurally with the first language, builds upon an underlying base common to both languages. There does not appear to be competition over mental resources by the two languages, and there are even possible cognitive advantages to bilingualism. It is evident that the duality of the languages per se does not hamper the overall language proficiency or cognitive development of bilingual children. Despite such conclusions, it is interesting to note the extent to which the debate over bilingual education has centered on the metaphor of languages in competition.

Bilingual Education

The policy debate over how best to educate students who enter school with limited ability in English has focused on the issue of native-language support in instruction (August & Garcia, 1988; Baker & de Kanter, 1983). There is hardly any dispute over the ultimate goal of the programs—to "mainstream" students in monolingual English classrooms with maximal efficiency. The tension has centered on the specific instructional role of the native language: How long, how much, and how intensely should it be used?

On one side of this debate are supporters of native-language instruction. Proponents of bilingual education recommend aggressive development of the native language prior to the introduction of English. This approach is based on the argument that competencies in the native language, particularly as they relate to decontentualized language skills, provide important cognitive foundations for second-language acquisition and academic learning in general. The ease of transfer of skills acquired in the native language to English is an important component of this argument.

On the other side of the debate, some recommend the introduction of the English curriculum from the very beginning of the student's schooling experience, with minimal use of the native language. This strategy calls for the use of simplified English to facilitate comprehension. The approach is typically combined with an English as a Second Language (ESL) component. One intuitive appeal of this English-only method is its consistency with time-in-task arguments—that spending more time being exposed to English should aid students in their acquisition of English (Rossel & Ross, 1986).

Research and Evaluation of Bilingual Education

Bilingual education programs have been in existence for over two decades, and thus the reasonable question arises as to whether there is evidence of the relative effectiveness of the different approaches. Summative evaluations of programs that compare these different approaches have run into difficulty on a number of fronts. Willig (1985), in a meta-analysis of studies of the effectiveness of bilingual education, complained that evaluation research in this area is plagued with problems ranging from poor design to bad measurement. She concluded that "most research conclusions regarding the effectiveness of bilingual education reflect weaknesses of research itself rather than effects of the actual programs" (p. 297).

The range of variability among the research approaches chosen is instructive. Almost all of the program evaluation studies concentrate on the effectiveness of the programs in teaching the students English, rather than focusing on students' overall academic development or factors other than traditional measures of school success. Furthermore, the studies tend to observe children over only a limited duration, often no more than two years. The research defines its treatments and outcomes in strictly linguistic terms. At stake is the question of which ap-

proach would lead to faster and stronger acquisition of English. This question is a scientifically legitimate one, but it is dwarfed when compared to the outcomes that are of real long-term interest to society: the social and economic advancement of linguistic-minority populations through education.

Paulston (1980) expressed concern with the narrowness of the definition of program success in the following way:

It makes a lot more sense to look at employment figures upon leaving school, figures on drug addiction and alcoholism, suicide rates, and personality disorders, i.e., indicators which measure the social pathology which accompanies social injustice, rather than in terms of language skills. . . . The dropout rate for American Indians in Chicago public schools is 95 percent; in the bilingual-bicultural Little Big Horn High School in Chicago the dropout rate in 1976 was 11 percent, and I found that figure a much more meaningful indicator for evaluation of the bilingual program than any psychometric assessment of students' language skills. (p. 41)

It is not always the case that English language proficiency has guided educational research with bilinguals. The Significant Bilingual Instructional Features Study, funded in 1980, was a federal study that described instructional strategies in selected "effective" bilingual education classrooms around the country (Tikunoff, 1983). It was able to identify instructional attributes in these classrooms that were similar to those reported in effective nonbilingual classrooms as well as a set of attributes specifically common to the effective bilingual classrooms. More recent research, particularly that of Carter and Chatfield (1986) and Krashen and Biber (1988), has followed this earlier example of describing the organizational and instructional attributes of schools and classrooms that produce academically successful bilingual students. However, even the more recent federal initiatives regarding program evaluation continue to look almost exclusively at English-language skills as the primary outcome variable (Ramirez, 1986).

Bilingual Education Policy

Continued focus on instructional language as treatment and English language as outcome can be directly traced to the judicial and legislative impetus for the development of programs and the related student eligibility criteria. The courts and Congress have repeatedly spoken directly to the disadvantages that students face as the result of their limited English proficiency. In the landmark 1974 United States Supreme Court decision in *Lau v. Nichols,* the court directly addressed the issue of language: "There is no equality of treatment merely by providing students with the same facilities, textbooks, teachers, and curriculum: for students who do not understand English are effectively foreclosed from meaningful education" (p. 26). In that same year, Congress addressed the issue in the Equal Education Opportunity Act (EEOA, 1974). The EEOA was an effort by Congress to specifically define what constitutes a denial of equal educational opportunity, including "the failure by an educational agency to take appropriate action to overcome language barriers that impede equal participation by students in its instructional programs" (EEOA, 1974, p. 1146).

Federal program initiatives in the form of targeted bilingual education legislation (in 1968, 1974, 1978, 1984, and 1988) have provided over a billion dollars in support for local school-district programs. In concert with the aims of the legislature and the courts, the main goal of these programs is to increase English-language proficiency. Guidelines for student inclusion in these programs have required evidence of limited English oral ability as assessed by a standardized English measure; a similar assessment of English proficiency is required prior to program exit. States with large numbers of bilingual students have adopted similar requirements. Moreover, these state and federal programs have focused their attention on the instructional strategies, frequently defined with respect to language of instruction, that will ensure the development of English-language proficiency.

The narrow linguistic definition of bilingualism in such programs has meant problems in accounting for all of the data. For example, as Cummins (1986) pointed out, linguistic mismatch between home and school may be a viable explanation for the school failure of some Spanish-speaking groups, but it fails to explain why some Asian-language groups have not experienced similar degrees of difficulty. Larger social and cultural factors embedded in the histories of different linguistic-minority groups may need to be taken into account (Ogbu & Matute-Bianchi, 1986), as well as differences in learning styles that interact with instructional approaches (Wong Fillmore & McLaughlin, 1986).

That the linguistic definition of bilingualism in these programs can lead to imperfect predictability with respect to different groups of students should come as no surprise. Obviously, no quick fix for larger issues of social and cultural adjustment is likely to result from the manipulation of a single variable such as instructional language. We do not mean to suggest that the language variable is unimportant; rather, we are warning that the isolation of this single attribute as the only variable of significance ignores our present understanding of language as a complex interaction of linguistic, psychological, and social domains. The

linguistic handle may have served policymakers well in focusing on an educationally vulnerable population of students, but it is clearly inadequate as the single focus of educational intervention aimed at ensuring academic competence for this population.

Future Research

A considerable amount of knowledge has accumulated on bilingualism in recent years (summaries have been offered by Garcia, 1983; Grosjean, 1982; Hakuta, 1986; Haugen, 1973), and the topic has captured the attention of scholars from diverse disciplines. Inevitably, this body of research has overlapped with issues in education, particularly linguistic-minority education. The potpourri of concerns closely related to bilingualism constitutes a fertile meeting ground for social scientists with widely different research interests. We believe that future research should be directed at expanding the knowledge to be gained at the junctures of those diverse interests, as described in the following sections.

The Language-Cognition-Affect Connection

How language is related to general cognition and how both of these are involved with affective variables such as attitude, self-awareness, and identity formation can be fruitfully studied in bilingual individuals. Bilinguals, for example, provide test cases that disassociate variables in cognitive and language development that are otherwise conflated (Slobin, 1973). On the affective dimension, the relationship between affective variables and changes in language proficiency (e.g., greater degrees of acquisition of a second language or attrition of the native language) has been well explored in some settings (Gardner, 1983; R. D. Lambert & Freed, 1982). However, specific mechanisms about the relationship (e.g., Clark & Fiske, 1982) have yet to be proposed, and a coherent framework that takes into account issues of social identification processes (Gumperz, 1982) and emotions (Ervin-Tripp, 1987) must be developed. Bilinguals, as individuals who possess different configurations of affect toward the two languages, provide important empirical evidence on such relationships.

Individual/Societal Levels of Analysis

Bilingualism also offers an important area where the connections between individual and societal levels of a phenomenon can be studied. One example would be the notion of language vitality (Giles & Johnson, 1981) in individuals and in social groups. It is well known that bilingualism in social groups undergoes shift, often resulting in a monolingual community within two or three generations (Veltman, 1988). The rate of this language shift is a function of language vitality.

One argument for advocating aggressive development of the native language of linguistic-minority youngsters prior to introduction of English is that there is little environmental support for the home language because the social milieu (aside from the home and the immediate community) is overwhelmingly English (W. E. Lambert, 1984). Lower levels of language vitality at the larger community level presumably lead to lower levels of individual development in language proficiency. This relationship between the social milieu and the individual child has not been rigorously studied, but it provides an ideal "preparation" in which the impact of a societal level variable on individual development can be mapped out in detail.

Research, Practice, and Policy Interface

There continues to be a great need for quality research on the basic processes of bilingualism as well as on the nature and effectiveness of educational programs that serve linguistic-minority students. The need is made greater because this topic readily invites "folk" speculation based, for example, on the experiences of immigrant relatives.

Among the various dilemmas confronting socially minded researchers is balancing responsiveness to this pressing need of society against standard scholarly attitudes toward applied research. Scientists with a sense of social responsibility often have resorted to bifurcating their energy, and scholars who have ventured into social policy have at times endangered their own scientific credibility. As in many areas of child development, bilingualism and education is an exciting arena in which basic research can be conducted with educational and policy emphases, and with mutual enrichment rather than compromise (Zigler & Finn-Stevenson, 1987).

Indeed, in our view, scholars who conduct such research must step away from their traditional relationships with educators and policymakers. Rather than interpreting ivory tower research for practitioners, a collaborative structure and program of research must be formed through an ongoing dialogue between all parties involved in the education of linguistic-minority students, and new research questions can be generated from such discourse. An important by-product of such collaboration would be the efficient translation of research into practical and political deliberations, as well as deep inquiry into the role

relationships between the various parties involved (Cummins, 1987).

Linguistic Minorities and the Linguistic Majority

We believe that work in the area of bilingualism must establish continuities between the phenomenon as it occurs in minority and majority populations. For example, is second-language acquisition in principle the same process when operative in linguistic minority and majority individuals? How is the acquisition of English by a Hmong refugee child different from the acquisition of French by a native speaker of English?

At the programmatic level, it is important to recognize the paradox that the educational system continues to convert linguistic-minority bilingual children into English monolinguals yet, at the same time, deplores the lack of competence of Americans in foreign languages, many of which were natively spoken by minority children (Simon, 1980). So-called bilingual immersion programs (M. A. Snow, 1986), which combine language programs designed for minority students with those for majority students, should be encouraged and rigorously researched because they provide important continuity between the two groups and address an important societal need for a bilingually competent workforce.

Acknowledgment of the Complexity

As we have argued throughout this article, the linguistic aspects of bilingualism provide only a window into a complex set of psychological and social processes in the development of bilingual children. A broad multidisciplinary perspective must be applied to the increasingly important problems faced by linguistic-minority students throughout the socialization process. How else are we to capture, understand, and respond to the sentiments of many immigrants, so eloquently expressed by this 10th-grade Chinese-born girl who had immigrated at age 12?

I don't know who I am. Am I the good Chinese daughter? Am I an American teenager? I always feel I am letting my parents down when I am with my friends because I act so American, but I also feel that I will never really be an American. I never feel really comfortable with myself anymore. (Olsen, 1988, p. 30)

There is, indeed, more to issues confronting the bilingual individual than can be summarized by language proficiency measurements. As social scientists and educators, it is our obligation to capture the complexity of the situation and in the process to enrich our own science and practice.

References

August, D., & Garcia, E. E. (1988). *Language minority education in the United States: Research, policy and practice.* Springfield, IL: Charles C Thomas.

Ayres, L. P. (1909). *Laggards in our schools.* New York: Russell Sage Foundation.

Baker, K., & de Kanter, A. (Eds.). (1983). *Bilingual education: A reappraisal of federal policy.* Lexington, MA: Lexington Books.

Brown, R., & Bellugi, U. (1964). Three processes in the child's acquisition of syntax. *Harvard Educational Review, 34,* 133–151.

Carter, T. P., & Chatfield, M. L. (1986). Effective bilingual schools: Implications for policy and practice. *American Journal of Education, 95,* 200–234.

Chomsky, N. (1957). *Syntactic structures.* The Hague: Mouton.

Clark, M. S., & Fiske, S. T. (Eds.). (1982). *Affect and cognition: The Seventeenth Annual Carnegie Symposium on Cognition.* Hillsdale, NJ: Erlbaum.

Cummings, J. (1984). *Bilingualism and special education.* San Diego, CA: College Hill Press.

Cummings, J. (1986). Empowering minority students: A framework for intervention. *Harvard Educational Review, 56,* 18–36.

Cummings, J. (1987). *Empowering minority students.* Unpublished book manuscript, Ontario Institute for Studies in Education.

Diaz, R. M. (1983). Thought and two languages: The impact of bilingualism on cognitive development. *Review of Research in Education, 10,* 23–54.

Equal Education Opportunity Act of 1974, 42 U.S.C. §6705 (1975).

Ervin-Tripp, S. (1987, February). *La emoción en el bilinguismo.* Paper presented at the International Symposium on Bilingualism, San Juan, Puerto Rico.

Fallows, J. (1986, November 24). Viva bilingualism. *The New Republic,* pp. 18–19.

Fishman, J. A., Cooper, R. L., & Ma, R. (1966). *Bilingualism in the barrio.* Bloomington: Indiana University Press.

Garcia, E. E. (1983). *Early childhood bilingualism.* Albuquerque: University of New Mexico Press.

Gardner, R. C. (1983). Learning another language: A true social psychological experiment. *Journal of Language and Social Psychology, 2,* 219–239.

Giles, H., & Johnson, P. (1981). The role of language in ethnic group relations. In J. C. Turner & H. Giles (Eds.), *Intergroup behavior* (pp. 199–241). Oxford, England: Blackwell.

Grosjean, F. (1982). *Life with two languages.* Cambridge, MA: Harvard University Press.

Gumperz, J. (1982). *Discourse strategies.* New York: Cambridge University Press.

Hakuta, K. (1986). *Mirror of language: The debate on bilingualism.* New York: Basic Books.

Haugen, E. (1973). Bilingualism, language contact and immigrant languages in the United States: A research report 1956–1970. In T. Sebeok (Ed.), *Current trends in linguistics* (Vol. 10, pp. 505–591). The Hague: Mouton.

Krashen, S., & Biber, D. (1988). *On course: Bilingual education success in California.* Sacramento: California Association for Bilingual Education.

Lambert, R. D., & Freed, B. F. (Eds.). (1982). *The loss of language skills.* Rowley, MA: Newbury House.

Lambert, W. E. (1984). An overview of issues in immersion education. In *Studies on immersion education* (pp. 8–30). Sacramento: California State Department of Education.

Lau v. Nichols, 414 U.S. 563 (1974).

McLaughlin, B. (1987). *Theories of second-language learning.* London: Arnold.

Ogbu, J., & Matute-Bianchi, M. E. (1986). Understanding sociocultural factors: Knowledge, identity, and school adjustment. In California State Department of Education (Ed.), *Beyond language: Social and cultural factors in schooling language minority students* (pp. 73–142). Los Angeles: Evaluation, Dissemination and Assessment Center, California State University.

Olsen, L. (1988). *Crossing the schoolhouse border: Immigrant students and the California Public Schools.* San Francisco: California Tomorrow (Fort Mason, Building B, San Francisco, CA 94123).

Paulston, C. B. (1980). *Bilingual education: Theories and issues.* Rowley, MA: Newbury House.

Ramirez, J. D. (1986). Comparing structural English immersion and bilingual education: First year results of a national study. *American Journal of Education, 95,* 122–148.

Rossel, C., & Ross, J. M. (1986). *The social science evidence on bilingual education.* Boston: Boston University Press.

Simon, P. (1980). *The tongue-tied American: Confronting the foreign language crisis.* New York: Continuum.

Slobin, D. I. (1973). Cognitive prerequisites for the development of grammar. In C. A. Ferguson & D. I. Slobin (Eds.), *Studies of child language development* (pp. 175–208). New York: Holt, Rinehart & Winston.

Snow, C. E. (1987). Beyond conversation: Second language learners' acquisition of description and explanation. In J. P. Lantolf & A. Labarca (Eds.), *Research in second language learning: Focus on the classroom* (pp. 3–16). Norwood, NJ: Ablex.

Snow, M. A. (1986). *Innovative second language education: Bilingual immersion programs* (Education Report 1). Los Angeles: Center for Language Education and Research, University of California.

Sternberg, R. (1985). *Beyond IQ: A triarchic theory of human intelligence.* New York: Cambridge University Press.

Thompson, G. G. (1952). *Child psychology.* Boston: Houghton Mifflin.

Tikunoff, W. J. (1983). *Significant Bilingual Instructional Features Study.* San Francisco: Far West Laboratory.

Veltman, C. (1988). *The future of the Spanish language in the United States.* New York: Hispanic Policy Development Project.

Willig, A. (1985). A meta-analysis of selected studies on the effectiveness of bilingual education. *Review of Educational Research, 55,* 269–317.

Wong Fillmore, L., & McLaughlin, B. (1986). *Oral language learning in bilingual classrooms: The role of cultural factors in language acquisition.* Unpublished manuscript, School of Education, University of California, Berkeley.

Zentella, A. C. (1981). Language variety among Puerto Ricans. In C. A. Ferguson & S. B. Heath (Eds.), *Language in the USA* (pp. 218–238). New York: Cambridge University Press.

Zigler, E., & Fin-Stevenson, M. (1987). *Children: Development and social issues.* Lexington, MA: D. C. Heath.

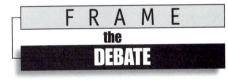

Form at end of book

WiseGuide Wrap-Up

The authors of Readings 3 and 4 suggest that bilingual education will not only benefit individuals but also society. They note that some of the problems associated with the successful acquisition of English have less to do with language learning than the social stigma attached to the speakers of languages other than English. The social setting must be taken into account to understand the problems of bilingual teaching. One of these problems is the concern for performance on standardized tests of intelligence.

Some believe that language may be used as a dumping ground for social problems and that the native language must be eliminated to avoid these effects. Recent research suggests the opposite: Being able to speak, read, and write more than one language is not a burden, but instead, an asset. English is actually acquired more quickly when the first language is maintained and strengthened. So why is bilingual education such a politically charged issue?

R.E.A.L. Sites

This list provides a print preview of typical **Coursewise** R.E.A.L. sites. (There are over 100 such sites at the **Courselinks**™ site.) The danger in printing URLs is that web sites can change overnight. As we went to press, these sites were functional using the URLs provided. If you come across one that isn't, please let us know via email to: webmaster@coursewise.com. Use your Passport to access the most current list of R.E.A.L. sites at the **Courselinks** site.

Site name: National Association for Bilingual Education
URL: http://www.nabe.org/
Why is it R.E.A.L.? The National Association for Bilingual Education promotes bilingual education in the schools. Its web site contains a variety of information on teaching pedagogy, successful bilingual education programs, and symposiums and other conferences on bilingual education.
Key terms: bilingual education

Site name: National Clearinghouse for Bilingual Education
URL: http://www.ncbe.gwu.edu/
Why is it R.E.A.L.? The National Clearinghouse for Bilingual Education is funded by the U.S. Department of Education's Office of Bilingual Education and Minority Affairs to collect, analyze, and disseminate information about the effective education of linguistically and culturally diverse learners. The web site provides information on developing programs, links to other organizations, and news on the topic of bilingual education.
Key terms: bilingual education, cultural diversity

section 3 | Should English Be Our Official Language?

Take a Closer Look

1. Should all Americans speak the same language?

2. Should English be the official language of the United States? What are the advantages and disadvantages of this?

3. Is Anglo cultural dominance the real issue behind the English-only debate?

4. Does becoming American entail not just learning English but also rejecting the language and culture of your parents?

5. Is lack of English a handicap to learning to live in a democracy?

Is the human race condemned to everlasting linguistic conflict? Is this the image of life in the United States today? Can we create a brighter future by demanding linguistic homogeneity in every nation-state? If our nations are monolingual, can we communicate with one another at all? In the future, will we all live in monolingual, monocultural nation-states?

The nation-state is a rather recent development in human history, and in the latter half of the twentieth century, its definition has changed radically. The nation-state has gone from being a predominantly political entity to which any and all individuals could potentially belong, depending on their political loyalty, to a concept that focuses on socioanthropological factors. A new sense of community is based on a common language, culture, and religion, and calls for an unprecedented degree of homogeneity.

Is the need for a common language to transact the business of the society a reason to remove other languages from the community? Is the state's insistence on a common language to be used in all areas of social and political life an infringement on citizens' privacy? Is language diversity a threat to the development of a common society? To what lengths can the state go to demand linguistic conformity? Are mass compulsion, expulsion, or genocide the only ways to achieve this?

In Reading 5, Geoffrey Nunberg takes a look at American history and notes that language has not been a major theme in our political life. He notes, "More than 97 percent of Americans speak English well, a level of linguistic homogeneity unsurpassed by any other large nation in history." Nunberg explores the connection between English and American political values and practices. In the past, learning English was also associated with understanding the fundamental concepts of democratic society.

In Reading 6, Eric Hobsbawm discusses the development of national languages, and the relationship between language and culture as a new definition of nation. He notes that a single national language only became important when ordinary citizens became an important component of the state. The reading also explores the role of education in this process.

Issue 3: Should English be our official language?

Lingo Jingo:
English Only and the New Nativism

Geoffrey Nunberg

Abstract

The current English-only movement has focused the public eye on the question of the continued status of English as the common language of public discourse in the society. The movement is not only insulting to immigrants but is more disturbing because it reflects doubt in the ability of English-language culture to flourish in an open market. The English-only movement reflects the defensiveness linked to linguistic nationalism in other countries.

Since Slovakia became an independent state a few years ago, the Slovak majority has been imposing increasingly stringent language restrictions on the ethnic Hungarian minority, whom they suspect of irredentist leanings. Hungarian place-names must be changed to accord with Slovak spellings, all official business must be transacted in Slovak even in districts that are almost entirely Hungarian-speaking, and so forth. It's a familiar enough pattern in that part of the world, where antique ethnic antagonisms are routinely fought out on the field of language, except that in this case, the Slovakians have insisted that their policies are in fact thoroughly modern—even American. By way of demonstrating this, the Slovak State Language Law of 1995 cites the example of American official-English bills, and the drafters of the law made a point of entertaining a delegation from the U.S. English organization. In American eyes, though, the similarities might lead to another, more disquieting conclusion: What if it's we who are becoming more like them?

For most of our history, language has not been a major theme in American political life. The chief reason for that, to be sure, is that God in his wisdom has given us a single dominant language, with few real dialects or patois of the sort that European nations have had to deal with in the course of their nation building. (One notable exception is the post-Creole variety spoken by many African Americans.) It's true that America has always had substantial communities of speakers of non-English languages: indigenous peoples; groups absorbed in the course of colonial expansion, like the Francophones of Louisiana and the Hispanics of the Southwest; and the great flows of immigrants from 1880 to 1920 and during the past 30 years. And since the eighteenth century there have been recurrent efforts to discourage or suppress the use of other languages by various minorities, particularly at the time of the nativist movement of the turn of the century. But the focus on language has always been opportunistic, a convenient way of underscoring the difference between us and them; the issue has always subsided as minorities have become anglicized, leaving little symbolic residue in its wake. Unlike the Slovakians, the Italians, the Germans, or those paragons of official orality, the French, we have not until now made how we speak an essential element of what we are.

Given the minor role that language has played in our historical self-conception, it isn't surprising that the current English-only movement began in the political margins, the brainchild of slightly flaky figures like Senator S. I. Hayakawa and John Tanton, a Michigan ophthalmologist who co-founded the U.S. English organization as an outgrowth of his involvement in zero population growth and immigration restriction. (The term "English-only" was originally introduced by supporters of a 1984 California initiative opposing bilingual ballots, a stalking horse for other official-language measures. Leaders of the movement have since rejected the label, pointing out that they have no objection to the use of foreign languages in the home. But the phrase is a fair characterization of the goals of the movement so far as public life is concerned.)

Until recently, English-only was not a high priority for the establishment right. President Bush was opposed to the movement, and Barbara Bush once went so far as to describe it as "racist." And while a number of figures in the Republican leadership have been among the sponsors of official-language bills, most did not become vocal enthusiasts of the policy until the successes of English-only measures and of anti-immigrant initiatives like California's Proposition 187 persuaded them that anti-immigrant politics might have broad voter appeal. Senator Dole endorsed English-only in the 1996 presidential campaign, and Newt Gingrich recently described bilingualism as a menace to American civilization.

The successes of English-only are undeniably impressive. Polls show between 65 percent and 86 percent of Americans favoring making English the official language, and the U.S. English organization currently claims more than 650,000 members. Largely owing to its efforts, 18 states have adopted official-language measures via either referenda or legislative action, with legislation pending in 13 more (four other states have official-language statutes that date from earlier periods). The majority of these laws are largely symbolic, like the 1987 Arkansas law—which President Clinton now says it was "a mistake" to sign—that states merely, "The English language shall be the official language of the state of Arkansas." But a few are more restrictive, notably the measure adopted by Arizona voters in 1988, which bars the state or its employees from conducting business in any language other than English, apart from some narrow exceptions for purposes like health and public safety. In 1996 the House passed H.R. 123, which is similar in most respects to the Arizona law. (Its title is the "English Language Empowerment Act," which as the writer James Crawford has observed is a small assault on the language in its own right.) The Senate did not act on the bill, but it has been reintroduced in the current session; given the present makeup of the Congress, there is a fair chance that some legislation will be enacted in this session—though perhaps in the watered-down version preferred by some Senate Republicans who are apprehensive about offending Hispanic constituents. In that form, as little more than a symbolic affirmation of the official status of English, the bill would likely win the support of some Democrats, and might prove difficult for President Clinton to veto.

In any case, to the extent that the bill is symbolic, its adoption is more or less facultative; the movement achieves most of its goals simply by raising the issue. At the local level, the public discussion of English-only has encouraged numerous private acts of discrimination. In recent years, for example, dozens of firms and institutions have adopted English-only workplace rules that bar employees from using foreign languages even when speaking among themselves or when on breaks. More generally, the mere fact that politicians and the press are willing to take the proposals of English-only seriously tends to establish the basic premise of the movement: that there is a question about the continued status of English as the common language of American public discourse. In the end, the success of the movement should be measured not by the number of official-language statutes passed, but by its success in persuading people—including many who are unsympathetic to the English-only approach—to accept large parts of the English-only account of the situation of language in America.

Is English Really Endangered?

In rough outline, the English-only story goes like this: The result of recent immigration has been a huge influx of non-English speakers, who now constitute a substantial proportion of the population. Advocates of English-only often claim that there are 32 million Americans who are not proficient in English, a figure that will rise to 40 million by the year 2000. Moreover, these recent arrivals, particularly the Hispanics, are not learning English as earlier generations of immigrants did. According to Senator Hayakawa, "large populations of Mexican Americans, Cubans, and Puerto Ricans do not speak English and have no intention of learning."

The alleged failure to learn English is laid to several causes. There are the ethnic leaders accused of advocating a multiculturalist doctrine that asserts, as Peter Salins describes it, that "ethnic Americans [have] the right to function in their 'native' language—not just at home but in the public realm." Government is charged with impeding linguistic assimilation by providing a full range of services in other languages, even as bilingual education enables immigrant children to complete their schooling without ever making the transition to English. Moreover, it is claimed, the peculiar geographic situation of Hispanics creates communities in which linguistic or cultural assimilation is unnecessary. For example, Paul Kennedy (himself no supporter of English-only) writes of an impending "Hispanicization of the American Southwest," where

Mexican-Americans will have sufficient coherence and critical mass in a defined region so that, if they choose, they can preserve their distinctive culture indefinitely. They could also undertake to do what no previous immigrant group could ever have dreamed of doing: challenge the existing cultural, political, legal commercial, and educational systems to change fundamentally not only the language but also the very institutions in which they do business.

Once you accept all this, it is not hard to conclude, as Congressman Norman Shumway puts it, that "the primacy of English is being threatened, and we are moving to a bilingual society," with all the prospects of disorder and disunity that bilingualism seems to imply. As Senator Hayakawa wrote:

For the first time in our history, our nation is faced with the possibility of the kind of linguistic division that has torn apart Canada in recent years; that has been a major feature of the unhappy history of Belgium, split into speakers of French and Flemish; that is at this very moment a bloody division between the Sinhalese and Tamil populations of Sri Lanka.

A U.S. English ad makes the point more graphically: A knife bearing the legend "official bilingualism" slashes through a map of the United States.

But the English-only story is nonsense from the beginning to end. Take, for starters, the claim that there are 32 million Americans who are not proficient in English. To see how wild that figure is, consider that the total number of foreign-born residents over five years old is only 18 million, some of them immigrants from other English-speaking countries and most of the rest speaking English well. The actual Census figure for residents over five who speak no English is only 1.9 million—proportionately only a quarter as high as it was in 1890, at the peak of the last great wave of immigration. And even if we include people who report speaking English "not well," the number of residents with limited English proficiency stands at around six million people in all. This is not a huge figure when you consider the extent of recent immigration and the difficulty that adults have in acquiring a new language, particularly when they are working in menial jobs that involve little regular contact with English speakers. (Or to put it another way: More than 97 percent of Americans speak English well, a level of linguistic homogeneity unsurpassed by any other large nation in history.)

What is more, recent immigrants are in fact learning English at a faster rate than any earlier generations of immigrants did—and by all the evidence, with at least as much enthusiasm. Whatever "multiculturalism" may mean to its proponents, it most assuredly does not involve a rejection of English as the national lingua franca. No ethnic leaders have been crazy enough to suggest that immigrants can get along without learning English, nor would any immigrants pay the slightest attention to such a suggestion if it were made. According to a recent Florida poll, 98 percent of Hispanics want their children to speak English well. And the wish is father to the deed: Immigrants of all nationalities are moving to English at a faster rate than ever before in our history. The demographer Calvin Veltman has observed that the traditional three-generation period for a complete shift to English is being shortened to two generations. A recent RAND Corporation study showed that more than 90 percent of first-generation Hispanics born in California have native fluency in English, and that only about 50 percent of the second generation still speak Spanish.

That latter figure suggests that for recent Hispanic arrivals, as for many groups of immigrants that preceded them, becoming American entails not just mastering English but also rejecting the language and culture of one's parents. It is a regrettable attitude (and the very one that English-only has battened on), but the process seems inevitable: Relatively few Hispanics display the fierce religious or patriotic loyalty to their mother tongue that the Germans did a hundred years ago. The only exception is the Cubans, who have a special political motivation for wanting to hang on to Spanish, but even here the preference for English is increasingly marked—a survey of first- and second-generation Cuban college students in Miami found that 86 percent preferred to use English in speaking among themselves. It is only the assimilated third- and fourth-generation descendants of immigrants who feel the loss of languages keenly, and by then it is almost always too late. (For a linguist, there is no more poignant experience than to watch a class of American college freshmen struggling to master the basic grammar of the language that their grandparents spoke with indifferent fluency.)

A number of factors contribute to the accelerated pace of language shift among immigrants: the increased mobility, both social and geographical, of modern life; the ubiquity of English-language media; universal schooling; and the demands of the urban workplace. In the nineteenth century, by contrast, many immigrants could hold on to their native language for several generations at no great cost: some because they lived in isolated farming communities and required very little contact with English speakers, others because they lived in one of the many states or cities that provided public schooling in their native tongues. At the turn of the century, in fact, more than 6 percent of American schoolchildren were receiving most or all of their primary education in the German language alone—programs that were eliminated only around the time of the First World War.

All of this underscores the irony of the frequent claims that unlike earlier generations, modern immigrants are refusing to learn English—or that modern bilingual education is an "unprecedented" concession to immigrants who insist on maintaining their own language. In point of fact, there's a good chance that great-grandpa didn't work very hard to learn English, and a fair probability that his kids didn't, either. Today, by contrast, all publicly supported bilingual education programs are aimed at facilitating the transition to English. The programs are unevenly implemented, it's true, owing to limited funding, to the resistance of school administrators, and to the shortage of trained teachers. (An early study found that 50 percent of teachers hired in "bilingual" programs lacked proficiency in their students' native languages.) And in any case such programs are available right now for only about 25 percent of limited-English students. Still, the method clearly works better than any of the alternatives. An extensive 1992 study sponsored by the National Academy of Sciences found that, compared with various types of "immersion" programs, bilingual education reduces the time to reach full English fluency by between two and three years.

What of the other government programs that critics describe as opening the door to "official bilingualism"? Measured against the numerous social and economic motivations that limited-English immigrants have for learning English, the availability of official information in their own language is a negligible disincentive, and there are strong arguments for providing these services. To take an example that the English-only people are fond of raising, why in the world would we want to keep immigrants with limited English from taking their driver's license tests in their native languages? Do we want to keep them from driving to work until they have learned the English word pedestrian? Or to be more realistic about it—since many of them will have no choice but to drive anyway—do we want to drive to work on roads full of drivers who are ignorant of the traffic laws?

In any event, these programs are extremely, even excessively, limited. Federal law mandates provision of foreign-language services only in a handful of special cases—interpreters must be provided for migrant worker health care centers and for certain Immigration and Naturalization Service procedures, for example—and a recent General Accounting Office survey found that the total number of federal documents printed in languages other than English over the past five years amounted to less than one-tenth of 1 percent of the total number of titles, hardly a sign of any massive shift to multilingualism in the public realm.

Language As Symbolism

Considered strictly in the light of the actualities, then, English-only is an irrelevant provocation. It is a bad cure for an imaginary disease, and moreover, one that encourages an unseemly hypochondria about the health of the dominant language and culture. But it is probably a mistake to try to engage the issue primarily at this level, as opponents of these measures have tried to do with little

success. Despite the insistence of English-only advocates that they have launched their campaign "for the immigrants' own good," it's hard to avoid the conclusion that the needs of non-English speakers are a pretext, not a rationale, for the movement. At every stage, the success of the movement has depended on its capacity to provoke widespread indignation over allegations that government bilingual programs are promoting a dangerous drift toward a multilingual society. The movement's supporters seem to have little interest in modifying that story to take the actual situation of immigrants into account. To take just one example, there are currently long waiting lists in most cities for English-language adult classes—around 50,000 people in Los Angeles County alone—but none of the English-only bills that have been introduced in the Congress make any direct provision for funding of such programs. Who, after all, would care about that?

One indication of just how broadly the movement transcends any immediate, practical concerns about immigrants is the success it has had in regions where issues like immigration and multiculturalism ought by rights to be fairly remote concerns. Of the states that have passed official-English laws in recent years, only four (California, Florida, Arizona, and Colorado) have large immigrant populations. The remainder consist of western states like Montana, North and South Dakota, and Wyoming; Indiana and New Hampshire; and all of the southern and border states except Louisiana (apart from Florida, the only state in the region with substantial numbers of non-English speakers). The breadth of support for these measures seems to increase as its local relevance diminishes, as witness the 89 percent majority that the measure won in an Alabama referendum and the unanimous or near-unanimous legislative votes for English-only measures in states like Arkansas, Georgia, Tennessee, Kentucky, and Virginia. These are not the sorts of places where voters could feel any imminent threat to English from the babel alien tongues, or indeed, where we would expect to see voters or legislators giving much attention to immigration at all.

At the national level, then, English-only is not strictly comparable to explicit anti-immigrant measures like Proposition 187, which raise genuine substantive issues. The English-only movement has been successful because it provides a symbolic means of registering dissatisfaction with a range of disquieting social phenomena—immigration, yes, but also multiculturalism, affirmative action, and even public assistance. (Not missing a trick, U.S. English advocates like to describe bilingual programs as "linguistic welfare.") By way of response, the movement offers an apparently minimal conception of

American identity: We are at the very least a people who speak English.

It seems an unexceptionable stipulation. Even Horace Kallen, who introduced the notion of "cultural pluralism" 70 years ago as a counter to the ideology of the melting pot, readily acknowledged that all Americans must accept English as "the common language of [our] great tradition." But the decision to invest a language with official status is almost never based on merely practical considerations. Language always trails symbolic baggage in its wake and frames the notion of national identity in a particular way. That is why the designation of a national language is controversial wherever the matter arises.

However, the actual significance varies enormously from one nation to the next. Sometimes language is made the embodiment of a liturgical tradition, as in various Balkan countries, and sometimes of a narrowly ethnic conception of nationality, as in Slovakia or the Baltic states. In the recent French debates over the status of the language and the use of English words, the language is standing in more than anything else for the cultural authority of traditional republican institutions—a recent constitutional amendment declared French not the national language, but a langue de la Republique.

Even in the American context, the case for English has been made in very different ways over the course of the century. For the nativists of Kallen's time, language was charged with a specifically ideological burden. The imposition of English was the cornerstone of an aggressive program of Americanization, aimed at sanitizing immigrant groups of the undemocratic doctrines they were thought to harbor. The laws passed in this period undid almost all the extensive public bilingualism of the late nineteenth century, particularly in the civic and political domains. The ability to speak English was made a condition for citizenship in 1906, and in 1915 an English-literacy requirement was added, over President Wilson's veto. A 1919 Nebraska statute stipulated that all public meetings be conducted in English; Oregon required that foreign-language periodicals provide an English translation of their entire contents. More than 30 states passed laws prohibiting or restricting foreign-language instruction in primary schools.

The justification provided for these measures was a peculiar doctrine about the connection between language and political thought, which held that speaking a foreign language was inimical to grasping the fundamental concepts of democratic society. The Nebraska supreme court, for example, warned against the "baneful effects" of educating children in foreign languages, which must "naturally inculcate in them the ideas and sentiments foreign to the best interests of their country." English was viewed as

a kind of "chosen language," the consecrated bearer of "Anglo-Saxon" political ideals and institutions. A New York official told immigrants in 1916: "You have got to learn our language because that is the vehicle of the thought that has been handed down from the men in whose breasts first burned the fire of freedom." (Like many other defenders of this doctrine, he dated the tradition from the Magna Carta, a text written, as it happens, in Latin.)

Taken literally, the chosen-language doctrine does not stand up under scrutiny, either linguistically or philosophically. Nothing could be more alien to the Enlightenment universalism of the Founders than the notion that the truths they held to be "self-evident" were ineffable in other languages. But it is almost always a mistake to take talk of language literally. It was not our democratic ideals that seemed to require expression in English, but the patriotic rituals that were charged with mediating the sense of national identity in the period, such as the obligatory schoolroom declamations of the sacred texts of American democracy; and more broadly, the Anglo culture in which those rituals were embedded. Theodore Roosevelt made the connection clear when he said: "We must . . . have but one language. That must be the language of the Declaration of Independence, of Washington's Farewell Address, of Lincoln's Gettysburg speech and second inaugural." The list is significant in its omissions. English might also be the language of Shakespeare, Emerson, and Melville, but its claim to merit official recognition had to be made on political grounds, as the only cloth from which our defining ideals could be woven.

In this regard, the "new nativism" is greatly different from the old. The modern English-only movement makes the case for a national language in what seem to be apolitical (or at least, nonideological) terms. English is important solely as a lingua franca, the "social glue" or "common bond" that units all Americans. Indeed, advocates are careful to avoid suggesting that English has any unique virtues that make it appropriate in this role. A U.S. English publication explains: "We hold no special brief for English. If Dutch (or French, or Spanish, or German) had become our national language, we would now be enthusiastically defending Dutch." (It is hard to imagine Theodore Roosevelt passing over the special genius of English so lightly.)

On the face of things, the contemporary English-only movement seems a less coercive point of view. Indeed, the movement often seems eager to discharge English of any cultural or ideological responsibility whatsoever. Its advocates cast their arguments with due homage to the sanctity of pluralism. As former Kentucky

Senator Walter Huddleston puts it, Americans are "a generous people, appreciative of cultural diversity," and the existence of a common language has enabled us "to develop a stable and cohesive society that is the envy of many fractured ones, without imposing any strict standards of homogeneity." At the limit, advocates seem to suggest that Americans need have nothing at all in common, so long as we have the resources for talking about it.

That is misleading, though. Language is as much a proxy for culture now as it was at the turn of the century, except that now neither English nor Anglo culture needs any doctrinal justification. This explains why English-only advocates are so drawn to comparisons with polities like Canada, Belgium, and Sri Lanka. Turn-of-the century nativists rarely invoked the cases of Austria-Hungary or the Turkish empire in making the case against multilingualism, not because such scenarios were implausible—after all, the nativists had no qualms about invoking equally implausible scenarios of immigrant hordes inciting revolution—but because they were irrelevant: What could Americans learn about their national identity from comparisons with places like those? And the fact that Americans are now disposed to find these specters plausible is an indication of how far the sense of national identity has moved from its doctrinal base. The ethnic divisions in Canada and Belgium are generally and rightly perceived as having no ideological significance, and the moral seems to be that cultural differences alone are sufficient to fragment a state, even this one.

There are a number of reasons for the shift in emphasis. One, certainly, is a generally diminished role for our particular political ideology in an age in which it seems to lack serious doctrinal rivals. Over the long term, though, the new sense of the role of a common language also reflects the emergence of new mechanisms for mediating the sense of national community—radio, film, television—which require no direct institutional intervention. And the effects of the new media are complemented by the techniques of mass merchandising, which ensure that apart from "colorful" local differences, the material setting of American life will look the same from one place to another. ("To be American is to learn to shop," Newt Gingrich observed not long ago, without apparent irony.)

As Raymond Williams noted, the broadcast media aren't direct replacements for traditional institutions: They do not inculcate an ideology so much as presuppose one. In this sense they are capable of imposing a high degree of cultural and ideological uniformity without explicit indoctrination, or indeed, without seeming to "impose" at all. This may help to explain why the English-only movement appears indifferent to the schools or the courses in citizenship that played such an important part in the program of the turn-of-the-century Americanization movement, as well as to the theories about the special mission of English that were so prominent then. It's hard to imagine anyone making the case for English as the language of Washington's farewell speech or Lincoln's second inaugural, when students are no longer required to memorize or even read those texts anymore. Of all our sacred texts, only the Pledge of Allegiance and the national anthem are still capable of rousing strong feelings. But these are, notably, the most linguistically empty of all the American liturgy (schoolchildren say the first as if it were four long words, and I have never encountered anybody who is capable of parsing the second), which derive their significance chiefly from their association with the non-linguistic symbol of the flag.

Cherished Conformity

It is inevitable, then, that modern formulations of the basis of national identity should come to focus increasingly on the importance of common experience and common knowledge, in place of (or at least, on an equal footing with) common political ideals. Michael Lind, for example, has argued that American identity ought to be officially vested in a national culture, which has native competence in American English as its primary index but is also based on American "folkways" that include

particular ways of acting and dressing; conventions of masculinity and femininity; ways of celebrating major events like births, marriages, and funerals; particular kinds of sports and recreations; and conceptions of the proper boundaries between the secular and religious spheres. And there is also a body of material—ranging from historical events that everyone is expected to know about to widely shared but ephemeral knowledge of sports and cinema and music—that might be called common knowledge.

Once we begin to insist on these cultural commonalities as necessary ingredients of national identity, it is inevitable that the insistence on English will become more categorical and sweeping. Where turn-of-the-century Americanizationists emphasized the explicitly civic uses of language, English-only casts its net a lot wider. It's true that the movement has tended to focus its criticism on the government bilingual programs, but only because these are the most accessible to direct political action; and within this domain, it has paid as much attention to wholly apolitical texts like driver's license tests and tax forms as to bilingual ballots. Where convenient, moreover, English-only advocates have also opposed the wholly apolitical private-sector uses of foreign languages. They have urged the California Public Utilities Commission to prohibit Pac Tel from publishing the Hispanic Yellow Pages; they have opposed the FCC licensing of foreign-language television and radio stations; they have proposed boycotts of Philip Morris for advertising in Spanish and of Burger King for furnishing bilingual menus in some localities. For all their talk of "cherished diversity," English-only advocates are in their way more intolerant of difference than their nativist predecessors. "This is America; speak English," English-only supporters like to say, and they mean 24 hours a day.

The irony of all this is that there was never a culture or a language so little in need of official support. Indeed, for someone whose first allegiance is to the English language and its culture, what is most distressing about the movement is not so much the insult it offers to immi-grants as its evident lack of faith in the ability of English-language culture to make its way in the open market—and this at the very moment of the triumph of English as a world language of unprecedented currency. (A Frenchman I know described the English-only measures as akin to declaring crabgrass an endangered species.) The entire movement comes to seem tainted with the defensive character we associate with linguistic nationalism in other nations. I don't mean to say that English will ever acquire the particular significance that national languages have in places like Slovakia or France. But it's getting harder to tell the difference.

Form at end of book

Language, Culture, and National Identity

Eric Hobsbawm

Abstract

The use of a single standard spoken and written language to help define nationality is relatively recent. Throughout history people of different ethnicities and linguistic backgrounds coexisted peacefully within the same nation. National languages arose with the growth of literacy and popular political participation because people needed to communicate with each other more fully in a democratic context. Multilingualism is returning because of modern non-written communications media and the dominance of English as a worldwide universal language.

Language, culture, and national identity is the title of my paper, but its central subject is the situation of languages in cultures, written or spoken languages still being the main medium of these. More specifically, my subject is "multiculturalism" insofar as this depends on language. "Nations" come into it, since in the states in which we all live political decisions about how and where languages are used for public purposes (for example, in schools) are crucial. And these states are today commonly identified with "nations" as in the term United Nations. This is a dangerous confusion. So let me begin with a few words about it.

Since there are hardly any colonies left, practically all of us today live in independent and sovereign states. With the rarest exceptions, even exiles and refugees live in states, though not their own. It is fairly easy to get agreement about what constitutes such a state, at any rate the modern model of it, which has become the template for all new independent political entities since the late eighteenth century. It is a territory, preferably coherent and demarcated by frontier lines from is neighbors, within which all citizens without exception come under the exclusive rule of the territorial government and the rules under which it operates. Against this there is no ap-

peal, except by authoritarian of that government; for even the superiority of European Community law over national law was established only by the decision of the constituent governments of the Community. Within the state's territory all are citizens who are born and live there except those specifically excluded as "foreigners" by the state, which also has the power to admit people to citizenship—but not, in democratic states, to deprive them of it. Foreigners are taken to belong to some other territorial state, though the growth of inhumanity since World War I has produced a growing, and now very large, body of officially invisible denizens for whom special terms had to be devised in our tragic century: "stateless," "apartide," "illegal immigrant," or whatever.

At some time, mainly since the end of the nineteenth century, the inhabitants of this state have been identified with an "imagined community" bonded together, as it were laterally, by such things as language, culture, ethnicity, and the like. The ideal of such a state is represented by an ethnically, culturally, and linguistically homogeneous population. We now know that this standing invitation to "ethnic cleansing" is dangerous and completely unrealistic, but out of the almost 200 states today only about a dozen correspond to this program. Moreover, it would have surprised the founders of the original nation-states. For them, the unity of the nation was political and not socio-anthropological. It consisted in the decision of a sovereign people to live under common laws and a common constitution, irrespective of culture, language, and ethnic composition. "A nation," said the Abbe Sieyes, with habitual French lucidity, "is the totality of the individuals united by living under a common law and represented by the same legislative assembly" (Schieder, 1985, p. 122). The assumption that communities of ethnic descent, language, culture, religion, and so on ought to find expression in territorial states, let alone in a single territorial state, was, of course, equally new. It could actually be a reversal of historic values, as in

Zionism. "Strangers have arisen," wrote an orthodox rabbi in 1900,

who say that the people of Israel should be clothed in secular nationalism, a nation like all other nations, that Judaism rests on three things, national feeling, the land and the language, and that national feeling is the most praiseworthy element in the brew and the most effective in preserving Judaism, while the observance of the Torah and the commandments is a private matter depending on the inclination of each individual. May the Lord rebuke these evil men and may He who chooseth Jerusalem seal their mouths (Kedourie, 1960, p. 76).

The Dzikover Rebbe, whom I have here quoted, undoubtedly represented the tradition of judaism.

A third observation brings me closer to the main theme of this lecture. The concept of a single, exclusive, and unchanging ethnic or cultural or other identity is a dangerous piece of brainwashing. Human mental identities are not like shoes, of which we can only wear one pair at a time. We are all multi-dimensional beings. Whether a Mr. Patel in London will think of himself primarily as an Indian, a British citizen, a Hindu, a Gujarati-speaker, an ex-colonist from Kenya, a member of a specific caste or kin-group, or in some other capacity depends on whether he faces an immigration officer, a Pakistani, or Sikh or Moslem, a Bengali-speaker, and so on. There is no single platonic essence of Patel. He is all these and more at the same time. David Selbourne, a London ideologue, calls on "the jew in England" to "cease to pretend to be English" and to recognize that his "real" identity is as a jew. The only people who face us with such either-or choices are those whose policies have led or could lead to genocide.

Moreover, historically multiple identity lies behind even national homogeneity. Every German in the past, and vestigially even today, had simultaneously two or three identities: as members of a "tribe"—the Saxons, the Swabians, the Franks—German principality or state, and a linguistic culture combining a single standard written language for all Germans with a variety of spoken dialects, some of which also had begun to develop a written literature. (The Reformation brought not only one, but several Bible translations into German languages. Indeed, until Hitler, people were regarded as Germans by virtue of being Bavarians, Saxons, or Swabians who could often understand one another only when they spoke the written standard culture-language.

This brings me naturally to my central theme of multilingualism and multiculturalism. Both are historically novel as concepts. They could not arise until the combination of three circumstances: the aspiration to universal literacy, the political mobilization of the common people, and a particular form of linguistic nationalism.

Historically, the coexistence of peoples of different languages and cultures is normal or, rather, nothing is less common than countries inhabited exclusively by people of a single uniform language and culture. Even in Iceland, with its 300,000 inhabitants, such uniformity is only maintained by a ruthless policy of Icelandization, including forcing every immigrant to take an ancient Icelandic name. At the time of the French Revolution, only half the inhabitants of France could speak French, and only 12–13 percent spoke it "correctly"; and the extreme case is Italy, where at the moment it became a state only 2 or 3 Italians out of a hundred actually used the Italian language at home. So long as most people lived in an oral universe, there was no necessary link between the spoken and the written language of the literate minority. So long as reading and writing were strictly affairs for specialized minorities, it did not even have to be a living language. The administration of India in the 1830s switched from written classical Persian, which nobody in India spoke, to written English, which was equally incomprehensible. If illiterates needed to communicate with those who spoke other languages, they relied on intermediaries who could speak or else learned enough of the older language to get by, or developed pidgins or creoles which became unwritten but effective means of communication and have become a fashionable topic for study among linguists.

A single national language only became important when ordinary citizens became an important component of the state; and the written language had to have a relation to the spoken language only when these citizens were supposed to read and write it. But remember that universal primary education, outside of a few exceptional countries, is not much more than a century old.

The original case for a standard language was entirely democratic, not cultural. How could citizens understand, let alone take part in, the government of their country if it was conducted in an incomprehensible language—for example, in Latin, as in the Hungarian parliament before 1840? Would this not guarantee government by an elite minority? This was the argument of the Abbe Gregoire in 1974 (Hobsbawm, 1990, p. 103 n). Education in French was, therefore, essential for French citizens, whatever the language they spoke at home. This remained essentially the position in the United States, another product of the same age of democratic revolution. To be a citizen, an immigrant had to pass a test in English, and readers of *The Education of Hyman Kaplan* will be familiar with this process of linguistic homogenization. I need not add that Mr. Kaplan's struggles with the English language were not intended to stop him from talking Yiddish with his wife at home, which he certainly did; nor did they affect his children, who obviously went to

English-speaking public schools. What people spoke or wrote among themselves was nobody's business but their own, like their religion. You will remember that even in 1970—that is to say before the onset of the present wave of mass immigration—33 million Americans, plus an unknown percentage of another 9 million who did not answer the relevant question, said that English was not their mother-tongue. Over three quarters of them were second generation or older American-born (Thernstrom et al., 1980, p. 632).

In practice, education in languages other than the standard national language was traditionally left to private effort, to special voluntary provision by minority communities, as in the case of the Czech Comenius schools which were set up in Vienna after 1918 with help from the Czech government for the large Czech minority in the city, or by local option, as often happened in America. Thus, bilingual education in English and German was introduced in Cincinnati in 1840. Most such arrangements—and there were several in the second half of the century—had quietly faded away by the time the demand for official federal bilingual education surfaced in the 1960s and 1970s. Let me say that this was a political rather than an educational demand. It was part of the rise of a new kind of ethnic and identity politics during this period.

The situation was different, of course, where there was no single predominant national language, spoken or even written, or where a linguistic community resented the superior status of another language. In the multinational Habsburg empire, "the language of (public) office and school" became a political issue from 1848, as it did somewhat later in Belgium and Finland. The usual minimum formula here was—and I quote the Hungarian Nationality Law of 1868—that people should be educated in their own language at primary school level and under certain circumstances at secondary school level, and that they should be allowed to use it directly or through interpreters in dealings with public authorities (But note that what was a language was politically defined. It did not include Yiddish nor the creole spoken in Istria, where experts in the 1850s counted thirteen different national varieties [Worsdorfer, 1994, p. 206].) To have a language, as distinct from a dialect or "jargon" you needed to be classified as a nation or nationality. The minimum formula could work in areas of solid settlement by one language group, and local or even regional government could be substantially conducted in what was called the "language of common use" (Umgangssprache), but it raised big problems in areas of mixed settlement and in most cities. The real educational issue, of course, was not primary, but secondary and tertiary education. This is where the major battles were fought. Here, the issue was not mass literacy,

but the linguistic status of unofficial elites. For we must remember that until World War II not more than 2 percent of the age group 15–19 went to high school, even in countries with a reputation for democracy like Denmark and the Netherlands. Under the circumstances, any Fleming or Finn who had gotten to university level was certainly capable of pursuing it in French or Swedish. In short, once again the issue was not educational, but political.

Basically, this system of one official language per country became part of everyone's aspiration to become a nation-state, though special arrangements had to be made for minorities which insisted on them. Multilingual nations like Switzerland were regarded as freaks; and *de facto*, given the great cantonal autonomy of that country, even Switzerland is hardly multilingual because every canton except one—Grisons—is in fact monoglot. Colonies winning their independence after World War II automatically thought in terms of some home-grown national language as the base of national education and culture—Urdu in Pakistan, Hindi in India, Sinhala in Sri Lanka, Arabic in Algeria. As we shall see in a moment, this was a dangerous delusion. Small peoples which define themselves ethnic-linguistically still hanker after this ideal of homogeneity: Latvia only for Lettish-speakers, Moldavia only for Rumanians. As it so happened in 1940, when this area once again passed to Russia, almost half its population consisted not of Rumanians, but of Ukrainians, Russians, Bulgarians, Turks, Jews, and a number of other groups (Seton-Watson, 1977, p. 182). Let us be clear: in the absence of a willingness to change languages, national linguistic homogeneity in multi-ethnic and multi-lingual areas can be achieved only by mass compulsion, expulsion, or genocide. Poland, which had a third non-Polish population in 1939, is today overwhelmingly Polish, but only because its Germans were expelled to the West, its Lithuanians, Bielorussians, and Ukrainians were detached to form part of the USSR in the East, and its Jews were murdered. Let me add that neither Poland nor any other homogeneous country can stay homogeneous in the present world of mass labour migration, mass flight, mass travel, and mass urbanization except, once again, by ruthless exclusion or the creation *de jure* or *de facto* of apartheid societies.

The case for the privileged use of any language as the only language of education and culture in a country is, thus, political and ideological or, at best, pragmatic. Except in one respect, it is not educational. Universal literacy is extremely difficult to achieve in a written language that has no relation to the spoken vernacular—and it may be impossible unless the parents and the community are particularly anxious for their children to become literate in that language, as is the case with most immigrants into anglophone countries today. Whether this requires formal bilingual education is another matter. Basically, the demand for official education in a language other than the already established one, when this does not bring obvious advantages to the learners, is a demand for recognition or for power or for status, not for easier learning. However, it may also be a demand for ensuring the survival and development of a non-competitive language otherwise likely to fade away. Whether official institutionalization is necessary to achieve this today is an interesting question, but, according to the best expert in the field, bilingual education alone will not do the trick (Fishman, 1980, p. 636).

Let me just add one important point. Any language that moves from the purely oral to the realm of reading and writing, that is, *a fortiori* any language that becomes a medium for school teaching or official use, changes its character. It has to be standardized in grammar, spelling, vocabulary, and perhaps pronunciation. And its lexical range has to be extended to cover new needs. At least a third of the vocabulary of modern Hebrew has been formed in the twentieth century, since biblical Hebrew, rather like the Welsh of the Mabinogion, belonged to a people of ancient herdsmen and peasants. The established culture-languages of modern states—Italian, Spanish, French, English, German, Russian, and one or two others—went through this phase of social engineering before the nineteenth century. Most of the world's written languages did so in the past hundred years, insofar as they were "modernized," and some, like Basque, are still in the process of doing so. The very process of turning language into a medium of writing destroys it as a vernacular. Suppose we say, as champions of African-Americans sometimes say: our kids should not be taught in standard English, which is a language they do not speak, but in their own black English, which is not a "wrong" version of standard English, but an independent idiom of its own. So it may be. But if you turned it into a school language, it would cease to be the language that the kids speak. A distinguished French historian, whose native language was Flemish, once said: "The Flemish they now learn in school in Flanders is not the language the mothers and grandmothers of Flanders taught their children." It is no longer a "mother tongue" in the literal sense. A lady who looked after my apartment in New York, bilingual in Spanish and Galician like all from her region in Spain, has difficulty in understanding the purified and standardized Gallego which is now an official language in Galacia. It is not the language of common use in the region, but a new social construct.

What I have said so far may be true or not, but it is now largely out of date. For three things have happened which were not thought of in the heyday of nationalism and are still not thought of by the dangerous late-comers to nationalism. First, we no longer live entirely in a culture of reading and writing. Second, we no longer live in a world where the idea of a single all-purpose national language is generally feasible, that is, we live in a necessarily plurilingual world. And third, we live in an era when at least for the time being there is a single language for universal global communication, namely, a version of English.

The first development is basically the effect of film and television and, above all, the small portable radio. It means that spoken vernacular languages are no longer only face-to-face, domestic, or restricted idioms. Illiterates are, therefore, directly within the reach of the wider world and wider culture. This may also mean that small languages and dialects can survive more easily, insofar as even a modest population is enough to justify a local radio program. Minority languages, thus, can be cheaply provided for. However, exposure to some bigger language through the media may speed up linguistic assimilation. On balance, radio favors small language, television has been hostile to them, but this may no longer be true when cable and satellite television are as accessible as FM radio.[1] In short, it is no longer necessary to make a language official if it is to be moved out of the home and off the street into the wider world. Of course, none of this means that illiterates are not at a severe and growing disadvantage compared to literates, whether in written languages or in computer languages.

In Europe, national standard languages were usually based on a combination of dialects spoken by the main state people which was transformed into a literacy idiom. In the postcolonial states, this is rarely possible, and when it is, as in Sri Lanka, the results of giving Sinhalese exclusive official status have been disastrous. In fact, the most convenient "national languages" are either lingua francas or pidgins developed purely for intercommunication between peoples who do not talk each others' languages, like Swahili, Pilipino, or Bahasa Indonesia, or former imperial languages like English in India and Pakistan. Their advantages are that they are neutral between the languages actually spoken and put no one group at a particular advantage or disadvantage. Except, of course, the elite. The price India pays for conducting its affairs in English as an insurance against language-based civil wars such as that in Sri Lanka is that people who have not had the several years full-time education which make a person fluent in a foreign written language will never make it above a relatively modest level in public affairs or—today—in business. That price is worth paying, I think. Nevertheless, imagine the effect on Europe if Hindi were the only language of general communication in the European parliament, and the *London Times, Le Monde,* and the

Frankfurter Allgemeine Zeitung could be read only by those literate in Hindi.

All this is changing, or will profoundly change, the relation of languages to each other in multinational societies. The ambition of all languages in the past which aspired to the status of national languages and to be the basis of national education and culture was to be all-purpose languages at all levels, that is, interchangeable with the major culture-languages. Especially, of course, with the dominant language against which they tried to establish themselves. Thus, in Finland, Finnish was to be capable of replacing Swedish for all purposes, in Belgium Flemish of replacing French. Hence, the real triumph of linguistic emancipation was to set up a vernacular university: in the history of Finland, Wales, and the Flemish movement, the date when such a university was established is a major date in nationalist history. A lot of smaller languages have tried to do this over the past centuries, starting, I suppose, with Dutch in the seventeenth century and ending, so far, with Catalan. Some are still trying to do it, like Basque.

Now in practice this is ceasing to be the case operationally, although small-nation nationalism does what it can to resist the trend. Languages once again have niches and are used in different situations and for different purposes. Therefore, they do not need to cover the same ground. This is partly because for international purposes only a few languages are actually used. Actually the administration of the European Union spends one-third of its income on translation from and into all the eleven languages in it which have official status, it is a safe bet that the overwhelming bulk of its actual work is conducted in not more than three languages. Again, while it is perfectly possible to devise a vocabulary for writing papers in molecular biology in Estonian, and for all I know this has been done, nobody who wishes to be read—except by the other Estonian molecular biologists—will write such papers. They will need to write them in internationally current languages, as even the French and the Germans have to do in such fields as economics. Only if the number of students coming into higher education is so large and if they are recruited from monoglot families is there a sound educational reason for a full vernacular scientific vocabulary—and then only for introductory textbooks; for all more advanced purposes, students will have to learn enough of an international language to read the literature, and probably they also will have to learn enough of the kind of English which is today for intellectuals what Latin was in the Middle Ages. It would be realistic to give all university education in certain subjects in English today,

as is partly done in countries like the Netherlands and Finland which once were the pioneers of turning local vernaculars into all-purpose languages. There is no other way. Officially, nineteenth-century Hungary succeeded in making Magyar into such an all-purpose language for everything from poetry to nuclear physics. In practice, since only 10 million out of the world's 6000 million speak it, every educated Hungarian has to be, and is, plurilingual.

What we have today are not interchangeable, but complementary languages, whatever the official position. In Switzerland, there is no pressure to turn the spoken idiom of Schwyzerdutsch into a written language because there is no political objection to using high German, English, and French for this purpose. (In Catalunya, the cost of turning Catalan into an all-purpose language is to deprive poor and uneducated inhabitants of this bilingual region of the native advantage of speaking and writing one of the few major international languages, namely, Spanish.) In Paraguay everybody speaks Guarani (well, strictly speaking 45 percent of the population are bilingual), the Indian language which has ever since the colony served as a regional *lingua franca*. However, though it has long had equal rights, so far as I can see it is written chiefly for purposes of *felles letters*; for all other purposes, Spanish is used. It is extremely unlikely that in Peru, where Quechua (rightly) acquired official standing in the 1970s, there will be much demand either for daily newspapers or university education in that language. Why should there be? Even in Barcelona, where Catalan is universally spoken by the locals, the great majority of daily papers read, including the Catalan edition of national papers, are in Spanish. As for the typical third-world state, as I have pointed out, they cannot possibly have just one all-purpose language.

This is the situation which has encouraged the rise of lingua francas in countries and regions and of English as a worldwide medium of communication. Such pidgins or creoles may be culture and literary languages, but that is not their main purpose. Medieval clerk's Latin had very little to do with Virgil and Cicero. They may or may not become official languages—for countries do need languages of general public communication—but when they do, they should avoid becoming monopoly culture-languages. And the less we let the poets get their hands on such communication languages the better, for poetry encourages both incommunicability and linguistic nationalism. However, such languages are tempted to let themselves be dominated by bureaucratic or technical jargon since this is their primary use. This also should be fought in the interests of clarity. Since American English is already one of the most jargon-ridden idioms ever invented, the danger is real.

Let me conclude with some remarks about what one might call purely political languages—that is, languages which are created specifically as symbols of nationalist or regionalist aspiration, generally for separatist or secessionist purposes. The case for these is non-existent. The extreme example is the attempted reconstitution of the Cornish language, last spoken in the mid-eighteenth century, which has no other purpose except to demarcate Cornwall from England. Such constructed languages may succeed like Hebrew in Israel—that is, they may turn into real spoken and living languages—or they may fail, like the attempt by nationalist poets between the wars to turn the Scots dialect into a literacy language ("Lallans"), but neither communication nor culture is the object of such exercises. These are extreme cases, but all languages have elements of such political self-assertion, for in an era of national or regional secessionism there is a natural tendency to complement political independence by linguistic separatism. We can see this happening in Croatia at the moment. It has the additional advantage of providing a privileged zone of employment for a body of nationalist or regionalist militants, as in Wales. Let me repeat. Politics and not culture is at the core of this language manipulation, as the experts in the study of language purism have established.[2] Czech language purism was directed mainly at the elimination of German elements but did not resist the mass influx of French borrowings or the old Latin loan-words (Jernudd and Shapiro, 1989, p. 218). This is natural enough. The Ruthenes do not define themselves as a "nation" with a "language" in general, but specifically against the Ukrainians (Magocsi, 1992). Catalan nationalism is directed exclusively against Spain, just as linguistic Welsh nationalism is directed exclusively against English.

However, there is today a new element encouraging the political creation of languages, namely, the systematic regionalization of states, which assimilated regions without special linguistic, ethnic, or other characteristics, to the potentially separatist areas—for example, Murcia to Catalonia. If Spain is a guide, this will lead to the creation of localized "official" languages, no doubt eventually—as in Catalunya—demanding monopoly status. What is true of Valencia today may be true of Picardy tomorrow.

This raises the specter of general Balkanization. Given the European Union's policy of favoring regions against existing nation-states, which is de facto a policy favoring separatism, as the Scots and Catalan nationalists have quickly recognized, this is a real problem. Balkanization will not solve any problems of linguistic and cultural identity. We shall continue as before. Brussels may spend one-third of its income on translation and interpretation, and if Europe can afford it, why not? But the affairs of the community will not be primarily or at all conducted in Portuguese or Greek or even Danish and Dutch. What linguistic Balkanization will do is to multiply the occasions for conflict. If the Croats can create a separate language for themselves out of the unified Serbocroat which their forefathers constructed to unify the southern Slavs—not with much success—then anybody can. So long as language is not as firmly separated from the state as religion was in the United States under the American Constitution, it will be a constant and generally artificial source of civil strife.

Let us remember the Tower of Babel. It remained forever uncompleted because God condemned the human race to everlasting linguistic conflict.

Notes

1. In New York, in 1994, television programs were available in Italian, French, Chinese, Japanese, Spanish, Polish, Greek, and even occasionally in Albanian—though only at certain times of day, except for Spanish.
2. See Jernudd and Shapiro, 1989.

References

Fishman, Joshua, "Language Maintenance," in S. Thernstrom et al., eds., *Harvard Encyclopedia of American Ethnic Groups* (Cambridge, MA: Harvard University Press, 1980).

Jernudd, Bjorn and Shapiro, Michael, eds., *The Politics of Language Purism* (Berlin: Mouton de Gruyter, 1989).

Kedourie, Elie, *Nationalism* (London: Hutchinson, 1960).

Magocsi, Paul Robert, "The Birth of a New Nation or the Return of an Old Problem? The Rusyns of East Central Europe," *Canadian Slavonic Papers/Revue canadienne des slavistes*, 34:3 (September 1992): 199–223.

Schieder, Theodor, "Typoloogie und Erscheinungs-formdes Nationalistaats in Europa," in Heinrich August Winkler, ed., *Nationalismus* (Athanaeum, Konigstein/Ts, 1985), pp. 119–37.

Seton-Watson, Hugh, *Nations and States* (London: Methuen, 1977).

Thernstrom, S. et al., eds., *Harvard Encyclopedia of American Ethnic Groups* (Cambridge, MA: Harvard University Press, 1980).

Wordsdorfer, Rolf, "Ethnizitaet' und Entnationalisierung," *Oester reichische Zeitschrift fur Geschichtswissenchaften* 5 (Jg 2/1994): 201–31.

Form at end of book

WiseGuide Wrap-Up

Does the rise of the English-only movement mean that the use of English in U.S. society is endangered? Perhaps the movement has been successful because it symbolically registers dissatisfaction with a range of disquieting social phenomena, such as multiculturalism, affirmative action, and public assistance. Speaking English may be a minimal definition of what it is to be American. We may not all share the same religion, ethnicity, or culture, but at least we all speak English.

Multiculturalism does not involve a rejection of English as a national *lingua franca*. Nor does it impede the ability to function in a democratic society. Despite arguments presented by English-only proponents, we have had neither a monolinguistic nor monocultural past. The English-only movement seems to reflect defensiveness regarding Anglo cultural dominance and to indicate that some people are concerned with redefining America in cultural rather than political terms. Are we a society of individuals under common law with common institutions, or are we a nation-state defined by a single culture, language, and religion reinforced by the power of the state?

R.E.A.L. Sites

This list provides a print preview of typical **Coursewise** R.E.A.L. sites. (There are over 100 such sites at the **Courselinks**™ site.) The danger in printing URLs is that web sites can change overnight. As we went to press, these sites were functional using the URLs provided. If you come across one that isn't, please let us know via email to: webmaster@coursewise.com. Use your Passport to access the most current list of R.E.A.L. sites at the **Courselinks** site.

Site name: English for the Children

URL: http://www.onenation.org/

Why is it R.E.A.L.? This web site focuses on the issue of teaching all children in English only. It has information on the people involved in the issue and on initiatives in California. It also provides personal stories and links to other groups with similar goals.

Key terms: English only, education, minorities, immigrants

Site name: James Crawford's Language Policy Web Site and Emporium

URL: http://ourworld.compuserve.com/homepages/JWCRAWFORD

Why is it R.E.A.L.? James Crawford, a self-proclaimed specialist on the politics of language, reports on the English Only movement, English Plus, bilingual education, efforts to save endangered languages, and language rights. His web site contains news articles, updates on current issues, and links to other sources.

Key terms: English Only, bilingual education, endangered languages

section 4 | Does Ethnic Humor Improve Group Relations?

Take a Closer Look

1. According to David Segal, in what five ways does risqué humor benefit society?

2. What rules can serve as a guide to joking?

3. How is your view of joking affected by whether you are the teller or the listener?

4. How do Readings 7, 8, and 9 address the concerns of those who might be offended?

5. Do you think that jokes can improve ethnic relations?

WiseGuide Intro

Do the jokes you tell reflect or reveal your attitudes? Does laughing at a joke you may find offensive but funny express your agreement with the ideas and attitudes expressed in the joke? What do the jokes you tell say about you to others? Does a concern about being "politically incorrect" affect the kinds of jokes you tell and listen to? When you tell a joke are you looking to create a bond between you and your listeners, which is a friendly use of joke-telling? Or do you use joke-telling to establish a hierarchy among those who tell jokes and those who must listen, regardless of their personal feelings? The intent of joke-telling is important in a joke's reception.

Frank DeLima, one of the most popular local entertainers in Hawaii, uses a great deal of ethnic humor in his routines. His jokes are often told mainly in Hawaiian pidgin English and are therefore somewhat difficult for mainland visitors to understand. DeLima points out the stereotypic content of ethnic jokes, which is some of the reason why ethnic jokes can be offensive. At the end of his show, he concludes with a statement about being able to laugh about and with each other as essential to enabling different groups to get along. DeLima believes that humor has helped to successfully integrate ethnic groups in Hawaii.

Joking is one of the most common aspects of conversation. We tell each other favorite stories and email them to our friends. We are often surprised when our jokes are met with negative responses. Is the response "only joking" a defense to protect the joke-teller from negative consequences, or is it a disclaimer that suggests that the joke does not represent the teller's true attitudes or feelings toward the subject? Do some people use jokes to assert their more powerful positions? Do we increase the sting of epithets by making them off-limits? Does being cruel to each other in jokes obviate being cruel to each other for real? Does barring jokes on certain topics and issues impede a frank discussion of these concerns? Such questions make humor no joking matter.

In Reading 7, A. Michael Johnson reports on his study of college students' attitudes toward joking. In his research, Johnson was mainly concerned with the attitudes of joke-tellers and their audiences, and not with the specific content of the jokes. He found that joker-tellers are more focused on the intent to amuse than are their listeners. The audience is less aware of this intent and are more likely to see the joke as an expression of the teller's attitudes. The "only joking" defense is often regarded as a way to avoid negative responses.

In Reading 8, David Segal looks at the social benefits of risqué humor. He notes the decline in the use of such humor over the past few years in films and on television, and explains why he laments the loss. Segal feels that risqué humor defuses tensions, educates (exposing the weaknesses of stereotypes), disarms, undermines prejudice, and is funny. According to Segal, offensive humor is not a threat but a critical support in a multicultural society, where it functions as a safety valve and encourages discussion of socially sensitive topics.

Reading 9 looks at jokes that politicians tell and offers some joke-telling rules. The author notes that ethnic humor can be offensive, but that if it is funny, it is good to laugh. The toleration for some topics over others (drunkenness and greed being more acceptable than personal habits), the element of gloating superiority, and the actual humor in the joke are important elements, according to this reading. As the author points out, "An unfunny ethnic joke is merely an expression of contempt."

Issue 4: Does ethnic humor improve group relations?

The "Only Joking" Defense:
Attribution Bias or Impression Management?

A. Michael Johnson

Centenary College of Louisiana

Summary

The extent to which people believe that offensive jokes are consistent with joke tellers' attitudes was investigated. 135 college students indicated the extent to which they believe that there is congruence of joke and attitude when they tell offensive jokes or when others tell offensive jokes. Subjects who rated themselves as joke tellers attributed far less congruence between jokes and attitudes than subjects who rated others as joke tellers. The results are discussed in terms of the fundamental bias in attribution.

During the 1990 Texas gubernatorial campaign, candidate Clayton Williams received national attention for a "joking" remark he made which some perceived as sexist (Murchison, 1990). When confronted, Williams apologized and explained that he was "only joking." After the fact disclaimers such as Williams' are commonplace. Many people, like Williams, sometimes deny that their jests reflect their attitudes and values while those they have offended insist the opposite, that the remark was congruent with the attitude. This produces a peculiar situation in social communication. Listeners are convinced that what was said was what was intended. The joke teller, on the other hand, argues that what was intended was not received. All this poses an intriguing problem.

The difference between the joker's and the audience's perceptions may be understood within the framework of the fundamental bias in attribution (Watson, 1982). The joker focuses on situational variables such as the intent to amuse and the perceived, immediate expectations of the audience. These predominate. When reflecting on their own motives jokers sincerely believe that they did not intend to offend, only to amuse. Observers, on the other hand, are focused on the teller and concomitant stable, in-

ternal, attitudinal, motivational, or personality factors. They are less aware of the teller's intent to amuse and so more likely to attribute the offensive content of the joke to teller's attitudes.

Suls and Miller (1976), in the only empirically based study concerning this hypothesis in the literature, showed that people sometimes attribute consistency between sexist jokes and a teller's attitudes. Congruent joke/attitude attributions were made when subjects knew that the audience shared feminist attitudes and when the audience did not respond with amusement. Suls and Miller enlighten us by showing that people assume that jokes are attitude congruent at least part of the time. But this study may be of limited generalizability for several reasons. First, it measured the attributions of observers of rather than participants in joking situations. We cannot be certain that observers make the same sort of attributions as do actual audiences when they hear potentially offensive jokes. Second, it is uncertain if the effect is linked in some way to the particular topic operationalized by Suls and Miller. Therefore, we do not know the extent to which people are generally inclined to use another's jokes as an index of their attitudes. And finally, Suls and Miller do not address the sincerity of tellers of offensive jokes when they claim the defense "only joking."

The attributional account of the defense of "only joking" assumes that tellers are sincere in their claims. However, it is also possible that the defense is used as an expedient lie. Some authors have suggested that the "only joking" defense is invoked only when a joke draws unintended negative responses. For instance, Mendel (1971) speculated that joking provides a medium for the expression of risky feelings in a social context. Because humorous rather than attitudinal intent can be claimed if a joke does not find a receptive audience, the joker has a backdoor through which escape from association with the offensive attitude can be made. Kane, Suls, and Tedeschi (1977) expanded this speculation by suggesting that, in addition to providing a managed risk media for social probing and indirect self-disclosure, joking and the ability to "take it back" or "decommit" allow face-saving impression management. Unlike the attributional explanation, this view of the invocation of the defense of "only joking" is based on the teller's intention to maintain a socially desirable impression. This account differs from the attributional account in that jokers are insincere in claiming the defense of "only joking."

These two views make different and testable predictions concerning the defense of "only joking." We need only assume that, removed from a situation in which they might be judged for their attitudes and assured anonymity people will be honest. If the view of the fundamental attribution bias is correct, we expect that people are less likely to believe that their own jokes are attitude congruent than they are to believe the jokes of others are attitude congruent. On the other hand, if the hypothesis of impression management is correct and if anonymous reports concerning joke/attitude congruence are used to remove the need to manage impression, there ought not be significant differences between attributions for self and other teller.

Method

Subjects were college students (92 men and 43 women) who participated for course credit. Each subject completed one of two versions of a brief questionnaire. These questionnaires varied in one respect. One, the "self-attribution" version, began with the question, "When *you* tell jokes which might be perceived as mocking, hostile, or insensitive to the feelings of members of specific groups (e.g., African Americans, women, Polacks, Catholics, etc.), the jokes are representative of *your* attitudes toward those groups." In the "other-attribution" version this question was modified to read, "When *people* tell jokes . . . the jokes are representative of the *teller's* attitudes . . ." The question, "When people laugh at jokes like those described in the first item, their laughter reflects acceptance of or agreement with the attitude expressed by the jokes," appeared in both versions of the questionnaire. This question was included to determine whether the self vs other manipulation generally sensitized subjects to the relation of offensive humor and attitudes. Hence, it is referred to as the "other-amusement" question. Subjects rated these questions on seven-point Likert scales with the following descriptors attached to the scale values: never (1), rarely (2), occasionally (3), half of the time (4), often (5), usually (6), and always (7). Subjects also reported their sex. Questionnaires were completed privately and no identifying information was recorded.

Results

A 2 (attributional condition) × 2 (sex) analysis of variance was conducted. Attitudinal attributions were significantly lower in the self-attribution condition than the other-attribution condition ($F_{1,131}$ = 87.32, $p<.0001$). Group means and standard deviations were 2.3 (1.0) and 4.0 (1.16), respectively. The interaction between sex and attribution condition was also significant ($F_{1,131}$ = 4.12, $p<.05$), indicating that women in the self-attribution condition made lower attitude-congruent attributions (M = 1.8, SD = .73) than did men (M = 2.6, SD = 1.1). Women and men did not differ significantly in their attributions of joke and attitude congruence to others. These group means and standard deviations were 4.0 (1.1) and 4.0 (1.2), respectively.

A second 2 (attributional condition) × 2 (sex) analysis of variance in which the "other-amusement" question was the dependent variable showed no significant effects. These means and standard deviations were 3.4 (1.2) and 3.6 (1.1) for the self and other conditions and 3.3 (1.2) and 3.6 (1.1) for women and men, respectively. This result seems to indicate that the manipulated forms of the questionnaire did not generally affect subjects' judgments concerning humor.

Finally, the two teller condition means (self and other) were compared with the "other-amusement" means. Attitude attributions for "other-amusement" were significantly lower than "other as teller" attributions ($F_{1,60}$ = 5.68, $p<.01$) and significantly higher than "self as teller" attributions ($F_{1,71}$ = 37.59, $p<.0001$).

Discussion

This evidence suggests that people believe that their own jokes do not usually reflect their attitudes even when other people are offended. Using the descriptors of the rating scale as guidelines, people attribute attitude consistency to the jokes they tell somewhere between occasionally and rarely. This seems to support the view that jokers are often sincere when they claim that they were only joking. In contrast, people seem inclined to attribute consistency of attitude to others' jokes about half of the time. This is a tremendous gulf and no doubt a significant source of conflict between tellers and audiences, likely to leave tellers feeling misunderstood and audiences first offended and then later deceived.

The fact that people feel that others are reflecting their own attitudes in the joking situation only about half of the time is consistent with the predictions we might derive from Suls and Miller (1976). Situational variables such as audiences' responses and attitudes allow people to find other explanations for offensive humor, at least part of the time. When the present subjects reflected on their experiences with offensive humor, they may have taken into account those times when situations and audiences' responses left them with the *feeling* that the offending joke teller had not intended to convey an authentic personal attitude. This line of evidence will be furthered if studies assess the differential effects of subjects' amusement on attitude-congruent attributions.

The interaction effect between attribution condition and sex was not predicted and is difficult to interpret. Empirically it shows that women are less likely to attribute congruence between their attitudes and the jokes they tell than are men. Since we do not know what the "true" relationship between jokes and attitudes is we cannot tell if men or women are more accurate or more distorting. This is further complicated by the fact that there is no guarantee that the jokes which women tell are as offensive as the jokes which men tell. Therefore, when reflecting on their attitudes, women may also be reflecting on an internal repertoire of jokes which is less offensive than those in men's repertoires. There is some indication that such content differences in the joke repertoires of men and women are real (Johnson, 1990). Although women were actually more likely than men to tell racist and ethnic jokes, these tended to be of fairly benign varieties. Men, on the other hand, were more likely to tell sick, highly aggressive, and sexual jokes and were exclusive from women in telling jokes which aggressively victimize others, especially women and homosexuals. These data were drawn from a different sample than the data presented in the current study, and so direct comparisons cannot be made. However, *prima facie,* the offensive potential of the average Polack joke, which women tell more than do men, is probably not as great as the offensive potential of the average "gay bashing," "dead baby," or "sorority girl" joke. Therefore, very tentatively, the observed interaction is probably best understood as evidence that women tell less offensive jokes and so feel less that they have intended to offend.

These results also indicated that people sometimes interpret the laughter of others as evidence that their attitudes are consistent with the attitude a joke conveys. These attributions are more moderate than the attributions people make about tellers' attitudes. We can only speculate about why there should be a significant difference between the attributions made concerning tellers' and laughers' attitudes. But it makes sense that people recognize we sometimes laugh at offensive jokes told in social situations to conform rather than as an expression of amusement. Expressing amusement by laughing at offensive jokes is more excusable than is telling such jokes.

To summarize the major findings of this study, when people tell jokes which target members of identifiable groups, some people will be offended, at least part of the time. Even if the teller does not intend the offense, it is felt. Further, tellers generally believe that their jokes are not attitude-congruent. This raises another question. Why do people tell jokes which offend others if the jokes are not consistent with their attitudes? Several tentative arguments can be put forward for the reader's consideration.

One might argue that people who are insensitive to others or poor predictors of the reactions of others are more likely to make unintended offense. As a subhypothesis we might continue that such people misread social cues and tell their jokes with the expectancy that their jokes will match the attitudes of their audiences if not their own. Poor readers of social cues would, in this construction, be more likely to blunder by offending and then to claim honestly they were only joking.

The alternate explanation of the fact that people sometimes accidentally tell offensive jokes would elevate the common-sense meaning of the defense of "only joking" to include it as a member of the class of psychoanalytic defense mechanisms. This would be in keeping with Freud's (1960) pioneering work in the psychology of humor. Freud contended that joking represents an avenue for the expression of motives which are too threatening to express directly, too threatening even to acknowledge consciously. Assuming this for a moment, the defense of "only joking" may operate like a classical defense mechanism by preventing awareness of anxiety-producing motives while simultaneously allowing their indirect and disguised expression. This view offers the humor researcher new and testable hypotheses concerning the telling of offensive jokes, the claiming of the "only joking" defense, and the underlying motives of those who do such things.

In conclusion, let us briefly consider the heuristic value of this study. All of us will, at one time or another, be offended by a joking remark which someone makes. It will be worth remembering, when they begin claiming that they were only joking, that they are probably at least consciously sincere. On the other hand, for those times when some of us, not the least of whom is this author, accidentally offends someone else with a joke, it will be wise to recall that, even if we claim we were only joking, the chances are that no one will believe us. We will probably only further inflame the offended party by seeming, to them, to lie to save our own investment in the situation.

References

Freud, S. (1960) *Jokes and their relation to the unconscious.* New York: Norton.

Johnson, A. M. (1990) Reproductive humor: an unobtrusive, omnidirectional estimate of attitudes and sex differences. (Unpublished manuscript, Centenary College)

Kane, T. R., Suls, J., and Tedeschi, J. T. (1977) Humour as a tool of social interaction. In A. J. Chapman & H. C. Foot (Eds.), *It's a funny thing, humour.* Elmsford, NJ: Pergamon. Pp. 13–16.

Mendel, W. M. (1971) Humor as in index of emotional means. *Worm Runner's Digest,* 13, 53–61.

Murchison, W. (1990) "Me Bubba, you Jane." *National Review,* May, 24–26.

Suls, J. M., and Miller, R. L. (1976) Humor as an attribution index. *Personality and Social Psychology Bulletin,* 2, 256–259.

Watson, D. (1982) The actor and the observer: how are their perceptions of causality divergent? *Psychological Bulletin,* 92, 682–700.

Form at end of book

Excuuuse Me: The Case for Offensive Humor

Politically correct movies now evade any sexist, racial or gay jokes. This is too bad, because risque humor can actually reduce tension and prejudice and be very funny. Because humorless activists and multiculturalists dominate public opinion, violence dominates pop entertainment.

David Segal

David Segal is a Washington writer.

It was inevitable that the chill of sensitivity now felt in public discourse and academic life would eventually come to comedy. But p.c. humor has arrived more swiftly—and completely—than even ardent activists could have hoped. Take three films written and directed by David and Jerry Zucker and Jim Abrahams. *Airplane,* released in 1980, has a slew of gay bits, two black men speaking indecipherable jive over subtitles, close to a minyan of Jewish jokes, drug gags, references to bestiality, nun jokes, five obscenities, and one gratuitous front shot of a naked woman. *Naked Gun,* released in 1989, contains only one drug joke, one obscenity, no nudity, not a single Jewish joke, and three gay lines. In 1991 and *Naked Gun 2 1/2,* there were no obscenities, no frontal nudity, just two ethnic slurs, three tentative gay jokes, and one muttered "mazel-tov." Moreover, an earnest stripe of environmentalism is painted down the movie's middle. At the end of the film, the protagonist says, "Love is like the ozone layer: you only miss it once it's gone" without a hint of irony.

It's been a long slide downhill. Like the deficit, off-color humor touches everyone but has no constituency, and neither politicians nor pundits will be clamoring for its return soon. But there are good reasons to lament its passing. Let me count the ways.

Risque Humor Defuses Tensions.

Lenny Bruce used to do a stand-up routine in which he'd gesture to each ethnic minority in the room and call them the most offensive names in the book: "I got a nigger here, two spics there. . . ." When his audience was ready to assault him, he'd reveal his point: that epithets get at least part of their sting precisely by being placed off-limits. By spreading the abuse about, you take the sting out of it. (The caveat, of course, is that if you're going to use ethnic humor, you should avoid singling out any particular group for derision.) Today's puritans, in contrast, are a drag on our culture, impeding frank talk about race, sex, class, and sexuality, and deadening our public wit at the same time. It's no coincidence that in the 1980s, before multiculturalism killed racial jokes, productive discussions of race were more common.

Risque Humor Educates.

The experience of American Jews in this country may be the best example of how this works. For decades the capacity of Jewish comedians to poke fun at the peculiar tics of their people helped make Jewish otherness, a quality that aroused suspicion and hatred in bygone eras, something disarming. It's a safe bet that the films of Mel Brooks and Woody Allen did more to stymie anti-Semitism in the past twenty years than all the wide-eyed vigilance and arm-waving of the Anti-Defamation League. When a quick cut-away shot in Annie Hall reveals that the grandmother of Allen's WASPY girlfriend sees him as a bearded and yarmulked rabbi, we laugh even as we empathize with his discomfort. Gays have used humor the same way. You'd be hard-pressed to watch "La Cage Aux Folles," a musical about a troupe of mincing gay entertainers, and have your homophobia strengthened. *Airplane* had a character—John, an air traffic controller—whose jokes, improvised by gay actor and activist Steve Stucco, made fun of gay sensibility without attacking it. When someone hands him a piece of paper and asks what he can make of it, Stucco begins folding it and says, "Oh a brooch, or a hat, or a pterodactyl."

Risque Humor Disarms.

A classic—and rare—modern example is "In Living Color," which showcases merciless skits about black culture. (The reason it survives the p.c. police is that it's largely written and acted by blacks.) Witness a "Star Trek" spoof, "The Wrath of Farrakhan," a vicious lampoon of the black Muslim leader; or a sketch making fun of West Indians' hard-work habits. The feature "Men on Films," starring Damon Wayans and David Alan Grier (a.k.a. Antoine and Blaine), breaks taboos and wows both gay and straight audiences—while enraging the humorless activists. One regular skit centers on "Handi Man," a caped, spastic superhero who foils villains with his dwarf sidekick. To believe this hardens prejudice against people with disabilities is to believe that people are fundamentally barbaric; and assuming the handicapped are too tender a subject, humor is more patronizing than outright disdain. Indeed, there may be no better way to perpetate a myth of disabled otherness than coming up with euphemisms like "the differently abled" and making irreverent utterances off-limits.

Risque Humor Undermines Prejudices.

A black comic I recently saw had the right idea: he said he got so mad when a grocery clerk snickered about his purchase of frozen fried chicken that "I just grabbed my watermelon and tap-danced on out of there." The joke both played with stereotypes and ridiculed them: sometimes the best offense is offense. The major problem with ethnic humor—that it is often deployed by the powerful against the powerless—is best answered not by silencing the powerful (that hardly takes away their power) but by unleashing the humorous abilities of the powerless. Allowing ethnic humor means that blacks are allowed to make fun of whites (Eddie Murphy), gays are allowed to make fun of straights (Harvey Fierstein), and women are allowed to make fun of men (Roseanne Barr). In today's more ethically and sexually diverse media, little of this opportunity for humor is being realized. Diversity is being achieved;

and the result, ironically, is more piety. This is not only a bore, but an insult to the rich traditions of gay, black, Jewish, female, fat, ugly, disabled humor—and a boon to society's wealthy, powerful, and largely unfunny elites.

Risque Humor Is Funny.

Ethnic humor's final defense is that it makes people laugh. In a free society, this is an irrepressible—and admirable—activity, and one I suspect we did more of some years back. Ask yourself: Were you laughing harder a decade ago? When Buck Henry hosted "Saturday Night Live" in the 1970s, he'd do a skit in which he played a pedophilic baby sitter who got his jollies by playing games with his two nieces, like "find the pocket with the treat" and "show me your dirty laundry." In 1967 Mel Brooks won a best screenplay Academy Award for *The Producers*, which was full of Jewish, gay, and Nazi jokes and is now a confirmed classic. Brooks's 1991 offering was *Life Stinks*, which was bereft of anything off-color and rightly panned.

As we've pushed the risque off-stage, we've brought violent slapstick back on as a means of keeping the audience's attention. "Saturday Night Live" has abandoned racy material in favor of skits like "Horrible Headwound Harry," which features Dana Carvey as a party guest bleeding from the head. And last year *Home Alone*, the story of a little boy, played by Macaulay Culkin, who fends off two burglars from his house by, among other things, dropping a hot iron on their heads, became the most lucrative comedy of movie history, grossing more than $285 million. The violence was far more explicit than anything the Three Stooges ever came up with, and all of it was done by a 12-year-old. Compare this with *Animal House*, which used to be the top-grossing comedy; it was filled with sexist—and hilarious—moments like the one in which the conscience of Tom Hulce's character advises him to take advantage of his passed-out, underage date.

In a multicultural society like ours, humor is not a threat, it's critical support. It keeps us sane, and it's a useful safety valve. If we can't be cruel about each other in jest, we might end up being cruel to each other in deadly seriousness. The politically correct war against insensitive humor might end up generating the very social and racial tension it is trying to defuse.

Form at end of book

Tell Me Another One

Have you heard the one about the new movie called *Jews?* It's the story of a small resort town terrorized by a loan shark.

Now, I think that's pretty funny. And, I'm sorry, I just can't find enough high-mindedness within me to wish that this sort of joke didn't exist.

President Reagan told a good one in Venice the other day. As per usual, he thought the microphone was off. It seems there was this gondolier singing "O Solo Mio" and the Lord wondered what would happen if he lost 25 percent of his brainpower. Result: he sang, "O sole, O sole." So the Lord took away half his brains and he sang, "O so, O so." Finally, the Lord took away all his brains and he sang, "When Irish Eyes Are Smiling." Reagan noted, "See, I can tell that, being Irish."

In fact, it's amazing he got away with it. In other circumstances, it could easily have become a political-life-threatening gaffe. Imagine if George Bush had said it in New Hampshire. Yet there's been no fuss at all. Reagan being Irish had less to do with this than Reagan being Reagan. He has uttered so many boners, faux pas, and non sequiturs over the past seven years that people have become numb and the media have wearied of trying to stir up trouble. In the 1980 campaign he told a joke about a Pole and an Italian at a cock fight. Confronted at a press conference, he explained that he was just illustrating the kind of joke politicians shouldn't tell. Now he doesn't bother to explain because no one asks.

But maybe Reagan's bizarre immunity on matters of this sort will help to set a new standard, and we will be spared episodes like the one in the 1984 campaign when Walter Mondale made Gary Hart apologize repeatedly for making a little joke about New Jersey. After all, it's not as if there's a surfeit of good jokes in the world. We don't need more reasons not to laugh.

Of course it's undeniably true that ethnic jokes affront the brotherhood and sisterhood of all humankind, as well as the individuality of each person. In America, we have a special need to minimize ethnic friction and resentment. But a world of universal and constant respect for these ideals might be hard to live in—and, in any event, is not on the horizon.

There are those, no doubt, who can refrain from telling ethnic jokes. And there may even be some—a much smaller group, and one you probably wouldn't care to share a long cruise or jail term with—who can refrain from laughing at any of them. As for the rest of us, what we need are some etiquette guidelines aimed at providing maximum gaiety with minimum offense. Pending congressional hearings, here are a few suggestions.

Rule 1. As Reagan noted, it's better to tell jokes on your own ethnic group. He's Irish, I'm Jewish. Of course Reagan doesn't really believe that the Irish are inordinately stupid and I don't really believe that Jews are inordinately avaricious. But an ethnic joke told on oneself can become a way of laughing at the stereotype, thereby undermining it, rather than promoting it.

Rule 2. If the joke is about some other ethnic group, a good seat-of-the-pants test is whether you would tell it in the presence of a friend from that group. If you'd be embarrassed to tell the joke in front of your friend, maybe you shouldn't tell it elsewhere. If you don't even have a friend from this particular group, that's an even better signal to stay away.

Rule 3. Jokes about some groups are less offensive than jokes about others. This is a double standard, but a valid one. Black Americans are still everyday victims of oppression and discrimination based on ethnic stereotypes; Italian, Irish, and Jewish Americans far, far less so. Of the common subjects of ethnic jokes, I would rank them in order of legitimate sensitivity as: blacks, Hispanics, Poles, Jews, Italians, Irish, WASPS.

Unfortunately, most WASP jokes just aren't very funny. (From *Truly Tasteless Jokes* by "Blanche Knott": "How can you tell the only WASP in a sauna? He's the one with the *Wall Street Journal* on his lap." Not terribly tasteless.) WASP jokes have a sense of strain, almost a sense of duty about them, not a sense of natural vicious inspiration. Many are actually jokes at the expense of other groups—variations on "What do you get when you mix a WASP and a Puerto Rican?" and so on. This illustrates the unavoidable truth that a good ethnic joke must contain an element of gloating superiority. It can be vestigial, but it must be there. A well-meaning naif once suggested that we should invent an all-purpose imaginary group to be the butt of ethnic humor. Unfortunately, it wouldn't work.

Rule 4. Jokes about certain alleged traits are more offensive than jokes about others. This has nothing in particular to do with the validity of the stereotype involved. For example, it is not true that certain ethnic groups inherently smell bad and/or attract insects, and jokes based on this premise are pointless and disgusting. On the other hand, a whole genre of jokes has surfaced in recent years based on the equally absurd premise that all Jewish women are frigid (exactly the opposite of the historical stereotype). In that case, it seems to me, the patent falsity of the premise turns it into a harmless convention. Meanwhile, jokes that turn on blacks having curly hair are stupid and offensive even though—or actually because—it's true. Where's the joke?

Of course all ethnic stereotypes are invalid generalizations. But jokes about drunkenness, laziness, greed are more tolerable than jokes about physical characteristics or personal habits. The tough call is stupidity, since (unlike, say, bad table manners) it implies genuine and immutable inferiority, and yet is the basis of probably half of all ethnic jokes, including some good ones. One comfort here is that the literature lacks any clear consensus about which groups are ostensibly dumber than others. Reagan's joke turned on the Irish being dumber than Italians. *Totally Gross Jokes, Volume II* has a similar joke about progressive loss of brainpower whose punch line is "Oh, mamma mia!"

Rule 5. If you tell an ethnic joke, make sure it's funny. Most ethnic humor in the recent rash of paperbacks and on those gross-out radio talk shows is witless. Wittiness is important not only for its own sake—to compensate for any offense—but as a test of motive. An unfunny ethnic joke is merely an expression of contempt. A funny one need not be.

Rule 6. If you hear one you think is good, feel free to laugh. Examine your conscience later. It's healthier that way.

Form at end of book

WiseGuide Wrap-Up

Joking is one of the most common ways we interact with each other. We applaud people who can tell jokes well. Joke-telling is a valuable social skill that many people cultivate to be successful in business and politics. Joking can also be a way in which we establish control of a situation and draw attention to ourselves. Most people do not want their joke-telling to be a way of alienating people.

The readings in this section raise a number of concerns about jokes that may not achieve our intentions. Risqué jokes and jokes about sensitive ethnic and racial issues may do more social harm than good. Wise selection is important when telling a joke, since the response to the joke may not be what we expect. Even an audience laughing at a joke does not mean that the joke-teller has been socially successful. Laughing at a joke may indicate a willingness to conform, rather than real amusement. Laughing at an offensive joke is more excusable than telling one. Poor readers of social cues are more likely to blunder in this regard.

Freud suggested that joking might be one way to express motives and attitudes that are too threatening to express directly. Do jokes reflect subconscious attitudes of which the joke-teller is not even aware? The "only joking" defense may not get the teller off the hook.

One concern that the authors of the readings in this section do not deal with is identifying a suitable audience. Should young children be protected from certain kinds of humor? Are cartoons such as "South Park" meant for adults only? When children watch this type of cartoon, do they learn negative attitudes about the subjects of the jokes? What kind of humor is appropriate for young children?

What is offensive and what is acceptable constantly fluctuates. And identifying the line between what is funny and what is offensive is not always easy.

R.E.A.L. Sites

This list provides a print preview of typical **Coursewise** R.E.A.L. sites. (There are over 100 such sites at the **Courselinks**™ site.) The danger in printing URLs is that web sites can change overnight. As we went to press, these sites were functional using the URLs provided. If you come across one that isn't, please let us know via email to: webmaster@coursewise.com. Use your Passport to access the most current list of R.E.A.L. sites at the **Courselinks** site.

Site name: American Association for Therapeutic Humor
URL: http://www.aath.org/
Why is it R.E.A.L.? This site offers information on the therapeutic use of humor. It includes an affirmation of intent to use humor only for beneficial purposes and provides links to jokes of various kinds.
Key terms: inoffensive humor

Site name: Humor Space
URL: http://www.humorspace.com/
Why is it R.E.A.L.? This site is a source of jokes and various other kinds of humor. It has a humor archive, dictionaries, and links to action groups opposed to exploitative humor.
Key terms: jokes, cartoons

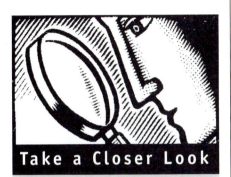

Take a Closer Look

1. Should First Amendment rights be restricted in cases of hate speeches?

2. According to Kleinig, what are the main policy considerations that hate crime legislation poses?

3. What impact will enhanced penalties have on defendants? If juveniles are the main offenders, is legislation the best method to modify their behavior?

4. Is revenge through the law the best way to decrease tensions in a multicultural society?

WiseGuide Intro

Hate and crimes inspired by hatred, prejudice, and bigotry are harmful to individuals, minority groups, and society as a whole. There is, however, little agreement on how to deal with these problems. According to James Jacobs (Reading 10), most hate crimes committed in the United States are not the hard-core actions of racists and anti-Semites, but the result of impulsive behavior or situational disputes. Most often, juveniles commit these crimes, which means that hate crime legislation will have little effect in limiting the crimes committed. Juveniles are dealt with differently under the law, and current laws do not apply to juvenile cases. Minors are most likely to be charged with "delinquency" and thus not come under the specific codes that regulate hate crimes. Educational programs might be more effective in such cases than jail time.

Another important aspect of hate crimes is prejudice. Prejudice is difficult to define but relates to ideas and thoughts rather than action. Is prejudice the primary motivation for hate crimes or simply a contributing factor? Should a prosecutor focus on proving the prejudice of an individual by investigating the person's reading materials, manner of joking, and membership in questionable organizations? Should the defense conduct a similar investigation as a way of eliminating prejudice? Either course would substantially change the focus of the trial and turn it into a series of character tests and inquisitions into the defendant's beliefs, attitudes, and personality. Would this lead to greater social harmony or increased social conflict?

If crime control is the objective, then hate crime legislation may be the wrong tool for achieving it. Current hate crime laws are often vague and open the door to arbitrary application. They are often overbroad and thus may have a chilling effect on free and protected speech. Some of the proposed laws criminalize thought and may lead to the punishing of motives, not acts. The laws can deny equal protection under the law by basing the treatment of offenders on the beliefs that they hold.

Tolerance is not the same as acceptance. In a free society, the majority may have to tolerate the unacceptable behavior of individuals and minority groups. The freedom to express ideas enables discussion of the ideas and can assist individuals in making choices. Criminal law is a last resort for resolving hate crimes because it does not promote intergroup respect and acceptance.

In Reading 10, James Jacobs's concern is with the criminal justice system. What role do courts have in dealing with issues of hate and prejudice? Should the courts, the police, and the society deal with the prejudicial aspects of hate crimes when there is sufficient law to deal with the actual behavior of individuals? While Jacobs concedes that to denounce hate crimes affirms the goal of a fair and tolerant society, he fears that this will transform the crime problem into a prejudice problem and will encourage groups to keep score of how such cases are handled. He suggests that this will lead to greater social conflict and have no direct effect on reducing hate crimes.

In Reading 11, John Kleinig reviews the points made by Susan Gellman, an assistant Ohio public defender who not only sees the enhancement of penalties for crimes with a hate component as threatening to First Amendment rights but also as ineffective. Kleinig believes that such laws result in greater costs than benefits to society and that they do little to deter crime or to eliminate prejudice.

Should Hate Be a Crime?

James B. Jacobs

Abstract

Hate crime in the United States is a controversial area. Many people favour the expansion of hate crime legislation to try and decrease the incidence of racism and prejudice. Existing legislation lacks clear definition of what constitutes a hate crime and law enforcers can find themselves in a no-win situation. About 50% of hate crime is undertaken by teenagers under the age of 19 years. With this in mind it might be more realistic to expand social services rather than continue to segregate criminal law into specialist areas. Continuation of this will result in a decline in race relations.

On May 29, 1989, a white man, David Wyant, occupied a campsite next to Jerry White, an African-American. White complained to the park authorities that Wyant was playing his music too loudly during "quiet hours." White and his companion later heard three comments directed at them from the Wyants' campsite: (1) "We didn't have this problem until those niggers moved in next to us"; (2) "The black motherfucker over there; I will take this gun and kill him"; (3) "In fact, I will go over and beat his black ass now."

On the basis of these statements, without any accompanying conduct or evidence that there actually was a gun, Wyant was convicted of "ethnic intimidation" and sentenced to eighteen months incarceration.

State v. Wyant is the kind of case that ought to be carefully considered by proponents of hate crime legislation. The imagery that animates the passage of such legislation posits hardcore racists and anti-Semites waging a systematic campaign against blacks and Jews. By contrast, most of the cases that are labeled hate crimes result from impulsive behavior or situational disputes, often involving juveniles. One could easily think of the *Wyant* case as a fight about noise at a campground that activated the defendant's racial prejudice. Such prejudice is certainly not pretty but, unlike hardcore neo-Nazism, is widespread and often bubbles to the surface in the arguments, altercations, and conflicts that punctuate life in a multi-racial and multi-ethnic society. This kind of prejudice certainly needs attention, but not the kind of attention that is provided by elevating an occasional low-level, harassment-type crime into a serious offense.

The Problem of Motive

Wyant also reveals a more serious flaw in hate crime legislation. Criminal law has long struggled to define the criminal intent (*mens rea*) that transforms a harm into a crime. Defining criminal motivation is even trickier, because it requires getting to the source of the defendant's intent. For this reason criminal law generally has steered clear of motivation.

Motivation is particularly problematic in hate crime cases because the presumed motive, "prejudice," defies precise definition. According to the *International Encyclopedia of the Social Sciences:*

Prejudice is not a unitary phenomenon . . . [I]t will take varying forms in different individuals. Socially and psychologically, attitudes differ depending upon whether they are the result of deep-seated personality characteristics, sometimes of the pathological nature, of a traumatic experience, or whether they simply represent conformity to an established norm.

Indeed, some people speak of prejudice as being unconscious as well as conscious. Consider the view of Charles Lawrence III, an influential professor of law at Stanford University:

Americans share a common historical and cultural heritage in which racism played and still plays a dominant role. Because of this shared experience, we also inevitably share many ideas, attitudes and beliefs that attach significance to an individual's race and induce negative feelings and opinions about non-whites. To the extent that this cultural belief system has influenced all of us, we are all racists. At the same time, most of us are unaware of our racism. . . . In other words, a large part of the behavior that produces racial discrimination is influenced by unconscious racial motivation.

If prejudice is this pervasive, subtle, and complex, the criminal justice system will certainly have a hard time sorting out which interracial crimes are motivated by prejudice and which are not. Moreover, recent efforts by law enforcement agencies and courts to define hate crimes more precisely do inspire confidence. For example, the U.S. Department of Justice Guidelines, which set out the government's criteria for labeling a hate crime, define ethnic prejudice as a "preformed negative opinion or attitude toward a group of persons of the same race or national origin who share common or similar traits, languages, customs, and traditions." If the prejudice required is no more than "a preformed negative opinion," most interracial crimes could be prosecuted as hate crimes.

Prosecutors in hate crime cases must prove not only that the defendant was prejudiced, but that prejudice motivated his crime. But must prejudice be the sole or primary motivation, or simply a contributing motivation? If prejudice must be the sole or the primary motivation, it will be very difficult to prove a hate crime, since criminal behavior, like all behavior, is almost always motivated by many factors.

If, however, prejudice must be merely a contributing factor, practically any interracial crime could be prosecuted as a hate crime. Contemplate, for example, the percentage of interracial muggings, robberies, and assaults in bars that might be said to be "in part" attributable to a preformed negative opinion about the victim's racial group. Thus far, courts and legislatures have opted for an inclusive interpretation, so that in most jurisdictions the prosecution has to prove only that the criminal conduct was "in whole or in part" attributable to prejudice.

In labeling hate crimes, there is immense potential for confusion and arbitrariness. In New York City, the police are instructed not to apply the hate crime label to an offense that started off as something else (e.g., a fight over a parking space) and then escalated into name calling. But they are also instructed: "If after applying the [even] criteria listed and asking the appropriate questions, substantial doubt exists as to whether or not the incident is bias motivated or not, the incident should be classified as bias motivated for investigative and reporting purposes."

It is uncertain where things will go from there. Police commissioners and politicians obviously will not wish to have their cities labeled the "hate crime capital." Yet they are also under constant pressure from advocacy groups to recognize racism, anti-Semitism, and homophobia, and they are vulnerable to criticism when they do not denounce, label, investigate, and prosecute various offenses as hate crimes. So there will probably be a tendency to err on the side of inclusion.

The First Amendment

In *R.A.V. v. St. Paul* (1991), the Supreme Court, in an opinion by Justice Scalia, held unconstitutional on First Amendment grounds a St. Paul hate ordinance that outlawed symbolic speech (including cross burning and swastikas) which insults or provokes violence on the basis of race, color, creed, religion, or gender.

Although *R.A.V.* dealt with an ordinance that prohibited offensive "fighting words," the decision also cast a cloud over laws that enhance sentences for ordinary crimes (e.g., harassment, assault, rape) motivated by particular prejudices. Critics of such laws charge that enhancing the sentence of an offender for conduct motivated by politically disfavored opinion, thought, or belief also violates the First Amendment. Adopting that view, the Wisconsin Supreme Court held the state's hate crime enhancement statute to be unconstitutional: "the Wisconsin legislature cannot prohibit bigoted thought with which it disagrees."

In *Mitchell v. Wisconsin* (1993), however, the U.S. Supreme Court overruled the Wisconsin Supreme Court. Chief Justice Rehnquist's opinion for a unanimous Court noted that, "whereas the ordinance struck down in *R.A.V.* was explicitly directed at expression, the statute in this case is aimed at conduct unprotected by the First Amendment." The Court also rejected as "simply too speculative" the defendant's argument that the statute would have a chilling effect on speech, causing citizens to fear making prejudiced or racist statements or engaging in politically disfavored activities (reading, memberships, etc.) lest their words or deeds be used against them at some future criminal trial.

In response to the defendant's claim, the Court explained that "the First Amendment does not prohibit the evidentiary use of speech to establish the elements of a crime or to prove motive or intent." Thus, according to the Court, the admissibility of speech, speech-related, or associational activity can be properly managed under long-established evidentiary rules of relevancy and reliability.

That may turn out to be wishful thinking. In *Mitchell*, there was testimony of a close relationship between racist speech and criminal conduct—the defendant said to his friends: "Do you feel hyped up to move on some white people?" and "You all want to fuck somebody up? There goes a white boy; go get him." Clearly, the racist speech immediately preceding the brutal assault was relevant to proving that Mitchell had selected his victim because of racial prejudice. But how will the criminal justice system deal with beliefs, words, or associations that are not as closely connected to the criminal conduct?

In interracial cases, should the police routinely investigate the defendant's prejudices: what publications he subscribes to, what organizations he's a member of, what jokes he tells, what stereotypes he holds? Suppose, in *Mitchell*, that several days or weeks earlier, the defendant had told friends or co-workers that he wanted to retaliate against whites for the injustice portrayed in the movie *Mississippi Burning*. Since prejudice would be an element of the offense, the defendant's conversations and activities regarding prejudice would definitely be relevant and, in my judgment, admissible. I am also led to this conclusion by cases like *People v. Aishman* (1993), where the fact that one of the defendants wore two tattoos, one a swastika and another reading "Thank God I'm White," was held admissible in considering whether the defendant selected his Mexican-American victim because of ethnicity. While admitting such evidence may not be unconstitutional, it certainly is not consistent with the spirit of a strong First Amendment. It bristles with potential for defendants to be convicted or sentenced more harshly because of their "bad" beliefs and attitudes.

In an effort to defend against a hate crime charge, some defendants may try to prove their lack of prejudice by introducing evidence of non-racist speech, memberships, and activities. How could a judge rule such evidence irrelevant? If the defendant is permitted to adduce such evidence, however, the prosecutor will almost certainly be allowed to introduce rebuttal evidence of the defendant's racism.

Thus, there is the all too likely possibility that hate crime trials will degenerate into inquisitions on the defendant's beliefs, attitudes, and personality. In *Wyant*, the attempt to determine the defendant's motivation led to the following cross-examination:

Q. And you lived next door to [Mrs. Ware, a 65-year-old black neighbor of the defendant's] for nine years and you don't even know her first name?

A. No.

Q. Never had dinner with her?

A. No.

Q. Never gone out and had a beer with her?

A. No.

Q. Never went to a movie?

A. No.

Q. Never invited her to a picnic at your house?

A. No.

Q. Never invited her to Alum Creek?

A. No, she never invited me nowhere, no.

Q. You don't associate with her, do you?

A. I talk with her when I can, whenever I see her out.

Q. All these black people that you have described that are your friends, I want you to give me one person, just one who was really a good friend of yours.

Examinations like this one are unlikely to ease racial tension. Rather, they seem more likely to turn hate crime trials into character tests of the most pernicious kind and to widen social divisions.

Even if judges find a way to limit cross-examination and the admissibility of speech and thought evidence, the defendant's arguably racist words and thoughts will still be ventilated at pretrial and trial hearings on the admissibility of evidence. Even if the jury does not hear the evidence, the media can and will seize on the defendant's beliefs as newsworthy. With prejudice the key factor distinguishing hate crime from ordinary crime, the inevitable result will be the further politicization of the criminal justice process. That can only have a negative effect on racial and other intergroup relations in American society.

Hate Crime Politics

On the one hand, to denounce hate crimes is to affirm the goal of a fair and tolerant society. On the other, to highlight the prejudicial and racial aspects of as many crimes as possible, transforming the crime problem into a prejudice problem, is to present an unduly bleak picture of the state of inter-group relations and rub salt into the wounds of festering angers and prejudices. Rather than defining violence as a social problem that unites all Americans in a search for a solution, this new approach defines the problem as a composite of different types of intergroup hate, and so may divide the political community.

In the last several years, New York City has experienced a new kind of political controversy: whether a particular crime merits denunciation as a hate crime by the criminal justice system, mayor, police commissioner, and media. These high visibility controversies put the politicians and police brass in a no-win situation. If they do not utter the words "hate crime," they are excoriated by the victim's group for bias and insensitivity. If they do apply the hate crime label, they are similarly criticized by the perpetrator's group for bias, hasty judgment, and double standards.

When the gang rape of the Central Park jogger was not classified as a hate crime (because of a few of the victims of the marauding youths were black or Hispanic), some journalists charged that there exists a double standard, whereby white-on-black crimes are labeled hate crimes, while black-on-white crimes are not. Some women expressed outrage that a gang rape was not considered a hate crime regardless of the racial element. Meanwhile, some black observers denounced the prosecution of the youths as itself racist. To take another example, after Mayor Dinkins forcefully denounced the beating of Ralph Nimmons, a homeless black man, as a bias crime, the Jewish Lubavitcher community reacted angrily to the hate crime charge, claiming that Nimmons had been apprehended burglarizing a school.

The very existence of the hate crime label raises the political and social stakes in intergroup crimes. Groups are beginning to keep score cards. Applying or failing to apply the hate crime label triggers heated political battles. The result is not greater racial and ethnic harmony, but exacerbated social conflict.

Adding hate crime charges in high-visibility interracial cases can make them even more socially divisive. Consider the pending trial in Los Angeles of two black defendants charged with pulling Reginald Denny, a white driver, out of his truck and brutally beating him. What good would be served in charging the defendants with a hate crime and trying to demonstrate their racial prejudice? Doing so would politicize the trial even more, and, given the seriousness of the charges, would have little effect on the actual punishment.

In cases like this, prosecutors frequently do not want the jury to focus on racial prejudice. The fear is a jury polarized along racial lines. Indeed, in the Denny trial and other high-visibility interracial prosecutions, defendants have attempted to turn their trials into referenda on the racist exercise of police and prosecutorial discretion.

The basic civil rights paradigm posits whites as the prototypical discriminators or offenders; it does not contemplate discrimination by minorities against whites or against one another. Blacks and Hispanics, however are disproportionately involved in violent crimes. Most of these are intragroup, but many are against whites and members of other minority groups.

While violence by whites against blacks occurs all too frequently, blacks also commit many crimes against whites. Thus, unlike other civil rights legislation and jurisprudence, hate crime laws will not necessarily work to advance the interests of all black Americans (although they might arguably advance the interests of nearly all gays and lesbians, who rarely engage in "heterosexual bashing"). Indeed, at some point in the future, some supporters of hate crime laws may be dismayed to find that these laws are frequently used against black offenders.

Anticipating this outcome, several student law review writers have urged that hate crime laws should apply only (or more easily) to white defendants. To my knowledge, these proposals have not been seriously considered by state legislatures.

The Politics of Victimization

Hate crime legislation attempts, as noted, to import the civil rights paradigm into criminal law. Some groups are defined as needing special protection against discriminatory treatment, albeit not at the hands of government officials or employers, but at the hands of criminals.

If such a status is available, every conceivable minority group will naturally lobby to be included. If the law says that criminal conduct motivated by racism warrants enhanced punishment, why shouldn't crime conduct motivated by sexism and homophobia also be covered? Not surprisingly, many women cannot understand why rape and spouse abuse do not qualify as hate crimes motivated by gender prejudice. Gays and lesbians, who in other contexts have not been fully successful in obtaining recognition as a bona fide minority group entitled to social, legal, and economic advantages, have argued with incontrovertible logic that to ignore the history of gay-bashing in the formulation of hate clime legislation would itself constitute an act of blatant prejudice.

Women and gays and lesbians are slowly obtaining inclusion in hate clime statutes, although their inclusion is by no means universal or uncontroversial. In the state of New York, for example, the legislature has refused to pass a hate crime law that includes gays and lesbians. Some state legislators also have argued that the victimization of women is already recognized in specific criminal statutes. Perhaps without fully realizing it, legislators are resisting the temptation to expand the hate crime label to the extent that it becomes nearly co-extensive with crime itself.

But some states, like Wisconsin, include prejudice based upon mental or physical disability in their hate crime statues. Many other prejudices will undoubtedly be recognized over time (age, marital status, political memberships and beliefs). To exclude any group, once it petitions to have its victimization recognized as equivalent to that of other groups, would provoke justifiable anger. Except where a particular prejudice enjoys substantial support (e.g., anti-gay sentiment in some states), politicians will almost certainly bestow hate crime victim status on practically any group that can make its voice heard; there is no political payoff in opposing such a demand. Eventually, a large percentage of all crimes could qualify for secondary condemnation as hate crimes. At that point, those whose victimizations do not fall within any hate crime category might feel discriminated against.

Hate crime law fits uneasily within the civil rights paradigm. Civil rights laws attempt to extend positive rights and opportunities to minorities and women. They are directed at the conduct of government officials and private persons who govern, regulate, or sell goods and services. By contrast, hate crime law deals with conduct that is already criminal and with wrongdoers who are already criminals. The possibility that criminals can be threatened into not discriminating in their choice of crime victims seems slight. Whether the criminal law can be employed successfully in eradicating or reforming deep-rooted prejudices is doubtful.

Enhancing Deterrence

The horrendous crimes that provide the imagery and emotion for the passage of hate crime legislation are already so heavily punished under American law that any talk of "sentence enhancement" must be primarily symbolic. In fact, we have all the criminal and sentencing law we need to respond severely and punitively to criminal conduct inspired, in whole or in part, by prejudice.

I do not mean to say that the availability of enhanced punishments for hate crimes can never have any practical implications. When new powers are given to police and prosecutors, they will be used and from time to time make a difference. This is more likely to happen in low-level crimes which, because of overloaded dockets and jails, would otherwise fall through the cracks but for the added emphasis that a hate crime label might provide.

In speculating about the possible deterrent effect of hate crime laws, we need also take into account some facts about the offenders who commit these crimes. According to data from New York City and Los Angeles, the majority are teenagers. In New York City in 1990, over 50 percent of hate crime arrestees were under the age of nineteen, and over 20 percent were under sixteen. Ironically, hate crime laws do not apply to juveniles, who are charged with "delinquency" rather than with specific code offenses. Moreover, when juveniles are convicted they are "committed" to juvenile institutions for indefinite terms, not "sentenced"; thus, sentencing enhancement statutes are not applicable. Even if they were, the youthful offenders who are arrested for such crimes are often alienated, impulsive, and generally hostile, hardly the kind of individuals likely to be deterred by sentencing enhancements.

Even if the new wave of hate crime laws does not deter any hate crimes, some advocates, believe these laws are justified because hate crimes are "worse" than other crimes in the same generic offense category and so deserve greater punishment. I agree that certain extremely violent, racist crimes warrant the most intense condemnation, but

I would not be prepared to say that these crimes are without moral equals. It is invariably worse to be raped by someone who hates you because of your race, rather than for your gender, appearance, social class, or for no reason at all? Is a racially bigoted rapist deserving of more condemnation than a "merely" hostile and anti-social rapist? Does it really matter whether the rapists in the Central Park jogger case were motivated in whole or in part by racism?

The most horrible crimes—murder, rape, kidnapping, arson—are so devastating that it seems to deprecate the victim's pain and anguish to conclude, as the hate crime laws do, that there is more trauma if the perpetrator is a bigot as well as a brute. If distinctions must be made, wouldn't a more neutral statute make more sense; i.e., a rape warrants enhanced punishment if it involves terror, torture, or substantial gratuitous violence beyond the rape itself? Sentencing law already provides this option in many states.

Those who lobby for more hate crime laws claim that a crime motivated by prejudice ought to be punished more severely than other crimes because the effects ripple out beyond the individual victim; all members of the victim's group are made less secure and, depending upon which groups are involved, there may be retaliation or group conflict. Once again, I believe that this conclusion is applicable to some hate crimes, but I do not believe that every hate crime (e.g., an act of shoving on the subway) generates serious social instability. Moreover, all sorts of crimes have serious social repercussions: carjackings, shootings and stabbings in schools and housing projects, "wildings" in parks, shootouts by rival gangs and drug dealers, and murderous attacks in subways. Over the last several decades, fear of crime has been a prime reason that hundreds of thousands, perhaps millions, of people have moved from cities to suburbs or from one neighborhood to another. Thus, it is surely an exaggeration to say that hate crimes are unique in their impact on people beyond the immediate victims.

The Wrong Tool

While many civil rights advocates view the passage of hate crime laws as a step toward the reduction of hate crimes and prejudice generally, I am skeptical. To fragment criminal law into specialized laws recognizing a moral hierarchy of motives and offender/victim configurations will have little, if any, crime-control benefit, while carrying serious risks for race relations and social harmony. The attempt to extend the civil rights paradigm to crimes committed by one private party against another is well-meaning but misguided. Prejudice and hate will not be stamped out by enhancing criminal penalties, and considerable damage may result from enforcing these laws. The new hate crime laws both reflect and contribute to the politicization of the crime problem and the criminal justice process, especially around issues of race, and thereby exacerbate social divisions and social conflict.

Reducing prejudice and hate must be a high priority for American society, but more criminal law is the wrong tool. We should exhaust all other strategies of social education and institution-building before pinning our hopes on the criminal law, which has, at best, a very unimpressive record in ameliorating social problems.

Form at end of book

Issue 5: Should hate be a crime?

Penalty Enhancement for Hate Crimes

John Kleinig

Editor's Introduction

The recent Supreme Court decision in *R.A.V. v. City of St. Paul*[1] has tended to overshadow a more complex problem that has been confronting the courts. In *R.A.V.*, following the conviction of a St. Paul (Minn.) resident for planting a burning cross on the front lawn of a black family, the Court was asked to rule on the constitutionality of the ordinance under which the defendant had been convicted, one banning the display of a swastika, the burning of a cross, or use of other symbols that "arouse anger, alarm, or resentment in others on the basis of race, color, creed, religion or gender."[2] The Court's decision has already generated much discussion. It appears to have focussed on a subject-matter restriction in the Minnesota ordinance, in contravention of an equal protection commitment implicit in the First Amendment. In any case, it dealt with conduct that was primarily expressive.

The more complex problem concerns statutes that enhance penalties when conduct that is independently criminal in character has been motivated by racial, religious, or sexual- or gender-based considerations, to take those considerations most commonly involved. Do such enhancements fall foul of First Amendment or other protections, or may they stand as a legitimate exercise of state and judicial discretion? Although some have argued that the recent Supreme Court decision will have a bearing on such penalty enhancement statutes, others believe that it does not, and that the issue of penalty enhancement can stand apart from decisions concerned more centrally with what is predominantly expression.

In 1991, Susan Gellman, an Assistant Ohio Public Defender, published an important article[3] in which she argued that penalty enhancement statutes violate First Amendment and other protections. Gellman's arguments were recently endorsed by the Wisconsin and Ohio Supreme Courts in cases that overturned hate crime convictions. And, following *R.A.V.*, she (along with Martin Redish) reaffirmed her position before a House subcommittee called to consider whether that decision would impact on penalty enhancement legislation.

In her article, Gellman speaks uniformly of the statutes that would enhance penalties for hate crimes as "ethnic intimidation" laws, though she intends this label to cover "violent or harassing offenses motivated by racism, antisemitism, sexism, or other forms of bias" [333]. Their paradigm is a model statute drafted in 1981 by the Anti-Defamation League of B'nai B'rith, and since then adapted or paralleled by over twenty state legislatures. The courts have given them a mixed reception. It is Gellman's contention that such laws are unconstitutional, unwise, and likely to be ineffective.

I Constitutional Considerations

Following a brief overview of the development of ethnic intimidation statutes, the purpose of which, she says, is to provide redress not only to those directly attacked, but also to other members of disempowered groups for the added injury that a bias motivated crime works, Gellman turns to the constitutional questions such statutes raise.

She considers three possible ways in which the statutes may be viewed: (i) they "bump-up" the penalty for criminal offenses motivated by bigotry; (ii) they recognize a qualitative difference in criminal conduct that is bias-motivated; or (iii) they identify a new class of speech not protected by the First Amendment. Whichever way they are construed, Gellman considers them constitutionally defective. She suggests four deficiencies.

1. They are *vague* in important respects, and thus not only fail to provide people with a reasonable opportunity to avoid violating them but open the door to their discriminatory and arbitrary application. It is not clear, for example, whether such statutes are intended to reach cases

From John Kleinig, "Penalty Enhancement for Hate Crimes" (as appeared in *Criminal Justice Ethics*, Volume 11, Number 2, Summer/Fall 1992, pp. 3–6. Reprinted by permission of The Institute for Criminal Justice Ethics, 899 Tenth Avenue, New York, NY 10019–1029.

in which, say, one Jew threatens another in an argument about Yasir Arafat, or one white harasses another for supporting Nelson Mandela, and so [356]. Nor is it clear what mental state is appropriate to them—whether, for example, the intimidator must "know" that s/he is motivated by bigotry, whether such motives must be under one's immediate control, and whether a person whose motives are mixed should be liable, even if other reasons contribute to the conduct as or even more substantially [356–57]. Gellman acknowledges that more precise drafting might avoid these deficiencies.

Even so, she considers that there is a more subtle problem. If (following (i) above) a suitably specified motive is permitted to enhance an existing non-vague crime, it will run foul of the First Amendment by criminalizing pure thought. But if, on the other hand, it is said that the motive changes the character of the conduct that it prompts (as in (ii) above), it lapses into unconstitutional (Fourteenth Amendment) vagueness, since the resulting conduct is not defined.

2. They are *substantially overbroad,* and thus chill speech, thought, and discussion. Even though penalty enhancement statutes start from conduct that is on other grounds illegal, Gellman believes that they are susceptible of application to protected activity. Writing of the ADL model statute, she says that although it

does not include the making of bigoted statements as an element of the offense, . . . its enforcement must inevitably—and probably exclusively—rely upon defendants' speech and associations for evidence of the motive it seeks to punish. In practical effect, then, the model statute threatens to penalize the speech and associations themselves. . . . The distinction between the use of the actor's words as the sole—and perhaps the only possible—evidence of an element of an offense, and their use as an actual element of the offense, is so fine as to be often nonexistent [359].

She is not persuaded by the obvious objection that all one needs to do to avoid such consequences is to stay clear of one of the underlying offenses. For, she claims, "chill of expression . . . by definition occurs *before* any offense is committed, and even if no offense is *ever* committed" [361].

3. They *criminalize thought,* thus violating a basic First Amendment protection. Gellman's argument has two main thrusts.

(a) *The questionable constitutionality of punishing motives.* The fact that the conduct in question is punishable independently of the motives that propel it does not,

Gellman believes, remove the constitutional protective shield that is otherwise guaranteed to thoughts and ideas. Although she acknowledges the relevance of "intent" and "purpose" to criminality (since they enter into the "what" of conduct), she believes that "motive" (which is related to the "why" of conduct) is irrelevant, and has been so regarded by the mainstream of juridical opinion.

(b) *Bigotry and the First Amendment.* It might be argued that although bigotry ought not enter into the determination of criminality *qua* motive, it may be penalized *qua* nonprotected expression, as defined by *Chaplinsky v. New Hampshire.*[4] Gellman thinks otherwise. The "fighting words" provision of *Chaplinsky* would need considerable extension before it could accommodate the bigoted motivations that are envisaged in ADL-type statutes.

Perhaps a new class of nonprotected "hate speech" ought to be created? After all, isn't one of the effects of hate speech the *silencing* of its objects, thus constricting the "marketplace of ideas"? The trouble with this, Gellman claims, is that "the First Amendment is not simply a device to facilitate the search for truth; it exists to protect the expression of ideas by a minority, including those which may ultimately prove to be 'wrong' and harmful, from the pressures of the majority" [373].

As a further possibility, Gellman considers the argument that liberty is only one value, to be weighed against other values, such as equality, and therefore sometimes legitimately sacrificed. Does not "tolerance of bigoted expression for the sake of maintaining social tolerance of unpopular expression . . . place the burden wholly upon disempowered groups" [374]? Gellman is unconvinced. To treat First Amendment liberties in this way would depart from the strict scrutiny standard to which exceptions are subject. Moreover, the elimination of bigoted attitudes has not been accepted as a "compelling state interest" that would survive strict scrutiny.

In sum, by enhancing penalties for hate crimes, the state "is not regulating conduct *despite* its expressive elements, but actually penalizing already proscribed conduct *because* of its expressive elements . . . precisely what the First Amendment forbids" [376].

Can this conclusion be avoided if we understand the statutes in question to be not simply adding a penalty for the motive to penalty already warranted by the underlying crime (under interpretation (i) above), but as criminalizing a distinct form of conduct, compounded out of the underlying conduct and its motivation (as in (ii) above)?

Do not hate crimes possess a threatening character not possessed by the underlying conduct—a threat that affects not only their victim but also other members of the victim's group?

Gellman believes, however, that it is not the specificity of the victim's identity that give them this more generally intimidating character, for the same reverberations may be produced by entirely random attacks—for example, the poisoning of bottles of Tylenol [377]. All crimes, in fact, have indirect victims.

4. They *deny equal protection,* by basing treatment of offenders on the beliefs that they hold and express. Since equal protection is a Fourteenth Amendment interest, exceptions must be strictly scrutinized to see whether they are "precisely tailored to serve a compelling governmental interest."[5] But though combatting bigotry is a laudable social goal, the promotion of interethnic harmony *inter alia* by penalizing bigoted motives does not rise to the level of compellingness necessary to pass the strict scrutiny test.

II Policy Considerations

Whatever position we ultimately take on the First Amendment issues, there are, Gellman believes, strong policy reasons for refusing to adopt ethnic intimidation statutes. Such statutes will exact significant costs from both society as a whole and the disempowered groups they are intended to protect, and they will do so without commensurate benefits.

1. *Costs to society.* Because of their limiting or chilling effect, ethnic intimidation statutes will detract from some of the First Amendment's major underlying values: the importance of ensuring that the marketplace of ideas has available to it the broadest possible range of ideas and expression, the presumption that in a civilized society people are capable of making responsible choices between ideas, and the notion that the state should not function as arbiter of the worthiness of ideas.

To the extent that the state becomes involved in arbitrating between ideas, there is a danger that small encroachments on expressive liberty will be followed by ever larger ones. Indeed, even those few encroachments that are now countenanced by *Chaplinsky* have been appealed to as a basis for further encroachments. And if such decisions are to be made, who should make them? And using what criteria? Gellman believes that these are questions on which reasonable people will disagree, and that in a free society the toleration of all kinds of ideas is

both a value and an indication of the society's strength. Toleration is not the same as acceptance, and the lively refutation of pernicious ideas gives truth the vitality that keeps it from becoming mere dogma.

2. *Costs to disempowered groups.* Although the social benefits of ethnic intimidation statutes may outweigh their costs, Gellman believes that the costs to protected groups will be very significant. Ethnic intimidation statutes manifest a patronizing and paternalistic attitude, implying the special vulnerability of such groups and their incapacity to "hold their own." In so doing they reinforce the group's differentness. For members of such groups, the effect may be an undermining of self-esteem.

3. *The question of efficacy.* If the benefits that ethnic intimidation statutes produce are great enough, their costs may be acceptable. But Gellman does not believe that they achieve the ends that supposedly sustain them. There is no evidence of decreased bigotry in states with ADL-type intimidation statutes.

But may not the fact that government has "taken a stand" on an issue as important as this be a significant value in itself? Gellman is skeptical: symbols and gestures may in fact divert us from attending to effective solutions to the problems of bigotry. To the contrary. In some circles it will breed resentment paralleling that evoked by the "teacher's pet."

Education and positive incentives may do much more to eradicate discriminatory attitudes than recourse to criminal law. The latter creates an environment of indignation and evasion. Criminal law is to be seen as a device of last resort. It is an "acknowledgement of defeat in the quest for interethnic acceptance and respect" [391]. To see it as the "quick fix" for an extremely complex social ill is to show scant recognition of the rich resources for social change that are available to a civilized society. Repression and bigotry have the same roots, and the path from one must also be the path from the other—a nurturing of civilizing and civilized attitudes.

*   *   *

The present symposium had its beginnings in a Law School Colloquium at Arizona State University, at which Ms. Gellman was invited to discuss her *U.C.L.A. Law Review* article. Respondents at the colloquium were Professors James Weinstein and Jeffrie Murphy, both of Arizona State University.

In order to further the debate, the Editors of *Criminal Justice Ethics* invited a number of other legal and First Amendment scholars to offer their responses—to

Gellman's initial article, to her respondents, or to other issues raised by the issue of penalty enhancement for hate crimes. We are pleased to have the responses of Ms. Gellman, Professor Martin Redish of Northwestern University, Professor Martin Margulies of the University of Bridgeport Law School, Professor Ralph Brown of Yale Law School, Professor Larry Alexander of the San Diego Law School, Professor Frederick Schauer of Harvard University, and Professor James Jacobs of New York University Law School. Professor Weinstein has appended a brief rejoinder.*

*The responses of the law professors and the rejoinder by Professor Weinstein do not appear in this publication.

Notes

1. 112 S.Ct. 2538 (1992).
2. St. Paul Leg. Code §292.02 (1990).
3. 39 *UCLA Rev.* 333 (1991). Bracketed numbers in the text refer to pages in this article.
4. 315 U.S. 568 (1942). *Chaplinsky* included in nonprotected expression "the lewd and obscene, the profane, libelous, and insulting or 'fighting' words—those which by their very utterance inflict injury or tend to incite an immediate breach of the peace" (at 571).
5. Plyer v. Doe, 457 U.S. 202, at 216-17 (1982), as quoted in Gellman, *supra* note 3, at 379.

Form at end of book

WiseGuide Wrap-Up

How do we inhibit expressions of bigotry and prejudice? The display of swastikas, the burning of crosses, and the casting of racial slurs do not enhance multicultural life in the United States. While we wish to eliminate intergroup intimidation, is limiting First Amendment rights the only way to do it?

Frequently, education is believed to be the solution to such problems. However, the type of education that will accomplish this is rarely discussed. Has integrating schools decreased hate behavior among juveniles? Does proximity solve such problems, or are more proactive lessons necessary? Education must deal directly with issues of prejudice, bigotry, and discrimination to eliminate such behavior. Young men and women must learn that engaging in hate crimes is not "cool" or a sign of maturity and adulthood.

Hate groups recruit juveniles who are on the edge of society. These groups can provide a sense of membership by identifying an out-group to feel superior to and toward which to direct antisocial behavior.

The prejudice often follows, not precedes, involvement in hate crimes and serves as a justification for behavior that would not be acceptable if directed toward the perpetrator.

If hate crime legislation signals our failure to deal with these divisive issues, how can we signal success? If one of the effects of hate speech is the constriction of the "marketplace of ideas," then encouraging open discussion is one way to counteract this. The strength of our society may be in its ability to tolerate and refute these ideas, rather than punish.

R.E.A.L. Sites

This list provides a print preview of typical **Coursewise** R.E.A.L. sites. (There are over 100 such sites at the **Courselinks**™ site.) The danger in printing URLs is that web sites can change overnight. As we went to press, these sites were functional using the URLs provided. If you come across one that isn't, please let us know via email to: webmaster@coursewise.com. Use your Passport to access the most current list of R.E.A.L. sites at the **Courselinks** site.

Site name: Anti-Defamation League

URL: http://www.adl.org/

Why is it R.E.A.L.? The Anti-Defamation League is a nongovernmental organization and the world's leading organization on anti-Semitism and other hate crimes. It provides programs and services to counteract bigotry, hatred, and prejudice. Its web site contains articles, book references, and links to other relevant web sites.

Key terms: hate crimes, prejudice, bigotry

Site name: Southern Poverty Law Center

URL: http://www.splcenter.org/

Why is it R.E.A.L.? The Southern Poverty Law Center is a nongovernmental organization that is active in litigation against hate groups. Its web site includes information on its activities and its Teaching Tolerance project, as well as material provided by Klanwatch on various hate groups around the United States.

Key terms: tolerance, hate groups

Site name: Hatewatch

URL: http://www.hatewatch.org/

Why is it R.E.A.L.? Hatewatch is a nongovernmental organization dedicated to combating online bigotry. It monitors various organizations known for violence against ethnic and religious minorities, gays, and others who are the victims of hate groups. It identifies the web sites of these organizations and reports monthly on hate crimes in the United States and Europe. It also maintains a list of activist groups combating hate groups.

Key terms: bigotry, hate crimes

section 6 | Should the United States Be Involved in Human Rights Issues in Other Countries?

Take a Closer Look

1. Are human rights universal, or can they be interpreted in the framework of different cultural experiences?

2. How do human rights issues affect minority groups within the United States?

3. Should we be tolerant of all minority groups, regardless of their culture and practices?

4. Where does freedom end and license begin?

5. Do states have the right to intervene in the internal affairs of sovereign nations where human rights are being violated?

Americans are very conscious of their "rights" and are sensitive to any infringement upon those rights. Whichever term is used—inalienable rights, basic rights, civil rights, Bill of Rights—Americans believe that they know what is due them as U.S. citizens, as human beings. Therefore, they have no difficulty accepting the Universal Declaration of Human Rights adopted by the United Nations (see Reading 12), and they believe that these rights should be universally available to all.

The Universal Declaration of Human Rights seems like an extension of the American Bill of Rights. Americans assume that they are in compliance with all of the rights espoused in the Declaration, but some areas are problematic. For example, individual privacy (Article 12 of the Declaration) is not protected under the U.S. Constitution. Americans have difficulty understanding the difference between freedom and license. What limits can be placed on the right of the individual to do as he or she pleases? Americans have not enacted laws that provide equal pay for equal work (Article 23 of the Declaration). While they recognize the right to an education (Article 26 of the Declaration), not everyone who wants one gets it. Americans acknowledge the right of individuals to change their nationality (Article 15 of the Declaration), but they do not grant citizenship to everyone who asks or have open borders to enable freedom of movement. The death penalty is the law in many states, but organizations that oppose it are not only concerned with the issue of the state's right to take human life but also the arbitrary imposition of the penalty. Americans declare that everyone is created equal but do not apply that to all groups in the country—minorities, women, and homosexuals are still struggling for what they feel are their rights. Americans tend to look more at others' lack of compliance with the Universal Declaration of Human Rights than at their own.

When adopted in 1948, the Universal Declaration of Human Rights was proclaimed as a common standard of achievement for all peoples. Some, however, questioned its universality and saw it as a Western regional imposition. In 1993 at a World Conference on Human Rights in Vienna, the Declaration was modified to reflect issues regarding private rights. The 1993 Vienna Declaration reaffirmed many of the rights presented in the Universal Declaration of Human Rights but indicated that the international community would have to acknowledge regional differences to make progress.

Monitoring and enforcement of human rights is a major problem. Most states accept the legal norm of nonintervention in the internal affairs of other states. Amnesty International and other nongovernmental organizations try to monitor state abuses but are unable to directly interfere. The exception may be genocide, as seen in Rwanda, Bosnia, and Kosovo, where recent multilateral peacekeeping activities have been successful.

In Reading 13, Christina M. Cerna raises the question, "Can human rights norms be regional and universal at the same time?" Cerna discusses the debates between first- and third-world states over the implementation of sections of the Declaration that are contrary to their own religions and secular laws. One of the concerns these countries express is the right to regional differences that result from their historical past. They often feel that they should not be held to the same standards as other countries. Most of the concerns raised involve private rights in the areas of religion and culture. For example, Article 18 in the Declaration recognizes the right to change religion, while the Koran forbids Muslims from changing religion. In many societies, families, not individuals, make marriage choices, which is in discord with Article 16 of the Declaration. The states that raise these arguments are mostly third-world Asian, Middle Eastern, North African, and Latin American countries. They seek to redefine the term *human rights*. Western governments fear that this redefinition would allow authoritarian governments to perpetuate abuses.

In Reading 14, Jack Donnelly focuses on the problem of implementation that rests solely on individual governments. States are concerned with the rights of their own nationals, and nationals have little recourse when their own governments neglect or abuse them. At this time, no significant international recourse is available. States agree to implement the Universal Declaration of Human Rights only to the extent it does not conflict with national constitutions and laws. According to Donnelly, there are several areas where the declaration is not applied: war and embargo, business, and immigrants and refugees. He says, "When other states engage in behavior that would be called human rights violations if done by one's own government, we usually do not use the language of human rights." The activities of businesses and their impact on communities also do not fall under the category of human rights, even though the consequences of business decisions may affect the ability of people to make a living and to provide for their welfare. Refugees are largely seen as objects of charity, rather than as victims of human rights violations. Donnelly also questions the legally permissible discrimination against non-nationals. Most of his article focuses on the right to nondiscrimination and the group that he thinks is currently the most abused—homosexuals. If human rights are due to all on the basis of being human, then we cannot choose to grant them to groups of which we approve and withhold them from groups we don't.

Issue 6: Should the United States be involved in human rights issues in other countries?

Universal Declaration of Human Rights

Anuradha Mittal

On December 10, 1948, the General Assembly of the United Nations adopted and proclaimed the Universal Declaration of Human Rights, the full text of which appears in the following pages. Following this historic act, the Assembly called upon all member countries to publicize the text of the Declaration and "to cause it to be disseminated, displayed, read and expounded principally in schools and other educational institutions, without distinction based on the political status of countries or territories."

Preamble

Whereas recognition of the inherent dignity and of the equal and inalienable rights of all members of the human family is the foundation of freedom, justice and peace in the world,

Whereas disregard and contempt for human rights have resulted in barbarous acts which have outraged the conscience of mankind, and the advent of a world in which human beings shall enjoy freedom of speech and belief and freedom from fear and want has been proclaimed as the highest aspiration of the common people,

Whereas it is essential, if man is not to be compelled to have recourse as a last resort to rebellion against tyranny and oppression, that human rights should be protected by the rule of law,

Whereas it is essential to promote the development of friendly relations between nations,

Whereas the peoples of the United Nations have in the Charter reaffirmed their faith in fundamental human rights, in the dignity and worth of the human person and in the equal rights of men and women and have determined to promote social progress and better standards of life in larger freedom,

Whereas Member States have pledged themselves to achieve, in cooperation with the United Nations, the pro-

motion of universal respect for and observance of human rights and fundamental freedoms,

Whereas a common understanding of these rights and freedoms is of the greatest importance for the full realization of this pledge,

Now, Therefore,

The General Assembly proclaims this Universal Declaration of Human Rights as a common standard of achievement for all peoples and all nations, to the end that every individual and every organ of society, keeping this Declaration constantly in mind, shall strive by teaching and education to promote respect for these rights and freedoms and by progressive measures, national and international, to secure their universal and effective recognition and observance, both among the peoples of Member States themselves and among the peoples of territories under their jurisdiction.

Article 1. All human beings are born free and equal in dignity and rights. They are endowed with reason and conscience and should act towards one another in a spirit of brotherhood [or sisterhood].

Article 2. Everyone is entitled to all the rights and freedoms set forth in this Declaration, without distinction of any kind, such as race, color, sex, language, religion, political or other opinion, national or social origin, property, birth or other status. Furthermore, no distinction shall be made on the basis of the political, jurisdictional or international status of the country or territory to which a person belongs, whether it be independent, trust, non-self-governing or under any other limitation of sovereignty.

Article 3. Everyone has the right to life, liberty and security of person.

Article 4. No one shall be held in slavery or servitude; slavery and the slave trade shall be prohibited in all their forms.

Article 5. No one shall be subjected to torture or to cruel, inhuman or degrading treatment or punishment.

From Anuradha Mittal, "Universal Declaration of Human Rights" in *Earth Island Journal*, Winter 1997, Vol. 13, No. 1, Earth Island Journal.

Article 6. Everyone has the right to recognition everywhere as a person before the law.

Article 7. All are equal before the law and are entitled without any discrimination to equal protection of the law. All are entitled to equal protection against any discrimination in violation of this Declaration and against any incitement to such discrimination.

Article 8. Everyone has the right to an effective remedy by the competent national tribunals for acts violating the fundamental rights granted him [or her] by the constitution or by law.

Article 9. No one shall be subjected to arbitrary arrest, detention or exile.

Article 10. Everyone is entitled in full equality to a fair and public hearing by an independent and impartial tribunal, in the determination of his [or her] rights and obligations and of any criminal charge against him [or her].

Article 11. (1) Everyone charged with a penal offense has the right to be presumed innocent until proved guilty according to law in a public trial at which he has had all the guarantees necessary for his defense. (2) No one shall be held guilty of any penal offense on account of any act or omission which did not constitute a penal offense, under national or international law, at the time when it was committed. Nor shall a heavier penalty be imposed than the one that was applicable at the time the penal offense was committed.

Article 12. No one shall be subjected to arbitrary interference with his privacy, family, home or correspondence, nor to attacks upon his [or her] honor and reputation. Everyone has the right to the protection of the law against such interference or attacks.

Article 13. (1) Everyone has the right to freedom of movement and residence within the borders of each state. (2) Everyone has the right to leave any country, including his own, and to return to his [or her] country.

Article 14. (1) Everyone has the right to seek, and to enjoy in other countries, asylum from persecution. (2) This right may not be invoked in the case of prosecutions genuinely arising from nonpolitical crimes or from acts contrary to the purposes and principles of the United Nations.

Article 15. (1) Everyone has the right to a nationality. (2) No one shall be arbitrarily deprived of his [or her] nationality nor denied the right to change his [or her] nationality.

Article 16. (1) Men and women of full age, without any limitation due to race, nationality or religion, have the right to marry and to found a family. They are entitled to equal rights as to marriage, during marriage and at its dissolution. (2) Marriage shall be entered into only with the free and full consent of the intending spouses. (3) The family is the natural and fundamental group unit of society and is entitled to protection by society and the State.

Article 17. (1) Everyone has the right to own property alone as well as in association with others. (2) No one shall be arbitrarily deprived of his [or her] property.

Article 18. Everyone has the right to freedom of thought, conscience and religion; this right includes freedom to change his [or her] religion or belief, and freedom, either alone or in community with others and in public or private, to manifest his [or her] religion or belief in teaching, practice, worship and observance.

Article 19. Everyone has the right to freedom of opinion and expression; this right includes freedom to hold opinions without interference and to seek, receive and impart information and ideas through any media and regardless of frontiers.

Article 20. (1) Everyone has the right to freedom of peaceful assembly and association. (2) No one may be compelled to belong to an association.

Article 21. (1) Everyone has the right to take part in the government of his [or her] country, directly or through freely chosen representatives. (2) Everyone has the right of equal access to public service in his [or her] country. (3) The will of the people shall be the basis of the authority of government; this will shall be expressed in periodic and genuine elections which shall be by universal and equal suffrage and shall be held by secret vote or by equivalent free voting procedures.

Article 22. Everyone, as a member of society, has the right to social security and is entitled to realization, through national effort and international cooperation and in accordance with the organization and resources of each State, of the economic, social and cultural rights indispensable for his [or her] dignity and the free development of his [or her] personality.

Article 23. (1) Everyone has the right to work, to free choice of employment, to just and favorable conditions of work and to protection against unemployment. (2) Everyone, without any discrimination, has the right to equal pay for equal work. (3) Everyone who works has the right to just and favorable remuneration ensuring for himself [or herself] and his [or her] family an existence worthy of human dignity, and supplemented, if necessary, by other means of social protection. (4) Everyone has the right to form and to join trade unions for the protection of his [or her] interests.

Article 24. Everyone has the right to rest and leisure, including reasonable limitation of working hours and periodic holidays with pay.

Article 25. (1) Everyone has the right to a standard of living adequate for the health and well-being of himself [or herself] and of his [or her] family, including food, clothing, housing and medical care and necessary social services, and the right to security in the event of unemployment, sickness, disability, widowhood, old age or other lack of livelihood in circumstances beyond his [or her] control. (2) Motherhood [or fatherhood] and childhood are entitled to special care and assistance. All children, whether born in or out of wedlock, shall enjoy the same social protection.

Article 26. (1) Everyone has the right to education. Education shall be free, at least in the elementary and fundamental stages. Elementary education shall be compulsory. Technical and professional education shall be made generally available and higher education shall be equally accessible to all on the basis of merit. (2) Education shall be directed to the full development of the human personality and to the strengthening of respect for human rights and fundamental freedoms. It shall promote understanding, tolerance and friendship among all nations, racial or religious groups, and shall further the activities of the United Nations for the maintenance of peace. (3) Parents have a prior right to choose the kind of education that shall be given to their children.

Article 27. (1) Everyone has the right freely to participate in the cultural life of the community, to enjoy the arts and to share in scientific advancement and its benefits. (2) Everyone has the right to the protection of the moral and material interests resulting from any scientific, literary or artistic production of which he [or she] is the author.

Article 28. Everyone is entitled to a social and international order in which the rights and freedoms set forth in this Declaration can be fully realized.

Article 29. (1) Everyone has duties to the community in which alone the free and full development of his [or her] personality is possible. (2) In the exercise of his [or her] rights and freedoms, everyone shall be subject only to such limitations as are determined by law solely for the purpose of securing due recognition and respect for the rights and freedoms of others and of meeting the just requirements of morality, public order and the general welfare in a democratic society. (3) These rights and freedoms may in no case be exercised contrary to the purposes and principles of the United Nations.

Article 30. Nothing in this Declaration may be interpreted as implying for any State, group or person any right to engage in any activity or to perform any act aimed at the destruction of any of the rights and freedoms set forth herein.

Form at end of book

Issue 6: Should the United States be involved in human rights issues in other countries?

Universality of Human Rights and Cultural Diversity:
Implementation of Human Rights in Different Socio-Cultural Contexts

Christina M. Cerna

Abstract

The conflict regarding the universality of human rights was demonstrated at the UN World Conference on Human Rights in Vienna in June 1993 by the assertion by many Asian nations in the Bangkok Declaration that cultural and regional norms should be acknowledged in determining human rights compliance. Certain nations believe that their norms, based on ancient cultures, should allow for differing standards. The Vienna Declaration and Programme of Action included affirmation of human rights concerns, but the international community may have to acknowledge regional difference to make progress on human rights.

The Nature of the Debate

Forty-five years ago, on 10 December 1948, the international community adopted, by consensus, the Universal Declaration of Human Rights,[1] still the preeminent document in the growing corpus of human rights instruments. Today, a group of nations is seeking to redefine the content of the term "human rights" against the will of the Western states. This group sees the current definition as part of the ideological patrimony of Western civilization. They argue that the principles enshrined in the Universal Declaration reflect Western values and not their own. They complain that the West is interfering in their internal affairs when it imposes its own definition of human rights

upon them, and that it hampers their trade and weakens their competitiveness. Because of social and cultural differences in their countries, they say, they should not be held to the same standards. This attempt to undermine the notion of the universality of human rights is attributed to such countries as China, Columbia, Cuba, Indonesia, Iran, Iraq, Libya, Malaysia, Mexico, Myanmar, Pakistan, Singapore, Syria, Vietnam, and Yemen. These countries are all in the third world, although the strongest advocates of this position are the Asian states experiencing the most dynamic economic growth.

This debate was center-stage at the second UN World Conference on Human Rights, held in June 1993 in Vienna, Austria. The Western states were reportedly concerned that the universality of human rights might be eroded. Their first priority was damage control to ensure "that the conference issue[d] a strong endorsement of the universality of human rights and reject[ed] the idea that such rights can be measured differently in some countries."[2] The U.S. administration dismissed the argument that any definition of human rights should consider regional social and cultural differences. It countered that such a position is a screen behind which authoritarian governments can perpetuate abuses.

The Vienna Declaration and Programme of Action,[3] adopted by the World Conference on Human Rights on 25 June 1993, contained thirty-nine "paragraphs" (the term chosen in lieu of "principles," which was considered unacceptable by certain delegations) and a "programme of action." The universality of human rights was affirmed repeatedly:

Paragraph 1: The World Conference on Human Rights reaffirms the solemn commitment of all States to fulfil their obligations to promote universal respect for, and observance and protection of, all human rights and fundamental freedoms for all in accordance with the Charter of the United Nations, other instruments relating to human rights, and international law. The universal nature of these rights and freedoms is beyond question.

Paragraph 5: All human rights are universal, indivisible and interdependent and interrelated. The international community must treat human rights globally in a fair and equal manner, on the same footing, and with the same emphasis. While the significance of national and regional particularities and various historical, cultural and religious backgrounds must be borne in mind, it is the duty of States, regardless of their political, economic and cultural systems, to promote and protect all human rights and fundamental freedoms.

Paragraph 32: The World Conference on Human Rights reaffirms the importance of ensuring the universality, objectivity, and non-selectivity of the consideration of human rights issues.

Paragraph 37: Regional arrangements play a fundamental role in promoting and protecting human rights. They should reinforce universal human rights standards, as contained in international human rights instruments, and their protection. The World Conference on Human Rights endorses efforts under way to strengthen these arrangements and to increase their effectiveness, while at the same time stressing the importance of cooperation with the United Nations human rights activities.

The World Conference on Human Rights reiterates the need to consider the possibility of establishing regional and subregional arrangements for the promotion and protection of human rights where they do not already exist.[4]

Achieving a consensus on the reaffirmation of the universality of human rights, forty-five years after the adoption of the Universal Declaration, was perhaps the most significant success of the World Conference. To put the achievement in its proper perspective, however, it should be recalled that when the Universal Declaration was adopted, forty-eight states voted in favor of its adoption, none against, eight abstained (Byelorussia, Czechoslovakia, Poland, Saudi Arabia, the Ukraine, the Union of South Africa, the Soviet Union, and Yugoslavia), and two were absent (Honduras and Yemen). As we will examine further on, some of the states that abstained did so because they were unable to accept certain provisions of the Universal Declaration. In Vienna, 172 states participated in the adoption of the Vienna Declaration, having achieved a hard wrought consensus. Because of the repeat-

edly articulated challenge from diverse sectors, reaffirmation of the universality of human rights had to be hammered into the Vienna Declaration again and again, almost to the point of redundancy.

The preparatory work leading to Vienna did not bode well for a successful outcome on this issue. Three regional, preparatory meetings had been held prior to the World Conference: in Africa, in the Latin American and Caribbean region, and in Asia. At the end of each of these meetings, a "Final Declaration" was adopted which referred to the particular concerns of each region.[5] The preambles to the Latin American and Asian regional declarations referred to the regions' cultures. In the preamble to the San Jose Declaration, the Latin American states:

[r]eaffirm[ed] that our countries represent a broad grouping of nations sharing common roots within a rich cultural heritage based on a combination of various peoples, religions and races, and that our roots unite us in the search for collective solutions to present problems through friendly dialogue, peaceful coexistence and respect for pluralism and the principles of national sovereignty, non-interference in the internal affairs of States and self-determination of peoples.[6]

Similarly, in the preamble to the Bangkok Declaration, the Asian states also referred to their rich cultural traditions and noted "the contribution that can be made to the World Conference by Asian countries with their diverse and rich cultures and traditions."[7]

Unlike the ancient African and Latin American cultures which effectively have been destroyed by the ravages of colonialism, the Asian civilizations maintained a direct link with the cultures and traditions of their ancestors.[8] It is, without doubt, this ancient cultural heritage, the region's enormous population, and its dramatic, relatively recent economic prosperity which provided the Asian governments with the confidence to challenge international human rights as a Western ideological imposition.

The Bangkok Declaration made thinly veiled references to what the Asian states considered intervention in their internal affairs and the imposition of alien values:

Stressing the universality, objectivity and non-selectivity of all human rights and the need to avoid the application of double standards in the implementation of human rights and its politicization, Recognizing that the promotion of human rights should be encouraged by cooperation and consensus, and not through confrontation and the imposition of incompatible values . . .[9]

The Bangkok Declaration included a controversial statement that the Asian states "[r]ecognize that while human rights are universal in nature, they must be considered in the context of a dynamic and evolving process of international norm-setting, bearing in mind the significance of national and regional particularities and various historical, cultural and religious backgrounds."[10] Perhaps in order to facilitate the consideration of human rights in an Asian historical, cultural, and religious context, the Bangkok Declaration also supported the possibility of establishing a regional arrangement for the promotion and protection of human rights in Asia.[11]

Some Western delegations, such as the United States, dismissed the argument that any definition of human rights should take account of "national and regional particularities and various historical, cultural and religious backgrounds"[12]—a direct reference to the language of this paragraph in the Bangkok Declaration. What does it mean, in operational terms, to consider the significance of these issues? Other preparatory meetings of the World Conference, such as the Rights and Humanity Round Table on Strengthening Commitment to the Universality of Human Rights, held at Amman in April 1993, provided little guidance on this question. The participants in the Round Table simply recommended that "the universality of human rights requires respect for the diversity of faiths and cultures."[13]

The Challenge to Universality

The Vienna Declaration and the regional declarations reiterated that all human rights—civil and political, as well as economic, social, and cultural—should be implemented simultaneously, and that neither set of rights should take precedence over the other. The challenge to the concept of the universality of human rights coming primarily from Asia, had to do with "private" rights.

All states are willing to accept the universality of a certain core group of rights. These are the rights that are listed in the human rights treaties as "non-derogable" rights or are considered jus cogens.[14]

The major distinguishing feature of such rules [of jus cogens] is their relative indelibility. They are rules of customary law which cannot be set aside by treaty or acquiescence but only by the formation of a subsequent customary rule of contrary effect. The least controversial examples of the class are the prohibition of the use of force, the law of genocide, the principle of racial non-discrimination, crimes against humanity, and the rules prohibiting trade in slaves and piracy. . . .

Other rules which probably have this special status include the principle of permanent sovereignty over natural resources and the principle of self-determination.[15]

In further attempting to define the catalogue of rights which have achieved universal acceptance, it is useful to consult the positions of individuals who have been most critical of Western attitudes in the area of human rights. For example, Mr. Kishore Mahbubani, Deputy

Secretary of the Ministry of Foreign Affairs of the Republic of Singapore, was quite critical of "the aggressive Western promotion of democracy, human rights and freedom of the press to the Third World at the end of the cold war."[16] He conceded that

both Asians and Westerners are human beings. They can agree on minimal standards of civilized behavior that both would like to live under. For example, there should be no torture, no slavery, no arbitrary killings, no disappearances in the middle of the night, no shooting down of innocent demonstrators, no imprisonment without careful review. These rights should be upheld not only for moral reasons. There are sound functional reasons. Any society which is at odds with its best and brightest and shoots them down when they demonstrate peacefully, as Myanmar did, is headed for trouble. Most Asian societies do not want to be in the position that Myanmar is in today, a nation at odds with itself.[17]

(It is interesting to note that, while Singapore formed part of the consensus at Vienna, it has not ratified any of the UN human rights instruments for which there are treaty bodies monitoring implementation).

Some publicists of international law argue that all the rights set forth in the Universal Declaration of Human Rights have become customary international law and, as such, have achieved universal acceptance as legally binding obligations on states.[18] These civil, political, economic, and social rights have been most widely recognized in constitutions around the world.

In 1948, when the Universal Declaration was adopted, Eleanor Roosevelt, as Chair of the Commission on Human Rights, stated that the Declaration "is not and does not purport to be a statement of law or of legal obligation," but rather that it is "to serve as a common standard of achievement for all peoples of all nations."[19] In 1968, at the first World Conference on Human Rights, the international community proclaimed: "The Universal Declaration of Human Rights states a common understanding of the peoples of the world concerning the inalienable and inviolable rights of all members of the human family and constitutes an obligation for the members of the international community."[20]

Although the rights set forth in the Universal Declaration have been incorporated into many constitutions in the world, most publicists do not consider the entire Declaration to have become custom and thereby legally binding. The entire document failed to crystalize into custom because, since 1948, certain provisions have not been universally accepted. These provisions regard private rights which relate to the private sphere or personal life of the individual. These rights have traditionally been covered by religious law; they still are in many countries.

This private sphere, which deals with issues such as religion, culture, the status of women, the right to marry and to divorce and to remarry, the protection of children, the question of choice as regards family planning, and the like, is a domain in which the most serious challenges to the universality of human rights arise.

In 1948, the first clause of Article 18 of the Universal Declaration—"Everyone has the right to freedom of thought, conscience and religion"[21]—was acceptable to all religious faiths. However, the second clause—"this right includes freedom to change his religion or belief"[22]—created problems for some Muslim states. They pointed out that the Koran forbids a Muslim to change his religion and criticized the Christian missionaries who sought to convert Muslims to Christianity. Saudi Arabia abstained on the final vote on the Universal Declaration in 1948 because of this clause. (Saudi Arabia, it should be noted in this context, is another state that has not ratified any of the United Nations human rights instruments for which there are treaty bodies monitoring implementation).

The number of states parties to an international treaty provides some evidence of universality, or the acceptance of the norms in that treaty by the international community. As of 1 September 1993, the nine UN human rights instruments for which there are treaty bodies monitoring implementation have been ratified or acceded to by the following number of states (which are not necessarily member states of the United Nations):

1. the International Covenant on Economic, Social and Cultural Rights[23]—124 states parties;

2. the International Covenant on Civil and Political Rights (CCPR)[24]—122 states parties;

3. the Optional Protocol to the CCPR (on the right of individual petition)[25]—seventy-four states parties;

4. the Second Optional Protocol to the CCPR, Aiming at the Abolition of the Death Penalty[26]—nineteen states parties;

5. the International Convention on the Elimination of All Forms of Racial Discrimination[27]—137 state parties;

6. the International Convention on the Suppression and Punishment of the Crime of Apartheid[28]—ninety-seven states parties;

7. the Convention on the Elimination of All Forms of Discrimination against Women[29]—125 state parties;

8. the Convention Against Torture and Other Cruel, Inhuman or Degrading Treatment or Punishment[30] (Convention against Torture)—seventy-six states parties;

9. the Convention on the Rights of the Child[31]—146 states parties.

This list provides some information: for example, the international consensus on the abolition of the death penalty is still quite limited; on the other hand, there is an apparent consensus to protect the rights of the child. As of 1 September 1993, 169 member states of the United Nations (of a total membership of 184 states) and three non-member states were a party to one or more of these instruments and fifteen member states were not a party to any.

A state's ratification of an international human rights instrument is not sufficient evidence that the state, in fact, observes the provisions of that instrument. The four Geneva Conventions of 1949[32] have the greatest number of states parties of any human rights/humanitarian law instrument. Yet the Geneva Conventions are honored perhaps more in the breath than in their observance. The converse is also not conclusive evidence of the contrary. For example, seventy-six states have become parties to the Convention Against Torture; yet Amnesty International charges that more than 110 states today continue to practice torture[33]—it does not follow that all states which have not become parties to this Convention are engaging in the practice of torture.

Nonetheless, becoming party to an international human rights treaty is evidence of a state's intent to be legally bound by the provisions of that instrument. In that context, it is interesting to look at the reservations which states have made to the newest human rights treaty, the Convention on the Rights of the Child. A surprisingly large number of African and Asian states have made reservations to this Convention.

Kuwait, for example, reserved "on all provisions of the Convention that [were] incompatible with the laws of Islamic Shari's and the local statutes in effect."[34] Similarly, Afghanistan, Egypt, Iran, Jordan, the Maldives, Pakistan, and Qatar all invoked Shari's law as an obstacle to the full implementation of the provisions of the Convention.[35] Some states, such as Djibouti, undertook to adhere to the Convention to the extent that its provisions and articles were compatible with their religions and traditions.[36] Other states, such as Indonesia, ratified the Convention by stating that its ratification "[did] not imply the acceptance of obligations going beyond the Constitutional limits nor the acceptance of any obligation to introduce any right beyond those prescribed under the Constitution."[37] Several Western countries (Finland, Germany, Ireland, Norway, Portugal, and Sweden) objected to these reservations as "incompatible with the object and purpose of the Convention."[38] Curiously, they neither demanded the withdrawal of these reservations, nor did they object to the Convention entering into force for the states that formulated them.

The point here is that certain societies are unwilling to assume international human rights obligations in this private sphere—their own code of conduct, which is informed by their religious or traditional law, already covers this terrain. This tension between the universality of norms in the private sphere and the competing religious/traditional law renders all international human rights norms which have not become part of jus cogens suspect.

International human rights law has, in some sense, become the substitute for religion in secular societies. It aims to establish a minimum standard of decency, a common denominator of what is morally acceptable in a civilized society. For this reason, regional human rights arrangements have been more successful in securing compliance with international human rights norms; there is a shared history, geography, and, in some cases, language and religion, as well as a commonality of values. Interestingly, however, the regional supervisory human rights bodies have tended to defer to the religious or cultural particularities which generally are found within the private sphere—rather than finding the particularities incompatible with the common standard and the state's obligations under the regional instrument.

Regional Human Rights Bodies and Universality

The role of regional supervisory bodies for the protection of human rights is two-fold:

1. to provide an emergency device when something basically goes wrong in a country and to be able to inform the world as to what the problem is, and

2. to provide a common minimum human rights standard for the region, or what Professor Jochen Frowein has called (in the European context) the "constitutionalization of Europe."[39]

The Vienna Declaration reaffirms the universality of human rights, but also states that regional particularities should be borne in mind. Can human rights norms be regional and universal at the same time? Are there regional human rights norms? Probably not, but as the hard cases in the regional systems prove, deference to regional particularities slows down the creation of a regional common standard.

An example of a European regional particularity presented itself in the *Johnston v. Ireland*[40] case before the European Court of Human Rights. Petitioners in the case challenged the prohibition on divorce set forth in the Irish Constitution.[41] They argued that a right to divorce was inherent in the right to marry, protected by the European Convention on Human Rights;[42] that thousands of couples were denied their right to marry because they had been unable, under Irish law, to divorce their previous spouses.

On the day of the oral arguments before the European Court, the Irish government held an overwhelmingly supported referendum on the issue. Pressured by Irish public opinion on the issue, the constitutional status of the prohibition on divorce, and the importance of Catholicism in Ireland, the court issued a judgement denying the right claimed.[43] The court distinguished Article 12 of the European Convention from Article 16 of the Universal Declaration of Human Rights, upon which Article 12 was based.[44] Article 16 provided "equal rights as to marriage, during marriage and at its dissolution."[45] The court concluded that, because this phrase was not intended to guarantee a right to divorce;[46] therefore, the Irish prohibition on divorce was not incompatible with the European Convention.[47] The court effectively ignored the common, regional standard of the right to divorce, now available in most European states.

Similar deference to regional particularities has occurred in the inter-American system. A Catholic political action group, seeking to challenge the 1973 U.S. Supreme Court case legalizing abortion,[48] brought a case before the Inter-American Commission on Human Rights.[49] The class action, on behalf of fetuses aborted in Massachusetts in 1973, based its claim on Article 4 of the American Convention on Human Rights: "Every person has the right to have his life respected. This right shall be protected by law and, in general, from the moment of conception."[50]

Because the United States had not ratified the American Convention, the Commission, according to its governing rules, applied the American Declaration of the Rights and Duties of Man.[51] Article I of the American Declaration stated that "[e]very human being has the right to life, liberty and the security of his person."[52] As the American Declaration did not directly address the issue of abortion, the Commission looked to the American Convention, reasoning that the two human rights instruments were, by nature, compatible. The travaux preparatoires to the American Convention revealed that it was not the intent of the drafters to prohibit abortion where it was legal. To accommodate the countries in which abortion was legal and to render the protection of Article 4 less absolute, the drafters added the phrase "in general."[53] Consequently, the Commission was able to find that the U.S. Supreme Court decision legalizing abortion was not in violation of the American Declaration.[54]

Roe v. Wade, however, had virtually made abortion available upon request during the first trimester of pregnancy; abortion in the United States was not limited to emergency cases as were the few examples of Latin American legislation allowing abortion (for example, to save the mother's life or in the case of rape). The common regional standard was to criminalize abortion, in line with the dictates of the Catholic Church, which absolutely prohibits abortion, even in the case of rape.

Conclusion

What conclusion can be drawn from this conflict between the purported universality of international human rights law and the limitations placed on universal acceptance of these norms by the different cultural and religious systems prevailing in the world? Can a system of international human rights norms be called truly universal as long as one state still refuses to accept them?

For example, a common argument is that Islamic law stands in stark opposition to the Universal Declaration of Human Rights.[55] The Universal Declaration guarantees the freedom to choose one's religion[56] and spouse,[57] both of which are restricted under Islamic law. Some commentators argue that it is not Islam that the West has to fear as its great, new ideological competitor after the fall of Communism; rather the West should fear the ideology of "soft authoritarianism" coming from Asia's most prosperous states.[58] There is also the complication of states reserving the right to implement an international human rights instrument only to the extent that it does not conflict with national constitutions and laws. Are these all attacks on the universality of human rights?

The only possible answer is that achieving universal acceptance of international human rights norms is a process, and different norms occupy different places on the continuum. Change and acceptance of these norms must ultimately come from within the region and cannot be imposed by outside forces. The creation of a regional human rights arrangement provides for its participants an accelerated acceptance in the region of a catalogue of international human rights norms. States with similar history, language, geography, religion, and culture have a greater influence checking the behavior of states which fail to respect the common regional denominator of decency. States outside the region, which cannot claim such ties, do not have the same influence.

Finally, there are no regional human rights norms; there are only regional arrangements which supervise compliance with international standards. The international supervisory bodies must realize that the international norms dealing with rights that affect the private sphere of human activity will take the longest time to achieve universal acceptance.

Notes

1. Universal Declaration of Human Rights, adopted Dec. 10, 1948, G.A. Res. 217A, U.N. GAOR, 3rd Sess., at 71, U.N. Doc. A/810 (1948) (hereinafter Universal Declaration).
2. Alan Riding, A Rights Meeting; But Don't Mention the Wronged, *N.Y. Times,* 14 June 1993, at A3.
3. The Vienna Declaration and Programme of Action, adopted by The World Conference on Human Rights 24 June 1993, U.N. Doc. A/Conf. 157/24 (Part 1), at 20-46 (13 Oct. 1993).
4. Id.
5. Final Declaration of the Regional Meeting for Africa of the World Conference on Human Rights, Report of the Regional Meeting for Africa of the World Conference on Human Rights (Tunis, 2–6 Nov. 1992), at 1, A/Conf. 157/AFRM/14–A/Conf. 157/PC/57 (24 Nov. 1992); Final Declaration of the Regional Meeting for Latin America and the Caribbean of the World Conference on Human Rights, Report of the Regional Meeting for Latin America and the Caribbean of the World Conference on Human Rights (San Jose, 18–22 Jan. 1993), at 3, A/Conf. 157/LACRM/15–A/Conf. 157/PC/58 (11 Feb. 1993) (hereinafter San Jose Declaration); Final Declaration of the Regional Meeting for Asia of the World Conference on Human Rights, Report of the Regional Meeting for Asia of the World Conference on Human Rights (Bangkok, 29 Mar.–2 Apr. 1993), at 3, A/Conf. 157/ASRM/8–A/Conf. 157/PC/59 (7 Apr. 1993) (hereinafter Bangkok Declaration).
6. San Jose Declaration, supra note 5, preamble.
7. Bangkok Declaration, supra note 5, preamble.
8. For example, the Chinese characters, in which many modern Asians write today, were invented thousands of years ago, but have been in continuous use.
9. Bangkok Declaration, supra note 5, preamble.
10. Id. [paragraph] 8.
11. Id. [paragraph] 26.
12. Id. [paragraph] 8.
13. Rights and Humanity Round Table: Strengthening Commitment to the Universality of Human Rights, [paragraph] 1(iv), World Conference on Human Rights Preparatory Committee: Report of the Secretary-General, U.N. GAOR, 4th. Sess., Agenda Item 6, at 4, U.N. Doc. A/Conf. 157/PC/42/Add. 7 (28 Apr. 1993).
14. As regards the catalogue of non-derogable rights, see the International Covenant on Civil and Political Rights, adopted 16 Dec. 1966, art. 4, G.A. Res. 2200, U.N. GAOR, 21st Sess., Supp. No. 16, at 52, U.N. Doc. A/6316 (1966); the European Convention for the Protection of Human Rights and Fundamental Freedoms, concluded 4 Nov. 1950, art. 27(2), Europ. T.S. No. 5 [hereinafter European Convention]. See also Vienna Convention on the Law of Treaties, opened for signature 23 May 1969, art. 53, U.N. Doc. A/Conf. 39/27 (1969). A peremptory norm of general international law is defined as a "norm accepted and recognized by the international community of states as a whole as a norm from which no derogation is permitted and which can be modified only by a subsequent norm of general international law having the same character." Id.
15. Ian Brownlie, *Principles of Public International Law* 513 (1990) (footnotes omitted).
16. Kishore Mahbubani, An Asian Perspective on Human Rights and Freedom of the Press, [paragraph] 3, Status of Preparation of Publications, Studies and Documents for the World Conference, U.N. Doc. A/Conf. 157/PC/63/Add.28 (4 May 1993) (letter dated 29 Apr. 1993 from the Permanent Representative of the Republic of Singapore to the Coordinator of the World Conference on Human Rights).
17. Id. [paragraph] 47.
18. See, e.g., the Montreal Statement of the Assembly for Human Rights (22–27 Mar. 1968), Montreal Statement, reprinted in *J. Int'l Commission Jurists,* June 1968, at 94 (statement issued by nongovernmental meeting of experts on human rights issues).
19. General Assembly Adopts Declaration of Human Rights (statement by Mrs. Franklin D. Roosevelt, U.S. Representative to the U.N. GAOR, 9 Dec. 1948), *Dep't St. Bull.,* 19 Dec. 1948, at 751.

20. Proclamation of Teheran, [paragraph] 2, International Conference on Human Rights, 22 Apr.–13 May 1968, U.N. GAOR, 23rd Sess., U.N. Doc. A/Conf. 32/41 (1968) (emphasis added).

21. Universal Declaration, supra note 1, art. 18.

22. Id.

23. International Covenant on Economic, Social and Cultural Rights, adopted 16 Dec. 1966, G.A. Res. 2200, U.N. GAOR, 21st Sess., Supp. No. 16, at 49, U.N. Doc. A/6316 (1966).

24. International Covenant on Civil and Political Rights, supra note 14.

25. Optional Protocol to the International Covenant on Civil and Political Rights, adopted 16 Dec. 1966, G.A. Res. 2200, U.N. GAOR, 21st Sess., Supp. No. 16, at 66, U.N. Doc. A/6316 (1966).

26. Second Optional Protocol to the International Covenant on Civil and Political Rights, Aiming at the Abolition of the Death Penalty, adopted 15 Dec. 1989, G.A. Res. 44/128, U.N. GAOR, 44th Sess., Supp. No. 49, at 206, U.N. Doc. A/44/824 (1989).

27. International Convention on the Elimination of All Forms of Racial Discrimination, adopted 7 Mar. 1966, G.A. Res. 2106A, U.N. GAOR, 20th Sess., Supp. No. 14, at 47, U.N. Doc. A/6014 (1965).

28. International Convention on the Suppression and Punishment of the Crime of Apartheid, adopted 30 Nov. 1973, G.A. Res. 3068, U.N. GAOR, 28th Sess., Supp. No. 30, at 75, U.N. Doc. A/9030 (1973).

29. Convention on the Elimination of All Forms of Discrimination Against Women, adopted 18 Dec. 1979, G.A. Res. 34/180, U.N. GAOR, 34th Sess., Supp. No. 46, at 193, U.N. Doc. A/34/46 (1979).

30. Convention Against Torture and Other Cruel, Inhuman or Degrading Treatment or Punishment, adopted 10 Dec. 1984, G.A. Res. 39/46, U.N. GAOR, 39th Sess., Supp. No. 51, at 197, U.N. Doc. 39/51 (1984).

31. Convention on the Rights of the Child, adopted 20 Nov. 1989, G.A. Res. 44/25, U.N. GAOR, 44th Sess., U.N. Doc. A/RES/44/25 (1989).

32. Geneva Conventions, opened for signature 12 Aug. 1949, 75 U.N.T.S. 31.

33. See generally Amnesty Int'l, Amnesty Int'l Reports 1989–1993 (1990–1994).

34. U.N., Multilateral Treaties Deposited with the Secretary-General (Status as of 31 Dec. 1992), at 192, U.N. Doc. ST/LEG/SER.E/11, U.N. Sales No. E.93.V.11 (1993).

35. Id. at 190–92.

36. Id. at 190.

37. Id. at 192.

38. Id. at 194–95.

39. Jochen Frowein, Presentation at the 2d Joint Conference of the American Society of International Law and the Nederlandse Vereniging voor International Recht (The Hague, July 1993).

40. Johnston v. Ireland, App. No. 9697/82, 9 Eur. H.R. Rep. 20 (1987).

41. IR. Const. art. 41, [section]3, cl. 2.

42. European Convention, supra note 14, art. 12.

43. 9 Eur. H.R. Rep. at 228.

44. Id. at 219.

45. Universal Declaration, supra note 1, art. 16.

46. 9 Eur. H.R. Rep. at 219.

47. Id. at 228.

48. Roe v. Wade, 410 U.S. 113 (1973).

49. Case 2141, Inter-Am. C.H.R. 25, OEA/ser. L/V/11.54, doc. 9 rev. 1 (1981).

50. American Convention on Human Rights, signed 22 Nov. 1969, art. 4(1), O.A.S. Official Rec. OEA/ser.L/V/II. 23, doc. 21, rev. 6 (English 1979).

51. Regulations of the Inter-American Commission on Human Rights, art. 48, Inter-Am. C.H.R., 49th Sess., 660th mtg., in Handbook of Existing Rules Pertaining to Human Rights in the Interamerican System, at 138, OEA/ser. L/V 11.60, doc. 28 (1983).

52. American Declaration of the Rights and Duties of Man, signed 2 May 1948, art. 1, O.A.S. Official Rec. OEA/ser. L/V/II, 23, doc. 21, rev. 6 (English 1979).

53. Case 2141 at 39–42.

54. Id. at 43.

55. Martin Kramer, Islam vs. Democracy, Commentary, Jan. 1993, at 35, 38.

56. Universal Declaration, supra note 1, art. 18.

57. Id. art. 16.

58. James Walsh, Asia's Different Drum, Time (Int'l), 14 June 1993, at 50.

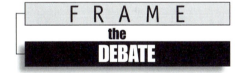

Form at end of book

Issue 6: Should the United States be involved in human rights issues in other countries?

Unfinished Business:
Failure of Imagination Preserves Inequality and Jeopardizes the Universality of Human Rights

Jack Donnelly

Abstract

The Universal Declaration of Human Rights has come short of its envisioned goals primarily because its implementation rests solely on individual governments. Individuals who have suffered abuse are rendered helpless if their governments fail to attend to them. Likewise, enforcers of the Declaration seemed to have neglected the rights of citizens in warring countries. The sanctions laid on Iraq, for instance, affect not just the state but also its hapless citizens.

Earlier articles in this symposium have shown the important role played by the Universal Declaration of Human Rights in the spread of international human rights ideas and practices. Forsythe, Henkin, Galley, and Sikkink have also documented considerable progress over the past half century in implementing internationally recognized human rights. My task here is to draw attention to some shortcomings and areas where further progress seems required. I will emphasize the limitations inherent in our system of state-based implementation and gaps in the coverage of contemporary international human rights norms.

National Implementation of Universal Rights

Human rights are "universal" in the sense that they are held by every person simply by virtue of being human. Human rights, however, typically target the state of which one is a national. International human rights treaties create obligations for states to respect, protect, and implement the rights of their own citizens (and foreigners temporarily under their jurisdiction). The human rights of non-nationals remain largely—although, as earlier essays

have indicated, no longer exclusively—matters for their own states to secure. International human rights treaties not only do not require coercive action to implement or protect the rights of foreigners abroad, they fail to provide international legal justification for doing so.

Human rights norms have been largely internationalized. Their implementation, however, remains almost entirely national. The general international legal norm of nonintervention remains paramount. Other states may encourage, condemn, and cajole. Human rights today, in sharp contrast to half a century ago, are almost universally accepted as a legitimate area of noncoercive international action. But coercion, and thus international enforcement in a strong sense of that term, remains largely prohibited.

Recent multilateral peacekeeping activities in Rwanda and Bosnia do suggest an emerging exception in cases of genocide. In addition, human rights concerns have been included in the mandate of many UN military missions in the past decade, including those sent to Guatemala, El Salvador, and Angola. But even in the post–Cold War period, coercive international enforcement of internationally recognized human rights has been rare and typically only in the context of broader peace and security operations. There has been little apparent spillover into more "normal" situations. Even severe violations in "ordinary" situations usually are not seen to authorize coercive international enforcement.

States are subject to international monitoring by NGOs, foreign governments, and regional and international organizations. Human rights violations regularly provoke diplomatic initiatives. In unusual cases, states may even find themselves subject to aid and trade sanctions. Nonetheless, international human rights law gives states ultimate, and virtually sole, responsibility to implement the rights of their citizens. Citizens can only make legal human rights claims against, and expect effective redress from, their own state. If national remedies are not forthcoming, no significant international recourse is available (except in the European regional regime).

This lingering statism, which reflects the primacy of the sovereign state in contemporary international society,[1] usefully draws attention to the special dual role of the state as an instrument for good (implementing human rights) and a source of suffering (violating human rights). Morally, a system of national implementation reflects the special value many people place on national identities and communities. Politically, it rests on a not entirely unreasonable fear of supranational political institutions. Nonetheless, this system of national implementation of international human rights leaves states, the principal violators of human rights, to police themselves. Thus the fate of "universal" human rights, at least in the short and medium run, typically rests almost entirely on national, not international, politics.

Furthermore, and less noted in recent discussions, this system of decentralized national implementation produces large gaps in the coverage of international human rights. Consider three brief examples.

War and Embargo

War is not ordinarily discussed in terms of human rights violations. Although the rights of civilians in war zones are regulated by the closely related body of international humanitarian law, the suffering inflicted as a result of legal means of warfare is not. For example, "collateral damage" from aerial bombardments of Iraq, and the suffering of Iraqi civilians under the continuing UN/U.S. embargo, have rarely been presented, even by critics, as human rights violations (Weiss et al. 1997).[2]

There are good moral, conceptual, and political reasons for distinguishing war (formal inter-state violence) from other forms of violence. And in the particular case of Iraq, it is far too simple to blame just the U.S. or the international community for the embargo. Nonetheless, the suffering associated with the war against Iraq and the ensuing embargo, which is in so many ways analogous to recognized human rights violations, is not generally seen as an international human rights issue. When other states engage in behavior that would be called human rights violations if done by one's own government, we usually do not use the language of human rights.

Business and Human Rights

The human rights consequences of the practices of national and international business practices are also largely ignored by dominant conceptions of human rights. For example, although economic globalization reduces the ability of states to engage in rights-protective welfare state policies, it remains awkward to talk about, say closing a factory and moving production to a country with lower wages as a violation (or even an infringement) of human rights. More generally, the unwillingness of many businesses to address the consequences of their activities for the health and welfare of employees and communities does not fit into standard human rights frameworks, despite the fact that such practices often determine the extent to which individuals are able to enjoy internationally recognized human rights.[3]

States have well-established rights to intervene in business activities to implement human rights. Governments may legitimately require businesses to do (or not do) many things on human rights grounds. In countries like Japan, major responsibility for many economic and social rights even lies with firms. Yet we generally accept that the proper business of business is making money—unless the state explicitly requires more.

Such arguments, however, assume that states are politically capable of controlling corporations. Even setting aside the often cozy relationships between government and business, growing economic globalization is making this an increasingly problematic assumption. We thus create, or at least tolerate, a kind of common deprivation and suffering that, if done directly by the state, would be called a violation of human rights—or at least a culpable failure to implement internationally recognized human rights—but is not ordinarily thought of as such when (the state allows it to be) done by another social institution.[4]

Immigrants and Refugees

The treatment of immigrants and refugees reveals a different sort of gap in the current state-based system of national implementation. Freedom of movement, although formally recognized in the Universal Declaration, does not in practice apply internationally. One of the ironies of the end of the Cold War is that citizens of the former Soviet bloc, now finally "free" to leave their own country, often are prohibited entry into another.

Furthermore, individuals and families that are able to take up residence elsewhere often face discrimination based on nationality. For example, even life-long residents find it extremely difficult to acquire German or Kuwaiti citizenship if their parents were not nationals. In the United States, even legal immigrants have been denied basic social welfare benefits, and both formal and informal discrimination against illegal immigrants is increasingly popular. Furthermore, aliens in almost all countries have their political rights restricted. This selective denial of internationally recognized human rights rest entirely on one's nationality, a category based on the system of sovereign states.

When borders can no longer contain massive suffering, and large numbers of refugees fleeing famine or civil strife create problems for neighboring countries, the international community typically responds with financial and logistical assistance. But such "humanitarian assistance," even when it involves military means, is typically provided without consideration of broader human rights issues.[5] The primacy of the principle of nonintervention usually precludes effectively responding to the human rights violations that caused the problem. Even in treating the symptoms associated with massive flight, refugees are seen largely as objects of charity, rather than as victims of rights violations. Consequently, humanitarian assistance responds only to relatively immediate, largely physiological, needs rather than to the full range of internationally recognized human rights that are being denied.

A Deficit of Imagination

In all these cases, "ordinary" suffering becomes so familiar that we fail to even see it as a problem. Such a lack of imagination, a failure to see suffering clearly, remains a common problem, despite the progress we have made in the field of human rights. To take still another example, largely unreflective statism leads most Americans to see malnutrition overseas as a problem for residents of other countries, not ours. As good, charitable people, we may choose to do something about it. But we have no obligation to act correlative to the human right to food. This "universal" right somehow does not bind us to act.

In a world of sovereign states, this lack of obligation is, almost by definition, true. This "truth," however, is neither natural nor inevitable; it is an artifact of the international political structure. Even if that structure is extremely resistant to change, as realists rightly remind us, the ways in which it contributes to differential opportunities to enjoy one's human rights ought to be much more prominent in our discussions than it is. At the very least, we ought to feel more ill at ease about these structural impediments than we typically do. And we probably ought to devote much more effort to trying to ameliorate some of the undesirable human rights consequences of operating within the current system of sovereign states.

Whatever the attractions and justifications of a state-based conception of human rights—and they are many—it leads to the profoundly problematic situation in which the rights one enjoys, and the kinds of systematic violations one must endure, are in significant measure determined by the morally arbitrary fact of where one was born (or has been able to move). By taking sovereign states for granted in discussions of human rights, most Americans typically don't even recognize the tragic ironies inherent in the contemporary system of national implementation of universal human rights. This failure of imagination thus often leads us not even to try to take steps to reduce systematic inequalities in prospects for the enjoyment of universal human rights.

The Right to Nondiscrimination

Nondiscrimination reveals a very different set of shortcomings in contemporary international human rights understandings and practices. Conceptually, the right to nondiscrimination arises from the basic moral equality of all human beings that underlies the idea of human rights. Practically, nondiscrimination provides a foundation for securing a host of other rights. People who suffer discrimination because of race, gender, religion, or membership in any other social group typically face systematic denials of numerous other internationally recognized human rights.

There has been immense political and moral progress toward nondiscrimination over the past half century. The Universal Declaration predates the decolonization of Africa and Asia, the civil rights movement in the United States, the struggle against apartheid in South Africa, and national and international movements for women's rights. All of these struggles drew support from the ideal of nondiscrimination, and in much of the world (although not the United States) the Universal Declaration was a significant resource for victims of discrimination. Nonetheless, I want to emphasize the persistence of pervasive discrimination in much of the world.

Women and members of racial, ethnic, and religious minorities, who already fall under well-established international legal guarantees of nondiscrimination, suffer systematic, and often severe, discrimination in most countries. Rather than focus on this sort of shortcoming, however, I want to call attention to people and groups that have not yet received even formal guarantees under international human rights law. The discussion of immigrants and refugees above has already highlighted the problem of legally permissible discrimination against non-nationals. Here, however, I want to focus on the remaining gaps in categories of prohibited discrimination. Among nationals, perhaps the most prominent contemporary example is systematic legal discrimination on the basis of sexual orientation or gender identification.

Discrimination against Homosexuals

The severe legal and social discrimination faced by lesbians, gay men, and bisexuals in most countries remains sanctioned by current international human rights law. It is, however, difficult to justify in moral terms. Even accepting, for the purposes of argument, that voluntary sexual relations among adults of the same sex and families headed by same-sex couples are a profound moral outrage, it is difficult to comprehend how discrimination against homosexuals can be justified from a human rights perspective. "Perverts," "degenerates," and "deviants"[6] have the same human rights as the morally pure, and should have those rights guaranteed by law. Homosexuals are still human beings, no matter how deeply they are loathed by the rest of society. Therefore, they are entitled to equal protection of the law and the equal enjoyment of all internationally recognized human rights.

Human rights rest on the idea that all human beings have certain basic rights simply because they are human. Human rights do not need to be earned. And they cannot be lost because one holds beliefs or leads a particular lifestyle, no matter how repugnant most others in a society finds them.[7] How one chooses to lead one's life, subject only to minimum requirements of law and public order, is a private matter—no matter how publicly one leads that life.

Discrimination on the basis of gender, birth, property, religion, race, ethnicity, and political opinion have been standard practices in many societies. All such discriminations have been backed by moral justifications as deep and extensive as those justifying discrimination against homosexuals. Each, however, came to be prohibited after lengthy struggles to establish that Jews, Protestants/Catholics, Africans, Asians, "foreigners," women, the poor, communists/capitalists, etc. were human beings, however much they were despised by the rest of society. In fact, one way to recount the history of human rights struggles is as a story of the growing range of members of the species homo sapiens who forced the dominant mainstream to recognize them as fully human—and thus protected by the human right to nondiscrimination. In many countries today, homosexuals are undertaking a similar struggle. In many others, repression is so severe that a serious political struggle has yet to begin.

Internationally recognized human rights prohibit the state, society, or dominant groups from imposing their moral values on "deviant" adults. The moral views of dominant groups do, of course, shape law and social policy in profound and often entirely legitimate ways. But human rights rest on the idea that the state should not impose the values of dominant groups on resistant adults, no matter how small or despised the minority to which they belong.

The prohibition of discrimination based on such moral differences does not, however, mean that "anything goes." Most obviously, criminal behavior may justify denial of many internationally recognized human rights, and notions of crime are, of course, tied to moral values. The "crime" in question, however, must be something more than leading a despised lifestyle or possessing some "natural" characteristic. Legal and political disabilities cannot be imposed on even the most reviled minorities, so long as they respect laws that are not aimed simply at punishing them for being who they are.[8] Furthermore, any restrictions on rights must be limited, and closely connected to the offense.

Discrimination against homosexuals clearly fails to meet such minimum standards of fairness. A state may act within its legitimate range of freedom if it, for example, criminalizes sex between unmarried persons. But if it prosecutes only unmarried partners of the same sex, it illegitimately discriminates. And if it imposes legal liabilities on or refuses to protect the personal and civil liberties of homosexuals, it is guilty of a serious offense. Likewise, a state may legitimately restrict adoption or legal guardianship to natural parents, married couples, or blood relatives. But if it denies parents or relatives custody solely on the basis of sexual orientation, it engages in illegitimate—although in most jurisdictions, still entirely legal—discrimination. In most states today, homosexuals suffer such systematic, discriminatory legal liabilities.

Tolerating, Respecting, and Embracing Diversity

Human rights, however, demand only toleration of others. The right to nondiscrimination does not require the state—let alone members of society—to embrace, or even respect, homosexuals, or any other "deviant" group. The state is not required to support homosexuals. But any goods, services, or opportunities it does provide must be made available equally to homosexuals and heterosexuals, just as they must be provided equally to whites and non-whites, men and women, Christians, Jews, Muslims, Hindus, and atheists.

But tolerating a despised minority is not a purely "negative" obligation; it requires more than restraint. The state, in addition to not actively discriminating, must also protect members of minorities from persecution by private individuals and groups. Offering such protections no more confers "special rights" than does providing extra police in high crime areas. Quite the contrary, the need for such special protections indicates the extreme threats facing such rightholders. To fail to provide "special" protection to those whose rights are under unusually severe attack would effectively amount to state-based denials of a right. Without those additional protections, the rights in question cannot be enjoyed (equally).

Nonetheless, to the extent that homosexuals or other minorities are reviled by powerful groups in society, effective measures of equal protection are likely to be resisted and resented. Social intolerance makes effective legal and political tolerance very difficult. Thus one might argue that "true" or "deep" nondiscrimination requires not merely toleration of, but respect for, difference. Human rights, however, do not even attempt to impose or legislate respect (even granting that respect is something that can be legislated). The active legal and political toleration required by human rights may over time undermine social intolerance, but there is no guarantee, even in the long run. This "limitation" of the human rights approach is a deeply rooted consequence of the special, yet restricted, place of human rights in our system of moral, legal, and political practices and justifications.

Not discriminating against people one respects is (relatively) easy. Not discriminating against those one reviles is much more difficult. And where mere tolerance represents substantial progress towards realizing the ideal of nondiscrimination, the right to nondiscrimination matters most. A right is often of greatest value when respect is not deeply institutionalized, when duty-bearers are not almost unthinkingly inclined to respect that right.[9] Human rights seek to provide a last—or, if one prefers, minimum—line of defense in such circumstances.

This points to the important difference between a human right and the moral ideal it seeks to implement; in this case, between the human right to nondiscrimination and the moral ideal of nondiscrimination. The right to nondiscrimination sets minimum legal and political standards that have their primary use in contentious cases. These rights-based standards fall far short of what would be needed to create a world without discrimination. A world in which all human rights were adequately formulated and perfectly enforced would still not be a morally perfect world. Human rights regulate only the behavior of individuals and groups, whose moral views remain a private matter of conscience beyond the domain of legitimate state control.

Rather than a universal moral or political panacea, human rights are principally a resource for those subject to the power of the state. Nondiscrimination has a special place in a system of human rights because it deals with those on the margins of society, those without the power, prestige, or respect to protect their legitimate interests through other means. It is a vital resource for those seeking full recognition and full membership in a society that would prefer to keep them disadvantaged, marginalized, or subordinated.

This implies that the struggle against nondiscrimination is likely to be a running, and constantly evolving, fight. Once substantial progress has been made in combating the forced, systematic marginalization of one group, another marginalized group is likely to move to the forefront of political attention. Particular targets change with time and place—in the modern West, religious tolerance, beginning in the seventeenth and eighteenth centuries; in the nineteenth and early twentieth centuries, the rights of those without property; and more recent prohibitions of racial discrimination and discrimination against women—but the general problem seems deeply rooted in the tendency of social groups to see some signs of difference as signs of moral inferiority. For all the progress we have made over the past century in implementing human rights in general, and in ensuring nondiscrimination in particular, in most of the world today—including, very prominently, the United States—we still deny human beings basic rights on the basis of morally suspect criteria such as where they were born and who they love.

Notes

I thank Dave Forsythe for his helpful comments on an earlier draft.

1. I discuss these and related theoretical issues in Donnelly (1998, chap. 2).
2. Although some nongovernmental organizations, such as Physicians for Human Rights, and even the World Health Organization have addressed this suffering in human rights terms, this remains rare, especially among states.
3. Prominent recent exceptions include clothing and footwear manufacturers such as Nike and Levi Strauss, which found it necessary to respond to pressure brought by nongovernmental organizations and public opinion in their home countries. Nonetheless, it remains rare—especially in the United States, where there is a continuing reluctance to conceptualize issues of economic and social rights in human rights terms—to talk about human rights violations by businesses, either at home or abroad.
4. An even stronger argument can be made in the case of internationally imposed structural adjustment programs, where Third World states are pressured by international financial institutions to engage in practices that reduce, at least in the short run, the enjoyment of internationally recognized economic and social human rights.
5. For an overview of humanitarian assistance issues, see Weiss and Collins (1996). For a strong critique of this orientation to refugee issues, see Loescher (1993).
6. This language is not chosen to be inflammatory, or because it expresses my own views. In order to focus on the central issue of the justifiability of discrimination, I merely repeat, for the sake of argument, some standard moral condemnations of homosexuality.
7. I am implicitly assuming here that sexual orientation is "chosen" rather than given at birth, and thus more like religion than race—although, of course, racial identity is largely socially

constructed. If homosexuality is "genetic," the case for discrimination is even more tenuous, and the appropriate analogy becomes more like disability (another area of lingering legal discrimination in most countries).

8. Although the dividing line is not crystal clear—such lines almost never are—it is for most purposes adequate. For example, pedophiles cannot plausibly claim to be a discriminated-against minority. Children are legitimately protected—or, if one insists, restricted in their freedom—in many other areas of activity, on comparable grounds. If children cannot, for example, make legal contracts with adults, it does not seem unreasonable or discriminatory to prevent them from having sexual relations with adults. In addition, the crime in question is not directed principally against a lifestyle, and enforcement is standard against those outside the alleged minority.

9. I discuss this and related features of human rights more extensively in Donnelly (1989, 12–19).

References

Donnelly, Jack. 1989. *Universal Human Rights in Theory and Practice.* Ithaca, NY: Cornell University Press.

———. 1998. *International Human Rights.* Second Edition. Boulder: Westview Press.

Loescher, Gil, 1993. *Beyond Charity: International Cooperation and the Global Refugee Crisis.* New York: Oxford University Press.

Weiss, Thomas G. and Cindy Collins. 1996. *Humanitarian Challenges and Intervention: World Politics and the Dilemma of Help.* Boulder: Westview Press.

———, David Cortright, George A. Lopez, and Larry Minear, eds. 1997. *Political Gain and Civilian Pain: Humanitarian Impacts of Economic Sanctions.* Lanham, MD: Rowman & Littlefield.

Form at end of book

WiseGuide Wrap-Up

Tolerance is the issue. We all expect others to tolerate our way of life. We all expect protection from the state for our religious and cultural choices, but are we willing to grant the same to others? We often seem contradictory in this regard sometimes even demanding that the state withhold from others (illegal aliens, non-nationals, terrorists, people of different religious or sexual practice) the rights we want guaranteed to us. The state has the power to provide and to violate human rights. The sovereignty of the nation state in this area is rarely questioned. The concern is only over who will direct the use of that power.

Can you think of an incident when someone treated you in a way that was discriminatory or showed lack of respect? Now can you think of something that you did that might have discriminated against others or transgressed their rights or shown disrespect? You probably had no difficulty recalling something that happened to you but were unable to recall how your behavior affected another. We are all sensitive to our own rights and readily speak out when we feel they have been violated but we are often insensitive to our own lack of tolerance for others.

R.E.A.L. Sites

This list provides a print preview of typical **Coursewise** R.E.A.L. sites. (There are over 100 such sites at the **Courselinks**™ site.) The danger in printing URLs is that web sites can change overnight. As we went to press, these sites were functional using the URLs provided. If you come across one that isn't, please let us know via email to: webmaster@coursewise.com. Use your Passport to access the most current list of R.E.A.L. sites at the **Courselinks** site.

Site name: Amnesty International On-Line

URL: http://www.amnesty.org/

Why is it R.E.A.L.? Amnesty International is the largest nongovernmental organization dedicated to promoting and achieving human rights for all people in all countries. Its web site offers news, information, campaigns, and links to other web sites.

Key terms: human rights

Site name: United Nations: Human Rights

URL: http://www.un.org/rights

Why is it R.E.A.L.? Sponsored by the UN Commission on Human Rights, this web site provides general information on many aspects of human rights, including human rights treaties, the War Crimes Tribunal, human rights research, and UN human rights activities around the world.

Key terms: United Nations, human rights

Site name: American Civil Liberties Union

URL: http://www.aclu.org/

Why is it R.E.A.L.? The American Civil Liberties Union is one of the most important organizations speaking out for the rights of minority groups, whether the groups are respected or not. It has taken stands in support of the First Amendment for Americans and noncitizens in the United States. Its web site offers information on all issues concerning free speech and minority groups, news updates on particular cases, and material on lobbying efforts in various levels of government.

Key terms: human rights, free speech

section 7 | Is Being Labeled a "Model Minority" a Blessing or a Curse?

Take a Closer Look

1. Is it accurate to call Asian Americans a "model minority"?

2. Does high educational attainment prevent discrimination?

3. If education is the means for social advancement, has high educational attainment enabled Asians to reach positions of influence and power?

4. Do Asians face a "glass ceiling" that keeps them from positions of power?

5. Must the media rely on stereotypical portrayals?

WiseGuide Intro

Stereotyping is one of the most important aspects of group relations. To make sense of the world in which we live, we create "ideal types." These are handy, simple guides to the world around us that enable us to identify things in our world and select our behavior accordingly. They are useful in helping us to distinguish a friendly from an unfriendly dog, and our mother from other women, but sometimes, they get in the way of real communication and understanding.

Stereotypes are not meant to be substitutes for real knowledge. We create stereotypes of groups other than ours as part of the process of boundary creation. Stereotypes help us to know who is and who is not a member of the group to which we belong. Stereotype usefulness ends when the stereotype substitutes for the unique qualities of individual group members. Individuals can have some of a group's stereotypical characteristics but differ in others.

When stereotypes become caricatures, they become the basis for some of our humor. Why do we repeat them? How can we change them? Can we totally discard them? Do we need them to feel comfortable with our surroundings?

As we explore the world in which we live, we take our previous experiences with us. When you go on a trip, what do you pack? Do you take an umbrella for rain, traveler's checks for ready funds, a sweater for cold weather? What do you expect when you encounter those outside your group? Do you expect friendship, hostility, or indifference? Xenophobia is the fear of outsiders that we bring with us in some form or another. We expect support and assistance from members of our group but are wary of what to expect from others. The further the group's characteristics are from our own, the less likely we are to identify the group with safety, warmth, protection, and support. Our expectations travel with us. It is not easy to cross boundaries at home or abroad, but it can be done.

Are all Asian women either Suzie Wong or Madame Butterfly? Are they sexual beings who are only able to love white males and ultimately be victims of that love? Does Dr. Fu Manchu haunt your dreams to terrify you with the threat of an Asian takeover through drugs, economic domination, or gangs? Are Asians the source of crime, vice, and unfair economic competition? Can Asians assimilate, or are they impossibly alien? For Americans whose relatives have come from parts of Asia, these questions have had and continue to have an impact on their treatment in the United States.

In Reading 15, Doobo Shim gives an historical account of the portrayal of Asians in the American media. He looks at the relationship between the images of Asians and American attitudes toward the home country and immigration policy. He demonstrates the reoccurring stereotypes and questions the practice of "yellowfacing" (the use of non-Asian actors to play

Asians). Shim also discusses the use of the "model minority" image to represent the Asian community and notes that this seemingly positive image may hide negative interpretations. Is it used as a way to criticize other ethnic groups? Shim suggests that it separates Asians from other minorities and even encourages interethnic conflict.

In Reading 16, Pan Suk Kim and Gregory B. Lewis look specifically at Asian occupational attainment in the public sector. The image of Asian Americans as a "model minority" conceals both diversity and discrimination. Because Asians are likely to acquire high levels of education and gain employment in middle-class, white-collar jobs, discrimination against them may not be visible or receive much interest. Yet, as Kim and Lewis point out, Asian men and women do not achieve the same advancement or salaries as whites and are frequently underrepresented in certain sectors of the workforce.

Issue 7: Is being labeled a "model minority" a blessing or a curse?

From Yellow Peril through Model Minority to Renewed Yellow Peril

Doobo Shim

Doobo Shim is a Ph.D. candidate in the School of Journalism and Mass Communication at the University of Wisconsin–Madison.

Abstract

Asian Americans have almost always been portrayed in mass media as stereotypes. Mid-19th-century articles and pamphlets warned white America of a Yellow Peril, a horde of Japanese and Chinese who would destroy U.S. civilization, and this led to Asian villains in books and films that persisted through the 1980s. The stereotype of Asians as model minorities began in the 1960s, and the false image returned to demonizing Asians in the 1980s.

Why have Asian Americans recently been depicted as villains in films?[1] Why were Korean Americans depicted mainly as merciless gun-toting vigilante shopkeepers in the Los Angeles riot news? These initial questions led me to pursue this study. In a time when Asian Americans are more and more aware of their portrayals in white-dominated mass media, one is led to ask where these stereotypes came from. To have a deeper understanding of those current stereotypes, this study of the history of Asian stereotypes in the media will show how they have been controlled by the ruling bloc in this society.[2]

Semiotic and ideological analysis will be applied to portrayals of Asians and Asian Americans in U.S. entertainment media. Furthermore, their meaning in society will be contextualized to investigate racial ideology underlying the history of Asian and Asian American stereotypes. The analysis of Asian American portrayal in the media is drawn mostly from films for several reasons. Asian Americans are relatively invisible in entertainment media other than films (see section 6). Furthermore, films are well preserved on videotape and are recycled constantly on television. The period of the historical research in this study ranges from the mid-nineteenth century through roughly the Reagan-Bush era. Among ethnic groups of Asian heritage, Chinese and Japanese Americans are the main focus of this research since they represent the largest segment of the Asian American population and receive the greatest attention from the media.

The term entertainment media (or text) is used to contrast with factual media (or text). Film, drama, and other entertainment-based texts in print media and television comprise the former; news, documentary, and current affairs programs are included in the latter category. The main utility of factual media is to provide information about external reality; that of fictional media is to provide diversion. On the audience's response to a given text, John Corner (1991) makes an interesting distinction between factual and fictional programs. According to him, "In the former, the viewer is often drawn quite directly into a 'response' which involves relations of belief and disbelief, agreement and disagreement" (pp. 272–73). On the other hand, after watching a television drama, audiences vary in their interpretation of particular scenes—or the drama as a whole—as well as in their degree of emotional involvement. This point leads us to the debate in audience reception research.

In the past, it was assumed that the power of television and cinema was so great and that the audiences were passive consumers (Fiske 1987, 1982; McQuail 1983). As communication research developed, this view was revised. For example, the popularity of postmodernism put emphasis on audience "activity." It was claimed that the media texts were polysemic, and the audience could make critical/oppositional readings to counter the power of media. Text is a site of hegemonic straggle. It not only embodies an "encoded" or "preferred" reading, through diverse "decodings," but it also enables resistant political formations (Comer 1991; Fiske 1987; Morley 1992). Even so, as David Morley (1992, 31) claims, "The power of viewers to reinterpret meanings is hardly equivalent to the discursive power of centralized media institutions to construct the texts which the viewer then interprets." The active audience argument overextends Stuart Hall's encoding/decoding model, which actually stressed "strategies of textual closure" (Morley 1992, 27). Furthermore, by unduly emphasizing the role of the reader, this perspective caused "a form of sociological quietism, or loss of critical energy," in questioning "the macro-structures of media and society" (Comer 1991, 269). Therefore, political economist Robert W. McChesney (1996) came to wonder, "Is there any hope for cultural studies?"

This study focuses not on cultural consumption but on the relations of cultural production. By examining stereotypes of Asians and Asian Americans and their effect on the latter, I aim to discover the racial ideology of mainstream media and society. Since the texts arise within the dynamics of socio-politico-economic practices of production, I will explore the sociohistorical contexts that gave rise to the given texts. Sumiko Higashi (1991, 116) remarks on this point: "Contextualization of readings, as opposed to textual analysis that focus on internal logic or processes, would be useful in clarifying issues about ethnicity both on and off screen." Contextualization is a process connecting the text to the social and historical conditions from which it was born.

The six major sections of this study each represent a recurring formula or theme specific to Asian stereotypes in the media or major factors that influenced the representations. Because these formulas or factors are the products of specific historical eras, the first five sections presenting them are in chronological order: Early Asian American Experience and the Appearance of Fu Manchu; Asians—Sexually Distorted; Asian Americans—Swayed by U.S. International Relations; Model Minority Stereotype Since the 1960s; and The Reagan-Bush Era. These sections are followed by Asian Americans As the "Other"/The Practice of Yellowfacing and, finally, the Conclusion.

1. Early Asian American Experience and the Appearance of Fu Manchu

Asian immigration began in the mid-1800s in response to a shortage of labor in California created by the Gold Rush. The industry of the region needed workers in diverse fields, and the white entrepreneurs saw Chinese "coolie" laborers as the solution. Chinese immigrants performed most of the labor-intensive and agricultural work essential to the development of local industry and commerce (Sue and Kitano 1973, 84; Tchen 1984).

The Chinese contribution goes mostly unmentioned, and when it is known, it is severely distorted. For

instance, Chinese workers made a great contribution to the building of the transcontinental railroad, which was the central element in the social-economic development of the United States from the end of the Civil War through the 1910s. Numbering about 12,000, Chinese workers constituted 90 percent of all labor employed by Central Pacific Railroad by 1867. However, in the photographs commemorating the completion of the construction, there are no Chinese; they were not invited to the ceremony (Hamamoto 1994, 48; Tchen 1984, 5). During the economic depressions of the time, Chinese came to be identified with large businesses and were regarded as enemies of small farmers and workers (Mazumdar 1989, 3; Tchen 1984, 6).[3] As John Tchen (1984, 7) says,

The increased integrated national capitalist economy reeled from periodic economy depressions in the 1870s and again in the 1890s. . . . Masses of unemployed, militant trade unions, and antimonopoly political rallies punctuated these periods of economic downturn. Although the much-hated "monopolists" were a main target of organizational agitation, the Chinese were increasingly often made the scapegoats for social problems.

Throughout the late nineteenth and early twentieth centuries, Chinese were evicted from their residences and sometimes lynched by whites. The frustrated whites justified their attack on the Chinese by claiming that the Chinese were unassimilable others and that Chinese laborers sent money made in the United States back to China. However, statistics show that Chinese contributions to the discriminatory Foreign Miners' Tax "accounted for at least half of California's entire state revenues from 1850 to 1870" (Tchen 1984, 5).

Penny-press journalism warned of the Yellow Peril, a popular term used to warn that Japanese and Chinese hordes were on the way to take over white America and destroy white civilization. Countless cartoons in the popular press fanned the flames of xenophobia by depicting Asians as grasshoppers attacking Uncle Sam or as subhuman-looking workers trying to take jobs from whites (Lai and Choy 1972; Morley and Robins 1995, 154). Anti-Chinese agitation increased, and both major political parties passed countless discriminatory laws during the 1870s and 1880s, anxious to secure white votes. The intention of the laws was not only to restrict Chinese immigration but also to expel the Chinese from America (Tchen 1984, 7).[4] Both the white ruling class and white workers marched under the banner of the Asian exclusion movement. In race politics, the majority race unites regardless of class lines when its racial superiority and economic interests are threatened. As Hall (1986) notes, before apartheid, the South African state had been "sustained by the forging of alliances between white ruling-class interests and the interests of white workers against blacks." The same phenomenon—white racial unity to protect economic interests—took a renewed guise in the 1980s (see section 5).

The "Chinese Question" was resolved by expulsion and restriction. Chinese were forced to return to China or to retreat to a collective residence called Chinatown. The Chinese found safety in trades in which whites did not disturb them as competitors—laundries and restaurants—and as houseboys (Isaacs 1958, 115). Those residential districts "became more and more a segregated ghetto that kept the Chinese in one area, and whites out" (Mazumdar 1989, 4).

The dark and "exotic" Chinatown intensified the stereotype of Chinese "inscrutability." In his recollection of his boyhood early in this century in a New Jersey town, writer Robert Lawson described the Chinese as follows:

The Chinese, of course, were by far the most foreign and outlandish. They ran laundries, no work for a man anyway, they had no families or children, they were neither Democrats nor Republicans. They wrote backwards and upside down, with a brush, they worked incessantly night and day, Saturdays and Sundays, all of which stamped them as the most alien heathen. . . . We knew that they lived entirely on a horrible dish called chopsooey which was composed of rats, mice, cats, and puppydogs (quoted in Isaacs 1958, 109).

In this context, the image of the Chinese as the "unassimilable other" and as the Yellow Peril led whites to create Chinese villain characters. The story of Chinese villains in Chinatowns became a popular genre first in magazines and later in films. During the 1920s, American screens were filled with Chinese crime-and-gangster characters. Chief among these villains was arguably the best-remembered figure, Fu Manchu. First gaining popularity in a novel—*The Mystery of Dr. Fu Manchu* by the English writer, Sax Rohmer—Fu Manchu became an extraordinary attraction in films, starting in 1929 with *The Mysterious Dr. Fu Manchu* (Isaacs 1958, 115–16). Sequels of Fu Manchu films appeared: *The Return of Dr. Fu Manchu* (1930), *Daughter of the Dragon* (1931), *The Mask of Fu Manchu* (1932), and *The Drums of Fu Manchu* (serial, 1940).[5] As an incarnation of evil challenging the sanity of white civilization, Fu Manchu always miraculously reappeared in the next episode. He vanished when the Chinese commanded general sympathy during World War II. As we shall see, the Fu Manchu syndrome gives us an insight into the phenomenon of Asians' portrayals as villains in the Reagan-Bush era, when Asians loomed as "unfair" economic competitors (Hamamoto 1994; Isaacs 1958).

2. Asians Sexually Distorted

Westerners have tried to control and stereotype nonwhites' sexuality as a form of racial domination. First, sexist and racist stereotypes of "subservient and sexual" Asian women satisfied the needs of Western colonialism. During the colonial period, Westerners developed contrasting images of West and East: "strong," "rational," "virtuous" "mature" and "normal" for the West and "weak," "irrational," "depraved," "childish," and "abnormal" for the East. The East became the setting for exotic stories in the colonialist era. According to Marlo Praz (1951), "A love of the exotic is usually an imaginative projection of a sexual desire, and the Orient symbolized a type of licentious romantic sexual experience that titillated the European imagination." These exotic stories incited Westerners to seek colonial adventures, equating Asian women with the Asian continent.

According to Edward Said (1978, 190), what Westerners looked for "was a different type of sexuality, perhaps more libertine and less guilt-ridden." "Oriental sex" became a commodity in the mass culture, "with the result that readers and writers could have it if they wished without necessarily going to the Orient" (p. 190). American adoption of this idea is illustrated in Madame Butterfly, popular as a play, an opera, and, in 1915, a narrative film. Madame Butterfly, the prototype of the stereotypical Asian woman, commits suicide after her affair with an American naval officer comes to an end (May 1993, 84). This plot has been recycled in the popular culture. In the film *Sayonara* (1957), a Japanese woman (Miyoshi Umeki) chooses to kill herself when faced with the prospect of parting with her white boyfriend (Red Buttons). A recent European musical, "Miss Saigon," is a Vietnamese version of Madame Butterfly: the narrative structure is the same, only the locale has changed. As the presence of Asian women in a film is to fulfill white men's sexual desires, when their lovers leave they disappear from a narrative. The Chinese American actress Anna May Wong (1907–1961) commented, "When I die, my epitaph should be she died a thousand deaths. That was the story of my film career. . . . They didn't know what to do with me at the end, so they killed me off" (quoted in Moy 1993, 86).

Beside their representations in films, we must note the harshness of the real living conditions of Asian women. During the early stage of Chinese immigration, the San Francisco press focused on the problem of Chinese prostitution. Stereotyped as immoral and oversexed, Asian women were a threat to white "purity." It led to an exclusion of Chinese women. In 1870, "An Act to Prevent the Kidnapping and Importation of Mongolian, Chinese, and Japanese Females for Criminal and Demoralizing Purposes" was passed as one of a series of anti-Chinese laws (Mazumdar 1989, 3; Wong 1978, vii). As the immigration of Chinese females was cut off, the disparity in numbers between Chinese men and women widened. By 1870, the ratio of Chinese American men to women was no less than twelve to one. In 1900, this ratio increased to twenty-six males to one female (Mazumdar 1989, 2–5).

The film *The World of Suzie Wong* (1961) is arguably the best-remembered film satisfying the white male fantasy of Asian women as sexual slaves. When Robert Lomax (William Holden) meets Suzie (Nancy Kwan), a Hong Kong hooker, in a bar, she says, "You're looking for a girlfriend? I'm here for rent for a whole month." In the final scene, Suzie's last line symbolizes the subservience of Asian women: "I will love you until you let me go." The ideology of white racial domination directs this presentation of Asian females as under white male patronage. On the other hand, Asian females do not fall in love with Asian males in films: even in modern films such as *Year of the Dragon* (1985), *Rising Sun* (1993), and *Deadly Target* (1994), they fall in love with whites, not with Asians. In *Deadly Target,* a Chinese American woman who falls in love with a white man says, "I'm kinda safe having you around," implying that only a white male can protect her from the dangerous Asian gangs.

For Asian men, the sexual stereotype was different. In most cases, Asian men were portrayed as asexual in films, in contrast with the stereotype of black males as "beast-rapists."[6] However, regardless of the direction of sexual distortion, these stereotypes ultimately serve the same goal: as abnormalities, minorities should be contained. In the film *Broken Blossoms* (1919), a Chinese man who falls in love with a white girl is presented as asexual. James Moy describes the Chinese character: "Characterized as dreamy, frail, and sensitive, the 'Yellow Man' can offer only a love devoid of sexuality" (Moy 1993, 85). By killing off the lovers in the end, the film warned against the horrors of miscegenation. According to Richard Oehling, most films that dealt with Asian-white relations in the 1920s suggested that "interracial love affairs and marriages cannot work out in the long run. There are no happy endings" (Oehling 1980, 187).

This early stereotype of the asexual Asian male has been perpetuated. The famous Chinese detective Charlie Chan, featured in forty-eight films in the 1930s and 1940s, was effeminate and asexual in his walk and gestures. According to Eugene Franklin Wong (1978, 106–8), the motion picture producers, considering public sentiment, were very cautious in the creation of the Oriental who was on the side of the law. Therefore, Chan was made effeminate and comical with his abundance of aphorisms, so that he would not be rejected by the audience.[7] TV programs such as "Bachelor Father" (1957–1962), "Have Gun Will Travel" (1957–1963) "Bonanza" (1959–1973), "Valentine's Day" (1964–1965), "Star Trek" (1966–1969), "Highcliffe Manor" (1979), "Falcon Crest" (1981–1990), "General Hospital" (1985), and "Ohara" (1987–1988) all featured Asians as bachelors. Among these programs in the westerns, Asian bachelors are houseboys without sexuality (Hamamoto 1994, 7–12; James 1991, 164). In modern times, the male protagonist of *M. Butterfly* (1988) embodies the Western perception and stereotyping of the East as feminine.

3. Asian Americans—Swayed by U.S. International Relations

The year 1924 was a turning point in the portrayal of Asian Americans. With the 1924 Immigration Act, no more Asians were allowed into the United States, and growth of the Asian American community was stopped. Film industry's interest in Asian alien residents declined and, instead, China and Japan as foreign powers emerged as a theme in Hollywood films (Oehling 1980, 183). As we shall see, fluctuating relationships between the United States and Asian countries affected U.S. treatment of Asian Americans. As a result, Asian Americans have been easy scapegoats whenever the United States clashes with an Asian country. Before 1924, the Chinese were the major incarnations of evil in American media, as seen in Fu Manchu and related figures. When Japan revealed its expansionist ambitions and invaded China in 1937, the Chinese and Japanese changed places as "the bad guys." Moreover, the Japanese attack on Pearl Harbor reinforced the bad guy image of Japan (Chin 1973, 43–46). An opinion poll in July 1942 showed that while only 3 percent of Americans described the Chinese as "cruel," 56 percent of them applied this adjective to the Japanese (Isaacs 1958, 107). The war ended the career of a relatively positive Japanese American film character, Mr. Moto, a brilliant and humble sleuth. In its place arose the fanatical kamikaze "Jap" who brutally tortured and raped "white purity" in such diverse war films as *Wake Island* (1942), *The Purple Heart* (1944), and *Objective Burma* (1945) (Woll and Miller 1987, 192; Wong 1978).

During World War II, Japanese Americans suffered ineradicable psychological scars at the hands of the U.S. government. In 1942, President Franklin D. Roosevelt signed Executive Order 9066. By this order, the civil rights of 120,000 Japanese Americans—77,000 of them U.S.-born citizens—were suspended, and these individuals were evacuated to concentration camps solely due to their Japanese origin. Upon "clearance," Japanese American males older than age seventeen were required to sign a loyalty oath. After encampment for up to three years, the detainees were released without apology or compensation. The Japanese community never recovered culturally or economically. What awaited them was racially motivated violence, and their property was rifled, stolen, or sold during their absence (Mazumdar 1989, 10; Hamamoto 1994, 66–75; Matsumoto 1989). However, German and Italian

Americans, whose motherlands fought America and who belonged to the white race, did not experience the same treatment. In propaganda cartoons during the war, while Japanese were described as monkeys, Hitler and Germans were human. For the most part, Germans and Italians were portrayed in films as pitiful, ordinary people who were regrettably misled by dictators while the Japanese were a crazy subhuman race running wild (Dower 1986; Wong 1978).

On the other hand, "the American people became fascinated by the stubborn and heroic resistance of the Chinese against the better-equipped and better-trained Japanese troops" (Wong 1978, 127). The Chinese began to be portrayed as smiling and hardworking peasants, or otherwise favorably in films such as *The Good Earth* (1937), *Daughter of Shanghai* (1938), *King of Chinatown* (1939), *Dragon Seed* (1944), and *Thirty Seconds over Tokyo* (1944) (Woll and Miller 1987, 192; Wong 1978, 136–37). A remark by an American in *Thirty Seconds over Tokyo* demonstrates American feeling about the Chinese: "You're our kind of people" (Oehling 1980, 197). During the war, the Office of War Information (OWI) pronounced that the Charlie Chan series was included in the list of official anti-Japanese films since Chan was regarded as a "good Chinese American" who worked well with the authorities. Chinese Americans began to be regarded as the "ideal American minority"; in contrast with this fact, the very existence of the "good guy" Charlie Chan reminded Americans of "bad guy" Japanese (Chin 1973, 43–46). In the context of this favorable aura, in 1943 the U.S. Congress repealed the Chinese Exclusion Act of 1882 and established an annual quota of 105 for Chinese immigrants (U.S. Commission on Civil Rights 1992, 4). However, an astute scholar named Rose Hum Lee worried about the future of Chinese Americans even in 1944. She noted, "As violently as the Chinese were once attacked, they are now glorified and mounted on a pedestal. It is impossible to predict how lasting this change will be. . . . Largely grounded on the sandy loam of sentimentality, one is left conjecturing what the tone of literature toward the Chinese will be in 1954" (quoted in Isaacs 1958, 120).

Her predicted concern was realized. When the Communists took over in China in 1949, fought against the United States in the Korean War (1950–1953), and dealt "cruelly" with American prisoners, the Chinese became the bad guys again. Again, a series of anti-Chinese communist films were made during the 1950s. Fu Manchu, who died a natural death in movies produced in earlier years, made another of his miraculous reappearances during the 1950s in the form of serial stories in *Collier's Magazine* (1957) and in the TV series "The Adventures of Fu Manchu" (1955), which included seventy-eight half-hour episodes, with crueler portrayals than previous ones (Hamamoto 1994, 111; Paik 1971, 30;

Wong 1978, 102). As Wong (1978, 180) states, "By the end of the 1950s, the industry had clearly re-established the Chinese as America's main enemy, overshadowing the Russians if only on the basis of race." In the minds of many Americans, the Chinese were not only inhumane humans but bestial subhumans (Isaacs 1958, 108).

In contrast, Japanese became the good guys again after Japan adopted Western democracy following its defeat in World War II. Especially after the speech by Douglas MacArthur to Congress in 1951, "the Japanese thrift, enterprise, and acumen have been restored to high American regard, Japanese art exhibits draw admiring American audiences, and a visiting company of Kabuki dancers has scored a critical and popular triumph" (quoted in Isaacs 1958, 108 n27). In this favorable atmosphere, the McCarran-Walter Act of 1952 was passed finally allowing Japanese to become U.S. citizens (U.S. Commission on Civil Rights 1992; 4). The cameras began to focus favorably on Japan and Japanese geisha girls who were kind to American GIs in *Teahouse of the August Moon* (1956) and *Sayonara* (1957) (Hamamoto 1994, 11).[8] The Japanese began to be portrayed as less hostile and more human even in World War II films such as *Bridge on the River Kwai* (1957), *Hell to Eternity* (1960), and *Tora! Tora! Tora!* (1970). In contrast, from the start of the Korean War (1950) to the shifting of diplomatic ties from Taipei to Beijing (1978), *National Geographic* "virtually ignored" mainland China. During this period, *National Geographic* reported on Japan more "than on any other non-western nation" (Lutz and Collins 1993, 126–29). As seen in the concentration camp experience of the Japanese Americans, the welfare and the media portrayals of the Asian American community were influenced by the U.S. relationship with Asian countries.

4. Model Minority Stereotype Since the 1960s

In addition to being victimized by international affairs, Asian Americans were also made into puppets by racial politics. This changed circumstance was brought about in the context of African Americans assertively demanding their civil rights during the 1960s. As a counterblow to the African American attack on the U.S. social system, the power bloc needed Asian Americans to justify African Americans' own economic failure. At this time, it seemed that Chinese and Japanese Americans were regarded as one group, under the name of "model minority." Later, as Korean Americans and Asian Indians were included in the model minority category, it seemed that all Asian American groups were renamed as model minority, a notion used against African and Latino Americans (Espiritu 1992; Omi and Winant 1994).

The 1965 publication of *The Negro Family: The Case for National Action,* written by then Assistant Secretary of Labor Daniel Patrick Moynihan, and President Lyndon B. Johnson's commencement speech at Howard University based on this report sparked a controversy among government officials, civil rights leaders, social scientists, and the public. The so-called Moynihan report attributed the perpetual economic subordination of blacks to their lack of family values (Rainwater and Yancey 1967). Soon afterward, Asian success stories appeared in the media. Examples include "Success Story: Japanese American Style" in *The New York Times Magazine* (1966) and *Japanese Americans: Oppression and Success* (1971), both by William Petersen. The author unanimously attributed the success to Asian family values and called the Japanese Americans a "model American minority." Another success story article in *U.S. News & World Report* ("Success Story of One Minority Group" 1966) begins with the following:

Visit "Chinatown U.S.A." and you find an important racial minority pulling itself up from hardship and discrimination to become a model of self-respect and achievement in today's America. At a time when it is being proposed that hundreds of billions be spent to uplift Negroes and other minorities, the nation's 300,000 Chinese-Americans are moving ahead on their owns—with no help from anyone else. (p. 73)

And the article closes with the following:

At the same time, it must be recognized that the Chinese and other Orientals in California were faced with even more prejudice than faces the Negro today. We haven't stuck Negroes in concentration camps, for instance, as we did the Japanese in World War II. "The Orientals came back, and today they have established themselves as strong contributors to the health of the whole community." (p. 76)

The article contrasts Chinese Americans and blacks. Specifically, it emphasizes the admirable reluctance of Chinese, in contrast with blacks, to receive welfare checks. This idea is captured in the lead: "Still being taught in Chinatown is the old idea that people should depend on their own efforts—not a welfare check—to reach America's 'promised land' " (p. 73). The comparison between Asians and black's seemed to foster conflict between these two minorities. According to Frank Chin (1973, 46), some people in Chinatown said that on the same date that the *U.S. News & World Report* story appeared, mainstream papers in San Francisco began to report a story about black gangsters killing Chinese grocers.

The appreciation of Asians set the stage for a change in immigration policy. After a long period of restriction on Asian immigration, the Immigration Act of 1965 replaced the national origins system with a fixed annual quota of 20,000 per country, permitting a sizable increase in the influx of Asians (U.S. Commission on Civil Rights

1992, 5). Unlike the Chinese and Japanese, most Korean immigrants arrived in the United States after the Immigration Act of 1965; some believe that they were introduced to America to form a buffer zone between wealthy whites and poor blacks after the Watts riots.[9]

Just as Charlie Chan movies had been used to divide and conquer Japanese and Chinese Americans in the previous generation (see section 3), *Flower Drum Song* (1961) can be interpreted as a blow to African Americans. In this film, all the Asians rejoice over their identity as Asian "Americans" as they happily sing a song, "Chop Suey"—a mixed Chinese dish in American style, invoking the concept of Americanized Chinese. This film projects Asians as a "humble and quiet" model minority struggling to assimilate into white America without asking for anything. All Asians in the film are middle or upper middle-class, reflecting the realization of the "American Dream." Even the illegal immigrants are portrayed favorably. What is lacking is the reality: no racism exists in the film.

Despite the depiction of Asians as a model minority, public and Hollywood attitudes toward Asian Americans had not changed. Except for *Flower Drum Song*, Asians were still portrayed in negative and misleading ways throughout the 1960s and 1970s in films and TV programs, such as "The Hawaiians" (1970), "Hawaii Five-O" (TV series, 1968–1980), and "Mission: Impossible" (TV series, 1966–1973). According to Wong (1978, 210–13), Hollywood had already begun its "renewed propensity to depict Asians as illegalists" with gangland connections in the 1970s. In marked contrast, black characters began to be depicted as ordinary persons, as Hollywood began to acknowledge black audiences. However, Asian Americans, a smaller audience with less purchasing power, were not recognized by the media industry. Only the news media occasionally reported Asian success stories, seemingly always with the aim to divide and conquer the racial minorities.

5. The Reagan-Bush Era

To understand race relations in the 1980s, we must first examine the political and economic changes that started more than a decade earlier. Regionally, jobs and industries in the Frostbelt, formerly the industrial hub of America, were uprooted and moved to the Sunbelt. Structurally, the U.S. economy shifted from manufacturing to high-tech industry, eliminating many workingclass jobs. In the international market, U.S. manufacturers lost out to their competitors in Germany and Japan, with these countries reemerging as economic superpowers, significantly increasing the U.S. trade deficit. Furthermore, U.S. influence dwindled with the rise to power of anti-American nationalist and Communist regimes in the Third World. Defeat in Vietnam and the Iran hostage crisis, in particular, damaged national prestige and fostered xenophobia. It was in this atmosphere that Ronald Reagan won the 1980 presidential election, promising a Reagan Revolution to "revive a great America" (Omi and Winant 1994, 114–15).

During the Reagan administration, economic dislocation continued, monopoly capitalism grew, and the concentration of wealth narrowed. Between 1977 and 1989, 60 percent of the increase in after-tax income accrued to the wealthiest 1 percent of American households; the poorest 40 percent suffered a decrease in inflation-adjusted income. During the same period, the salaries of top executives increased dramatically compared to those of their employees, from 35 to 120 times the average workers' wages (Robinson 1993, 75). Blacks seemed to suffer most from the deregulation policy of the Reagan administration. During the period 1982–1989, 131 factories in Los Angeles, the majority of whose employees were blacks, closed and moved to the Third World. This move cost 124,000 jobs. In 1992, U.S. Representative Maxine Waters claimed that about 40 to 50 percent of blacks in Los Angeles were unemployed (Fiske 1994, 153; Waters 1992, 26).

However, the conservatives saw a return to traditional values as a cure-all for these socioeconomic problems. From 1980 to 1996, all Republican presidential candidates put family values at the center of their campaigns. Their emphasis on individual responsibility reflected the view that the state should no longer assume primary responsibility for the amelioration of socioeconomic problems (Fiske 1994, 114). In addition, issues of race were revived in the form of a backlash. Conservatives questioned the value of the existing social welfare policy, reopened the debate on race, and blamed the government for "throwing good money after bad" (Omi and Winant 1994, 116). Such books as *Losing Ground: American Social Policy, 1950–1980* by conservative theorist Charles Murray (1984) supported the Reagan assertion that social welfare programs based on race had created massive socioeconomic problems. According to Murray,

My proposal for dealing with the racial issue in social welfare is to repeal every bit of legislation and reverse every court decision that in any way requires, recommends, or awards differential treatment according to race. . . . Race is not a morally admissible (sic) reason for treating one person differently from another. Period. (p. 223)

Again, Asian Americans became embroiled in a racial "divide and conquer" policy. The laissez-faire economy of the 1980s promoted the myth of the self-made man in the name of "entrepreneurialism." Vietnamese shrimp wholesalers, Korean greengrocers, and Chinese computer whizzes were recognized as the epitome of "family values" (Hamamoto 1994, 198). Asians' "promotion" thrust blacks to the "bottom rung of the ethnic lad-

der" (Daniels and Kitano 1970, 81) and brought envy and antagonism from blacks against Asians. The speeches of two Republican politicians in Los Angeles after the riots in 1992 placed Asian Americans on the opposite side of African Americans. Dan Quayle said, "I believe the lawless social anarchy which we saw is directly related to the breakdown of family structure, personal responsibility and social order in too many areas of our society. For the poor the situation is compounded by a welfare ethos that impedes individual efforts to move ahead in society" (quoted in Fiske 1994, 68–69). In a similar vein, Pat Buchanan said, "There were the brave people of Koreatown who took the worst of those L.A. riots, but still live the family values we treasure, and who still believe deeply in the American dream" (quoted in Fiske 1994, 56). Asian Americans were made puppets in racial politics without their consent.

At the same time, the image of Asian Americans was adversely affected by the trade struggle between Asia and the United States. The domestic economic ills were attributed to "unfair" trade practices of Asian countries such as Japan and the "tigers"—South Korea, Taiwan, Hong Kong, and Singapore. A nationwide survey conducted in 1982 concluded that 44 percent of Americans blamed the country's economic woes "almost completely" or "very much" on competition from Japanese corporations (Espiritu 1992, 138). In 1984, the U.S. trade deficit with Japan was $37 billion, and that with Canada was $20 billion; however, Canada was not a target of resentment (Omi and Winant 1994, 202 n7). During this period, the Japanese purchase of Rockefeller Center, MCA, CBS Records, and Columbia Pictures received media attention and caused public protest. On the other hand, European and Canadian ownership of U.S. real estate was condoned. For example, in 1985, the Dutch held $35 billion worth of U.S. real estate, and the British owned $44 billion (Espiritu 1992, 139; Funabiki 1992; Morley and Robins 1995, (149–52). Typical of expressions of racial views of Asians, Waldemar Januszczak once remarked that, like Europeans, "Canadians, after all, are just like Americans, only less so. The Japanese, according to the occidental popular imagination are aliens from the East who are probably trying to take over the West" (quoted in Morley and Robins 1995, 158). Both labor leaders and executives placed racist blame on Japan. For example, Chrysler Chairman Lee Iacocca ignited blacks' anti-Asian sentiment by claiming that while Chrysler ran auto plants in downtown Detroit where many African Americans lived, Japanese auto makers were discriminating against blacks by building plants in suburban and rural areas where blacks rarely lived. In short, even the Japanese economic investment in America was viewed in terms of racial ideology. Subsequent to Iacocca's claim, the executive director of the National Association for the Advancement of Colored People (NAACP),

Benjamin J. Hooks, urged blacks to boycott Japanese automobiles (Espiritu 1992, 138; Hamamoto 1994, 80).

The media played a large role in stirring up anti-Japanese sentiment, using a military metaphor. For the most part, Japanese businesses and people were described as "sinister marauders," seeking to make up for "their losses during the war" (Funabiki 1992, 13). For example, the following remarks adorned the cover of *The New York Times Magazine* (28 July 1985) below a graphic of the nationalistic "red sun" indicator for Japan: "Today, 40 years after the end of World War II, the Japanese are on the move again in one of history's most brilliant commercial offensives, as they go about dismantling American industry. Whether they are still only smart, or have finally learned to be wiser than we, will be tested in the next 10 years. Only then will we know who finally won the war." In the related article, "The Danger from Japan," by Theodore H. White (1985), two photos were juxtaposed, showing people shouting with their hands raised. One was of American workers demonstrating against the loss of jobs; the other was of Japanese workers cheering at a training school for managers. The aim of this illustration was to suggest that the first photo was the result of the second. In a cover story of *The Atlantic Monthly,* "Containing Japan: Japan's Runaway Economy Will Harm the Rest of the World If Some Limits Aren't Set," James Fallows (1989) described the Japanese as having "destructive compulsions." He accused Japan of conducting "one-sided trading." A survey taken on 7 August 1989 showed that Japan was feared more than any other country, even the former archvillian, Russia, by U.S. citizens: the reason was economic competition (Chang 1993, 14; Morley and Robins 1995, 158).

The anti-Japanese sentiment in the press spills over into the writing on the Asian American community. For example, under the headline, "Asian Invasion," *The Daily Breeze* (Torrance, California, 24 March 1991) featured a story on the growth of the region's Asian American community (Funabiki 1992, 14). Asian Americans are lumped together with Asians and are the direct recipients of anti-Asian sentiment. According to a report published by the U.S. Commission on Civil Rights (1992), Japan bashing by American leaders in diverse sectors has invoked envy and led to anti-Asian violence in America. On 19 June 1982, Chinese American Vincent Chin was killed by whites who mistook him for a Japanese man. Throughout the 1980s, this kind of violence continued around the country, especially in southern California. In 1986, the U.S. Justice Department reported that hate crimes committed against Asian Americans had risen by 62 percent (Espiritu 1992; Hamamoto 1994, 167).[11]

Nevertheless, the criminal image of Asians continued throughout the 1980s and 1990s. Since the early years of their immigration, Asian Americans have been seen largely as criminals, such as tong warriors and prostitutes, and such criminalization was a means to justify their exclusion. The factual programs disseminated the criminal image of Asians as a new threat that had to be contained. For example, in a special TV program, "The New Godfathers," (1993), after announcing that a global wave of terror was attacking the United States, Geraldo Rivera, the host, emphasized the Hong Kong-based Triads and the Japanese Yakuza as "especially fearsome" (Hamamoto 1994, 180–81). In a documentary, "Asian Gangs: Terror in the Streets" (1992), Little Saigon, a Vietnamese residence in Orange County, California, was described as a hangout for gangsters. Detective Marcus Frank was interviewed, saying that "of all the street gangs out there, there is no question in my mind that the Indochinese street gangs are by far the most criminally sophisticated element we have ever seen in this country" (quoted in Hamamoto 1994, 183). Little Saigon was thus a renewed version of criminalized Chinatown.

The entertainment media are the spearhead in spreading the Asian criminal theme. Today, when one reads the Movie Guide pages in *TV Guide* describing crime movies set in Los Angeles, one will probably see Asians cast as criminals. For example, on the evening of 3 January 1996, four films showing Asians aired on television, all of which were gangster films: *Bloodsport* (1988), *The Protector* (1985), both on TBS, and *Deadly Target* (1994) and *Blue Tiger* (1994), both on HBO. In *Bloodsport,* Jean-Claude Van Damme fights with an Asian martial arts player who is described as "cruel." In *The Protector,* two New York policemen, one Asian and the other white, go to Hong Kong to fight a criminal organization. In *Deadly Target,* a white Hong Kong policeman comes to Los Angeles to arrest Wu Chang, a drug dealer and gangster from Hong Kong. Throughout the film, every Asian is a gangster. In *Blue Tiger,* all Asians are gang members except for a policeman. After arresting the Asian killer, the Japanese American policeman says, "You know what really crawls my butt. It's assholes like you come over here and gives Asians like me a bad rap." In his discourse, it seems that all Asian immigrants are criminals.

In *Year of the Dragon* (1985), Chinatown is a hotbed of vice and crime, and a white male is a crime solver. The white detective Stanley White (Mickey Rourke) says, "The Chinese are always involved in something—never involved in nothing." Still, the major Asian female character is the white's mistress. Only dark images of Chinatown, such as a gambling parlor, a sweatshop, and gang shootings, are found in this film.[12]

In both fictional and factual programs dealing with Asian gangsters, it was assumed that they have connections with secret international criminal organizations uniting Asians here and abroad, further "foreignizing" Asian Americans. In this scenario, Hong Kong and Los Angeles were two strongholds for this secret society. In both factual and fictional programs, by criminalizing Asian Americans, white racial superiority, in the guise of law enforcement, was justified. The inferential theme under those programs and films is that Asians are undesirables who bring vice and crime with their "unfair" trade.

6. Asian Americans As the "Other": The Practice of Yellowfacing

Even after 150 years of an Asian American presence on U.S. soil, on TV they are still portrayed as "foreigners" who speak pidgin English, preserve only their "old country traditions," and refuse to assimilate into American culture. Charlie Chan's famous formula, "Confucius say . . . " leads the audience to think that all Asians are mysterious. In TV programs such as "Happy Days" (1974–1984), "Mr. T. and Tina" (1976), "Gung Ho" (1986–1987), and "Davis Rules" (1991–1992) and in the film *Falling Down* (1992), Asian Americans are portrayed as new immigrants speaking accented English (Hamamoto 1994, 12). This phenomenon reflects the fact that the white-dominated media ignore the history of Asian Americans and regard them as foreign.

In the ABC sitcom "All-American Girl" (1994), the main narrative structure is based on binary opposition between old country values and American values, represented in the struggle between a mother and a daughter who are intolerant of each other's values. Through the emphasis on the differences between the two sets of values, Asian Americans are seen as all the more alien. The 4 January 1996 episode of "Murder, She Wrote," set in Japan, continually referred to outmoded aspects of Japanese life. In it, the marriage of a CEO's son has been contracted since his birth. A rickshaw is shown as a vehicle. Since there is a reference to baseball player Hideo Nomo, the setting is contemporary, but the drama is filled with old Japanese practices. Asia is still regarded as a "different" place.

According to a study of soap operas by Cathy James, many Asian American characters appear mainly as "ethnic background scenery" when the white lead characters need a secret "hideout." For example, on the soap opera *As the World Turns*" (1983), Barbara Stenbeck, disguised as a man, hid out in a room above a male Japanese health spa. Most of the scenes in the bathhouse featured Japanese American men in the hot tub conversing with each other. They minded their own business, and none of them was interested in Barbara Stenbeck. It was the perfect refuge, complete with secretive people (James 1991,

151–52). Asians shown in the film *Another 48 Hours* (1990) include a man and his wife who run a hotel in Chinatown, two arguing men, and a man who is complaining to policemen. They speak only Chinese, without subtitles, supplying an ethnic aura—but not of the same language value as English.

The popular TV series "Kung Fu" (1972–1975) reinforced the "inscrutability" of Asians—solving problems with Zen and mystic martial arts. Even the modern Asian American cop in "Ohara" (1987–1988) solves crimes through Zen (Hamamoto 1994, 12). In the film *Remo Williams: The Adventure Begins* (1985), the Korean martial arts master Chiun watches TV sitting on a mat made of a tiger's skin. In *The Karate Kid, Part II* (1986), the Japanese karate master is seen catching flies with chopsticks. In *Rising Sun* (1993), Sean Connery, who is excluded from the LAPD because he is regarded as having sold himself to Japan, frequently talks in fortune cookie slogans, such as "Hide a sword in a smile" and "Beat the grass to startle the snakes," reminding the audience of mysterious Asia.

The stereotype of inscrutable or foreign Asians leads to their use as comic relief. In *Sixteen Candles* (1984), a Chinese exchange student, with his pidgin English and strange behavior, looks not like a normal person but like an extraterrestrial. His name is Long Duk Dong, sounding like "long duck dung." "Dung" is slang for excrement, and "dong" is slang for penis. His name is also associated with "ding-dong," which is slang for crazy. In *Gung Ho* (1986), the Japanese take off their shoes in front of the red carpet that was put out in the airport to welcome them. In *Collision Course* (1987), a Japanese policeman provides comic relief with his accented English. Entering Tony's (Jay Leno) apartment, Oshima (Pat Morita) flinches. Tony asks, "What're you doing now? . . . Take off shoes. Show respect for house." Finding some dirty fur on the floor, he puts on his shoes again, saying, "I think better show respect for foot." In many scenes, Oshima is funny because of his exaggeratedly Japanese behavior and broken English. In *The Fiendish Plot of Fu Manchu* (1980), Asian followers of Fu Manchu jump up and down, clapping their hands in an extreme exaggeration.

Aside from all these stereotypes of Asian Americans, it is difficult to find Asians in the media. Asian leading roles are given to white actors, and Asian actors play only the marginal roles.[13] In Hollywood, there has been a long-standing practice of "yellowfacing"—casting whites as Asians by the application of tape to the temples and cheekbones. This practice has its origins in the early American theater. When a drama called for black characters, white actors played blacks to avoid physical contact with them (Moss 1991, 124). This practice lingered in the motion picture era and was applied to any nonwhite character. Even though Asian character serials such as Fu

Manchu and Charlie Chan were an important stock in the American motion picture industry in the first half of the twentieth century, Asian actors were given only marginal roles (Wong 1978, 103).[14]

The practice of yellowfacing was not applied to subservient female roles. When the role called for a housekeeper or the object of white male sexual desire, it was assigned to an Asian female actor. However, when the role portrayed an honorable Asian woman, white female actors substituted: Louise Rainer in *The Good Earth* (1937), Katharine Hepburn in *Dragon Seed* (1944), and Jennifer Jones in *Love Is a Many-Splendored Thing* (1955).

There are several excuses for the perpetuation of this practice. During an era of supposedly pro-Chinese policy, the film *The Good Earth* (1937) was produced, and a vast talent search was initiated for an all-Chinese cast. However, Paul Muni, a white, was given the male leading role with the excuse of a dearth of good Asian male actors. The MGM staff did find a female Asian for the leading role, but the Motion Picture Producers and Distributors Association stepped in and replaced her with Louise Rainer, a white, to avoid a violation of the anti-miscegenation law (Paik 1971, 31). Even though the Supreme Court ruled the anti-miscegenation law unconstitutional in 1967, it still influenced television media. The television soap opera, "Love Is a Many-Splendored Thing" (1967–1973), was supposed to show the first interracial love scene between an American man and a Eurasian woman. After the show's premiere, CBS, bombarded by too many protests from viewers, forced the writer to change the story (Hamamoto 1994, 39; LaGuardia 1983, 38). In the 1971 NBC TV series, the title character Charlie Chan was played by a white actor, Ross Martin. NBC TV vice president David Tebet gave the excuse that "no Chinese could speak English in an accent understandable to the U.S. audience" (Choy 1978, 150).

The TV program "Kung Fu" (1972–1975) could have produced the first Asian heroic character played by an Asian actor. Action star Bruce Lee originally was to have starred in "Kung Fu" but was later denied the role because it was assumed that audiences were not ready to watch an Asian physically humiliating whites. Instead, the hero was presented as half white, half Asian, and was played by David Carradine (Hamamoto 1994, 60). Yellowfacing was still prevalent in Hollywood in the 1980s. In *The Fiendish Plot of Fu Manchu* (1980) and *Remo Williams: The Adventure Begins* (1985), white actors played the Asian roles.[15]

Associating visibility in the media with "love," independent filmmaker Loni Ding (1991, 48) talks about the power of the media: "possibly they have this power because we empower them with our attention. Someone once startled me with the proposal that if you were to gaze at anybody long enough, you could become enamored with them. . . . Perhaps the gaze of the camera does the same." Accepting this premise for the moment, the fact that Asians are invisible denies them the opportunity to be loved by the audience. Furthermore, when Asians are portrayed as villains, prostitutes, or perpetual foreigners, they are hated rather than loved by the audience. In short, the psychological function of the "other" is to be hated by "us" as an embodiment of alien culture and a possible threat to our "norm."

7. Conclusion

The Asian American experience can be epitomized as a process of assimilation into American culture, from Asian immigrants' ordeal when they first arrived here to their adaptation to racial domination. As immigrant laborers, Asian Americans have suffered from racist attacks by nativists whenever they have been seen as a threat to nativists' livelihood and whenever their motherlands and the United States have come into conflict. As a comparatively small racial minority in America, Asian Americans have been "inexorably entangled in a web of economic, political, and social complexities and conflicts" (Wong 1978, 187). As Hamamoto (1994, 1) puts it, "the simultaneous necessity and undesirability of Asian immigrant labor is a crucial political-economic contradiction that informs much of the past and present experience of Asians in the United States." Compared to what they endured a century ago, Asian Americans today are subject to stereotyping and life experiences that are less intense but, amazingly, similar in kind.

Overt racism, such as public exclusion and expulsion directed at early Chinese immigrants, and spiteful stereotypes, such as Fu Manchu, have gradually disappeared. However, inferential racism hidden behind rationality is on the increase through the control of "illegal" immigration, welfare reform law, and the stereotypes in seemingly innocuous films. Racial ideology is articulated in and through portrayals of race in the media. These portrayals have taught both Asian Americans and nativists lessons about who Asian Americans were and who they should be. In addition, with the development of new video technology such as cable and home video and television's increasing reliance on reruns of feature films, audiences have greater exposure to the accumulation of Asian American stereotypes. For example, as Norman Denzin (1995, 111) notes, "In the early 1970s the Chan movies would become staples on American television and suddenly found (sic) themselves the center of a new cult, part of the general craze for nostalgia of the thirties and forties." These days, not only Chan films but also others are easily available in any video rental stores.

It can be said that the foremost goal of the media is simply to make a profit by reaching as large an audience as possible. When networks buy programs or movies from Hollywood producers, they decide whether to underwrite these projects based on the marketability of these programs "in such a way as to ensure a sizable share of the audience" (Schulze 1990, 361). The sponsors favor not only the largest but also the most desirable audience—the young and affluent. By this mechanism, the media alienate and neglect the less desirable audiences—the old, the poor, and ethnic minorities such as Asian Americans (Bagdikian 1992). One of the criteria for marketable programs is familiarity: a program must be familiar "by its reference to the instantly recognizable" (Schulze 1990, 362). Television continuously offers viewers images and myths that are already familiar in structure and form, such as whites defending the community against Indians and, more recently, against hordes of "aliens" from the Third World. In this process, the stereotypes of specific groups are reproduced and recycled forever (Fiske 1987; Fiske and Hartley 1978; Mellencamp 1990).

For these reasons, it is difficult for producers to broadcast images that are unfamiliar to the mainstream audience. According to film director Wayne Wang, it was impossible for him to persuade Hollywood producers to fund his Asian-cast films (Sakamoto 1991). The absence or limited influence of Asian American producers and writers in the culture industry is partly responsible for the perpetuation of Asian stereotypes. Simply blaming the culture industry for its stereotyping cannot challenge and change long-standing conventions. Rather, the attempts to deal with Asian stereotypes and underrepresentation have come from the Asian American community itself. Some of these independent films and their filmmakers are Wayne Wang's *Chan Is Missing* (1981), Spencer Nakasako's *Monterey's Boat People* (1982), Karen Ishizuka and Robert Nakamura's *Fool's Dance* (1983), Steven Okazaki's *Unfinished Business* (1984), Wayne Wang's *Dim Sum* (1985), Loni Ding's *Color of Honor* (1987), Christine Choy and Renee Tajima's *Who Killed Vincent Chin?* (1988), and Wayne Wang's *Eat a Bowl of Tea* (1989) (Yee 1991, 251).

Although these independent films have limited influence on Hollywood productions, filmmakers with a track record, even in the "indies," are more likely to break into Hollywood. The film industry tends to be cautious and looks for "a sure thing" in its screenplays and personnel. The filming of *Joy Luck Club* (1993) by Wayne Wang was possible only because the original book was a huge bestseller and Wang was already an experienced director (Sakamoto 1991). One is reminded that the filming of *Flower Drum Song* (1961) with an all-Asian cast was possi-

ble only because it had established itself as a successful musical and best-selling novel (Chin 1991, 144). Considering these facts, Asian Americans need to participate more in the culture industry.

However, these few films without stereotypes will not solve the entire problem. The deeper cause is indifference or outright hostility toward multiculturalism, despite the official rhetoric that the United States is a nation of immigrants. In October 1994, a curriculum guide titled *National Standards for United States History: Exploring the American Experience* was released by the UCLA National Center for History for the public schools. It included "minorities and women who have been omitted from traditional history texts" and was regarded as the first step toward multiculturalism. Conservatives criticized the guide in that it "excludes white male heroes and emphasizes the negative in American history" ("Blueprint of History" 1994, A22). That the guide was finally rejected indicates there is a long and winding road ahead to a multicultural society.

The lack of multiculturalism breeds misunderstanding of racial reality, racial stereotypings, and the racist violence onto the minorities. Asian Americans do not share a common origin: for example, Koreans, Indians, and Filipinos are different in race, language, religion, and culture. In addition, not all of them are recent immigrants, as so many Americans assume. Many Asian American families have been in the United States for more than 100 years. Despite this, Asian Americans are still considered as the Asian "other," being made the easy target of anti-Asian violence, such as in the Vincent Chin case. Ironically, Asian stereotypes and anti-Asian violence promote pan-Asian American ethnicity. As Yen Le Espiritu (1992, 134) put it, "Because the public does not usually distinguish among Asian subgroups, anti-Asian violence concerns the entire group—cross-cutting class, cultural, and generational divisions."

I believe the current changes in race discourse come from our acknowledgment of the past because, as E.H. Carr (1961, 69) remarked in his book *What is History?*, understanding the society of the past is the prerequisite to the mastery over the society of the present." As we review the history of Asian and Asian American stereotypes and life experiences, we see that history not only produced the present but continues "to function as constraints and determinations on discursive articulation" (Grossberg 1996a, 148). However, as Hall has aptly noted, "People make history but in conditions not of their own making" (quoted in Grossberg 1996b, 163). Despite adversities, Asian Americans will create a new history in race discourse, leading toward a more equal society.

Notes

1. I conducted a content analysis of twenty-two texts (twenty-one films and one TV drama), made during the 1980s and early 1990s, that feature Asians. In sixteen of them, Asians were seen as criminal or violent. The sample of the analysis is the following: *The Fiendish Plot of Fu Manchu* (1980), *Sixteen Candles* (1984), *Year of the Dragon* (1985), *The Protector* (1985), *Remo Williams: The Adventure Begins* (1985), *Karate Kid Part II* (1986), *Gung Ho* (1986), *Collision Course* (1987), *Bloodsport* (1988), *Die Hard* (1988), *Do the Right Thing* (1989), *Another 48 Hours* (1990), *Falling Down* (1992), *Heaven and Earth* (1992), *Bloodfist V: Human Target* (1993), *Sidekicks* (1993), *Rising Sun* (1993), *Three Ninjas—Kick Back* (1994), *Blue Tiger* (1994), *Deadly Target* (1994), *Outbreak* (1995), and "Murder, She Wrote" (TV drama; 4 January 1996 on CBS).

2. First suggested by Antonio Gramsci, the term ruling bloc or power bloc was developed by cultural theorists such as Stuart Hall. Rather than referring to a specific group or class, it refers to "alliances of social interests" that are not stable but are categories formed and dissolved strategically to advance their interests. It could be the military-industrial complex, "the haves," the "conservatives" or, in the case of this study, the white media and whites regardless of their class (Fiske 1993, 9–10; Hall 1981).

3. The extent to which anti-coolieism influenced the allegiance of workers is evidenced by the fact that the Workingmen's Party and populist movement both collapsed when the Chinese Exclusion Act of 1882 was passed (Daniels 1966, 17–18).

4. In 1875, the Page Law severely limited the number of female Chinese immigrants. In 1882, the U.S. Congress passed the Chinese Exclusion Act, the first federal exclusion law against a specific group. A series of laws subsequently limited Asian immigration: Japanese and Korean immigration was restricted by the 1907 gentlemen's agreement; the 1917 Immigration Act banned all Asian immigrants except for Filipinos, who were U.S. nationals, and Japanese; Japanese immigration was terminated by the 1924 Immigration Act. Between 1924 and 1943, when the Chinese Exclusion Act of 1882 was repealed, all Asians were denied naturalization (Mazumdar 1989, 4; Tchen 1984, 8; U.S. Commission on Civil Rights 1992, 3–4).

5. As an evil incarnation, the Fu Manchu character is so deeply rooted in mass entertainment that it reappears as a theme in comic books targeted at children and adolescents. In comics series such as Batman, Flash Gordon, Iron Man, and Nick Fury Agent of S.H.I.E.L.D., heroes are found to fight with Asian villains resembling Fu Manchu.

6. During World War II, an exception to this asexual stereotype of Asian men was popularized, with "Japs" raping white females in films and political cartoons. According to Sumiko Higashi (1991, 139), "As the only Asian nation to imitate Western industrialization and imperialist expansion, Japan violated characterizations of the East as feminine and has thus been labeled barbaric."

7. Another Chinese detective character, Mr. Wong, was also effeminate.

8. However, these films reinforced the stereotypes of Asian women as submissive and sensual. Miyoshi Umeki won an Academy Award for her role in *Sayonara* during these times of favorable sentiment toward the Japanese. After filming in Japan, actor Marlon Brando said, "I was terribly impressed with Japan. The people are the nicest I've ever met in my life. They unquestionably are the most courteous, honorable, well-meaning, and self-respecting people; hypersensitively attuned to other people in their relationships" (quoted in Isaacs 1958, 108).

9. Author's interviews with five Korean Americans in Los Angeles and Portland, Oregon (November 1994).

10. In fact, the Asian American success story is deceptive. For example, according to the 1990 census, the reality for Korean Americans is in stark contrast with the myth: Korean American per capita income was $11,177, below the national per capita income of $14,143 (U.S. Bureau of the Census 1993). Considering that 71.7 percent of Korean American business owners work six or seven days per week for an average of 54.3 hours, the success story is even emptier (Min 1984).

11. In 1987, the Federal Court ruled the Vincent Chin killers not guilty.

12. While this film was playing in theaters, Asian Americans held protests and boycotts. After these activities received national media coverage, MGM-UA promised better roles for Asians in the future and added the following disclaimer before the opening titles (Marchetti 1991, 277):

    The film does not intend to demean or to ignore the many positive features of Asian-Americans and specifically Chinese-American communities. Any similarity between the depiction in this film and any association, organization, individual or Chinatown that exists in real life is accidental.

13. One may raise an objection to my argument, citing the example of an all-Asian cast film, *Flower Drum Song,* as early as in 1961. A comment by the film's director, Henry Koster, is quite revealing: *"Flower Drum Song* didn't cost very much to make because you don't have to pay Oriental actors as much as white actors" (quoted in Chin 1973, 44).

14. Japanese male actor Sessue Hayakawa was an exception to this rule. After a huge box office success in *The Cheat* (1915), Hayakawa became a prominent figure in the film industry. For a brief time during the late 1910s and early 1920s, he both directed and acted in films that portrayed the Japanese without stereotyping them. This boom in Asian films did not last long in the absence of a substantial Asian American audience. Restless with the treatment he received in American society, he left the United States (Kishi 1991, 165; Oehling 1980, 189–93).

15. Other examples of yellowfacing actors and films include Richard Barthelmess in *Broken Blossoms* (1919), Warner Oland in *The Mysterious Dr. Fu Manchu* (1929) and Charlie Chan movies (1931–37), Boris Karloff in *The Mask of Fu Manchu* (1932) and *Mr. Wong* (1938–39), Niles Asther in *The Bitter Tea of General Yen* (1933), Sidney Toler and Roland Winters in Charlie Chan movies (1937–49), J. Carrell Naish in *Charlie Chan on TV* (1957), Alec Guiness in *A Majority of One* (1961), James Darrell in *Diamond Head* (1961), Christopher Lee in *The Face of Fu Munchu* (1965) and in *The Brides of Fu Manchu* (1966), Victor Buono in *The Silencers* (1966), Peter Sellers in *The Fiendish Plot of Fu Manchu* (1980), Peter Ustinov and Angie Dickinson in *Charlie Chan and the Curse of the Dragon Queen* (1981), and Joel Grey in *Remo Williams: The Adventure Begins* (1985) (Choy 1978, 150; Paik 1971, 32; Sing and Seriguchi 1989, 23–26; Woll and Miller 1987, 193).

References

Bagdikian, Ben H. 1992. *The media monopoly.* Boston: Beacon.

Blueprint of history for American students. 1994. *The San Francisco Chronicle,* 29 October, A22.

Carr, E.H. 1961. *What is history?* New York: Vintage.

Chang, Edward T. 1993. Jewish and Korean merchants in African American neighborhoods: A comparative perspective. *Amerasia Journal* 19 (2):5–22.

Chin, Frank. 1973. Confessions of a number one son. *Ramparts,* March, 40–48.

———. 1991. James Wang Howe: The Chinaman eye. In *Moving the image: Independent Asian Pacific American media arts,* edited by Russell Leong, 144–56. Los Angeles: UCLA Asian American Studies Center.

Choy, Christine. 1978. Images of Asian-Americans in films and television. In *Ethnic images in American film and television,* edited by Randall M. Miller, 145–55. Philadelphia: Balch Institute.

Corner, John. 1991. Meaning, genre and context: The problematics of "public knowledge" in the new audience studies. In *Mass media and society,* edited by James Curran and Michael Gurevitch, 267–84. London: Edward Arnold.

Daniels, Roger. 1966. *Politics of prejudice.* Gloucester, MA: Peter Smith.

Daniels, Roger, and Harry H.L. Kitano. 1970. *American racism.* Englewood Cliffs, NJ: Prentice Hall.

Denzin, Norman K. 1995. *Cinematic society.* London: Sage.

Ding, Loni. 1991. Strategies of an Asian American filmmaker. In *Moving the image: Independent Asian Pacific American media arts,* edited by Russell Leong 46–59. Los Angeles: UCLA Asian American Studies Center.

Dower, John W. 1986. *War without mercy.* New York: Pantheon.

Espiritu, Yen Le. 1992. *Asian American panethnicity.* Philadelphia: Temple University Press.

Fallows, James. 1989. Containing Japan: Japan's runaway economy will harm the rest of the world if some limits aren't set. *The Atlantic Monthly,* May, 40–54.

Fiske, John. 1982. *Introduction to communication studies.* London: Methuen.

———. 1987. *Television culture.* London: Routledge Kegan Paul.

———. 1993. *Power plays, power works.* London: Routledge Kegan Paul.

———. 1994. *Media matters.* Minneapolis: University of Minnesota Press.

Fiske, John, and John Hartley. 1978. *Reading television.* London: Methuen.

Funabiki, Jon. 1992. "Asian invasion" cliches recall wartime propaganda. *EXTRA!,* July/August, 13–14.

Grossberg, Lawrence. 1996a. On postmodernism and articulation: An interview with Stuart Hall. In *Stuart Hall: Critical dialogues in cultural studies,* edited by David Morley and Kuan-Hsing Chen, 131–50. London: Routledge Kegan Paul.

———. 1996b. History, politics and postmodernism. In *Stuart Hall: Critical dialogues in cultural studies,* edited by David Morley and Kuan-Hsing Chen, 151–73. London: Routledge Kegan Paul.

Hall, Stuart. 1981. Notes on Deconstructing "the popular." In *People's history and socialist theory,* edited by Raphael Samuel, 227–40. London: Routledge Kegan Paul.

———. 1986. Gramsci's relevance for the study of race and ethnicity. *Journal of Communication Inquiry* 10 (2): 5–27.

Hamamoto, Darrell Y. 1994. *Monitored peril.* Minneapolis: University of Minnesota Press.

Higashi, Sumiko. 1991. Ethnicity, class, and gender in film: DeMille's *The Cheat.* In *Unspeakable images,* edited by Lester D. Friedman, 112–39. Urbana: University of Illinois Press.

Isaacs, Harold R. 1958. *Scratches on our minds.* New York: John Day.

James, Cathy L. 1991. Soap opera mythology & racial-ethnic social change. Ph.D. dissertation, University of California, San Diego.

Kishi, Yoshio. 1991. Final mix: Unscheduled. In *Moving the image: Independent Asian Pacific American media arts,* edited by Russell Leong, 157–65. Los Angeles: UCLA Asian American Studies Center.

LaGuardia, Robert. 1983. *Soap world.* New York: Arbor House.

Lai, Him Mark, and Philip Choy. 1972. *Outline history of the Chinese in America.* San Francisco: Chinese-American Studies Planning Group.

Lutz, Catherine A., and Jane L. Collins. 1993. *Reading* National Geographic. Chicago: University of Chicago Press.

Marchetti, Gina. 1991. Ethnicity, the cinema, and cultural studies. In *Unspeakable images,* edited by Lester D. Friedman, 277–307. Urbana: University of Illinois Press.

Matsumoto, Valerie. 1989. Nisei women and resettlement during World War II. In *Making waves,* edited by Asian Women United of California, 115–26. Boston: Beacon.

Mazumdar, Sucheta. 1989. General introduction: A woman-centered perspective on Asian American history. In *Making waves,* edited by Asian Women United of California, 1–22. Boston: Beacon.

McChesney, Robert W. 1996. Is there any hope for cultural studies? *Monthly Review* 47 (10): 1–18.

McQuail, Denis. 1983. *Mass communication theory.* London: Sage.

Mellencamp, Patricia. 1990. Prologue. In *Logics of television,* edited by Patricia Mellencamp, 1–13. London: BFI.

Min, Pyong Gap. 1984. From white-collar occupations to small business: Korean immigrants' occupational adjustment. *Sociological Quarterly* 25 (3): 333–52.

Morley, David. 1992. *Television, audiences and cultural studies.* London: Routledge Kegan Paul.

Morley, David, and Kevin Robins. 1995. *Spaces of identity.* London: Routledge Kegan Paul.

Moss, Carlton. 1991. For the Asian American, Afro-American, Native American and Mexican American filmmakers and their friends. In *Moving the image: Independent Asian Pacific American media arts,* edited by Russell Leong, 121–24. Los Angeles: UCLA Asian American Studies Center.

Moy, James S. 1993. *Marginal sights.* Iowa City: University of Iowa Press.

Moynihan, Daniel Patrick. 1965. *The Negro family: The case for national action.*

Murray, Charles A. 1984. *Losing ground: American social policy, 1950–1980.* New York: Basic Books.

Oehling, Richard A. 1980. The yellow menace: Asian images in American film. In *The kaleidoscopic lens,* edited by Randall M. Miller, 182–206. Englewood, NJ: Jerome S. Ozer.

Omi, Michael, and Howard Winant. 1994. *Racial formation in the United States.* New York: Routledge Kegan Paul.

Paik, Irvin. 1971. That oriental feeling. In *Roots,* edited by Amy Tachiki et al., 30–36. Los Angeles: Continental Graphics.

Petersen, William. 1966. Success story: Japanese American style. *The New York Times Magazine,* 9 January.

———. 1971. *Japanese Americans: Oppression and success.* New York: Random House.

Praz, Mario. 1951. *The romantic agony.* Translated by Angus Davidson. London: Oxford University Press.

Rainwater, Lee, and William L. Yancey. 1967. *The Moynihan report and the politics of controversy.* Cambridge: MIT Press.

Robinson, Cedric J. 1993. Race, capitalism, and antidemocracy. In *Reading Rodney King, reading urban uprising,* edited by Robert Gooding-Williams, 73–81. New York: Routledge Kegan Paul.

Said, Edward W. 1978. *Orientalism.* New York: Pantheon.

Sakamoto, Janice. 1991. "Of life and perversity": Wayne Wang speaks. In *Moving the image: Independent Asian Pacific American media arts,* edited by Russell Leong, 71–73. Los Angeles: UCLA Asian American Studies Center.

Schulze, Laurie. 1990. The made-for TV movie. In *Hollywood in the age of television,* edited by Tino Balio, 351–76. Boston: Unwin Hyman.

Sing, Bill, and Karen Seriguchi. 1989. *Asian Pacific Americans.* Los Angeles: National Conference of Christians and Jews.

Success story of one minority group in U.S. 1966. *U.S. News & World Report,* 26 December, 73–76.

Sue, Stanley, and Harry H.L. Kitano. 1973. Stereotypes as a measure of success. *Journal of Social Issues* 29 (2): 83–98.

Tchen, John Kuo Wei. 1984. *Genthe's photographs of San Francisco's Old Chinatown.* New York: Dover.

U.S. Bureau of the Census. 1993. *We the American . . . Asians.* Washington, D.C.: Government Printing Office.

U.S. Commission on Civil Rights. 1992. *Civil rights issues facing Asian Americans in the 1990s.* Washington, D.C.: Government Printing Office.

Waters, Maxine. 1992. Testimony before the Senate Banking Committee. In *Inside the L.A. riots,* edited by Don Hazen, 26–27. New York: Institute for Alternative Journalism.

White, Theodore H. 1985. The danger from Japan. *The New York Times Magazine,* 28 July, 18–23, 31, 37–43, 57–59.

Woll, Allen L., and Randall M. Miller. 1987. *Ethnic and racial images in American film and television.* New York: Garland.

Wong, Eugene Franklin. 1978. On visual racism. New York: Arno.

Yee, James. 1991. Public media: Serving the public interest? In *Moving the image: Independent Asian Pacific American media arts,* edited by Russell Leong, 248–53. Los Angeles: UCLA Asian American Studies Center.

Form at end of book

Issue 7: Is being labeled a "model minority" a blessing or a curse?

Asian Americans in the Public Service:
Success, Diversity, and Discrimination

Pan Suk Kim and Gregory B. Lewis

Pan Suk Kim is an assistant professor in the department of urban studies and public administration at Old Dominion University in Virginia. His research, which focuses on public bureaucracy and organizational change, has appeared in several public administration journals. Gregory B. Lewis is associate professor of public administration at the American University. His research focuses on employment patterns and factors influencing career dynamics in the federal service. He is currently working on a history of federal policy toward gay and lesbian employees and assessing the impact of sexual orientation on federal career success.

Does the experience of Asian Americans in the public support their image as a "model minority"? The image of Asian Americans as a "model minority" conceals both their diversity and the discrimination they face. Despite high average salaries, Asian federal employees earn less and wield less supervisory authority than comparably qualified nonminorities. For the men, the problem is not a "glass ceiling" that keeps highly educated and experienced Asians out of the top levels of the federal bureaucracy; instead, it is Asians without college degrees who receive worse treatment than comparable nonminorities. For the women, the pattern is more complex and more troubling.

Although high levels of schooling and occupational achievement suggest that Asian Americans have succeeded in American society (Taylor and Kim, 1980, p. 2), their image as a "model minority" conceals both their diversity and the discrimination they continue to face. In this article we investigate that diversity and discrimination and analyze the status of Asian Americans in the public sector, particularly the federal civil service. We begin with a general profile of Asian Americans in the United States, then narrow the focus to federal employees. We examine trends in employment and compensation of Asian Americans relative to nonminorities and questions where Asians face a "glass ceiling" that keeps them out of the top levels of the federal bureaucracy, perhaps by channeling them into professional occupations and away from supervisory authority.

General Profile of Asian Americans

The first Asians in the United States in large numbers were the Chinese who arrived as laborers in the mid-nineteenth century. The Chinese Exclusion Act of 1882 banned the immigration of Chinese laborers, but not merchants and students (Daniels, 1988). Shortly thereafter, large numbers of Japanese laborers immigrated and were followed by Filipinos and considerable numbers of Koreans, Indians, and other Asians. Restrictive immigration laws such as the Immigration Acts of 1917 and 1924 produced a 40-year break in Asian immigration starting in the 1920s (Ozawa v. United States, 260 U.S. 178, 1922; Thind v. United States, 261 U.S. 204, 1923). In 1965, when the United States lifted its anti-Asian immigration restrictions (by abandoning the national origins system of immigration), a new wave of immigration from Southeast Asia and other Asian countries began (U.S. Commission on Civil Rights, 1992; Takaki, 1989; U.S. Commission on Civil Rights, 1980).

By 1990, the U.S. Asian and Pacific Islander population was about 7.3 million, of whom 95 percent were Asian (U.S. Bureau of the Census, 1991). Asian Americans (hereinafter terms "Asians" and "Asian Americans" include Pacific Islanders) are the fastest growing minority group in the United States, primarily because of immigration, especially in the aftermath of the Vietnam War. Their numbers grew by 55 percent in the 1960s, by 141 percent in the 1970s, and by 76 percent in the 1980s (O'Hare and Felt, 1991). Asians nearly doubled their share of the U.S. population during the 1980s, increasing from 1.6 percent in 1980 to 2.9 percent of the population in 1990. The U.S. Census Bureau (1992a) projects that by 2020, Asians may comprise 7 percent of the U.S. population.

Although Asians have been classified as a single minority group in official U.S. statistics since 1976 (before that they were included in "other races"), they vary widely in culture, language, and recency of immigration. In 1980, nearly two-thirds of all Asian Americans (compared to only 6 percent of the U.S. population) were foreign-born, and one-quarter of Asian adults had immigrated in the previous five years, with considerable variation by national/ethnic origin (Table 1).* Only about one-fourth of Japanese Americans were foreign born, compared to two-thirds of Chinese, Flipinos, and Indians, and 90 percent or more of Vietnamese, Cambodians, and Laotians.

Asian Americans are falsely perceived to be largely exempt from economic problems such as high unemployment or poverty (O'Hare and Felt, 1991). Their average family income exceeded the U.S. average by about 28 percent in 1985 primarily because Asian American households are generally larger; their per capita income was lower than the U.S. average and that of non-Hispanic whites (U.S. General Accounting Office, 1990). High family incomes also reflect the concentration of Asian Americans in high cost-of-living areas—94 percent lived in metropolitan areas in 1991, compared to only 77 percent of whites (U.S. Bureau of the Census, 1992b).

The high median family income of Asians as a group hides their diversity. According to 1980 census data (the most recent available by national origin), the median family income for Asian Americans was $2,700 higher than that for the U.S. population as a whole (Table 1)* The Japanese median family income exceeded that of white non-Hispanics by 30 percent and the other populous Asian groups (Chinese, Flipinos, and Asian Indians) also fared better than white non-Hispanic families. Southeast Asian Americans (Cambodian, Laotian, and Hmong) had median family incomes far less than the national average in 1979 (U.S. Bureau of the Census, 1983, 1988). These groups were also the most likely to be foreign born, however, and were probably the most recent immigrants, so more recent data might reveal different patterns.

Educational achievements of Asian Americans are high: in 1991, similar percentages of Asians and whites age 25 or older had finished high school (82 percent and 80 percent, respectively), but Asians were almost twice as likely to have finished four years of college (39 percent compared to 22 percent) (Usdansky, 1992; U.S. Bureau of the Census, 1992b, p. 5). According to 1980 census data (the most recent available by national origin), educational attainment was lower in 1980 (only 75 percent instead of 82 percent of Asians had completed high school) and varied substantially by national origin. Over 80 percent of Japanese, Indonesians, Pakistanis, and Asian-Indians had

completed high school, but the majority of Cambodian, Laotian, and Hmong had not.

High educational attainment, however, does not prevent discrimination. Among male high school graduates in 1990, median earnings were only 79 percent as high for Asians as for whites. Asian male college graduates earned only 90 percent as much as white male college graduates. Asian females earned about 95 percent as much as comparable white females, both at high school and college levels of educators (U.S. Bureau of the Census, 1992b).

Asian Americans in the Public Service

Asian American employment has increased rapidly in all sectors of the U.S. economy: by 108 percent in the private sector between 1978 and 1990, by 82 percent in the state and local sector between 1980 and 1990, and by 46 percent in the federal sector between 1982 and 1990 (U.S. Equal Employment Opportunity Commission, 1991). No other group remotely approaches these rates of employment growth. Overall, Asian Americans comprise 2.6 percent of the civilian labor force. Oddly, they are overrepresented in the federal service (3.5 percent) and the U.S. Postal Service (4.3 percent) but underrepresented in the state and local sector (2.0 percent).

This pattern of underrepresentation holds for state, county, city, and town governments (though not for special districts). It also holds for positions in elementary and secondary education, where Asians made up only 0.7 percent of school teachers, principals, and assistant principals in the fiscal year 1990–91 (U.S. Equal Employment Opportunity Commission, 1991). Asian Americans are overrepresented among college and university faculty, however, while non-Asian minorities are underrepresented. In 1990, Asians comprised only 15 of 7,065 elected mayors/chairmen in municipal governments; only 8 of 5,056 chief appointed administrative officers (CAOs)/managers; and only 6 of 1,524 assistant managers or assistant CAOs. Overall, fewer than 1 percent of municipal officials are Asians (International City Management Association, 1991).

In federal white-collar employment, the mean annual salary of white non-Hispanics was $33,500 in 1990. On average, Asian Americans earned 97 percent as much, Hispanics 82 percent, African Americans 76 percent, and American Indians 74 percent as much. In the federal General Schedule and equivalent pay systems, the mean grade of Asian Americans (8.9) approached that of whites (9.3), while those of Hispanics (7.9), African Americans (7.2), and American Indians (7.1) lagged far behind (U.S. Office of Personnel Management, 1990, p. 44). Overall, Asians had a grade distribution much more like that of whites than of other minorities, but at the top levels,

*Table 1 is not included in this publication.

Asians were underrepresented. They held only 73 of 8,136 positions (0.9 percent) in the federal Senior Executive Service (SES), whereas white non-Hispanics held 92.0 percent of SES positions (U.S. Equal Employment Opportunity Commission, 1990).

Asian Americans in the Federal Service

The extensive literature on representation and employment discrimination in the federal bureaucracy has focused mostly on African Americans and women (e.g., Krislov, 1967, 1974; Meier, 1975, 1984; Kranz, 1976; Rosenbloom, 1977; Lewis, 1988; Kellough, 1990). It shows that women and minorities are concentrated at the lower job levels, hold less prestigious occupations in the federal bureaucracy, and earn substantially less than white males with similar qualifications. Only two studies (Taylor and Kim, 1980; Kim, 1993) focus on Asian Americans in the U.S. public service, although a few more general studies mention them in passing. They suggest that the situation for Asian Americans differs somewhat from that for other minority groups. Asian males tend to be concentrated in higher level occupations than other minorities (i.e., a higher proportion of Asians hold managerial and professional occupations) (U.S. Bureau of the Census, 1992b), and their salaries approach those of white males, but they still earn less than comparable white males. Asian females face double discrimination, but they seem to be held back more by their gender than their race.

We investigated several questions in this study. First, previous research (Taylor and Kim, 1980; Lewis, 1988) demonstrated that Asians were in lower grades and earned lower salaries than comparable white non-Hispanics, but the last detailed look at this issue (Taylor and Kim, 1980) used data that are now 15 years old. We examined whether grade gaps between comparable Asians and white non-Hispanics have widened or narrowed over time, and whether they were wider for men or women. We used a standard methodology in the economics of discrimination literature. Using multiple regression analysis, we controlled for a number of factors known to influence career success. We asked whether Asians earned less than white non-Hispanics with the same levels of education, experience, and age who were also comparable in veterans' preference and disability status. Because other factors also affect career success, the persistence of grade gaps after controlling for age, education, federal experience, veterans' preference, and disability status does not prove discrimination, but it does indicate problems that the government needs to investigate. Second, Asians are the group most similar to whites in grade, salary, and education, yet they remain underrepresented at grades 13 and above. Does this suggest that Asians face a glass ceiling, a general pat-

tern of fair treatment until they reach the portals of power, at which point they find themselves restricted from top positions largely reserved for white males? Conversely, the rapid expansion of Asian American employment in the federal service may come largely from the newer immigrants, who may be less assimilated into American society. Is discrimination concentrated on this group? Third, Asians seem to choose or be directed to professional rather than administrative occupations in the federal government. Does this lead them to less supervisory and managerial power than comparably qualified white non-Hispanics?

We analyzed a 1 percent sample of federal personnel records for 1978, 1985, and 1992, taken from the Central Personnel Data File (CPDF). The CPDF, which is maintained by the U.S. Office of Personnel Management (OPM), is the best data set available for studying federal careers, but it classifies all Asians and Pacific Islanders as a single group. This makes it impossible to determine to what extent the expansion of Asian employment represents older, assimilated nationalities or newer immigrant groups. To simplify the analysis and isolate the impact of being Asian rather than nonminority, we eliminated all blacks, Hispanics, and Native Americans from the data set and analyzed men and women separately. Because the patterns for men and women differ so much, we discuss them separately below.

Asian and White Non-Hispanic Men

Consistent with previous studies, white men held a higher mean grade in federal jobs than Asian men in our sample (10.9 vs. 10.4) in 1992 (Table 2), and they were almost twice as likely as Asian men to be supervisors (27 percent vs. 15 percent). Both differences were significant at the .05 level or better, allowing us to conclude that the basic patterns held true for the entire federal work force. The supervisory situation was much worse for Asians in 1992 than in 1978, when Asian men had the edge in the sample (although the difference was not statistically significant). The gap between the mean grades of Asians and whites was slightly wider in 1992 (10.4 vs. 10.9) than in 1978 (9.8 vs. 10.2) but narrower than in 1985 (9.8 vs. 10.5), suggesting no special trend.

Patterns for both education and federal experience suggest possible explanations for the worsening of the situation for Asians. Asians had more education than whites in each year in our sample (though none of the differences were statistically significant), but whites gained steadily in years of service between 1978 and 1992. White men's mean length of federal service rose by 0.9 of a year between 1978 and 1992, but that of Asian men declined by 1.3 years. Because experience influences grade levels,

Table 2 — Characteristics of Asians and White Non-Hispanics in the Federal Service, 1978, 1985, and 1992

Characteristic	Asian Females	White Females	Asian Males	White Males
Mean Grade				
1992	7.7	8.1	10.4	10.9*
1985	6.9	6.7	9.8	10.5**
1978	6.7	5.9*	9.8	10.2
Percentage with Supervisory Authority				
1992	7	12*	15	27**
1985	9	8	15	26***
1978	8	6	23	19
Mean Years of Education				
1992	14.4	13.7***	15.3	15.2
1985	14.1	13.3***	15.2	15.0
1978	13.6	12.9*	15.0	14.6
Mean Years of Federal Service				
1992	10.2	12.4***	11.6	14.1***
1985	9.5	11.0*	11.7	13.8**
1978	12.5	10.4*	12.9	13.2
Sample Size				
1992	203	4,436	209	5,569
1985	123	4,283	163	5,691
1978	76	3,883	110	5,965

Source: U.S. Office of Personnel Management, Central Personnel Data File, 1 percent sample, machine-readable data set.

* Asian-white difference significant at .05 level.

** Asian-white difference significant at .01 level.

*** Asian-white difference significant at .0001 level.

Table 3 — Differences between Expected Grades of Comparable Asians and Whites, 1978, 1985, and 1992

Characteristic	Women	Men
All Employees		
1992	0.6***	0.3*
1985	0.2	0.5**
1978	0.0	0.6**
With High School or Less		
1992	1.6***	1.0*
1985	0.6	1.4*
1978	0.5	1.1
With Some College		
1992	0.1	1.0**
1985	0.0	1.1**
1978	-0.1	1.3**
With Bachelor's Degrees		
1992	0.1	-0.2
1985	0.4	-0.3
1978	-0.2	-0.2
With Graduate Degrees		
1992	1.9**	-0.2
1985	-0.8	0.5
1978	-0.4	0.9

Note: Numbers are unstandardized regression coefficients on the variable White, which was coded 1 for whites and 0 for Asians. All regression models include years of education, years of service, year of service squared, age, age squared, and two dummy variables indicating whether the employee received veterans' preferences or was classified as disabled.

Source: U.S. Office of Personnel Management, Central Personnel Data File, 1 percent sample, machine-readable data set.

* Coefficient significant at .05 level.

** Coefficient significant at .01 level.

*** Coefficient significant at .0001 level.

Asians' relative decline in seniority could have caused their grade levels to slip relative to that of whites. Multiple regression supports that explanation (Table 3). In 1992, Asian men tended to be 0.3 of a grade lower than white men with the same amount of education, federal experience, and age who had the same handicap and veteran status. Earlier gaps between the grades of comparable Asians and white non-Hispanics had been wider (0.6 grade in 1978 and 0.5 grade in 1985). Thus, the gap tentatively attributed to discrimination rather than to the other factors in the model actually narrowed in the 1980s, despite the fact that the gap between the mean grades widened. In short, Asian men are in lower grades than comparable white men (consistent with an argument of discrimination), but the trend is toward greater equality.

Do the well-educated Asians nearing the glass ceiling feel the pinch of discrimination more than their less-educated brethren? For the men, the answer is a clear "no."

In the 1992 sample, Asian men with bachelor's or graduate degrees had slightly higher grades than comparable white men (that is, white men of the same level of education, age, length of service, veteran status, and handicap status), but Asian men who had not gone beyond high school or who had started college but had not finished were one grade behind comparable white men. (The latter differences were statistically significant, while the former were not.) Trends over time suggest improvements in treatment for Asians with some college and, especially, for those with graduate degrees (where whites had a statistically significant 0.9 grade advantage in 1978 but had a statistically insignificant 0.2 grade disadvantage in 1992). Gaps held reasonably constant for those with college diplomas or with high school only.

In 1992, identical percentages of Asian and white men in the sample held professional or administrative positions. Much higher percentages of Asians than whites

(50 and 34, respectively) held professional jobs, however, whereas much higher percentages of whites than Asians (39 and 23, respectively) filled administrative positions. Logit analysis confirms that Asians were more likely to be professionals than whites with the same years of education, federal experience, age, and with the same veteran and handicap status, while the opposite held true for administrative occupations.

Does this division of labor between professional and administrative occupations help explain why Asians attain less supervisory authority? No. Logit analysis confirms that Asian men are less likely to be supervisors than comparable white men. That difference remains virtually unchanged when controlling for occupational category in the logit analysis. Asian men are less likely than comparable white men to be administrators; they are also less likely to be supervisors; but there appears to be little connection between the two facts.

In sum, as a group, well-educated Asian men face little or no discrimination in achieving high grade positions and salaries, but they are less successful in attaining supervisory or managerial authority. Their choice of, or channeling into, professional rather than administrative occupations does not seem to explain this discrepancy. Less-educated Asian men face much greater obstacles to attaining the same grades as comparably educated and experienced white men. Asians without college diplomas were at least one grade behind comparable whites in all three years examined, although the gaps seemed to be narrowing somewhat. Asians' communication skills, especially less fluency in English, might account for some of the grade differences, if this group is made up largely of newer immigrants.

Asian and White Non-Hispanic Women

The story for Asian women is more complex and troubling. As shown in Table 2, the mean grades of Asian and white non-Hispanic women in our sample did not differ significantly in 1992 (7.7 vs. 8.1), although the mean grade of Asians had been significantly higher in 1978 (6.7 vs. 5.9). In 1992, 12 percent of the whites and only 7 percent of the Asians wielded supervisory authority (a difference significant at the .05 level), but in 1978 and 1985, Asian women in the sample had a (statistically insignificant) advantage over white women in supervisory authority.

The relative standing of Asian women in mean grades and supervisory status fell between 1978 and 1992, despite the fact that Asians had significantly more education than whites in all three years and that the education gap did not shrink at all over the period. On the other hand, Asians had two more years of federal service than whites in 1978, but whites had two more years of federal

service than Asians in 1992. The declining relative seniority of Asian women could be partially responsible for their declining status.

Multiple regression, however, shows that is not a complete explanation (Table 3). In 1978, white and Asian women with the same education, seniority, age, veteran status, and handicap status had nearly identical grades. By 1985, Asian women were a statistically insignificant 0.2 of a grade behind, and by 1992, that gap had widened to a statistically significant 0.6 of a grade. Thus, while the unexplained grade gap between Asians and whites was narrowing for the men, it was widening for the women.

Analysis by level of education suggests that the problem is primarily at the high school and graduate school level. White and Asian women with some college or a bachelor's degree held very similar grades in all three years, but Asians with high school only or with graduate degrees were 1.6 or 1.9 grades, respectively, below comparable whites in 1992. Both differences were clearly significant, and much larger than the gaps in 1978 and 1985. These findings provide marginal support for arguments of both the glass ceiling and discrimination against recent immigrants, but the evidence does not fall neatly into a coherent whole.

Similar percentages of Asian and white non-Hispanic women held professional or administrative positions in 1992 (47 percent vs. 45 percent). As with the men, however, the Asians were more likely than the whites to be in professional occupations (24 percent vs. 16 percent) and less likely to be in administrative occupations (23 percent vs. 29 percent). Logit analysis did not reveal significant differences between the two groups in choice of, or channeling into, professional or administrative occupations.

Logit analysis confirmed that in 1992 white women were significantly more likely to wield supervisory authority than comparably educated and experienced Asian women. Again, occupational differences between Asians and whites explained none of that difference in supervisory authority, although finer distinctions among occupations might reveal some effect.

Overall, Asian women fell in status relative to white women between 1978 and 1992. Asians and whites did not differ significantly in grades or supervisory authority in 1978, but by 1992 white women had a clear, statistically significant advantage on both measures. That advantage was apparent among both the most and least educated women (although not those in between), offering little insight into why the situation is worsening for Asian American women. This is especially surprising when the trend has been toward greater equality, not only for Asian men but for all minority and female groups. The most likely explanation is that white women are the group that has gained most from affirmative action in recent years (Lewis, 1988). Asian women have gained on white men, but not as rapidly as white women have, leading Asian women to fall behind relative to white women.

Conclusion

Asian Americans have often been stereotyped as the model minority (Taylor and Kim, 1980; Petersen, 1970), based partly on high family incomes, educational attainment, and occupational status (Hurh and Kim, 1989; Chun, 1980). As favorable as it might seem, this stereotype has damaging consequences. First, it masks the very real social and economic problems faced by many segments of the Asian American population and may result in the needs of poorer, less successful Asian Americans being overlooked. Second, emphasis on the model minority stereotype may also divert public attention from the existence of discrimination, even against more successful Asian Americans, in general employment practices and in discriminatory admissions policies in institutions of higher learning. Finally, the origin of this stereotype may be an effort to discredit other minorities by arguing that if Asian Americans can succeed, so can other minorities. Many Asian Americans resent being used in this fashion (Daniels, 1988; U.S. Commission on Civil Rights, 1992).

The Asian American community actually differs substantially from the myth of uniform success. The rapid expansion of the Asian population in the United States means that this population is changing more rapidly than others and that perceptions need to keep changing to keep up with the reality. The Japanese in this country have typically lived here for generations, speak English as their first language, are highly educated, and earn high salaries. The comparatively new Asian communities are composed primarily of recent immigrants who have learned or are learning English as a second language, have less education, and earn much less. If even the Japanese earn less than comparably educated and experienced whites, then newer Asian immigrants face much greater obstacles to success.

In the federal service, Asian Americans resemble white non-Hispanics in education, salary, grade, and supervisory authority more than they resemble other minority groups. Nonetheless, they continue to earn lower salaries, attain lower grades, and wield less supervisory authority than comparably educated and experienced whites. Among men, grade gaps between comparable Asians and whites have shrunk over the past decade and have essentially disappeared among the college educated. Sizable gaps remain, however, between Asian and white men who have not completed college. Among women, being Asian rather than white appeared to be no particular disadvantage in 1978, but the disadvantage has become apparent over the past 12 years, especially among the least- and best-educated women. These Asian women are still closing the gap relative to white men, but not as rapidly as white women. Being Asian has become a disadvantage for women more so than in the recent past.

The grade and salary gaps between Asians and comparable whites are smaller than for any other minority group, but even this model minority faces discrimination. Policy makers should not ignore this evidence and assume that the battle against discrimination has been won for Asian Americans. A problem remains, especially for those without a college education and probably for recent immigrants, although data currently available do not allow a clear test of the latter hypothesis. Diversity training needs to contain the truth about Asian Americans to battle false stereotypes and lessen discrimination. Recent immigrants from rural areas, where values and customs differ greatly from the predominant U.S. culture, may need special help to familiarize them with modern technology and American common culture. For a diverse group of Asian Americans, long-term recruitment and placement strategies, commitment to higher education funding and transcultural programs that include job-related social services should be developed or expanded to attract them to the public service. Increasing the representation of Asian Americans in higher grade positions is a slow process. The Asian American national contingents still lack the numbers to mount a strong political influence by themselves, so pan-Asian efforts and pan-Asian organizations could promote opportunities for the establishment and expansion of Asian political and economic interests.

References

Chun, Ki Taek 1980. "The Myth of Asian American Success and Its Educational Ramifications" *IRCD Bulletin* 15 (Winter/Spring), pp. 1–12.

Daniels, Roger, 1988. *Asian America: Chinese and Japanese in the United States Since 1850.* Seattle: University of Washington Press.

Hurh, Won M. and Kwang C Kim, 1989. "The Success Image of Asian Americans: Its Validity, and Its Practical and Theoretical Implications." *Ethnic and Racial Studies* 12 (October): 512–538.

International City Management Association, 1991. *The Municipal Year Book.* Washington DC: International City Management Association.

Kellough, J. Edward 1990. "Integration in the Public Workplace: Determinants of Minority and Female Employment in Federal Agencies." *Public Administration Review* 50 (September/October), pp. 557–564.

Kim, Pan Suk, 1993. "Racial Integration in the American Federal Government: With Special Reference to Asian Americans." *Review of Public Personnel Administration* 13 (Winter), pp. 52–66.

Kranz, Harry, 1976. *The Participatory Bureaucracy.* Lexington MA: Lexington.

Krislov, Samuel, 1967. *The Negro in Federal Employment.* Minneapolis: University of Minnesota Press.

Krislov, Samuel, 1974. *Representative Bureaucracy.* Englewood Cliffs, NJ: Prentice-Hall.

Lewis, Gregory B, 1988. "Progress toward Racial and Sexual Equality in the Federal Civil Service." *Public Administration Review* 50 (March/April) pp. 220–227.

Meier, Kenneth J., 1975. "Representative Bureaucracy: An Empirical Analysis." *"American Political Science Review* 69 (June), pp. 526–542.

———, 1984. "Teachers, Students and Discrimination: The Policy Impact of Black Representation." *Journal of Politics* 46 (February), pp. 252–263.

O'Hare, William P., and Judy C. Felt, 1991. *Asian Americans: America's Fastest Growing Minority Group.* Washington, DC: Population Reference Bureau.

Petersen, William, 1970. "Success Story, Japanese American Style." In *Minority Responses,* edited by Minako Kurokawa, pp. 169–178. New York Random House.

Rosenbloom, David H., 1977. *Federal Equal Employment Opportunity.* New York: Praeger.

Taylor, Patricia A., and Sung-Soon Kim, 1980. "Asian-Americans in the Federal Civil Service in 1977." *California Sociologist* 3 (Winter), pp. l–16.

Takaki, Ronald 1989. *Strangers from a Different Shore: A History of Asian Americans.* Boston: Little Brown.

U.S. Bureau of the Census, 1983, *General Social Economic Characteristics of U.S. Summary 1980 Census.* Washington, DC: U.S. Government Printing Office.

———, 1988. *We, the Asian and Pacific Islander Americans.* Washington, DC: U.S. Government Printing Office.

———, 1991. *Statistical Abstract of the United States 1990.* Washington, DC: U.S. Government Printing Office.

———, 1992a. *Current Population Reports: Population Projections of the United States, by Age, Sex, Race, and Hispanic Origin, 1992 to 2050.* Washington, DC: U.S. Government Printing Office.

———, 1992b. *Current Population Reports: The Asian and Pacific Islander Population in the United States, March 1991 and 1990.* Washington, DC: U.S. Government Printing Office.

U.S. Commission on Civil Rights, 1980. *Success of Asian Americans. Fact or Fiction?* Washington, DC: U.S. Government Printing Office.

———, 1992. *Civil Rights Facing Asian Americans in the 1990s.* Washington, DC: US. Government Printing Office.

Usdansky, Margaret L, 1992. "Report Spotlights Asian Diversity," *USA Today* (September 18), p. A10.

U.S. Department of Commerce, 1991. "Census Bureau Release 1990 Census Counts on Special Racial Groups." *U.S. Department Commerce News,* June 12).

U.S. Equal Employment Opportunity Commission, 1990. *Annual Report on the Employment of Minorities, Women and Handicapped Individuals in the Federal Government.* Washington, DC: U.S. Government Printing Office.

———, 1991. *Indicators of Equal Employment Opportunity: A Status and Trends.* Washington, DC: U.S. Government Printing Office.

U.S. General Accounting Office, 1990. *Asian Americans: A Status Report,* Washington, DC: U.S. General Accounting Office.

U.S. Office of Personnel Management, 1990. *Affirmative Employment Statistics.* Washington, DC: U.S. Office of Personnel Management.

Form at end of book

WiseGuide Wrap-Up

Underrepresented minorities are usually identified as those who need affirmative action assistance to attain the American Dream. Regardless of their actual percentage in the population, Asians are seen as not needing that assistance. It seems that they have been able to overcome great odds and succeed on their own. Have they? Or have they benefited from American anti-Communist propaganda, which chose to view them as allies or refugees? Are their advances due to rapid assimilation of U.S. cultural ideals or a congruence of values and practices? The readings in this section probe the stereotypes of Asians and their success.

Stereotypes of Asians remain relatively unchanged in the media, despite changes within the culturally diverse grouping and differences in generations. There seems to be a reluctance to recognize Asians as capable of leadership in organizations where they work with non-Asians, which does not reflect their abilities in their own businesses and community groups. Asians are still used as scapegoats in times of economic or political crisis. Stereotypes, scapegoating, and similar practices all obscure the reality of the situation, making real solutions to problems impossible. Can immigrants ever really be members of American society if they are not of European origin? Can we go beyond who is acting or speaking and get to the core of issues and problems?

R.E.A.L. Sites

This list provides a print preview of typical **Coursewise** R.E.A.L. sites. (There are over 100 such sites at the **Courselinks**™ site.) The danger in printing URLs is that web sites can change overnight. As we went to press, these sites were functional using the URLs provided. If you come across one that isn't, please let us know via email to: webmaster@coursewise.com. Use your Passport to access the most current list of R.E.A.L. sites at the **Courselinks** site.

Site name: Review of Data on Asian Americans

URL: http://www.pafb.af.mil/deomi/asir.htm

Why is it R.E.A.L.? This site, sponsored by the Coalition for Asian American Children and Families, provides information on the history of Asian immigration, the model minority myth, and the organization's accomplishments and projects. It also provides links to articles by different writers.

Key terms: model minority, Asian American history, media

Site name: Chinese American Identity

URL: http://www.owlnet.rice.edu/ ~jenlin/HIST310/main.html

Why is it R.E.A.L.? This web site is a result of a project at Rice University on Chinese identity. It provides links to materials on Chinese identity as seen by others and as seen by Chinese. It also provides some images of Chinese in America and offers a view of the difficulty of creating a sense of self in minority groups.

Key terms: stereotypes, media, prejudice

section 8 | Is Intelligence Genetically Determined?

Take a Closer Look

1. Is inequality inevitable?

2. What genetic factors determine your intelligence? Are they affected by nutrition? Hormones? Illness?

3. Can you take chemicals to alter your intelligence? Should you?

4. If your I.Q. score determined your social, educational, and occupational opportunities, how would that change your life?

5. How are race and ethnicity determined? Should we use detailed charts of ethnic and genetic heritage to make decisions about individuals?

WiseGuide Intro Is intelligence best expressed by a single number and best measured by a single test that explores cognitive ability? Or is intelligence composed of a number of factors and skills that change over time as the individual matures and best expressed by a series of tests not limited to cognitive ability? Is I.Q. influenced by culture and local environments, or is it primarily genetic?

While the intelligence debate is centered in science, the answers have an impact on governmental and educational policies. Leaders are looking for an easy way to make complex decisions, and an I.Q. score is presented as a way to handle complex social problems, such as educational and occupational opportunity.

The way in which we understand and measure intelligence affects the kind of education we provide. It affects the way a child is provided with opportunities or tracked into specific occupational choices. Often, unspoken social issues of inequality and social mobility underlie decisions made in these areas. Class and ethnicity are major factors present in the consideration of intelligence. If I.Q. is immutable and determined early in life, then money spent on programs to combat poverty and cultural limitations is wasted. If intelligence is dynamic, then programs to promote varied types of educational experiences are an important allocation of resources.

Research regarding I.Q. has generated controversy. Reading 17 gives a brief history of past research on intelligence and the stress on environment and heredity as sources for intelligence. It also indicates the way this research has had an impact on policy decisions. The author encourages beneficial use of I.Q. testing to identify and diagnose mental deficiencies and to ensure that educational opportunities are allocated on the basis of ability rather than family connections.

In the 1994 book *The Bell Curve*, Charles Murray and Richard Herrnstein raise some of the issues around the study of intelligence from the past. Instead of class differences, they use racial groupings to compare, and they use a single measure of intelligence, which they see as being determined at an early age. Numerous critics of *The Bell Curve* argue the validity of the research. These critics raise important research questions concerning the reliability of the information that Murray and Herrnstein collected.

In Reading 18, Reuven Feuerstein and Alex Kozulin point out some important areas to be explored in understanding intelligence. The first point they make is that *The Bell Curve* study by Charles Murray and Richard Herrnstein brings to our attention the importance of cognition in human performance and social achievement. It also makes us consider that, although the modern world is becoming more homogeneous in basic everyday activities, human diversity is observed in the very different cognitive operations, abilities, and styles that people exhibit. Feuerstein and Kozulin also raise an important question about the nature of intelligence. Is it a thing that can be measured, or is it a process?

In Reading 19, however, Charles Murray and Richard Herrnstein argue that "the best and indeed the only answer to the problem of group differences is an energetic and uncompromising recommitment to individualism."

Issue 8: Is intelligence genetically determined?

Measuring Intelligence:
Bell, Book, and Scandal

For more than a century intelligence testing has been a field rich in disputed evidence and questionable conclusions. *"The Bell Curve,"* **by Charles Murray and Richard Herrnstein, has ensured it will remain so.**

There is plenty of room for debate about which was the most amusing book of 1994, or which the best written. But nobody can seriously quibble about which was the most controversial. "*The Bell Curve: Intelligence and Class Structure in America Life,*" an 845-page tome by Charles Murray and Richard Hermstein, (New York: The Free Press, 1994), has reignited a debate that is likely to rage on for years yet, consuming reputations and research grants as it goes

The Bell Curve is an ambitious attempt to resuscitate I.Q. ("intelligence quotient") testing, one of the most controversial ideas in recent intellectual history; and to use that idea to explain some of the more unpalatable features of modern America. Mr. Murray, a sociologist, and Hermstein, a psychologist who died shortly before the book's publication, argue that individuals differ substantially in their "cognitive abilities"; that these differences are inherited as much as acquired; and that intelligence is distributed in the population along a normal distribution curve—the bell curve of the book's title—with a few geniuses at the top, a mass of ordinary Joes in the middle and a minority of dullards at the bottom (see chart, next page).[*]

Then, into this relatively innocuous cocktail, Messrs, Murray and Herrnstein mix two explosive arguments. The first is that different races do not perform equally in the I.Q.-stakes—that, in America, Asians score, on average, slightly above the norm, and blacks, on average, substantially below it. The second is that America is calcifying into impermeable castes. The bright are inter-marrying, spawning bright offspring and bagging well-paid jobs; and the dull are doomed to teenage pregnancy, welfare dependency, drugs and crime.

For the past three months it has been almost impossible to pick up an American newspaper or tune into an

[*]Chart is not included in this publication.

American television station without learning more about Mr. Murray's views. Dozens of academics are hard at work rebutting (they would say refuting) his arguments. Thanks to the controversy, *The Bell Curve* has sold more than a quarter of a million copies.

Undoubtedly, Mr. Murray has been lucky in his timing. Left-wingers point out that Americans have seldom been so disillusioned with welfare policy: the voters are turning not just to Republicans, but to Republicans who are arguing seriously about the merits of state orphanages and of compulsory adoption. Mr. Murray's arguments answer to a feeling that social policies may have failed not because they were incompetently designed or inadequately funded, but because they are incompatible with certain "facts" of human nature.

Right-wingers retort that it is liberals' addiction to "affirmative action" that has supplied Mr. Murray with much of his material. Affirmative action has institutionalised the idea that different ethnic groups have different cognitive abilities: "race norming", now *de rigueur* in academia, means that a black can perform significantly less well than, say, an Asian, and still beat him into a university. It has also resulted in America's having a compilation of statistics about race unequalled outside South Africa.

Differently Wired

The regularity with which discussion of I.Q. testing turns into an argument that ethnic groups differ in their innate abilities, with blacks at the bottom of the cognitive pile, has done more than anything else to make theorists and practitioners of I.Q. testing into figures of academic notoriety reviled everywhere from Haight-Ashbury to Holland Park. The early 1970s saw a furious argument about "Jensenism", named after Arthur Jensen, a psychologist at the University of California, Berkeley, who published an article arguing, among other things, that the average black had a lower I.Q. than the average white. William Shockley, also known as a co-inventor of the transistor, drew the anti-Jensenists' fire by saying that blacks' and whites' brains were "differently wired."

But, even if it could be extricated from arguments about ethnic differences, I.Q. testing would remain controversial. One reason is that few people like the idea that inequality might be inevitable, the result of natural laws rather than particular circumstances (and the more so, perhaps, when economic inequalities seem likely to widen as labour markets put an ever-higher premium on intelligence). The implication is that egalitarian policies are self-defeating: the more inherited prejudices are broken down, the more society resolves into intellectual castes.

A second reason for controversy is that I.Q. testers are all too prone to the fatal conceit of thinking that their discipline equips them to know what is best for their fellow men. To most parents the idea that a man with a book of tests and a clipboard can define what is best for their children is an intolerable presumption (who can know a child as well as its parents?) and an insupportable invasion of liberty (surely people should be free to choose the best school for their children?). Nor has the I.Q. testers' image been helped by their having often been asked—as in England in the days of the 11-plus school entry examination—to help make already contentious decisions.

A third reason I.Q. testers excite concern is that they seem to make a fetish of intelligence. Many people feel instinctively that intelligence is only one of the qualities that make for success in life—that looks, luck and charm also play their part; they also like to feel that intelligence is less important than what they call "character," which can turn even a dull person into a useful citizen.

But the thing which, in the end, really frightens people about I.Q. testing is its message of genetic Calvinism: that I.Q. both determines one's destiny, and is dictated by one's genes. This flies in the face of the liberal notion that we are each responsible for fashioning our own fate. It also upsets two beliefs held particularly firmly in America: that anybody can win out, provided they have "the right stuff"; and that everybody should be given as many educational chances as possible, rather than sorted out and classified at the earliest possible opportunity. (Thus *Forrest Gump*, a film that appeared shortly before publication of *The Bell Curve*, enjoyed great popularity and critical acclaim for its portrayal of a well-meaning simpleton who won all America's glittering prizes.)

Hunting Down Sir Humphrey

How, then, did so widely distrusted a discipline originate? To answer that question means a trip to a rather unexpected place, the Whitehall of the mid-19th century. Traditionally, jobs in the British civil service had been handed out on the basis of family connections, in a sort of affirmative-action programme for upper-class twits. But as

Britain developed a world-beating economy and a world-spanning empire, reformers argued that preferment should go to the most intelligent candidates, their identity to be discovered by competitive examinations.

This innovation proved so successful that policy-makers applied the same principle to the universities and schools. Their aim was to construct an educational system capable of discovering real ability wherever it occurred, and of matching that ability with the appropriate opportunities.

Ironically, it was children at the other end of the ability scale who inspired the first I.Q. tests as such. The introduction of compulsory schooling for the masses confronted teachers with the full variety of human abilities, and obliged them to distinguish between the lazy and the congenitally dull. Most investigators contented themselves with measuring children's heads. But in 1905 Alfred Binet, a French psychologist, came up with the idea of assigning an age level to a variety of simple intellectual operations, determined by the earliest age at which the average child could perform them, and ranking children both against their peers and against a normal development curve. Binet's idea was refined soon afterwards by introducing the arithmetical device of dividing mental age by chronological age and multiplying by 100.

Two English psychologists turned intelligence testing into a sort of scientific movement. The first was Francis Galton, a rich and well connected man (Charles Darwin was a cousin) who devoted his life to the nascent sciences of statistics and genetics. His motto was "wherever you can, count," and he measured everything from the distended buttocks of Hottentot women (with a theodolite) to the distribution of "pulchritude" in the British Isles. He compiled family trees of everybody from Cambridge wranglers to West Country wrestlers to prove his belief that "characteristics cling to families" and "ability goes by descent."

Combining his two passions, Galton speculated that abilities in the British population were distributed along a "bell curve," with the upper classes at the top and an underclass at the bottom. He was so worried that those at the bottom of the curve were outbreeding those at the top that he spent most of his fortune bankrolling another "science," eugenics.

Galton's mission was completed by a retired soldier, Charles Spearman. Deciding that the results of certain tests correlated with each other to a remarkable degree, Spearman concluded, in a seminal article published in 1904, that all mental abilities were manifestations of a single general ability, which he called "g": all individuals inherited a fixed quantity of mental energy, which infused every intellectual act they performed and determined what they were capable of in life. The right tests could capture how much "g" each individual possessed and express it as a single number.

Intelligence testing went on to enjoy decades of growing popularity. The American army used it on recruits in the first world war, employing more than 300 psychologists, and other armies followed. Schools used tests to help in streaming or selecting their pupils. Bureaucrats and businessmen used them to identify talented recruits. Tests were thought indispensable for discovering and diagnosing learning problems.

Only in the 1960s did opinion turn sharply against the I.Q. testers. Educationalists accused them of allowing an obsession with classification to blind them to the full range of human abilities. Sociologists (and sociologically minded psychologists) argued that intellectual differences owed more to social circumstances than to genes. In Britain, disillusionment with I.Q. tests hastened the introduction of comprehensive schools. In the United States, schools abandoned the use of I.Q. tests to classify children. In 1978 a district court in San Francisco even ruled unconstitutional the use of I.Q. tests to place children in classes for the backward if the use of such tests meant that the classes contained a "grossly disproportionate" number of black children.

Dropping Clangers

The Bell Curve thus represents an attempt to rehabilitate an idea that had fallen into two or three decades of disfavour. But have Messrs. Murray and Herrnstein got their science right?

So far, the debate on *The Bell Curve* has been billed as if it were psychometrists (mind-measurers) versus the rest. In fact, I.Q. testers divide among themselves on all sorts of key issues, from the structure of the mind to the reliability of tests; moreover, Messrs. Murray and Herrnstein occupy a rather eccentric position among psychometrists. They are unabashed supporters of Charles Spearman, believing that intelligence is a unitary quality expressible in a single number, such that people who are good at one thing will also be good at others. Yet this is one of the most hotly disputed topics within psychometry. A British pioneer, Godfrey Thomson, argued that the correlations which so excited Spearman might be explained by the laws of chance. He concluded that the mind had no fixed structure and that intelligence tests gave little more than a hint of a person's mental powers.

Among other psychologists, L.L. Thurstone argued for the existence of dozens of different types of mental abilities, such as mathematical, verbal and visio-spatial abilities. Liam Hudson has found I.Q. tests to reward a particular type of "convergent" thinker. Howard Gardner thinks there are many sorts of "intelligence."

Synaptitude

I.Q. testers have clashed and go on clashing over less arcane issues too. They endorse widely different estimates of the hereditability of I.Q. ranging from 40% to 80%. They squabble about the accuracy of I.Q. tests: some argue that such tests are nothing more than estimates that need to be repeated frequently and to be supplemented by personal interviews (and indeed, observably, children can learn, or be taught, to raise their I.Q. scores). Some of the most illustrious psychometrists are even starting to argue that I.Q. tests should be replaced by physical tests to measure the speed of reactions, the production of glucose in the brain, the speed of neural transmission and even the size of the brain.

Psychometrists disagree, too, about the validity of generalising about groups in the way that Murray and Hermstein do. It is widely accepted that differences within groups may reflect hereditary factors; but differences between groups are susceptible to other explanations (just as people in one place may be taller on average than people in another place, for example, but for reasons of nutrition, not genetics).

Oddly, Messers. Murray and Herrnstein have chosen to dispute (or ignore) one of the few arguments on which other psychometrists agree: that children do not necessarily have the same I.Q. as their parents. *The Bell Curve* argues that society is fixing itself into impermeable castes. But psychometry is a theory of social mobility, not social stasis. It tries to explain why bright people often have dull children and dull people often have bright children. Sex ensures that genes are re-sorted in each generation.

In fact, it is hereditarianism's sworn enemy, environmentalism, which is really a theory of social stasis: if the rich and educated can pass on their advantages to their children undisturbed by the dance of the chromosomes, then social mobility will always be something of a freak. Messers. Murray and Herrnstein are, perhaps, environmentalists in hereditarian clothing.

Politically, *The Bell Curve* has reinforced the impression that I.Q. testers are anti-welfare conservatives. Some are. But the I.Q. tests have been invoked in defence of a wide variety of political positions, respectable and otherwise. American psychologists have popped up to support abominations such as compulsory sterilisation and ethnically sensitive immigration laws. Others have been socialists, keen on upward mobility, child-centred education and generous provision for the backward. In Britain between the wars Labour Party intellectuals such as R.H.

Tawney argued for IQ testing as a way to ensure educational opportunities were allocated on the basis of innate ability rather than family connections; psychologists such as Cyril Burt have been passionate supporters of nursery-school education and better treatment of backward children. (The fusty T.S. Eliot, on the other hand, thought I.Q. tests were a plot to promote social mobility and debase education. A particularly crusty Cambridge don, Edward Welbourne, denounced them as "devices invented by Jews for the advancement of Jews.")

Too Clever by Half

What makes the I.Q. debate particularly frustrating is that both sides have long been addicted to exaggeration. The earliest I.Q. testers were guilty of hubris when they argued that they had invented an infallible technique for measuring mental abilities and distributing educational and occupational opportunities. As if that was not bad enough, they exacerbated their error by claiming that their method contributed to economic efficiency (by making the best use of human resources) and personal happiness (by ensuring that people were given jobs suited to their abilities).

The enemies of I.Q. testing were also guilty of terrible exaggeration when they accused testers of shoring up capitalism, perpetuating inequality, and justifying sexism, racism, even fascism. In fact, the I.Q. testers were never anywhere near as influential as they, or their opponents, imagined.

I.Q. theory played no part in persuading the American Congress to pass the Immigration Restriction Act of 1924; British grammar schools used I.Q. tests only to supplement other, more traditional selection procedures, such as scholastic examinations and interviews; Hitler and Mussolini had no time for I.Q. tests that were liable to contradict their own racial prejudices.

What the I.Q. debate needs now is a dash of cold water. Opponents of testing should forget their overheated rhetoric about legitimising capitalism and racism. Supporters should fold up their more grandiose blueprints for building the meritocracy, and limit themselves to helping with practical problems. They should point out that I.Q. tests are useful ways of identifying and diagnosing mental deficiency, just so long as they are administered along with other diagnostic tools by a trained psychologist. They should add that I.Q tests can also be useful in helping to allocate places in oversubscribed schools; that, indeed, they are less class-biased than scholastic texts (which favour the well-taught) or personal interviews (which favour the well-brought up). It is a pity that Charles Murray and Richard Herrnstein have chosen to douse the debate not with cold water but with petrol.

Form at end of book

Issue 8: Is intelligence genetically determined?

"The Bell Curve":
Getting the Facts Straight

Reuven Feuerstein and Alex Kozulin

Reuven Feuerstein is Director and Professor, and Alex Kozulin is Director of Research and Development, The International Center for the Enhancement of Learning Potential, P.O. Box 7755, Jerusalem 91077, Israel.

Abstract

The bestselling book The Bell Curve *by Richard Herrnstein and Charles Murray offers misleading claims about human intelligence. The book maintains, for instance, that intelligence quotient (I.Q.) tests are reliable measurements of human intelligence, thus negating the strides that have been made in the fields of cognitive and developmental psychology. It also contends that educational intervention programs are not effective as they do not have any effect on the I.Q. level.*

This best-seller puts a lot of faith in conventional notions of I.Q. and I.Q. tests, and little faith in the human propensity for intellectual growth and cognitive change.

In a slightly patronizing, but otherwise friendly and informal tone, Charles Murray and the late Richard Herrnstein have presented the public with an 850-page elaboration of a position that we paraphrase as follows:

- As conscientious scientists we simply cannot hide from the public the following bitter truth: All that politicians, journalists, educators, and others have told you about the social benefits of education and self-development is pure ideology devoid of empirical foundation. In reality, our achievements are directly dependent on the level of our intelligence, as measured by I.Q. tests, and largely predetermined genetically.

- Those with a higher I.Q. will move faster up the social ladder, while those with a lower I.Q. will slide down. This dynamic is an objective fact of nature.

- There is little sense in pouring our tax dollars into remedial educational or social rehabilitation programs, because their influence on I.Q. levels is very limited.

- However, you, dear readers, should not worry, because the very fact that you are reading this $40 volume is a clear sign of your high I.Q. and thus a guarantee of your social success (statistically speaking).

There is nothing particularly new in this position. It largely repeats the notorious thesis of educational psychologist Arthur Jensen: Intelligence is distributed unequally among races and is resistant to change. This viewpoint led Jensen to suggest curtailing all intervention programs, such as Head Start, and instead using simple repetitive exercises, orienting these children's education to what he referred to as Level I intelligence (Jensen and Inouye 1980).

Such conclusions so clearly fly in the face of scientific data and common sense that one might dismiss *The Bell Curve* as having no value whatsoever. And yet, the book does. It presents ideas and information that are both relevant and interesting, although some of its main claims are extremely misleading.

The Ring of Truth

First, a look at three aspects of the book that make it worth reading.

1. A general emphasis on cognition as an important factor in human performance and social achievement. All too often, human performance is presented either as a purely behavioral phenomenon or as a product of emotional and affective conditions and unconscious motives. *The Bell Curve* appropriately points to cognition and intelligence as a major force mediating human behavior and social conditions. Unfortunately, this strong emphasis on cognition leads to some faulty conclusions. This happens because the authors chose to reduce intelligence to the IQ score, which they consider immutable, stable, and resistant to change, whether by education, development, or rehabilitation.

2. The notion of human diversity. The modern world is becoming homogeneous in the more basic everyday activities. Yet people, fortunately, continue to exhibit very different cognitive operations, abilities, and styles. It is one thing to acknowledge that certain aspects of cognitive functioning are genetically linked, and quite another to claim that these characteristics are unalterable. Further, certain ethnic, cultural, and racial groups may display characteristic patterns of cognitive functions that are statistically distinguishable. But this does not imply that these groups can be plotted in a linear way from less intelligent to more intelligent, as argued in *The Bell Curve*.

Height is one aspect of human diversity that is transmitted genetically from generation to generation. And certain ethnic groups, such as the Japanese, are statistically shorter than other groups, such as the Dutch. At the same time, height is also a changeable characteristic, as evidenced by the rapid increase in the height of the Japanese in the second half of the twentieth century. Chromosomes do not have the last word, even in the case of highly heritable characteristics.

3. A very interesting, though somewhat frightening, portrait of contemporary American society. *The Bell Curve* pictures this society as being capable of reducing the most complex phenomenon—human intelligence—to arithmetic and word memory tasks, then building a whole industry of evaluation, selection, labeling, and promotion on this primitive foundation.

This is a society in which 5 percent of those with higher than average intelligence, together with 6 percent of those born to rich and very rich parents, are destined to live below the poverty line. Apparently neither your I.Q. nor the social status of your parents can guarantee you decent living standards in the United States.

Intelligence As a Thing

Most important among *The Bell Curve's* misleading claims is the contention that intelligence is a measurable substance and the I.Q. test is a reliable measuring device. This claim sets us back more than 50 years, ignoring all the achievements of cognitive and developmental psychology in the last half of the twentieth century. The fact that some manifestations of intelligence can be measured does not imply that intelligence itself is a stable substance. To present intelligence in this reified way—as a concrete, stable quantity—is a scientific anachronism.

Intelligence is a propensity, a tendency, or the power of the organism to change itself to adapt to a new situation. It is multidimensional and modifiable, the very qualities that have enabled humans to adapt so effectively to a multitude of environments. Only if one accepts the reified version of intelligence can one believe in its deterministic predictability.

The realization of intellectual power is dependent on a great variety of biological, social, and cultural variables. It may vary from individual to individual, depending on factors such as genetic endowment; prenatal, perinatal, and postnatal development; and so on. It is important to understand that we never observe this intelligence as a power directly, only through its various realizations.

Infallibility of I.Q. Tests

Human intelligence is so extraordinarily complex that we have been forced to expand our research approaches rather than reduce them. Unfortunately, the authors of The Bell Curve chose an extremely reductionist position, equating the assessment of intelligence with the I.Q. measurement.

Hernnstein and Murray's far-reaching conclusions are based on the following: First, intelligence is equated with test performance. Then the whole range of possible tests is reduced to a few knowledge-based tasks performed in a limited time period. Finally, the data obtained are interpreted far beyond their actual empirical base.

The authors rely on data from the National Longitudinal Survey of Youth, which is based on a large sample of young people aged 14–22 when the study began in 1979. As a measure of I.Q., the researchers used four subtests of the Armed Forces Qualification Test: word knowledge, paragraph comprehension, arithmetic reasoning, and mathematical knowledge.

There is little doubt that we can measure the number of words recognized or mathematical operations accurately performed, but by doing so, are we measuring intelligence? How is it possible to claim that I.Q. measured in this way is unaffected by education? In reality, the results of I.Q. testing are so compounded and contaminated by various processes that is impossible to distinguish which part reflects intelligence as a power and which reflects various irrelevant conditions. In *The Bell Curve*, excessive reliance on statistical correlations without proper analysis of the data creates a statistical mirage, presented to readers as fact.

There are sufficient data to suggest that I.Q. test scores reflect not only—even probably not so much—the central thinking capacities as the individual's ability to decode test items and respond in an expected way. The elaboration phase of cognition is traditionally associated with intelligence as such. Yet many low I.Q. scores result from specific problems during the perception (input) phase or response (output) phase. Slow information processing may also be interpreted as a failure of intelligence. Some studies of twins indicate that speed of information processing is a highly heritable characteristic. Thus, although results of tests taken under tight time constraints may appear to indicate a similar I.Q., they may in fact merely reflect a similar speed of processing.

Culture and Intelligence

More than half a century ago, Lev Vygotsky identified two major lines in the development of human intelligence: natural and cultural. In the course of a child's development, the natural forms of intelligence—including perceptual abilities, memory, attention, and problem solving—are structurally changed by the cultural tools society associates with literacy and education (Kozulin 1990).

Feuerstein's theory of mediated learning experience (1990) attributes people's differing capacities for modifiability to the unequal amount and type of mediated learning they have experienced. These capacities (or levels) are, however, dynamic; remediation in mediated learning can change the extent to which someone's cognitive level can be modified.

The paradox of I.Q. testing is that while it is strongly culturally embedded—problem solving depends on certain symbolic and representational systems—its results are interpreted in terms of natural intelligence. Testing situations are also culturally constructed: test items, modalities of presentation and response, time limitations—all these may affect test results in a variety of ways. Yet, instead of interpreting the results as an outcome of interaction between the individual and the socially constructed situation, the authors interpret them in terms of the individual's natural intellectual ability.

Persistence of I.Q.

Much of *The Bell Curve's* emphasis is on the stability of I.Q. scores and the deterministic effect on educational, professional, and social success or failure. To a large extent, however, repetition enters when the same type of tests are used at school, in college entrance exams, and in professional selection. It is little wonder that a successful test taker is rewarded each step of the way.

What is not discussed is that I.Q. score labeling becomes a self-fulfilling prophecy. If from an early age the child is told that his or her intelligence should be low because his or her I.Q. scores are low, how can one expect the child and parents to actively work toward higher achievements?

One particularly damaging thesis is the claim that one's intellectual level does not change after the age of 10 (p. 130). It is exactly at this age that children, after mastering such basic skills as reading, writing, and arithmetic, start acquiring the higher-order conceptual reasoning necessary for successful study of sciences and humanities.

These higher forms of reasoning do not appear spontaneously, but must be taught. If children are denied exposure to this conceptual reasoning because of their alleged low intelligence, they obviously will be at a disadvantage later in their schooling.

The claim that educational, mediational, and interventional programs cannot substantially change students' intellectual levels is a prime recipe for decline in education standards. Any attempt to urge teachers and students to raise standards will now be rejected on the grounds that they are unsuitable for average or low I.Q. students.

Dynamic Cognitive Assessment

We do not mean to suggest that we oppose any attempt to assess intellectual functioning. On the contrary, cognitive assessment can become an important source of information for educational and social intervention. To be useful, however, such assessment should conform to certain guidelines.

The following criteria are embodied in the Learning Potential Assessment Device (Feuerstein 1979), and a number of other dynamic cognitive assessment methods.

1. Evaluate rather than measure. Intelligence is not a "thing" to be measured, but a process to be evaluated. Thus assessment should take into consideration that intelligence is modifiable, complex, and multidimensional.

2. Attempt to reveal the propensity for cognitive change. Do not simply register the current level of performance.

3. Plan learning interaction based on mediated learning experience. Such a dynamic assessment, which generates samples of cognitive change, provides better insight into the student's cognitive potential than unaided performance registered by the static test.

4. Focus on the process rather than the product of cognitive change. Assess those cognitive processes and states that are responsible for performance and can be modified, rather than those that are rigid or inflexible. Note their relative significance and choose ways to modify them.

5. Aim to suggest the proper form of psychoeducational intervention. Do not classify or label.

The use of the Learning Potential Assessment Device with various groups of people has demonstrated the plasticity of human intelligence—far beyond that measured by I.Q. For example, low I.Q. individuals were quite capable of learning and applying the principles of analogical reasoning that are embodied in the nonverbal tasks of the

Raven Standard Progressive Matrices Test. This directly contradicted the claim of many I.Q. proponents—including Raven himself—that individuals classified as educable mentally retarded are incapable of mastering analogical reasoning (Raven 1965).

It was also shown that the performance of culturally different adults, who in preschool revealed a subnormal I.Q. (as measured by Raven Matrices and the Wechsler Intelligence Scale for Children), improved in a statistically significant way after exposure to the mediated learning experience and Instrumental Enrichment (Feuerstein 1980). So much for the alleged stability of intelligence test performance.

Socially disadvantaged adolescents, who performed at a subnormal level as measured by the Analogies Test, improved by a full standard deviation as a result of short-term cognitive training. Three months later their performance was indistinguishable from that of middle-class students.

Contrary to *The Bell Curve's* pessimistic prognosis, we have every reason to be optimistic. Human cognition is highly amenable to change. One should simply stop measuring what is not measurable, and start improving what can be improved.

References

Feuerstein, R. (1979). *The Dynamic Assessment of Retarded Performer: Learning Potential Assessment Device.* Baltimore: University Park Press.

Feuerstein, R. (1980). *Instrument Enrichment.* Baltimore: University Park Press.

Feuerstein, R. (1990). "The Theory of Structural Cognitive Modifiability." in *Learning and Thinking Styles,* edited by B. Presseisen. Washington, D.C.: National Education Association.

Jensen, A.R., and A.R. Inouye. (1980). "Level I and Level II Abilities in Asian, White, and Black Children." *Intelligence* 4:41–49.

Kaniel, S., D. Tzuriel, R. Feuerstein, N. Ben-Shachar, and T. Eitan. (1991). "Dynamic Assessment: Learning and Transfer Abilities of Ethiopian Immigrants in Israel." In *Mediated Learning, Experience,* edited by R. Feuerstein, P. Klein, and A. Tannenbaum. London: Freund.

Kozulin, A. (1990). *Vygotsky's Psychology.* Cambridge, Mass.: Harvard University Press.

Raven, J.C. (1965). *Guide to Using the Colored Progressive Matrices.* London: H.K. Lewis.

Form at end of book

Issue 8: Is intelligence genetically determined?

Race, Genes, and I.Q.— An Apologia:
The Case for Conservative Multiculturalism

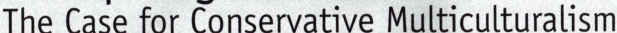

Charles Murray and Richard J. Herrnstein

Charles Murray and Richard Herrnstein are the authors of The Bell Curve (The Free Press), *from which Parts III and IV of this essay are adapted.*

I.

The private dialogue about race in America is far different from the public one, and we are not referring just to discussions among white rednecks. Our impression is that the private attitudes of white elites toward blacks is strained far beyond any public acknowledgment, that hostility is not uncommon and that a key part of the strain is a growing suspicion that fundamental racial differences are implicated in the social and economic gap that continues to separate blacks and whites, especially alleged genetic differences in intelligence.

We say "our impression" because we have been in a unique position to gather impressions. Since the beginning of 1990, we have been writing a book about differences in intellectual capacity among people and groups and what those differences mean for America's future. As authors do, we have gotten into numberless conversations that begin, "What are you working on now?" Our interlocutors have included scholars at the top-ranked universities and think tanks, journalists, high public officials, lawyers, financiers and corporate executives. In the aggregate, they have split about evenly between left and right of the political center.

With rare exceptions, these people have shared one thing besides their success. As soon as the subject turned to the question of I.Q., they focused on whether there was any genetic race differences in intelligence. And they tended to be scared stiff about the answer. This experience has led us to be scared as well, about the consequences of ignorance. We have been asked whether the question of racial genetic differences in intelligence should even be raised in polite society. We believe there's no alternative. A taboo issue, filled with potential for hurt and anger, lurks just beneath the surface of American life. It is essential that people begin to talk about this in the open. Because raising this question at all provokes a host of fears, it is worth stating at the outset a clear conclusion of our research: the fascination with race, I.Q. and genes is begotten. There are all sorts of things to be worried about regarding intelligence and American life, and even regarding intelligence and ethnicity. But genetics isn't one of them.

II.

First, the evidence, beginning with this furiously denied fact: intelligence is a useful construct. Among the experts, it is by now beyond much technical dispute that there is such a thing as a general factor of cognitive ability on which human beings differ and that this general factor is measured reasonably well by a variety of standardized tests, best of all by I.Q. tests designed for that purpose. These points are no longer the topic of much new work in the technical journals because most of the questions about them have been answered.

Intelligence as measured by I.Q. tests is predictive of many educational, economic and social outcomes. In America today, you are much better off knowing a child's I.Q. score than her parents' income or education if you want to predict whether she will drop out of high school, for example. If you are an employer trying to predict an applicant's job productivity and are given a choice of just one item of information, you are usually better off asking for an I.Q. score than a resume, college transcript, letter of recommendation or even a job interview. These statements hold true for whites, blacks, Asians and Latinos alike.

This is not to say that I.Q. is destiny—in each of these instances, I.Q. is merely a better predictor than the alternatives, not even close to a perfect one. But it should be stated that the pariah status of intelligence as a construct and I.Q. as its measure for the past three decades has been a function of political fashion, not science.

Ethnic differences in measured cognitive ability have been found since intelligence tests were invented. The battle over the meaning of these differences is largely responsible for today's controversy over intelligence testing itself. The first thing to remember is that the differences among individuals are far greater than the differences among groups. If all the ethnic differences in intelligence evaporated overnight, most of the intellectual variation in America would endure. The remaining inequality would still strain the political process, because differences in cognitive ability are problematic even in ethnically homogeneous societies.

Even using the word "race" is problematic, which is why we use the word ethnicity as well as race in this article. What does it mean to be "black" in America, in racial terms, when the word black (or African American) can be used for people whose ancestry is more European than African? How are we to classify a person whose parents hail from Panama but whose ancestry is predominantly African? Is he Latino? Black? The rule we follow here is a simple one: to classify people according to the way they classify themselves.

III.

We might start with a common question in America these days: Do Asians have higher I.Q.s than whites? The answer is probably yes, if Asian refers to the Japanese and Chinese (and perhaps also Koreans), whom we will refer to here as East Asians. How much higher is still unclear. The best tests of this have involved identical I.Q. tests given to populations that are comparable except for race. In one test, samples of American, British and Japanese students aged 13 to 15 were given a test of abstract reasoning and spatial relations. The U.S. and U.K. samples had scores within a point of the standardized mean of 100 on both the abstract and spatial relations parts of the test; the Japanese scored 104.5 on the test for abstract reasoning and 114 on the test for spatial relations—a large difference, amounting to a gap similar to the one found by another leading researcher for Asians in America. In a second set of studies, 9-year-olds in Japan, Hong Kong and Britain, drawn from comparable socioeconomic populations, were administered the Raven Standard Progressive Matrices. The children from Hong Kong averaged 113; from Japan, 110; and from Britain, 100.

Not everyone accepts that the East Asian-white difference exists. Another set of studies gave a battery of mental tests to elementary school children in Japan,

Taiwan and Minneapolis, Minnesota. The key difference between this study and the other two was that the children were matched carefully on many socioeconomic and demographic variables. No significant difference in overall I.Q. was found, and the authors concluded that "this study offers no support for the argument that there are differences in the general cognitive functioning of Chinese, Japanese and American children."

Where does this leave us? The parties in the debate are often confident, and present in their articles are many flat statements that an overall East Asian-white I.Q. difference does, or does not, exist. In our judgment, the balance of the evidence supports the notion that the overall East Asian mean is higher than the white mean. Three I.Q. points most resembles a consensus, tentative though it still is. East Asians have a greater advantage in a particular kind of nonverbal intelligence.

The issues become far more fraught, however, in determining the answer to the question: Do African Americans score differently from whites on standardized tests of cognitive ability? If the samples are chosen to be representative of the American population, the answer has been yes for every known test of cognitive ability that meets basic psychometric standards. The answer is also yes for almost all studies in which the black and white samples are matched on some special characteristics—juvenile delinquents, for example, or graduate students—but there are exceptions.

How large is the black-white difference? The usual answer is what statisticians call one standard deviation. In discussing I.Q. tests, for example, the black mean is commonly given as 85, the white mean as 100 and the standard deviation as fifteen points. But the differences observed in any given study seldom conform exactly to one standard deviation. In 156 American studies conducted during this century that have reported the I.Q. means of a black sample and a white sample, and that meet basic requirements of interpretability, the mean black-white difference is 1.1 standard deviations, or about sixteen I.Q. points.

More rigorous selection criteria do not diminish the size of the gap. For example, with tests given outside the South only after 1960, when people were increasingly sensitized to racial issues, the number of studies is reduced to twenty-four, but the mean difference is still 1.1 standard deviations. The National Longitudinal Survey of Youth (NLSY) administered an I.Q. test in 1980 to by far the largest and most carefully selected national sample (6,502 whites, 3,022 blacks) and found a difference of 1.2 standard deviations.

Evidence from the SAT, the ACT, and the National Assessment of Educational Progress gives reason to think that the black-white I.Q. difference has shrunk by perhaps three I.Q. points in the last twenty years. Almost all the improvement came in the low end, however, progress has stalled for several years and the most direct evidence, from I.Q. tests of the next generation in the NLSY, points to a widening black-white gap rather than a shrinking one.

It is important to understand that even a difference of 1.2 standard deviations means considerable overlap in the cognitive ability distribution for blacks and whites, as shown for the NLSY population in the figure on page 28.* For any equal number of blacks and whites, a large proportion have I.Q.s that can be matched up. For that matter, millions of blacks have higher I.Q.s than the average white. Tens of thousands have I.Q.s that put them in the top few percentiles of the white distribution. It should be no surprise to see (as everyone does every day) African Americans functioning at high levels in every intellectually challenging field. This is the distribution to keep in mind whenever thinking about individuals.

But an additional complication must be taken into account: in the United States, there are about six whites for every black. This means that the IQ. overlap of the two populations as they actually exist in the United States looks very different from the overlap in the figure on page 28.* The figure above* presents the same data from the NLSY when the distributions are shown in proportion to the actual population of young people in the NLSY. This figure* shows why a black-white difference can be problematic to society as a whole. At the lower end of the I.Q. range, there are about equal numbers of blacks and whites. But throughout the upper half of the range, the disproportions between the number of whites and blacks at any given I.Q. level are huge. To the extent that the difference represents an authentic difference in cognitive functioning, the social consequences are huge as well. But is the difference authentic? Is it, for example, attributable to cultural bias or other artifacts of the test? There are several ways of assessing this. We'll go through them one by one.

External Evidence of Bias

Tests are used to predict things—most commonly, to predict performance in school or on the job. The ability of a test to predict is known as its validity. A test with high validity predicts accurately; a test with poor validity makes many mistakes. Now suppose that a test's validity differs for the members of two groups. To use a concrete example: the SAT is used as a tool in college admissions because it has a certain validity in predicting college performance. If the SAT is biased against blacks, it will underpredict their college performance. If tests were biased in this way, blacks as a group would do better in college than the ad-

*Figure is not included in this publication.

missions office expected based just on their SATS. It would be as if the test underestimated the "true" SAT score of the blacks, so the natural remedy for this would be to compensate the black applicants by, for example, adding the appropriate number of points to their scores.

Predictive bias can work in another way, as when the test is simply less reliable—that is, less accurate—for blacks than for whites. Suppose a test used to select police sergeants is more accurate in predicting the performance of white candidates who become sergeants than in predicting the performance of black sergeants. It doesn't underpredict for blacks, but rather fails to predict at all (or predicts less accurately). In these cases, the natural remedy would be to give less weight to the test scores of blacks than to those of whites.

The key concept for both types of bias is the same: a test biased against blacks does not predict black performance in the real world in the same way that it predicts white performance in the real world. The evidence of bias is external in the sense that it shows up in differing validities for blacks and whites. External evidence of bias has been sought in hundreds of studies. It has been evaluated relative to performance in elementary school, in the university, in the military, in unskilled and skilled jobs, in the professions. Overwhelmingly, the evidence is that the standardized tests used to help make school and job decisions do not underpredict black performance. Nor does the expert community find any other systematic difference in the predictive accuracy of tests for blacks and whites.

Internal Evidence of Bias

The most common charges of cultural bias involve the putative cultural loading of items in a test. Here is an SAT analogy item that has become famous as an example of cultural bias:

Runner: Marathon (A) envoy: embassy (B) martyr: massacre (C) oarsman: regatta (D) referee: tournament (E) horse: stable.

The answer is "oarsman: regatta"—fairly easy if you know what both a marathon and a regatta are, a matter of guesswork otherwise. How would a black youngster from the inner city ever have heard of a regatta? Many view such items as proof that the tests must be biased against people front disadvantaged backgrounds. "Clearly," writes a critic of testing, citing this example, "this item does not measure students' 'aptitude' or logical reasoning ability, but knowledge of upper-middle-class recreational activity." In the language of psychometrics, this is called internal evidence of bias.

The hypothesis of bias again lends itself to direct examination. In effect, the SAT critic is saying that culturally loaded items are producing at least some of the black-white difference. Get rid of such items, and the gap will narrow, is he correct? When we look at the results for items that have answers such as "oarsman: regatta" and the results for items that seem to be empty of any cultural information (repeating a sequence of numbers, for example), are there any differences?

The technical literature is again clear. In study after study of the leading tests, the idea that the black-white difference is caused by questions with cultural content has been contradicted by the facts. Items that the average white test-taker finds easy relative to other items, the average black test-taker does, too; the same is true for items that the average white and black find difficult. Inasmuch as whites and blacks have different overall scores on the average, it follows that a smaller proportion of blacks get right answers for either easy or hard items, but the order of difficulty is virtually the same in each racial group. How can this be? The explanation is complicated and goes deep into the reasons why a test item is "good" or "bad" in measuring intelligence. Here, we restrict ourselves to the conclusion: *The black-white difference is generally wider on items that appear to be culturally neutral than on items that appear to be culturally loaded.* We italicize this point because it is so well established empirically yet comes as such a surprise to most people who are new to this topic.

Motivation to Try

Suppose the nature of cultural bias does not lie in predictive validity or in the content of the items but in what might be called "test willingness." A typical black youngster, it is hypothesized, comes to such tests with a mindset different from the white subject's. He is less attuned to testing situations (from one point of view), or less inclined to put up with such nonsense (from another). Perhaps he just doesn't give a damn, since he has no hopes of going to college or otherwise benefiting from a good test score. Perhaps he figures that the test is biased against him anyway, so what's the point. Perhaps he consciously refuses to put forth his best effort because of the peer pressure against "acting white" in some inner-city schools.

The studies that have attempted to measure motivation in such situations generally have found that blacks are at least as motivated as whites. But these are not wholly convincing, for why shouldn't the measures of motivation be just as inaccurate as the measures of cognitive ability are alleged to be? Analysis of internal characteristics of the tests once again offers the best leverage in examining this broad hypothesis, Here, we will offer just one example involving the "digit span" subtest, part of the widely used Wechsler intelligence tests. It has two forms: forward digit span, in which the subject tries to repeat a sequence of numbers in the order read to him, and backward digit span, in which the subject tries to repeat the sequence of numbers backward. The test is simple, uses numbers fa-

miliar to everyone and calls on no cultural information besides numbers. The digit span is informative regarding test motivation not just because of the low cultural loading of the items but because the backward form is a far better measure of "g," the psychometrician's shorthand for the general intelligence factor that I.Q. tests try to measure. The reason that the backward form is a better measure of g is that reversing the numbers is mentally more demanding than repeating them in the heard order, as you can determine for yourself by a little self testing.

The two parts of the subtest have identical content. They occur at the same time during the test. Each subject does both. But in most studies the black-white difference is about twice as great on backward digits as on forward digits. The question then arises: How can lack of motivation (or test willingness) explain the difference in performance on the two parts of the same subtest?

This still leaves another obvious question: Are the differences in overall black and white test scores attributable to differences in socioeconomic status? This question has two different answers depending on how the question is understood, and confusion is rampant. There are two essential answers and two associated rationales.

First version: If you extract the effects of socioeconomic class, what happens to the magnitude of the black-white difference? Blacks are disproportionately in the lower socioeconomic classes, and class is known to be associated with I.Q. Therefore, many people suggest, part of what appears to be an ethnic difference in I.Q. scores is actually a socioeconomic difference. The answer to this version of the question is that the size of the gap shrinks when socioeconomic status is statistically extracted. The NLSY gives a result typical of such analyses. The black-white difference in the NLSY is 1.2. In a regression equation in which both race and socioeconomic background are entered, the difference between whites and blacks shrinks to less than .8 standard deviation. Socioeconomic status explains 37 percent of the original black-white difference. This relationship is in line with the results from many other studies.

The difficulty comes in interpreting what it means to "control" for socioeconomic status. Matching the status of the groups is usually justified on the grounds that the scores people earn are caused to some extent by their socioeconomic status, so if we want to see the "real" or "authentic" difference between them, the contribution of status must be excluded. The trouble is that socioeconomic status is also a result of intelligence, as people of high and low cognitive ability move to high and low places in the class structure. The reason parents have high or low socioeconomic status is in part a function of their intelligence, and their intelligence also affects the I.Q. of the children via both genes and environment.

Because of these relationships, "controlling" for socioeconomic status in racial comparisons is guaranteed to reduce I.Q. differences in the same way that choosing black and white samples from a school for the intellectually gifted is guaranteed to reduce I.Q. differences (assuming race-blind admissions standards). These complications aside, a reasonable rule of thumb is that controlling for socioeconomic status reduces the overall black-white difference by about one-third.

Second version: As blacks move up the socioeconomic ladder, do the differences with whites of similar socioeconomic status diminish? The first version of the SES/I.Q. question referred to the overall score of a population of blacks and whites. The second version concentrates on the black-white difference within socioeconomic classes. The rationale goes like this: blacks score lower on average because they are socioeconomically at a disadvantage. This disadvantage should most seriously handicap children in the lower socioeconomic classes, who suffer from greater barriers to education and job advancement than do children in the middle and upper classes. As blacks advance up the socioeconomic ladder, their children, less exposed to these barriers, will do better and, by extension, close the gap with white children of their class.

This expectation is not borne out by the data. A good way to illustrate this is to use an index of parental SES based on their education, income and occupation and to match it against the mean I.Q. score, as shown in the figure. I.Q scores increase with economic status for both races. But as the figure shows, the magnitude of the black-white difference in standard deviations does not decrease. Indeed, it gets larger as people move up from the very bottom of the socioeconomic ladder. The pattern shown in the figure is consistent with many other major studies, except that the gap flattens out. In other studies, the gap has continued to increase throughout the range of socioeconomic status.

IV.

This brings us to the flashpoint of intelligence as a public topic: the question of genetic differences between the races. Expert opinion, when it is expressed at all, diverges widely. In the 1980s Mark Snyderman, a psychologist, and Stanley Rothman, a political scientist, sent a questionnaire to a broad sample of 1,020 scholars, mostly academicians, whose specialties give them reason to be knowledgeable about I.Q. Among other questions, they asked, "Which of the following best characterizes your opinion of the heritability of the black-white difference in IQ.?" The answers were divided as follows: The difference is entirely due to environmental variation: 15 percent. The difference is entirely due to genetic variation: 1 percent. The difference is

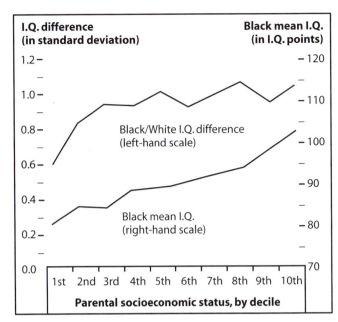

Black I.Q. scores rise with socioeconomic status, but the Black/White difference remains.

Illustration by Jim Holloway. Reprinted by permission.

a product of both genetic and environmental variation: 45 percent. The data are insufficient to support any reasonable opinion: 24 percent. No response: 14 percent.

This pretty well sums up the professional judgment on the matter. But it doesn't explain anything about the environment/genetic debate as it has played out in the profession and in the general public. And the question, of course, is fascinating. So what could help us understand the connection between heritability and group differences? A good place to start is by correcting a common confusion about the role of genes in individuals and in groups.

Most scholars accept that I.Q. in the human species as a whole is substantially heritable, somewhere between 40 percent and 80 percent, meaning that much of the observed variation in I.Q. is genetic. And yet this information tells us nothing for sure about the origin of the differences between groups of humans in measured intelligence. This point is so basic, and so misunderstood, that it deserves emphasis: that a trait is genetically transmitted in a population does not mean that group differences in that trait are also genetic in origin. Anyone who doubts this assertion may take two handfuls of genetically identical seed corn and plant one handful in Iowa, the other in the Mojave Desert, and let nature (i.e., the environment) take its course. The seeds will grow in Iowa, not in the Mojave, and the result will have nothing to do with genetic differences.

The environment for American blacks has been closer to the Mojave and the environment for American whites has been closer to Iowa. We may apply this general observation to the available data and see where the results lead. Suppose that all the observed ethnic differences in tested intelligence originate in some mysterious environmental differences—mysterious, because we know from material already presented that socioeconomic factors cannot be much of the explanation. We further stipulate that one standard deviation (fifteen I.Q. points) separates American blacks and whites and that one-fifth of a standard deviation (three I.Q. points) separates East Asians and whites. Finally, we assume that I.Q. is 60 percent heritable (a middle-ground estimate). Given these parameters, how different would the environments for the three groups have to be in order to explain the observed difference in these scores?

The observed ethnic differences in I.Q. could be explained solely by the environment if the mean environment of whites is 1.58 standard deviations better than the mean environment of blacks and .32 standard deviation worse than the mean environment for East Asians, when environments are measured along the continuum of their capacity to nurture intelligence. Let's state these conclusions in percentile terms: the average environment of blacks would have to be at the sixth percentile of the distribution of environments among whites and the average environment of East Asians would have to be at the sixty-third percentile of environments among whites for the racial differences to be entirely environmental.

Environmental differences of this magnitude and pattern are wildly out of line with all objective measures of the differences in black, Asian and white environments. Recall further that the black-white difference is smallest at the lowest socioeconomic levels. Why, if the black-white difference is entirely environmental should the advantage of the "white" environment compared to the "black" be greater among the better-off and better-educated blacks and whites? We have not been able to think of a plausible reason. Can you? An appeal to the effects of racism to explain ethnic differences also requires explaining why environments poisoned by discrimination and racism for some other groups—against the Chinese or the Jews in some regions of America for example—have left them with higher scores than the national average.

However discomfiting it may be to consider it, there are reasons to suspect genetic considerations are involved. The evidence is circumstantial, but provocative. For example, ethnicities differ not just in average scores but in the profile of intellectual capacities. A full-scale I.Q. score is the aggregate of many subtests. There are thirteen of them in the Wechsler Intelligence Scale for Children, for example. The most basic division of the subtests is into a verbal I.Q. and a performance I.Q. In white samples the verbal and performance I.Q. subscores tend to have about the same mean, because I.Q. tests have been standardized on predominantly white populations. But individuals can have imbalances between these two I.Q.s. People with high verbal abilities are likely to do well with words and logic. In school they excel in history and literature; in choosing a career to draw on those talents, they tend to choose law or journalism or advertising or politics. In contrast, people with high performance I.Q.s—or, using a more descriptive phrase, "visuospatial abilities"—are likely to do well in the physical and biological sciences, mathematics, engineering or other subjects that demand mental manipulation in the three physical dimensions or the more numerous dimensions of mathematics.

East Asians living overseas score about the same or slightly lower than whites on verbal I.Q. and substantially higher on visuospatial I.Q. Even in the rare studies that have found overall Japanese or Chinese I.Q.s no higher than white I.Q.s, the discrepancy between verbal and visuospatial I.Q. persists. For Japanese living in Asia, a 1987 review of the literature demonstrated without much question that the verbal-visuospatial difference persists even in examinations that have been thoroughly adapted to the Japanese language and, indeed, in tests developed by the Japanese themselves. A study of a small sample of Korean infants adopted into white families in Belgium found the familiar elevated visuospatial scores.

This finding has an echo in the United States, where Asian American students abound in science subjects, in engineering and in medical schools, but are scarce in law schools and graduate programs in the humanities and social sciences. Is this just a matter of parental pressures or of Asian immigrants uncomfortable with English? The same pattern of subtest scores is found in Inuits and American Indians (both of Asian origin) and in fully assimilated second- and third-generation Asian Americans. Any simple socioeconomic, cultural or linguistic explanation is out of the question, given the diversity of living conditions, native languages, educational systems and cultural practices experienced by these groups and by East Asians living in Asia. Their common genetic history cannot plausibly be dismissed as irrelevant.

Turning now to blacks and whites (using these terms to refer exclusively to Americans), ability profiles also have been important in understanding the nature, and possible genetic component, of group differences. The argument has been developing around what is known as Spearman's hypothesis. This hypothesis says that if the black-white difference on test scores reflects a real underlying difference in general mental ability (g), then the size of the black-white difference will be related to the degree to which the test is saturated with g. In other words, the better a test measures g, the larger the black-white difference will be.

By now, Spearman's hypothesis has been borne out in fourteen major studies, and no appropriate data set has yet been found that contradicts Spearman's hypothesis. It should be noted that not all group differences behave similarly. For example, deaf children often get lower test scores than hearing children, but the size of the difference is not correlated positively with the test's loading on *g*. The phenomenon seems peculiarly concentrated in comparisons of ethnic groups. How does this bear on the genetic explanation of ethnic differences? In plain though somewhat imprecise language: the broadest conception of intelligence is embodied in *g*. At the same time, *g* typically has the highest heritability (higher than the other factors measured by I.Q. tests). As mental measurement focuses most specifically and reliably on *g*, the observed black-white mean difference in cognitive ability gets larger. This does not in itself demand a genetic explanation of the ethnic difference but, by asserting that "the better the test, the greater the ethnic difference," Spearman's hypothesis undercuts many of the environmental explanations of the difference that rely on the proposition (again, simplifying) that the apparent black-white difference is the result of bad tests, not good ones.

There are, of course, many arguments against such a genetic explanation. Many studies have shown that the disadvantaged environment of some blacks has depressed their test scores. In one study, in black families in rural Georgia, the elder sibling typically had a lower I.Q. than the younger. The larger the age difference is between the siblings, the larger is the difference in I.Q. The implication is that something in the rural Georgia environment was depressing the scores of black children as they grew older. In neither the white families of Georgia, nor white or black families in Berkeley, California, were there comparable signs of a depressive effect of the environment.

Another approach is to say that tests are artifacts of a culture, and a culture may not diffuse equally into every household and community. In a heterogeneous society, subcultures vary in ways that inevitably affect scores on I.Q. tests. Fewer books in the home mean less exposure to the material that a vocabulary subtest measures; the varying ways of socializing children may influence whether a child acquires the skills, or a desire for the skills, that tests test; the "common knowledge" that tests supposedly draw on may not be common in certain households and neighborhoods.

So far, this sounds like a standard argument about cultural bias, and yet it accepts the generalizations that we discussed earlier about internal evidence of bias. The supporters of this argument are not claiming that less exposure to books means that blacks score lower on vocabulary questions but do as well as whites on culture-free items. Rather, the effects of culture are more diffuse.

Furthermore, strong correlations between home or community life and I.Q. scores are readily found. In a study of 180 Latino and 180 non-Latino white elementary school children in Riverside, California, the researcher examined eight sociocultural variables: (1) mother's participation in formal organizations, (2) living in a segregated neighborhood, (3) home language level, (4) socioeconomic status based on occupation and education of head of household, (5) urbanization, (6) mother's achievement values, (7) home ownership, and (8) intact biological family. She then showed that once these sociocultural variables were taken into account, the remaining group and I.Q. differences among the children fell to near zero.

The problem with this procedure lies in determining what, in fact, these eight variables control for: cultural diffusion, or genetic sources of variation in intelligence as ordinarily understood? By so drastically extending the usual match for socioeconomic status, the possibility is that such studies demonstrate only that parents matched on I.Q. will produce children with similar I.Q.s—not a startling finding. Also, the data used for such studies continue to show the distinctive racial patterns in the subtests. Why should cultural diffusion manifest itself by differences in backward and forward digit span or in completely nonverbal items? If the role of European white cultural diffusion is so important in affecting black I.Q. scores, why is it so unimportant in affecting Asian I.Q. scores?

There are other arguments related to cultural bias. In the American context, Wade Boykin is one of the most prominent academic advocates of a distinctive black culture, arguing that nine interrelated dimensions put blacks at odds with the prevailing Eurocentric model. Among them are spirituality (blacks approach life as "essentially vitalistic rather than mechanistic, with the conviction that nonmaterial forces influence people's everyday lives"); a belief in the harmony between humankind and nature; an emphasis on the importance of movement, rhythm, music and dance, "which are taken as central to psychological health"; personal styles that he characterizes as "verve" (high levels of stimulation and energy) and "affect" (emphasis on emotions and expressiveness); and "social time perspective," which he defines as "an orientation in which time is treated as passing through a social space rather than a material one." Such analyses purport to explain how large black-white differences in test scores could coexist with equal predictive validity of the test for such things as academic and job performance and yet still not be based on differences in "intelligence," broadly defined, let alone genetic differences.

John Ogbu, a Berkeley anthropologist, has proposed a more specific version of this argument. He suggests that we look at the history of various minority groups to understand the sources of differing levels of intellectual attainment in America. He distinguishes three types of minorities: "autonomous minorities" such as the Amish, Jews and Mormons, who, while they may be victims of discrimination, are still within the cultural mainstream; "immigrant minorities," such as the Chinese, Filipinos, Japanese and Koreans within the United States, who moved voluntarily to their new societies and, while they may begin in menial jobs, compare themselves favorably with their peers back in the home country; and, finally, "castelike minorities," such as black Americans, who were involuntary immigrants or otherwise are consigned from birth to a distinctively lower place on the social ladder. Ogbu argues that the differences in test scores are an outcome of this historical distinction, pointing to a number of castes around the world—the untouchables in India, the Buraku in Japan and Oriental Jews in Israel—that have exhibited comparable problems in educational achievement despite being of the same racial group as the majority.

Indirect support for the proposition that the observed black-white difference could be the result of environmental factors is provided by the worldwide phenomenon of rising test scores. We call it "the Flynn effect" because of psychologist James Flynn's pivotal role in focusing attention on it, but the phenomenon itself was identified in the 1930s when testers began to notice that I.Q. scores often rose with every successive year after a test was first standardized. For example, when the Stanford-Binet I.Q. was restandardized in the mid-1930s, it was observed that individuals earned lower I.Q.s on the new tests than they got on the Stanford-Binet that had been standardized in the mid-1910s; in other words, getting a score of 100 (the population average) was harder to do on the later test. This meant that the average person could answer more items on the old test than on the new test. Most of the change has been concentrated in the nonverbal portions of the tests.

The tendency for I.Q. scores to drift upward as a function of years since standardization has now been substantiated in many countries and on many I.Q. tests besides the Stanford-Binet. In some countries, the upward drift since World War II has been as much as a point per year for some spans of years. The national averages have in fact changed by amounts that are comparable to the fifteen or so I.Q. points separating whites and blacks in America. To put it another way, on the average, whites today may differ in I.Q. from whites, say, two generations ago as much as whites today differ from blacks today. Given their size and speed, the shifts in time necessarily have been due more to changes in the environment than to changes in the genes. The question then arises: Couldn't the mean of blacks move fifteen points as well through environmental changes? There seems no reason why not—but also no reason to believe that white and

Asian means can be made to stand still while the Flynn effect works its magic.

V.

As of 1994, then, we can say nothing for certain about the relative roles that genetics and environment play in the formation of the black-white difference in I.Q. All the evidence remains indirect. The heritability of individual differences in I.Q. does not necessarily mean that ethnic differences are also heritable. But those who think that ethnic differences are readily explained by environmental differences haven't been tough-minded enough about their own argument. At this complex intersection of complex factors, the easy answers are unsatisfactory ones.

Given the weight of the many circumstantial patterns, it seems improbable to us—though possible—that genes have no role whatsoever. What might the mix of genetic and environmental influences be? We are resolutely agnostic on that.

Here is what we hope will be our contribution to the discussion. We put it in italics; if we could, we would put it in neon lights: *The answer doesn't much matter.* Whether the black-white difference in test scores is produced by genes or the environment has no bearing on any of the reasons why the black-white difference is worth worrying about. If tomorrow we knew beyond a shadow of a doubt what role, if any, were played by genes, the news would be neither good if ethnic differences were predominantly environmental, nor awful if they were predominantly genetic.

The first reason for this assertion is that what matters is not whether differences are environmental or genetic, but how hard they are to change. Many people have a fuzzy impression that if cognitive ability has been depressed by a disadvantaged environment, it is easily remedied. Give the small child a more stimulating environment, give the older child a better education, it is thought, and the environmental deficit can be made up. This impression is wrong. The environment unquestionably has an impact on cognitive ability, but a record of interventions going back more than fifty years has demonstrated how difficult it is to manipulate the environment so that cognitive functioning is improved. The billions of dollars spent annually on compensatory education under Title I of the Elementary and Secondary Education Act have had such a dismal evaluation record that improving general cognitive functioning is no longer even a goal. Preschool education fares little better. Despite extravagant claims that periodically get their fifteen minutes of fame, preschool education, including not just ordinary Head Start but much more intensive programs such as Perry Preschool, raises I.Q. scores by a few points on the exit test, and even those small gains quickly fade. Preschool programs may be good for children in other ways, but they do not have important effects on intelligence. If larger effects are possible, it is only through truly heroic efforts, putting children into full-time, year-round, highly enriched day care from within a few months of birth and keeping them there for the first five years of life—and even those effects, claimed by the Milwaukee Program and the Abecedarian Project, are subject to widespread skepticism among scholars.

In short: if it were proved tomorrow that ethnic differences in test scores were entirely environmental, there would be no reason to celebrate. That knowledge would not suggest a single educational, preschool, day care or prenatal program that is not already being tried, and would give no reason to believe that tomorrow's effects from such programs will be any more encouraging than those observed to date. Radically improved knowledge about child development and intelligence is required, not just better implementation of what is already known. No breakthroughs are in sight.

The second reason that the concern about genes is overblown is the mistaken idea that genes mean there is nothing to be done. On the contrary, the distributions of genetic traits in a population can change over time, because people who die are not replaced one-for-one by babies with matched DNA. Just because there might be a genetic difference among groups in this generation does not mean that it cannot shrink. Nor, for that matter, does genetic equality in this generation mean that genetic differences might not arise within a matter of decades. It depends on which women in which group have how many babies at what ages. More broadly, genetic causes do not leave us helpless. Myops see fine with glasses and many bald men look as if they have hair, however closely myopia and baldness are tied to genes. Check out visual aids and gimmicks on any Macintosh computer to see how technology can compensate for innumeracy and illiteracy.

Now comes the third reason that the concern about genes needs rethinking. It is to us the most compelling: there is no *rational reason* why any encounter between individuals should be affected in any way by the knowledge that a group difference is genetic instead of environmental. Suppose that the news tomorrow morning is that the black-white difference in cognitive test scores is rooted in genetic differences. Suppose further that tomorrow afternoon, you—let us say you are white—encounter a random African American. Try to think of any way in which anything has changed that should affect your evaluation of or response to that individual and you will soon arrive at a truth that ought to be assimilated by everyone: nothing has changed. That an individual is a member of a group with a certain genetically based mean and distribution in

any characteristic, whether it be height, intelligence, predisposition to schizophrenia or eye color has no effect on that reality of that individual. A five-foot man with six-foot parents is still five feet tall, no matter how much height is determined by genes. An African American with an I.Q. of 130 still has an I.Q. of 130, no matter what the black mean may be or to what extent I.Q. is determined by genes. Maybe for some whites, behavior toward black individuals would change if it were known that certain ethnic differences were genetic—but not for any good reason.

We have been too idealistic, one may respond. In the real world, people treat individuals according to their membership in a group. Consider the young black male trying to catch a taxi. It makes no difference how honest he is; many taxi drivers will refuse to pick him up because young black males disproportionately account for taxi robberies. Similarly, some people fear that talking about group differences in I.Q. will encourage employers to use ethnicity as an inexpensive screen if they can get away with it, not bothering to consider black candidates.

These are authentic problems that need to be dealt with. But it puzzles us to hear them raised as a response to the question, "What difference does it make if genes are involved?" Two separate issues are being conflated: the reality of a difference versus its source. An employer has no more incentive to discriminate by ethnicity if he knows that a difference in ability is genetic than if he knows it is "only" environmental. To return to an earlier point, the key issue is how intractable the difference is. By the time someone is applying for a job, his cognitive functioning can be tweaked only at the margins, if at all, regardless of the original comparative roles of genes and environment in producing that level of cognitive functioning. The existence of a group difference may make a difference in the behavior of individuals toward other individuals, with implications that may well spill over into policy, but the source of the difference is irrelevant to the behavior.

VI.

In *The Bell Curve*, we make all of the above points, document them fully and are prepared to defend them against all comers. We argue that the best and indeed only answer to the problem of group differences is an energetic and uncompromising recommitment to individualism. To judge someone except on his or her own merits was historically thought to be un-American, and we urge that it become so again.

But as we worked on the discussion in the book, we also became aware that ratiocination is not a sufficient response. Many people instinctively believe that genetically caused group differences in intelligence must be psychologically destructive in a way that environmentally caused differences are not. In a way, our informal survey of elites during the writing of the book confirmed this. No matter what we said, we found that people walked away muttering that it does make a difference if genes are involved. But we nonetheless are not persuaded. It seems to us that, on the contrary, human beings have it in them to live comfortably with all kinds of differences, group and individual alike.

We did not put those thoughts into the book. Early on, we decided that the passages on ethnic differences in intelligence had to be inflexibly pinned to data. Speculations were out, and even provocative turns of phrase had to be guarded against. The thoughts we are about to express are decidedly speculative, and hence did not become part of our book. But if you will treat them accordingly, we think they form the basis of a conversation worth beginning, and we will open it here.

As one looks around the world at the huge variety of ethnic groups that have high opinions of themselves, for example, one is struck by how easy it is for each of these clans, as we will call them, to conclude that it has the best combination of genes and culture in the world. In each clan's eyes, its members are blessed to have been born who they are—Arab, Chinese, Jew, Welsh, Russian, Spanish, Zulu, Scots, Hungarian. The list could go on indefinitely, breaking into ever smaller groups (highland Scots, Glaswegians, Scotch-Irish). The members of each clan do not necessarily think their people have gotten the best break regarding their political or economic place in the world, but they do not doubt the intrinsic, unique merits of their particular clan.

How does this clannish self-esteem come about? Any one dimension, including intelligence, clearly plays only a small part. The self-esteem is based on a mix of qualities. These packages of qualities are incomparable across clans. The mixes are too complex, the metrics are too different, the qualities are too numerous to lend themselves to a weighting scheme that everyone could agree upon. The Irish have a way with words; the Irish also give high marks to having a way with words in the pantheon of human abilities. The Russians see themselves as soulful; they give high marks to soulfulness. The Scotch-Irish who moved to America tended to be cantankerous, restless and violent. Well, say the American Scotch-Irish proudly, these qualities made for terrific pioneers.

We offer this hypothesis: Clans tend to order the world, putting themselves on top, not because each clan has an inflated idea of its own virtues, but because each is using a weighting algorithm that genuinely works out that way. One of us had a conversation with a Thai many years ago about the Thai attitude toward Americans. Americans have technology and capabilities that the Thais do not have, he said, just as the elephant is stronger than a human. "But," he said with a shrug, "who wants to be an elephant?" We do not consider his view quaint. There is an internally consistent logic that legitimately might lead a Thai to conclude that being born Thai gives one a better chance of becoming a complete human being than being born American. He may not be right, but he is not necessarily wrong.

If these observations have merit, why is it that one human clan occasionally develops a deep-seated sense of ethnic inferiority vis-à-vis another clan? History suggests that the reasons tend to be independent of any particular qualities of the two groups, but instead are commonly rooted in historical confrontations. When one clan has been physically subjugated by another, the psychological reactions are complex and long-lasting. The academic literature on political development is filled with studies of the reactions of colonized peoples that prove this case. These self-denigrating reactions are not limited to the common people; if anything, they are most profound among the local elites. Consider, for example, the deeply ambivalent attitudes of Indian elites toward the British. The Indian cultural heritage is glittering, but that heritage was not enough to protect Indian elites from the psychological ravages of being subjugated.

Applying these observations to the American case and to relations between blacks and whites suggests a new way of conceptualizing the familiar "legacy of slavery" arguments. It is not just that slavery surely had lasting effects on black culture, nor even that slavery had a broad negative effect on black self-confidence and self-esteem, but more specifically that the experience of slavery perverted and stunted the evolution of the ethnocentric algorithm that American blacks would have developed in the normal course of events. Whites did everything in their power to explain away or belittle every sign of talent, virtue or superiority among blacks. They had to—if the slaves were superior in qualities that whites themselves valued, where was the moral justification for keeping them enslaved? And so everything that African Americans did well had to be cast in terms that belittled the quality in question. Even to try to document this point leaves one open to charges of condescension, so successfully did whites manage to coopt the value judgments. Most obviously, it is impossible to speak straightforwardly about the dominance of many black athletes without being subject to accusations that one is being backhandedly anti-black.

The nervous concern about racial inferiority in the United States is best seen as a variation on the colonial experience. It is in the process of diminishing as African Americans define for themselves that mix of qualities that makes the American black clan unique and (appropriately in the eyes of the clan) superior. It emerges in fiction by black authors and in a growing body of work by black scholars. It is also happening in the streets. The process is not only normal and healthy; it is essential.

In making these points, there are several things we are not saying that need to be spelled out. We are not giving up on the melting pot. Italians all over America who live in neighborhoods without a single other Italian, and who may technically have more non-Italian than Italian blood, continue to take pride in their Italian heritage in the ways we have described. The same may be said of other ethnic clans. For that matter, we could as easily have used the examples of Texans and Minnesotans as of Thais and Scotch-Irish in describing the ways in which people naturally take pride in their group. Americans often see themselves as members of several clans at the same time—and think of themselves as 100 percent American as well. It is one of America's most glorious qualities.

We are also not trying to tell African Americans or anyone else what qualities should be weighted in their algorithm. Our point is precisely the opposite: no one needs to tell any clan how to come up with a way of seeing itself that is satisfactory; it is one of those things that human communities know how to do quite well when left alone to do it. Still less are we saying that the children from any clan should not, say study calculus because studying calculus is not part of the clan's heritage. Individuals strike out on their own, making their way in the Great World according to what they bring to their endeavors as individuals—and can still take comfort and pride in their group affiliations. Of course there are complications and tensions in this process. The tighter the clan, the more likely it is to look suspiciously on their children who depart for the Great World—and yet also, the more proudly it is likely to boast of their success once they have made it, and the more likely that the children will one day restore some of their ties with the clan they left behind. This is one of the classic American dramas.

We are not preaching multiculturalism. Our point is not that everything is relative and the accomplishments of each culture and ethnic group are just as good as those of every other culture and ethnic group. Instead, we are saying a good word for a certain kind of ethnocentrism. Given a chance, each clan will add up its accomplishments using its own weighting system, will encounter the world with confidence in its own worth and, most importantly, will be unconcerned about comparing its accomplishments line-by-line with those of any other clan. This is wise ethnocentrism.

In the context of intelligence and I.Q. scores, we are urging that it is foolish ethnocentrism on the part of European Americans to assume that mean differences in I.Q. among ethnic groups must mean that those who rank lower on that particular dimension are required to be miserable about it—all the more foolish because the group I.Q. of the prototypical American clan, white Protestants, is some rungs from the top.

It is a difficult point to make persuasively, because the undoubted reality of our era is that group differences in intelligence are intensely threatening and feared. One may reasonably ask what point there is in speculating about some better arrangement in which it wouldn't matter. And yet there remain stubborn counterfactuals that give reason for thinking that inequalities in intelligence need not be feared—not just theoretically, but practically.

We put it as a hypothesis that lends itself to empirical test: hardly anyone feels inferior to people who have higher I.Q.s. If you doubt this, put it to yourself. You surely have known many people who are conspicuously smarter than you are, in terms of sheer intellectual horsepower. Certainly we have. There have been occasions when we thought it would be nice to be as smart as these other people. But, like the Thai who asked, "Who wants to be an elephant?" we have not felt inferior to our brilliant friends, nor have we wanted to trade places with them. We have felt a little sorry for some of them, thinking that despite their high intelligence they lacked other qualities that we possessed and that we valued more highly than their extra I.Q. points.

When we have remarked upon this to friends, their reaction has often been, "That's fine for you to say, because you're smart enough already." But we are making a more ambitious argument: it is not just people with high I.Q.s who don't feel inferior to people with even higher I.Q.s. The rule holds true all along the I.Q. continuum.

It is hard to get intellectuals to accept this, because of another phenomenon that we present as a hypothesis, but are fairly confident can be verified: people with high I.Q.s tend to condescend to people with lower I.Q.s. Once again, put yourself to the test. Suppose we point to a person with an I.Q. thirty points lower than yours. Would you be willing to trade places with him? Do you instinctively feel a little sorry for him? Here, we have found the answers from friends to be more reluctant, and usually a little embarrassed, but generally they have been "no" and "yes," respectively. Isn't it remarkable: just about everyone seems to think that his level of intelligence is enough, that any less than his isn't as good, but that any more than his isn't such a big deal.

In other words, we propose that the same thing goes on within individuals as within clans. In practice, not just idealistically, people do not judge themselves as human beings by the size of their I.Q.s. Instead, they bring to bear a multidimensional judgment of themselves that lets them take satisfaction in who they are. Surely a person with an I.Q. of 90 sometimes wishes he had an I.Q. of 120, just as a person with an I.Q. of 120 sometimes wishes he had an I.Q. of 150. But it is presumptuous, though a curiously common presumption among intellectuals, to think that someone with an I.Q. of 90 must feel inferior to those who are smarter, just as it is presumptuous to think a white person must feel threatened by a group difference that probably exists between whites and Japanese, a gentile must feel threatened by a group difference that certainly exists between gentiles and Jews or a black person must feel threatened by a group difference between blacks and whites. It is possible to look ahead to a world in which the glorious hodgepodge of inequalities of ethnic groups—genetic and environmental, permanent and temporary—can be not only accepted but celebrated.

This difficult topic calls up an unending sequence of questions. How can intelligence be treated as just one of many qualities when the marketplace puts such a large monetary premium on it? How can one hope that people who are on the lower end of the I.Q. range find places of dignity in the world when the niches they used to hold in society are being devalued? Since the world tends to be run by people who are winners in the I.Q. lottery, how can one hope that societies will be structured so that the lucky ones do not continually run society for their own benefit?

These are all large questions, exceedingly complex questions—but they are no longer about ethnic variations in intelligence. They are about human variation in intelligence. They, not ethnic differences, are worth writing a book about—and that's what we did. Ethnic differences must be dreaded only to the extent that people insist on dreading them. People certainly are doing so—that much is not in dispute. What we have tried to do here, in a preliminary and no doubt clumsy way, is to begin to talk about the reasons why they need not.

Form at end of book

WiseGuide Wrap-Up

The old but engrossing debate about which explains human behavior—environment (social circumstances) or genetics (physical characteristics)—is revised in the study of intelligence. Choosing either one or the other is sterile, but in combination, these two aspects of human existence can help us better understand who we are and of what we are capable. As long as we stay away from simple deterministic perspectives and recognize that human flexibility and adaptability are important to human survival, we can debate the relative merits of one contribution as compared to others.

Geneticists have not yet completely charted human DNA, but they are getting close. In the process, they are learning a lot about how DNA works, and it is not as deterministically simple as some people would like to believe. Which are the "white" genes?

Which are the ethnic genes? Where are they found in the DNA? Do the genes connected with intelligence function singly or in concert with other genes? Do nutrition and the health of the individual affect these genes? Are chromosomes variable? Don't mutations crop up from time to time? Where do exceptionally intelligent people come from? If intelligence were all determined by heredity, then wouldn't it be impossible to be smarter than your parents?

One of the areas missing from the debate is the measurement of ethnicity. While all of the arguments are concerned with errors in the measurement of cognitive ability, none of the issues raised deals with the reliability of measures of ethnicity. How do we measure ethnicity? The U.S. Census Bureau reports difficulties in identifying which individuals

belong in which category. Categories change, depending on social changes and interest in ethnic background. Intermarriage has made it difficult to determine how to classify many individuals. In an individual of mixed parentage, which group's characteristics predominate genetically? And what effect does intermarriage have on intelligence? The political importance of this can be seen in the arguments over affirmative action, Head Start, and other social programs.

In Reading 19, Murray and Herrnstein indicate that they want to move the discussion from group-based differences to comparisons of individuals. While this shift does raise interesting questions, it does not detract from the fact that the initial study focused on groups and that we live in groups and that this aspect of being human has a tremendous influence on individual lives.

R.E.A.L. Sites

This list provides a print preview of typical **Coursewise** R.E.A.L. sites. (There are over 100 such sites at the **Courselinks**™ site.) The danger in printing URLs is that web sites can change overnight. As we went to press, these sites were functional using the URLs provided. If you come across one that isn't, please let us know via email to: webmaster@coursewise.com. Use your Passport to access the most current list of R.E.A.L. sites at the **Courselinks** site.

Site name: The Gene Letter

URL: http://www.geneletter.org/

Why is it R.E.A.L.? The Gene Letter is a web site supported with a grant from the U.S. Department of Energy, Human Genome Project. It has lists of resources, articles by researchers, and essays on various topics relating to genetics mapping and research.

Key terms: eugenics, research

Site name: The Council for Responsible Genetics

URL: http://www.gene-watch.org/

Why is it R.E.A.L.? This web site, sponsored by the Council for Responsible Genetics, is concerned with the use of genetic research in discrimination. The Council for Responsible Genetics was founded in 1983 and is a national nonprofit organization of scientists, public health advocates, and others who monitor the development of new genetic technologies and advocate their responsible use. The organization also fosters public debate about the social, ethical, and environmental implications of genetic research.

Key terms: genetics, discrimination, biotechnology

section 9 | Is Race a Meaningful Concept in Understanding Human Behavior?

Take a Closer Look

1. What is a race, and is it a useful way to understand human nature?

2. Does knowledge of a person's race increase our understanding of the person? Does it help us to predict behavior?

3. How has race consciousness affected social policies with regard to educational and economic opportunities? Has this consistently produced policies that benefit the community?

4. Will the instant communication of the computer age nullify the diversity necessary for creativity?

5. Of what value is categorizing people by their biological features? What categories other than race might be more useful in accomplishing this?

What does it mean to be human? Scholars and researchers in many fields are trying to answer this fundamental question. How can we best understand what we are? Does the nature of our environment or biology provide the best answers? Both of these areas are much more complex than they appear. What aspects of our biology are most important? Is the individual or the group the best subject of study? Which group level—small groups of a few individuals or large societies of millions—should be studied? Can all of humanity be understood by the three racial classifications created in the eighteenth century, and why does this concept, which is of little scientific use, remain such an important focus of our social discussions?

Race, culture, and *ethnicity*—three seemingly simple words that carry explosive hidden meanings, history, and stereotypes. When we speak these words, we seem sure of their meanings, but when we try to use them to do research, defining them and collecting data about them are difficult. The readings in this section illustrate some of the problems that arise when using these terms to explain individual and group behavior.

Human life is dynamic. Diversity, rather than singularity, enables survival. Yet, many people still try to define themselves as having pure descent from a particular group. And they see the group that they belong to as better than other groups. Isolation has not produced great societies. As Claude Levi-Strauss clearly states in Reading 20: "The great creative epochs in history were those in which communication had become adequate for distant individuals to stimulate each other, but not frequent or rapid enough for those obstacles, indispensable between individuals as they are between groups, to be reduced to the point at which diversity becomes leveled out and nullified by excessively facile interchange."

In Reading 21, Jonathan Marks questions the role of the concept of race in American society. He relates race to the concerns of social policies and to using biology as a means of justifying particular positions in funding, education, and immigration debates. According to Marks: "Teaching that racial categories lack biological validity can be as much of a challenge as teaching in the seventeenth century that the earth goes round the sun—when anyone can plainly see the sun rise, traverse a path along the sky, and set beyond the opposing horizon. How can something that seems so obvious be denied?"

Issue 9: Is race a meaningful concept in understanding human behavior?

Race, History and Culture

Claude Levi-Strauss

Claude Levi-Strauss is a French social anthropologist and university teacher whose work has exerted considerable influence on the development of the contemporary social sciences. His works published in English include: The Savage Mind *(1968),* Elementary Structures of Kinship *(1969),* Structural Anthropology I and II *(1974 and 1981), and* Myth and Meaning *(1987).*

One of the world's leading anthropologists, Claude Levi-Strauss twice set forth his ideas on racism for UNESCO, first in Race and History *(1952) and later in* Race and Culture *(1971). On the following pages we publish long extracts from these two important studies.*

Race and History[1]

The development of human life is not everywhere the same but rather takes form in an extraordinary diversity of societies and civilizations. This intellectual, aesthetic and sociological diversity is in no way the outcome of the biological differences, in certain observable features, between different groups of men; it is simply a parallel phenomenon in a different sphere. But, at the same time, we must note two important respects in which there is a sharp distinction. First, the order of magnitude is different. There are many more human cultures than human races, since the first are to be counted in thousands and the second in single units. . . . Second, in contrast to the diversity of races, where interest is confined to their historical origin or their distribution over the face of the world, the diversity of cultures gives rise to many problems; it may be wondered whether it is an advantage or a disadvantage for human kind. . . .

Last and most important, the nature of the diversity must be investigated even at the risk of allowing the racial prejudices whose biological foundation has so lately been destroyed to develop again on new grounds. . . . We cannot therefore claim to have formulated a convincing denial of the inequality of the human races, so long as we fail to consider the problem of the inequality—or diversity—of human cultures, which is in fact—however justifiably—closely associated with it in the public mind. . . .

Collaboration between Cultures

. . . A culture's chance of uniting the complex body of inventions of all sorts which we describe as a civilization depends on the number and diversity of the other cultures with which it is working out, generally involuntarily, a common strategy. Number and diversity: a comparison of the Old World with the New on the eve of the latter's discovery [in 1492] provides a good illustration of the need for these two factors.

Europe at the beginning of the Renaissance was the meeting-place and melting-pot of the most diverse influences: the Greek, Roman, Germanic and Anglo-Saxon traditions combined with the influences of Arabia and China. Pre-Columbian America enjoyed no fewer cultural contacts, quantitatively speaking, as the various American cultures maintained relations with one another and the two Americas together represent a whole hemisphere. But, while the cultures which were cross-fertilizing each other in Europe had resulted from differentiation dating back several tens of thousands of years, those on the more recently occupied American continent had had less time to develop divergencies; the picture they offered was relatively homogeneous. Thus, although it would not be true to say that the cultural standard of Mexico or Peru was [in 1492] inferior to that of Europe at the time of the discovery (we have in fact seen that, in some respects, it was superior), the various aspects of culture were possibly less well organized in relation to each other. . . . Their organization, less flexible and diversified, probably explains their collapse before a handful of conquerors. And the underlying reason for this may be sought in the fact that the partners to the American cultural "coalition" were less dissimilar from one another than their counterparts in the Old World.

Reprinted from the *UNESCO Courier,* March 1996, Claude Levi-Strauss.

No society is therefore essentially and intrinsically cumulative. Cumulative history is not the prerogative of certain races or certain cultures, marking them off from the rest. It is the result of their conduct rather than their nature. It represents a certain "way of life" of cultures which depends on their capacity to "go along together." In this sense, it may be said that cumulative history is the type of history characteristic of grouped societies—social super-organisms—while stationary history (supposing it to exist) would be the distinguishing feature of an inferior form of social life, the isolated society.

The one real calamity, the one fatal flaw which can afflict a human group and prevent it from achieving fulfillment is to be alone.

We can thus see how clumsy and intellectually unsatisfactory the generally accepted efforts to defend the contributions of various human races and cultures to civilization often are. We list features, we sift questions of origin, we allot first places. However well-intentioned they may be, these efforts serve no purpose for, in three respects, they miss their aim.

In the first place, there can never be any certainty about a particular culture's credit for an invention or discovery. . . . In the second place, all cultural contributions can be divided into two groups. On the one hand we have isolated acquisitions or features, whose importance is evident but which are also somewhat limited. . . . At the other end of the scale (with a whole series of intermediates, of course), there are systematized contributions, representing the peculiar form in which each society has chosen to express and satisfy the generality of human aspirations. There is no denying the originality and particularity of these patterns, but, as they all represent the exclusive choice of a single group, it is difficult to see how one civilization can hope to benefit from the way of life of another, unless it is prepared to renounce its own individuality. Attempted compromises are, in fact, likely to produce only two results: either the disorganization and collapse of the pattern of one of the groups; or a new combination, which then, however, represents the emergence of a third pattern, and cannot be assimilated to either of the others. The question with which we are concerned, indeed, is not to discover whether or not a society can derive benefit from the way of life of its neighbours, but whether, and if so to what extent, it can succeed in understanding or even in knowing them. . . .

World Civilization

Finally, wherever a contribution is made, there must be a recipient. But while there are in fact real cultures which can be localized in time and space, and which may be said to have "contributed" and to be continuing their contribu- tions, what can this "world civilization" be, which is supposed to be the recipient of all these contributions? It is not a civilization distinct from all the others, and yet real in the same sense that they are. . . . [It is] an abstract conception, to which we attribute a moral or logical significance—moral, if we are thinking of an aim to be pursued by existing societies; logical, if we are using the one term to cover the common features which analysis may reveal in the different cultures. In both cases, we must not shut our eyes to the fact that the concept of world civilization is very sketchy and imperfect, and that its intellectual and emotional content is tenuous. To attempt to assess cultural contributions with all the weight of countless centuries behind them . . . by reference to the sole yardstick of a world civilization which is still a hollow shell, would be greatly to impoverish them, draining away their life-blood and leaving nothing but the bare bones behind.

. . . The true contribution of a culture consists, not in the list of inventions which it has personally produced, but in its difference from others. The sense of gratitude and respect which each single member of a given culture can and should feel towards all others can only be based on the conviction that the other cultures differ from his own in countless ways. . . .

We have taken the notion of world civilization as a sort of limiting concept or as an epitome of a highly complex process. If our arguments are valid, there is not, and never can be, a world civilization in the absolute sense in which that term is often used, since civilization implies, and indeed consists in, the coexistence of cultures exhibiting the maximum possible diversities. A world civilization could, in fact, represent no more than a worldwide coalition of cultures, each of which would preserve its own originality.

Race and Culture[2]

[In 1952], in a booklet written for UNESCO, I suggested the concept of "coalition" to explain why isolated cultures could not hope to create single-handed the conditions necessary for a truly cumulative history. To achieve this, I said, different cultures must, voluntarily or involuntarily, combine their respective stakes in the great game of history, to increase their chances of making that long run of winning plays by which history progresses. Geneticists are at present [1971] putting forward very similar views on biological evolution, in pointing out that a genome is in reality a system within which certain genes function as regulators and others act in concert on a single characteristic (or the contrary, if several characteristics depend on a single gene). What is true of the individual genome is also true of a population, in which the combination of a number of genetic inheritances—in which until recently a "racial type" would have been identified—must always be such as to allow the establishment of an optimum equilibrium and improve the group's chances of survival. In this sense, it might be said that in the history of populations, genetic recombination plays a part comparable to that played by cultural recombination in the evolution of the ways of life, techniques, knowledge and beliefs by which different societies are distinguished. . . .

The Nature-Culture Debate

[But] one fact cannot be too strongly emphasized: while selection makes it possible for living species to adapt to their natural environment or to resist its changes more effectively, in the case of man this environment ceases to be natural in any real sense. Its characteristics arise from technical, economic, social and psychological conditions which, through the operation of culture, create a particular environment for each human group. We can go a step further, and consider whether the relation between organic ovulation and cultural evolution is not merely analogical, but also complementary. . . .

In the dawn of humanity, biological evolution perhaps selected such pre-cultural traits as upright posture, manual dexterity, sociability, the capacity to think in symbols, speech and the ability to communicate. But once a culture existed, these traits were consolidated and propagated by cultural factors. When cultures became specialized, it was again cultural factors which consolidated and encouraged other traits, such as resistance to heat or cold for those societies which had willy-nilly to adapt themselves to extreme climatic conditions; aggressive or contemplative dispositions, technical ingenuity, etc. None of these traits, as perceived at a cultural level, can clearly be attributed to a genetic basis, although we cannot exclude the possibility that such a connexion—even if partial, remote and indirect—may sometimes exist. In that case, it would be true to say that every culture selects genetic aptitudes which then, by reflex action, influence those cultures by which they were at first stimulated.

An Ideological Cover

By pushing back the earliest beginnings of humanity to an ever more remote past—according to recent estimates, some millions of years ago—physical anthropology has undermined one of the principal bases for racialist theory, since the number of unknowable factors concerned thus increases much more rapidly than the number of landmarks available to stake out the paths followed by our earliest ancestors in the course of their evolution.

Geneticists delivered even more decisive blows to these theories when they replaced the concept of type by

that of population and the concept of race by that of the genetic stock, and again when they demonstrated that there is a gulf between hereditary differences attributable to a single gene—which are of little significance from the point of view of race, since they probably always have an adaptive value—and those attributable to the combined action of several, which makes it virtually impossible to determine them. . . .

Only in the last ten years have we begun to understand that we were discussing the problem of the relation between organic and cultural evolution in terms which Auguste Comte would have described as metaphysical. Human evolution is not a by-product of biological evolution, but neither is it completely distinct from it. A synthesis of these two traditional points of view is now possible, provided that biologists are not content with answers not based on fact, or with dogmatic explanations, and realize both the help they can give each other and their respective limitations.

The unsatisfactory nature of the traditional solutions to the problem perhaps explains why the ideological struggle against racialism has proved so ineffective on a practical level. There is nothing to indicate that racial prejudice is declining and plenty of evidence to suggest that, after brief periods of localized quiescence, it is reappearing everywhere with increased intensity. It is for this reason that UNESCO feels called upon to renew from time to time a battle whose outcome appears uncertain, to say the least.

But can we be so sure that the racial form taken by intolerance results primarily from false beliefs held by this or that people about the dependence of culture on organic evolution? Are these ideas not simply an ideological cover for a more real form of antagonism, based on the will to subjugate and on relations of power? This was certainly the case in the past, but, even supposing that these relations of power become less marked, will not racial differentiation continue to serve as a pretext for the growing difficulty of living together, unconsciously felt by mankind, which is undergoing a demographic explosion and which . . . is beginning to hate itself, warned by a mysterious prescience that its numbers are becoming too great for all its members to enjoy freely open space and pure, non-polluted air?

Racial prejudice is at its most intense when it concerns human groups confined to a territory so cramped and a share of natural resources so meager that these peoples lack dignity in their own eyes as well as in those of their more powerful neighbours. But does not humanity today, on the whole, tend to expropriate itself and, on a planet that has grown too small, reconstitute, to its own cost, a situation comparable to that inflicted by some of its representatives on the unfortunate American or Oceanic tribes? Finally, what would happen to the ideological struggle against racial prejudice, if it were shown to be universally true—as some experiments conducted by psychologists suggest—that if subjects of any origin whatever are divided into groups, which are placed in a competitive situation, each group will develop feelings of bias and injustice towards its rivals?

Minority groups appearing in various parts of the world today, such as the hippies, are not distinguished from the bulk of the population race, but only by their way of life, morality, hair style and dress; are the feelings of repugnance and sometimes hostility they inspire in most of their fellows substantially different from racial hatred? Would we therefore be making genuine progress if we confined ourselves to dissipating the particular prejudices on which racial hatred—in the strict sense of the term—can be said to be based?

The Mirage of Universal Entente

In any case, the contribution ethnologists can make to the solution of the race problem would be derisory; nor is it certain that psychologists and educators could do any better, so strong is the evidence—as we see from the evidence of the so-called primitive peoples—that mutual tolerance presupposes two conditions which in contemporary society are further than ever from being realized: one is relative equality; the other is adequate physical separation.

. . . No doubt we cherish the hope that one day equality and fraternity will reign among men without impairing their diversity. But if humanity is not to resign itself to becoming a sterile consumer of the values it created in the past and of those alone . . . , it will have to relearn the fact that all true creation implies a certain deafness to outside values, even to the extent of rejecting or denying them. For one individual cannot at the same time merge into the spirit of another, identify with another and still maintain his own identity. Integral communication with another, if fully realized, sooner or later dooms the creative originality of both. The great creative epochs in history were those in which communication had become adequate for distant individuals to stimulate each other, but not frequent or rapid enough for those obstacles, indispensable between individuals as they are between groups, to be reduced to the point at which diversity becomes levelled out and nullified by excessively facile interchange.

. . . Convinced that cultural and organic evolution are inextricably linked, [biologists and ethnologists] know, of course, that a return to the past is impossible, but they know, too, that the course humanity is at present following is building up tensions to such a degree that racial hatred is a mere foretaste of the greater intolerance that may hold sway tomorrow, without even the pretext of ethnic differences. To forestall the dangers threatening us today and those, still more formidable, that we shall have to face tomorrow, we must accept the fact that these causes are much deeper than mere ignorance or prejudice: we can only hope for a change in the course of history, which is even more difficult to bring about than progress in the march of ideas.

Notes

1. Extract from *Race and History,* first published in *The Race Question in Modern Science,* Paris, UNESCO, 1952.
2. Extract from *Race and Culture,* published in UNESCO's *International Social Science Journal,* Vol. XXIII, No. 4, 1971.

Form at end of book

Science and Race

Jonathan Marks

The scientific study of human biological variation has consistently produced knowledge that contradicts widespread popular, or folk, wisdom. Although people and the populations they belong to certainly differ from one another, they do not appear to do so in such a manner that permits the identification of a small number of human subspecies or races. Classification of people into races involves cultural, not biological, knowledge; and race is inherited according to cultural rules that stand in opposition to biology. Thus race is not a useful biological concept. To understand whether differences exist between populations in cognitive ability (or any other inherent "gifts") requires confronting the limits of scientific knowledge.

From the standpoint of biological anthropology, there are two general contributions we can make to the discourse of race in America. The first is to understand the empirical pattern of biological or genetic diversity among indigenous human populations and its relation to structured behavioral or cultural variation. The second involves demonstrating that the focus of human biological variation in American society represents simply one more example of how biology has been regularly recruited into discussions of social issues as a means of falsely justifying a position.

Race As an Empirical Issue

Teaching that racial categories lack biological validity can be as much of a challenge as teaching in the seventeenth century that the earth goes around the sun—when anyone can plainly see the sun rise, traverse a path along the sky, and set beyond the opposing horizon. How can something that seems so obvious be denied?

Of course, that is the way all great scientific breakthroughs appear, by denying folk wisdom and replacing it with a more sophisticated and analytic interpretation of the same data. We can break down race into four separate

empirical issues, each of which has been comprehensively answered by anthropology in this century.

Is the Human Species Naturally Divisible into a Small Number of Reasonably Discrete Groups?

Whether we examine people's bodies or sample their genes, the pattern that we encounter is very concordant. People are similar to those from geographically nearby and different from those far away. We refer to this pattern as clinal, a cline being simply a geographic gradient of a particular biological feature (Huxley, 1938; Livingstone, 1962).

Dividing human populations into a small number of discrete groups results in associations of populations and divisions between populations that are arbitrary, not natural. Africa, for example, is home to tall, thin people in Kenya (Nilotic), short people in Zaire (Pygmies), and peoples in southern Africa who are sufficiently different from our physical stereotypes of Africans (i.e., West Africans) as to have caused an earlier generation to speculate on whether they had some southeast Asian ancestry (Hiernaux, 1974). As far as we know, all are biologically different, all are indigenously African, and to establish a single category (African/Black/Negroid) to encompass them all reflects an arbitrary decision about human diversity, one that is not at all dictated by nature.

Further, grouping the peoples of Africa together as a single entity and dividing them from the peoples of Europe and the Near East (European/White/Caucasoid) imposes an exceedingly unnatural distinction at the boundary between the two groups. In fact, the "African" peoples of Somalia are far more similar to the peoples of, say, Saudi Arabia or Iran—which are close to Somalia—than they are to the Ghanaians on the western side of Africa. And the Iranis and Saudis are themselves more similar to the Somalis than to Norwegians. Thus associating the Ghanaians and Somalis on one hand and Saudis and

From Jonathan Marks, "Science and Race" in *American Behavioral Scientist,* Nov.–Dec. 1996, V. 40, No. 2, p. 123, copyright © 1996 Sage Publications, Inc. Reprinted by permission of Sage Publications, Inc.

Norwegians on the other generates an artificial pattern that is contradicted by empirical studies of human biology.

The reason why this clinal pattern exists lies in the processes of microevolution in the human species. Natural selection adapts people to their environment, yet environments generally change gradually over geography—consequently, adaptive differences in the human species might be expected to track that pattern. In addition, people interbreed with people nearby, who in turn interbreed with people nearby, and over the long run this reinforces the gradual nature of biological distinctions among populations. Indeed, the "isolation" of traditional indigenous peoples is a feature that has been consistently overestimated in the history of anthropology—all peoples trade, and where goods flow, so do genes (Terrell and Stewart, 1996; Wolf, 1972).

We know very little about the time frame in which these clines originated, but genetic and paleontological evidence points to a recent origin for the genetic diversity within our species. For example, we find two randomly chosen chimpanzees or gorillas to be considerably more different genetically than two randomly chosen humans, even though chimps, gorillas, and humans diverged from one another about 7 million years ago and are all consequently the same age (Ferris, Brown, Davidson, and Wilson, 1981; Ruano, Rogers, Ferguson-Smith, and Kidd, 1992). Genetic diversity in the human species is surprisingly ephemeral—only on the scale of tens of thousands of years—and seems in some large measure to have been replaced by cultural diversity.

The reason why Americans tend to see three "races" of people is simply an artifact of history and statistics. Immigrants to America have come mostly from ports where seafaring vessels in earlier centuries could pick them up—hence our notion of African is actually West African, and our notion of Asian is actually East Asian (Brace, 1995). When we realize that people originating from very different parts of the world are likely to look very different and combine that with the fact that most European immigrants came from north-central Europe, it is not hard to see why we might perceive three types of people.

If there were a larger immigrant presence in America representing the rest of the world—western Asia, Oceania, East or South Africa, the Arctic—we would be more struck by our inability to classify them easily as representatives of three groups. Perhaps the most obvious example involves the people of South Asia (India and Pakistan), who are darkly complected (like Africans), facially resemble Europeans, and live on the continent of Asia!

To an earlier generation, dividing humans into three types harmonized well with a mythical history that saw humans as descended from Noah's three sons. Although the far reaches of the continents were unknown to them, the ancient Hebrews ascribed the North Africans to the lineage of Ham, central and southern Europeans to the lineage of Japheth, and West Asians (including themselves) to the lineage of Shem, "after their families, after their tongues, in their lands, in their nations" (Genesis 10:20). This origin myth spread in the Roman Empire through the popularity of the Antiquities of the Jews by Flavius Josephus (Hannaford, 1996).

However, if there were three geographic types of people in nature, it is difficult to know in the light of modern knowledge what they might represent biohistorically. Did one ancestral lineage (Ham) settle near Ghana, one (Shem) settle near Korea, and one (Japheth) settle near Norway, their descendants becoming rather distinct from one another and remaining rather homogeneous as they spread outward and mixed at the fringes—as some 19th century writers essentially believed? No; humans have always been living and evolving in the in-between places, and there is no basis on which to regard the most divergent peoples as somehow the most primordial.

Actually, our racial archetypes represent not some pure ancestors but symbolic representations of the most biologically extreme peoples on earth. We may note in this context that the father of biological classification, Linnaeus, defined Europeans as blond and blue-eyed. Linnaeus, of course, was Swedish. But people with these features are the most extreme Europeans, not the most European, nor the most representative.

Dividing and classifying are cultural acts and represent the imposition of arbitrary decisions on natural patterns. This is most evident in the legalities of defining races, so that intermarriage between them could be prohibited—the miscegenation laws (Wright, 1995). In general, a single black great grandparent was sufficient to establish a person as "Black," whereas seven white great-grandparents were insufficient to establish one as "White." Here, race can be seen as inherited according to a symbolic or folk system of heredity, in contrast to biological inheritance. Thus racial heredity is qualitative, all or nothing, whereas biological heredity is quantitative and fractional.

Can We Compare People from Different Parts of the World?

The primary basis of all science is comparison. Peoples of the world differ from one another, and to understand the nature of those differences we are obliged to compare them. The social issues overlying such comparisons, however, necessitate considerably more introspection than would be taken for granted by a scientist accustomed to comparing spiders or earthworms (Marks, 1995).

The skin, hair, face, and body form all vary across the world's populations. In humans, these biological differences are complemented and exaggerated by differences in language, behavior, dress, and other components of the cumulative historical stream we call culture. The skeletal differences among the world's most different peoples are actually quite subtle, however, so that although a trained forensic anthropologist can allocate modern remains into a small number of given categories, it is virtually impossible to do so with prehistoric remains (Clark, 1963).

The fact that skeletal remains can be sorted into pre-existing categories does not mean that those categories represent fundamental divisions of the human species (Brace, 1995; Sauer, 1992). When asked to sort blocks of various sizes into large and small, a child can do so easily and replicably, but that is not a testimony to the existence of two kinds of blocks in the universe. It is a testament only to the ease with which distinctions can be imposed on gradients.

By the 18th century, European sailors had demonstrated unambiguously that all known human populations were interfertile and were thus biologically a single taxonomic unit in spite of the perceptible differences among them. Indeed, reconciling the obvious differences among humans to a single creative act in the Bible led 18th-century European scientists (such as Buffon) to the first theories of microevolution. On the other hand, theories of multiple origins of different peoples (polygenism, as opposed to monogenism) persisted in the United States through the Civil War. These biological theories helped to justify the subjugation of non-Whites by emphasizing their biological separation (Stanton, 1960). In the 1920s, geneticists still debated whether race-crossing might be genetically harmful because of the apparently profound differences among human populations (Davenport and Steggerda, 1929; Provine, 1973). Those differences are not so genetically substantial, however, for such interbreeding among human populations has not shown evidence of biologically harmful effects (Shapiro, 1961).

Are Consistently Detectable Differences between Human Populations Genetic?

This is quite possibly the most widely misunderstood aspect of human biology, in spite of nearly a century of study. If I study 1,000 Ibos from Nigeria and 1,000 Danes from Denmark, I can observe any number of differences between the two groups. One group, for example, is darkly complected; the other is lightly complected. This difference would probably be the same whether I selected my sample in the year 1900, 2000, or 2100, and it is presumably genetic in etiology.

On the other hand, one group speaks Ibo and the other speaks Danish. That difference would also be there if I selected my sample in 1900, 2000, or 2100, but it is presumably not genetic. At least, generations of immigrants attest to the unlikelihood of a genetic component to it.

How, then, can we know from the observation of a difference whether the difference is biologically based or not?

European explorers were well aware that the people who looked the most different from them also acted the most differently. Linnaeus had invoked broad suites of personality ("impassive, lazy") and culture traits ("wears loose-fitting clothes") in his diagnosis of four geographic subspecies of humans in 1758. The next generation of researchers recognize that these traits were both overgeneralized (if not outright slanderous) and exceedingly malleable, and they sought to establish their formal divisions of the human species solely on biological criteria. (One can also observe that cultural boundaries [political, linguistic, etc.)] are generally discrete, in contrast to clinal biological variation, which makes it unlikely that the two are causally connected.)

It was widely assumed by the middle of the 19th century that regardless of the degree of malleability of mental or behavioral traits of human groups, the features of the body were fundamentally immutable. Thus traits like the shape of the head could be taken as an indicator of transcendent biological affinity—groups with similarly shaped heads were closely related, and those with differently shaped heads were more distantly related (Gould, 1981).

The first to challenge this assumption empirically was Boas (1912), who measured skulls of immigrants to Ellis Island and compared them to those of relatives already living in the United States. He found that the human body is indeed very sensitive to the conditions of growth and that there was a decided tendency of diverse immigrant groups to become more physically convergent in America—in spite of marrying within their own groups—than they were when they arrived.

In particular, the shape of the head turned out to be a very malleable, and not at all a reliable indicator of genetics or race. Subsequent studies of other immigrant groups, notably Japanese immigrants to Hawaii by Shapiro and Hulse (1930), supported this discovery. Thus the observation of consistent difference between groups of people—even of the body—is not necessarily indicative of a genetic basis for that difference (Kaplan, 1954; Lasker, 1969). This work effectively shifted the burden of proof from those who question a genetic basis for the observation of difference to those who assert it.

To establish a genetic basis for an observed difference between two populations, therefore, requires more than just observing the difference to be consistent. It requires presumably genetic data. The inference of a genetic difference in the absence of genetic data thus represents not a scientific theory of heredity but a folk theory of heredity. To the extent that behavioral and mental traits—such as test scores and athletic performances—are even more developmentally plastic than are strictly physical traits, the same injunction must hold even more strongly for them. Genetic inferences require genetic data.

Do Different Groups Have Different Potentials?

One of the catch-phrases of 1995's best-selling *The Bell Curve* (Herrnstein and Murray, 1994) was "cognitive ability." Eluding a scientifically rigorous definition, the phrase is left to be explained by a common sense or folk definition—cognitive ability presumably means the mental development possible for a person under optimal circumstances. But it would take an extraordinarily naive or evil scientist to suggest seriously that such circumstances are, in fact, broadly optimized across social groups in our society. Consequently, not only can we not establish that abilities are different, we have no reliable way even to measure such an innate property in the first place. What we have is performance—on tests or just in life—which is measurable, but which is the result of many things, only one of which is unmeasurable innate ability.

Once again, we encounter the problem of a burden of proof for a biological assertion. If the concept itself is metaphysical, the burden of proof must obviously be very heavy. On one hand, it is not at all unreasonable to suggest that different people have different individual "gifts"—we all possess unique genetic constellations, after all. On the other hand, those gifts are not amenable to scientific study, for they are only detectable by virtue of having been developed or cultivated. Thus no scientific statements can be responsibly made about such genetic gifts in the absence of the life history of the person to whom they belong.

In other words, ability is a concept that is generally easy to see only in the past tense. I know I had the ability to be a college professor, because I am one; but how can I know in any scientifically valid sense whether I could have been a major-league third baseman? I can't, so it is simply vain for me to speculate on it. A life is lived but once, and what it could have been—while fascinating to contemplate—is not a scientific issue.

There is also an important asymmetry about the concept of ability. A good performance indicates a good ability, but a poor performance need not indicate poor ability. As noted above, many factors go into a performance, only one of which is ability. Thus, when we encounter the question of whether poor performance—even over the long term—is an indication of the lack of cognitive ability, the only defensible position from the standpoint of biology is agnosticism. We do not know whether humans or human groups differ in their potentials in any significant way. More than that, we cannot know—so this question lies outside the domain of scientific discourse and within the domain of folk knowledge.

Further, this raises a darker question: What are we to make of scientists who assert the existence of constitutional differences in ability? If we cannot gauge differences in ability in any reliable manner, it is a corruption of science to assert in its name that one group indeed has less ability than another. From the mouth or pen of a politician, the assertion might reflect ignorance or demagoguery; from that of a scientist, it reflects incompetence or irresponsibility. Scientists are subject to the cultural values of their time, place, and class and historically have found it difficult to disentangle those values from their pronouncements as scientists. We now recognize the need to define the boundaries of science in order to distinguish the authoritative voice of scientists speaking as scientists from the voice of scientists speaking as citizens. This distinction is vital to keeping science from being tarnished by those few scientists who have chosen to invoke it as a validation of odious social and political doctrines.

A reliable inference of differences in ability from the observation of differences in performance requires the control of many cultural and life history variables. The first step toward controlling those variables is to develop a society in which children from diverse social groups and upbringings have equal opportunities to cultivate their diverse gifts.

Human Biology through the Lens of History

Because ability is a metaphysical concept, there is no valid evidence from the fields of science that groups of people have similar abilities, any more than there is evidence that they have different abilities.

There is evidence bearing on this issue from the humanities, however—namely, history. Ours is not the first generation in which the claim has been put forward that human groups are of unequal worth, ostensibly based on science. Leading geneticists of the 1910s and 1920s avidly promoted the recent discoveries of chromosomes and Mendel's laws. Breakthroughs in genetics suggested that it might be fruitful to look there for a solution to America's social problems. Crosscutting political lines, Americans widely embraced a social philosophy known as eugenics, whose cardinal tenet was that antisocial traits represented the effects of a gene for "feeblemindedness," which had a very uneven distribution in the world (Davenport, 1911). It was found commonly among the rural and urban poor, and across the world in the techno-economically backward nations.

Among the most widely cited data was the pseudonymous Kallikak family, whose 18th-century genitor had sired a child by a "feeble-minded tavern girl" and another by his lawful Quaker wife. Several generations later, the descendants of the illegitimate son were primarily social outcasts, whereas those of the legitimate sons were upstanding citizens (Goddard, 1912). This was cited for decades, even in genetics textbooks, as evidence for the transmission of feeble-mindedness through one side of the family—in spite of the fact that it could hardly be diagnosed as a biological trait.

Scientific solutions to America's problems readily presented themselves on this basis: (a) restriction of immigration for the "feebleminded" hoping to enter the country and (b) sterilization for the "feebleminded" already here (Grant, 1916). The latter was upheld by the Supreme Court's 1927 decision in *Buck v. Bell,* in which the right of the state to sterilize the feebleminded, who "sap the strength of our nation," was upheld, on the grounds that "three generations of imbeciles are enough." This was not about enabling the poor to control their own reproduction, by giving them both the life options and the technology to implement them, but rather about the elimination of the gene pool of the poor, on the basis that it was irredeemably corrupt. Immigration restriction was enacted by the Johnson Act of 1924 and had an ultimate effect of denying asylum to many who would later suffer at the hands of the Nazis. Both were based on the expert voices of geneticists (Allen, 1983; Kevles, 1985; Paul, 1995).

The eugenics movement was not so much racist as classist—asserting the genetic superiority of the rich over the poor—but the Depression showed widely that economic status was not a reliable basis on which to infer genetic constitution. It was, curiously enough, geneticists themselves whose blind faith in (and promotion of) their subject proved them to be the least able to distinguish their own science from the folk prejudices that merely claimed that particular science as its basis.

Nearly a century later, however, some of these ideas are undergoing a renaissance. Promoting the Human Genome Project, James Watson declared that "we used to think our fate was in the stars. Now we know, in large measure, our fate is in our genes" (Jaroff, 1989, p. 67). With such a blank check for the power of genetics, it is no wonder we now hear routinely about hypothetical genes for crime, personality, intelligence, and sexual preference—often with evidence no more substantive than was presented in the 1920s (Nelkin and Lindee, 1995).

The eugenics movement was predicated on the apocalyptic fear that high reproductive rates in the lower classes would doom the nation to ever-growing numbers of constitutionally stupid people. And yet the descendants of those poor people became educated and socially mobile, and they have shown themselves indeed capable of running the nation. Ironically, the group targeted most strongly by I.Q. zealots of that era—poor immigrant Ashkenazi Jews—are now identified in *The Bell Curve* as comprising a "cognitive elite." With such extraordinary intellectual leapfrogging documentable in the history of this subject, we are consequently obliged to regard skeptically any broad criticisms of the gene pools of large classes of people. The issue revealed itself to be a social one—how to allow the children of the poor access to the means to develop their abilities—not a biological one, their lack of abilities.

Conclusions

Racial classifications represent a form of folk heredity, wherein subjects are compelled to identify with one of a small number of designated human groups. Where parents are members of different designated groups, offspring are generally expected to choose one, in defiance of their biological relationships.

Differing patterns of migration, and the intermixture that accompanies increasing urbanization, are ultimately proving the biological uselessness of racial classifications. Identification with a group is probably a fundamental feature of human existence. Such groups, however, are genetically fluid, and to the extent that they may sometimes reflect biological populations, they are defined locally. Races do not reflect large fundamental biological divisions of the human species, for the species does not, and probably never has, come packaged that way.

Merely calling racial issues "racial" may serve to load the discussion with reified patterns of biological variation and to focus on biology rather than on the social inequities at the heart of the problem. Racism is most fundamentally the assessment of individual worth on the basis of real or imputed group characteristics. Its evil lies in the denial of people's right to be judged as individuals, rather than as group members, and in the truncation of opportunities or rights on that basis. But this is true of other "isms"—sexism, anti-Semitism, and prejudices against other groups—and points toward the most important conclusion about human biology: Racial problems are not racial. If biologically diverse peoples had no biological differences but were marked simply on the basis of language, religion, or behavior, the same problems would still exist. How do we know this? Because they do exist, for other groups. The problems of race are social problems, not biological ones; and the focus on race (i.e., seemingly discontinuous bio-geographic variation) is therefore a deflection away from the real issues (Montagu, 1963).

The most fundamental dichotomy we can emphasize from the standpoint of biology is that between identity and equality. Identity is a relationship defined by biology; equality is a relationship conferred by culture and society. Genetic processes operate to guarantee that we are not biologically identical to others, although we are more or less similar to others; however, our laws guarantee equality, independently of biology (Dobzhansky, 1962). A society in which individual talents can be cultivated without regard to group affiliations, social rank, or other a priori judgments will be a successful one—acknowledging biological heterogeneity while developing the diverse individual gifts of its citizenry.

For Further Information

Marks, J. (1995). *Human Biodiversity.* Explores the overlap between genetics and anthropology, searching for areas of mutual illumination.
Montagu, A. (1963). *Man's Most Dangerous Myth.* A classic work by an outstanding and outspoken scholar.
Nelkin, D., and Lindee, M. S. (1995). *The DNA Mystique.* A popular account of the American infatuation with heredity, and the ways in which it has been exploited by science in this century.

References

Allen, G. (1983). The misuse of biological hierarchies: The American eugenics movement, 1900–1940. *History and Philosophy of the Life Sciences,* 5, 105–127.
Boas, F. (1912). Changes in the bodily form of descendants of immigrants. *American Anthropologist,* 14, 530–562.
Brace, C. L. (1995). Region does not mean "race"—Reality versus convention in forensic anthropology. *Journal of Forensic Sciences,* 40, 171–175.
Buck v. Bell, 274 U.S. 200 (1927).
Clark, W. E. Le Gros. (1963, January 12). How many families of man? *The Nation,* pp. 35–36.
Davenport, C. B. (1911). *Heredity in Relation to Eugenics.* New York: Henry Holt.
Davenport, C. B., and Steggerda, M. (1929). *Race Crossing in Jamaica* (Publication No. 395). Washington, D.C.: Carnegie Institution of Washington.
Dobzhansky, T. (1962). *Mankind Evolving.* New Haven: Yale University Press.
Ferris, S. D., Brown, W. M., Davidson, W. S., and Wilson, A. C. (1981). Extensive polymorphism in the mitochondrial DNA of apes. *Proceedings of the National Academy of Sciences, USA,* 78, 6319–6323.

Goddard, H. H. (1912). *The Kallikak Family: A Study in the Heredity of Feeblemindedness.* New York: Macmillan.
Grant, M. (1916). *The Passing of the Great Race.* New York: Scribner.
Gould, S. J. (1981). *The Mismeasure of Man.* New York: Norton.
Hannaford, I. (1996). *Race: The History of an Idea in the West.* Baltimore: Johns Hopkins University Press.
Herrnstein, R., and Murray, C. (1994). *The Bell Curve.* New York: Free Press.
Hiernaux, J. (1974). *The People of Africa.* London: Weidenfeld & Nicolson.
Huxley, J. (1938). Clines: An auxiliary taxonomic principle. *Nature,* 142, 219–220.
Jaroff, L. (1989, March 20). The gene hunt. *Trine,* 62–67.
Johnson Act (Immigration), ch. 190, 43 *Star,* 153 (May 26, 1924).
Kaplan, B. A. (1954). Environment and human plasticity. *American Anthropologist,* 56, 780–800.
Kevles, D. J. (1985). *In the Name of Eugenics.* Berkeley: University of California Press.
Lasker, G. W. (1969). Human biological adaptability. *Science,* 166, 1480–1486.
Livingstone, F. (1962). On the non-existence of human races. *Current Anthropology,* 3, 279.
Marks, J. (1995). *Human Biodiversity: Genes, Race, and History.* Hawthorne, N.Y.: Aldine.
Montagu, A. (1963). *Man's Most Dangerous Myth: The Fallacy of Race.* Cleveland: World Publishing.
Nelkin, D., and Lindee, M. S. (1995). *The DNA Mystique: The Gene As Cultural Icon.* New York: Freeman.
Paul, D. B. (1995). *Controlling Human Heredity.* Atlantic Highlands, N.J.: Humanities Press.
Provine, W. (1973). Geneticists and the biology of race crossing. *Science,* 182, 790–796.
Ruano, G., Rogers, J., Ferguson-Smith, A. C., and Kidd, K. K. (1992). DNA sequence polymorphism within hominoid species exceeds the number of phylogenetically informative characters for a HOX2 locus. *Molecular Biology and Evolution,* 9, 575–586.
Sauer, N. (1992). Forensic anthropology and the concept of race: If races don't exist, why are forensic anthropologists so good at identifying them? *Social Science and Medicine,* 34, 107–111.
Shapiro, H. (1939). *Migration and Environment.* London: Oxford University Press.
———. (1961). Race mixture. In *The Race Question in Modern Science* (pp. 343–389). New York: Columbia University Press/UNESCO.
Stanton, W. H. (1960). *The Leopard's Spots: Scientific Attitudes toward Race in America, 1815–59.* Chicago: University of Chicago Press.
Terrell, J. E., and Stewart, P. J. (1996). The paradox of human population genetics at the end of the twentieth century. *Reviews in Anthropology,* 25, 13–33.
Wolf, E. (1972). *Europe and the People without History.* Berkeley: University of California Press.
Wright, L. (1995, July 25). One drop of blood. *The New Yorker,* pp. 46–55.

Form at end of book

WiseGuide Wrap-Up

There is greater diversity within racial categories than among them. Racial categories do not offer much insight into the lives or characteristics of the people that they are used to categorize. The secondary characteristics of skin color, hair texture, and facial features do not explain more important issues of intelligence, morality, or personality. There is no clear genetic connection between melanin in the skin and human behavior. So why do we persist in using these categorizations?

Maybe it can be explained by a preference for information we can see over information that must be more carefully acquired. We want to believe that what we see is a guide to the person because that is easier than actually getting to know the person. We want easy categorizations that make the world predictable and safe. The categories of race seem to provide a ready-made way to sort people—our kind versus not our kind. We are reluctant to give this up, even if it isn't really useful.

Diversity and creativity go together. During creative periods, diverse peoples and interests come together to excite and challenge one another. Many see this as the reason behind America's success. Purity and isolation do not increase individual or group success. Fear of others who are different diverts energies away from constructive uses. Continued interest in ethnic and racial differences may prevent us from improving our understanding of the important facets of being biologically human.

R.E.A.L. Sites

This list provides a print preview of typical **Coursewise** R.E.A.L. sites. (There are over 100 such sites at the **Courselinks**™ site.) The danger in printing URLs is that web sites can change overnight. As we went to press, these sites were functional using the URLs provided. If you come across one that isn't, please let us know via email to: webmaster@coursewise.com. Use your Passport to access the most current list of R.E.A.L. sites at the **Courselinks** site.

Site name: The Center for the Study of White American Culture
URL: http://www.euroamerican.org/
Why is it R.E.A.L.? The Center for the Study of White American Culture is not a white supremacist organization but a group of multiracial scholars looking into the meaning of "whiteness" in American culture. The site offers articles and information on white culture and links to other relevant sites.
Key terms: culture, race

Site name: The Nizkor Project
URL: http://www.nizkor.org/
Why is it R.E.A.L.? This site, sponsored by the Nizkor Project, provides insight into the Holocaust, an important event in modern history that suggests the meaning of race in human behavior. The site includes information on the Holocaust, the Nuremberg trials, various Nazi leaders, and revisionists' attempts to redefine the meaning of events during World War II.
Key terms: race, ethnicity, Holocaust

section 10

STAND!

Is Participation in Sports the Best Avenue to Minority Success and Acceptance?

Take a Closer Look

1. What role do sports play in promoting economic opportunities for minorities?

2. Are sports an accurate description of American society? How does the notion of teamwork define the way society operates?

3. Should minority Americans devote their talents and energies to sports as a means of achieving social acceptance and economic success?

4. Is the percentage of minority coaches, owners, and promoters as great as that of minority players? Are minorities part of the decision-making groups in sports?

WiseGuide Intro

The United States has always prided itself on being the land of opportunity. While everyone might not be economically equal, the theory is that, in the long run, talent and ability win out, and those with talent and the willingness to work hard are accepted into society. The history of blacks and Native Americans in U.S. society raises interesting questions concerning the validity of this view.

In the past, white power brokers obstructed the careers of talented minority athletes. White team owners and coaches determined the extent of black and Native American participation and exposure in sports. The media portrayed minority athletes in stereotypical ways that disadvantaged them and reinforced notions of Anglo moral superiority. It was not until the Civil Rights movement, beginning in the 1950s, that minority athletes began to get the recognition and opportunities they deserved.

In Reading 22, Gerald R. Gems presents a concise history of black and Native American football players. He discusses this history in light of the roadblocks to these groups' acceptance into professional sports and also in the context of the developing identities of these athletes as men, professionals, and ethnic group members. Gems explores the impact of sports participation on the changing identity of individuals in these groups and the use of sports as a means of entering the wider society. According to Gems: "Whereas boxing pitted black against white in an individual and hostile encounter, football incorporated black players within the cooperative framework of the team, symbolically portraying their inclusion in the greater polity."

For minority athletes, being as good as white players was insufficient. To get an opportunity to play, they had to be twice as good. This meant placing a greater emphasis on developing talent in sports. In Reading 23, Robert M. Sellers and Gabriel P. Kuperminc explore the degree to which an emphasis on sports has skewed the goals of the black community. They note that black athletes are overrepresented in various professional sports, such as football and basketball, and they explore the impact this has had on producing unrealistic goals for black male athletes. Their research indicates that while some goal discrepancy exists, it is not an impediment to academic success or other forms of occupational attainment.

Issue 10: Is participation in sports the best avenue to minority success and acceptance?

The Construction, Negotiation, and Transformation of Racial Identity in American Football:
A Study of Native and African Americans

Gerald R. Gems

Gerald R. Gems currently serves as the chairperson of the Health and Physical Education Department at North Central College in Naperville, Illinois. He is the coeditor of book reviews for the Journal of Sport History, *and has authored two books and numerous articles.*

Introduction

This study assumes that its subjects have multiple identities: as men, football players, members of distinct racial and socio-economic groups, Americans, sons, fathers, and husbands. It attempts to analyze only some of these roles in relation to the subjects' sporting experiences, which generated meanings that were interpreted by themselves and others. Furthermore, such meanings changed over time, and proved negotiable through human agency. Racial identity, a problematic construct, assumed physiological differences during the period of this study, which extends from 1890 to the 1960s. The practices of the dominant white culture defined the boundaries of racial interaction, and attempted to define the meanings of a collective racial identity. To that extent, non-white groups such as Native Americans and African Americans underwent similar experiences in their exclusion, then limited inclusion in the dominant society and in white construction of alternative groups' identity.[1]

Construction of Identity

For the Native Americans, even the term *Indian* proved a descriptive misnomer. Ascribed by whites, they also as-signed roles such as savage, child of nature, earthly steward, and ultimate victim. Blacks, too, fell victim to slavery, the loss of their African cultures, and white characterizations of them as brutes, inept children, and even subhumans. Social Darwinists stereotyped non-whites as inferior and subordinate groups and rationalized white dominance as a benevolent practice of deculturation and assimilation to white norms. That process included the humiliating experiences of plantation or reservation life, the imposition of sedentary agricultural lifestyles, white dress and housing styles, and shorn braids for Indians or facial hair for blacks. Both slavery and boarding school experiences sought to segregate non-whites from white society, break down clan and kinship ties, and produce white generalizations of racial identity that had, in fact, differed greatly by tribe affiliation. Thus unable to define their own identities, both blacks and Indians struggled to overcome whites' stereotypes and the self-doubts that such characterizations as "others" produced.[2]

Such training or schooling brought inevitable cultural change as it brought non-whites into contact with whites' language, education, economy, and religious, political, and social practices. For many Indians and blacks it eventually meant a transition from a rural lifestyle to an urban, industrial existence. Part of that commercial world included sporting enterprises as an expression of power relations, and football, in particular, enjoyed a late nineteenth century boom, as elite white institutions contested with each other for prestige and national recognition. That process began with the first Princeton–Rutgers game in 1869, and reached nationwide proportions by the 1890s.

Reprinted from *American Indian Culture and Research Journal,* Volume 22, Number 2, by permission of the American Indian Studies Center, UCLA. © 1998 Regents of the University of California.

For non-whites the football field proved an arena of contested terrain, where they might mediate and transform the white construction of their identities. For non-white football players that meant a measure of assimilation, but not full enculturation in the white world.[3]

Negotiation of Identity

Football, a game that had started among and for the northeastern elites, could not remain so, once it spread westward and southward. Students at land grant colleges, the burgeoning public high schools, and even boys' sandlot teams adopted the game by the 1880s, bringing greater democratization to the sport. Although Social Darwinists of the time assumed white, Anglo, upper-class superiority, they did not fully intend to test it on the football field. Walter Camp claimed that "it is a gentleman's game—that, as the 'Dandy' gentlemen regiments in the Civil War outmarched, out fought, and out plucked the 'bloody rebs,' so gentlemen teams and gentlemen players will always hold the football field. Brutes haven't the pluck. . . . "[4] The elites' own insistence on winning dismantled the amateur code and its pretensions of gentlemanly posture. Victories required talent, regardless of lineage, and the spread of football induced an inevitable leveling effect. As early as 1894, a proponent of the game claimed that it "dissapated [sic] bigotry and intolerance."[5]

Among the first to dispel the myths of Social Darwinism were African Americans. Systematically excluded from the upper echelons of professional baseball after 1877, boxing, for a time, offered blacks the opportunity to challenge the belief in white superiority. When George Dixon, the black featherweight champ, bloodied and knocked out Jack Skelly in an 1892 New Orleans title fight, however, a racist backlash ensued in a move to ban interracial bouts. Heavyweights refused to give the black Peter Jackson a deserved chance at the crown. Thus, when Jack Johnson finally wrested it from Tommy Burns in Australia in 1908, it engendered the search for the "Great White Hope," Johnson's flight from federal prosecution, race riots, and his eventual imprisonment.[6] It remained for the more docile Joe Louis to rekindle African American hopes in the 1930s. Until that time football provided the only continuous, highly visible athletic enterprise for African American athletes. Moreover, whereas boxing pitted black against white in an individual and hostile encounter, football incorporated black players within the cooperative framework of the team, symbolically portraying their inclusion in the greater polity.

Within that framework blacks seemed less threatening than in the singular encounters of the boxing ring, yet stellar play might be recognized by all. Given the game's similarity to military combat, football may have served a surrogate function for African American players, allowing them to attain a measure of hero status denied them in other arenas, even though they served with distinction in the Civil War as so-called Buffalo Soldiers, and in the Spanish-American War. Such disregard for black contributions to war efforts continued throughout World Wars I and II.[7]

On the football field, however, African American players, literally fought for and earned respect. George Jewett, star of the Ann Arbor High School team in 1889, entered the University of Michigan the next year. As a halfback and kicker, Jewett scored six touchdowns in one game against the Detroit Athletic Club, but his play in a 56–10 win over Albion resulted in a riot as opponents and fans tried to "kill the nigger." Police restored order and Jewett remained in the game. A teammate admitted that Jewett was "very fast. . . . He undoubtedly was the best player on the Michigan team of 1890." When an Indianapolis hotel manager refused him a room, white teammates caused him to retract his decision. Nevertheless, Jewett left Michigan the following year and reappeared in 1893 on the Northwestern team, whose fans apparently appreciated his play. In a game against Michigan that year a "special student train with all kinds of money to bet on their team" from Northwestern traveled to Ann Arbor. When Jewett scored the first touchdown they doubled their bets, only to be humiliated when Michigan beat Northwestern 72–6.[8]

While Jewett's fame proved transitory, he led the way for others. The year after his appearance two African Americans played for the Amherst team. William Tecumseh Sherman Jackson starred at halfback, and William Henry Lewis captained the team at center. Lewis, the son of former slaves, entered Harvard Law School and earned All-America honors at center in 1892 and 1893, the first black to gain such distinction. Lewis coached Harvard teams in later years and won election to the Cambridge city council and state legislature. He then served as assistant United States attorney general for Boston and held that national office during the Taft administration.[9]

Lewis earned respect beyond the football field, but it was due at least initially and in no small part to his prowess on it. When a local barber refused service to Lewis, fellow students boycotted his shop. Yet they took no action when Monroe Trotter, Harvard's first black Phi Beta Kappa, suffered a similar fate. W.E.B. DuBois, who obtained his bachelor's, master's, and doctoral degrees at the institution during the same period, stated that he did not feel a part of the school. Within a few short years, DuBois penned the scholarly treatise on the black experience in America, and in 1903 *The Souls of Black Folk*, which illuminated the "double-consciousness" of African American identity and his opposition to the accommodationist philosophy of Booker T. Washington, who accepted the policy of racial exclusion.[10]

In the South, segregation laws forced African Americans to play each other, and they did so by 1890 when Biddle began intramural football. Two years later it engaged in the first black intercollegiate game with Livingstone at Salisbury, North Carolina. The Lincoln-Howard series, initiated in 1894, became a Thanksgiving spectacular in Washington, D.C., which paralleled white festivities in New York as black identity blossomed. The Tuskegee–Atlanta series opened in 1897 and black sandlot teams competed in the South by the mid-1890s. Where excluded, African Americans thus constructed a parallel sporting culture and thereby gained some sense of inclusion in the mainstream sporting activities.[11]

Somewhat more fluid social conditions allowed greater opportunities for African Americans in the North. In 1902 Minnesota featured a multiracial front line with an Indian, an African American, a German, two Englishmen, and two Irishmen, all led by a Jewish quarterback. Such cosmopolitanism appeared throughout urban areas where the children of ethnic immigrants and African American migrants increasingly attended the public schools after the turn of the century. In Chicago the Pollard brothers began earning athletic laurels in the 1890s. By 1902 Chicago newspapers regularly praised Sam Ransom, a multi-sport star and teammate of Walter Eckersall at Hyde Park High School. Hyde Park arranged a post-season game in Louisville with Manual Training School in November of 1902; however, the Southerners refused to let Ransom play. He later showcased his brilliance in a national championship game against a Brooklyn team in which he scored seven touchdowns. Despite the presence of future All-Americans who also played in the game, the *Chicago Tribune* asserted that "Ransom was the particular star of the game. It was Sammy who was always in evidence, running now around one end and now the other, gaining twenty, thirty, forty yards with ease, always on hand when a fumble was made ready to fall on the ball. Ransom it was who made touchdown after touchdown, Ransom the irresistible."[12] Despite such prowess, white power brokers limited his future options.

Relatively few African Americans were able to showcase their talents at the collegiate level. Coaches Amos Alonzo Stagg of Chicago and Fielding Yost of Michigan fought over Eckersall, Ransom's white teammate, but neither apparently tried to recruit Ransom, who ended up at tiny Beloit College. Yost paid no heed in 1904 when a Michigan supporter wrote about Abner Powell, a black schoolboy sensation in Salt Lake City. At 180 pounds Powell allegedly ran one hundred yards in ten seconds. "This young man is a *human whirlwind* . . . the equal of Heston . . . a thorough gentleman, always knows his

place . . . fine punter." Such attributes proved to no avail, as white coaches determined the extent of black participation and exposure.[13]

Likewise, Stagg bypassed the numerous black stars on local high school teams. Southern schools adhered to strict segregation of the races, so when Dan McGugin, the Vanderbilt coach, requested a game with Chicago he wanted assurances that Chicago had no blacks on its team. Stagg replied, "No, we have no Negroes on the University of Chicago football team, and there is no chance of there being any candidates for the team next fall. Up to date there has never been a Negro on a University of Chicago team. In twenty-four years only three Negroes have competed . . . in track athletics."[14] Such coaches thus negated the promise of education and equal opportunity by limiting the complexion of the squads. African Americans might compete in individual sports, like track, but could not be part of the team on or off the field.

The athletes who got a chance made the most of it. Bob Marshall earned All-America recognition at Minnesota in 1905 and 1906, as did Edward Gray at Amherst in the latter year. Archie Alexander gained All-Missouri Valley honors for Iowa in 1910, even though opponents in Missouri refused to let him play. Alexander worked as hard in the classroom, earning a degree in civil engineering. Two years later, Roy Young coached linemen at Northwestern, one of the few blacks accorded a leadership role. Fritz Pollard, in 1916, and Paul Robeson, in 1917 and 1918, became the first African Americans to make the All-American first team, thereby becoming national heroes in the black community.[15]

The *Chicago Defender,* perhaps the most prominent of all African American newspapers, charged that football had become an "obsession" in black colleges as early as 1910. The craze included the trustees, alumni, faculty, and women. The paper claimed that players experienced tremendous pressure to bring glory to their schools and their female fans, for whom they risked injury and death. Failure to win brought disgrace.[16] In football blacks had found a means to challenge Social Darwinism, and when excluded they mobilized their own resources.

The black media began choosing its own All-American team in 1911. In 1912 Lincoln University of Pennsylvania joined three southern schools to form the Colored Intercollegiate Athletic Conference. The *Pittsburgh Courier* began naming a black national champion in 1920. In 1922 black promoters staged a black versus white football game in Chicago, which the black team won. By 1933 Florida A&M hosted the Orange Blossom Classic in Jacksonville, an African American bowl game that served as the unofficial national championship for black colleges. Still laboring under the Jim Crow laws that forced segregation, African Americans adopted the game as their own within their own administrative framework and commercialized structure. By that time dozens of black players had competed with and against whites on northern teams, slowly dismantling the precepts of Social Darwinism and providing the African American community with continued hope in the promise of democracy. Blacks demonstrated that trust by donating the proceeds of the 1942 Tuskegee–Wilberforce game, held in Chicago's Soldier Field, to the army emergency relief fund. The game itself, between two black schools, and the symbolic contribution signified an ongoing dilemma of dual identity for African Americans.[17]

Ironically, it was often in the small towns and among the less educated working class that black players won begrudging respect for their prowess on the burgeoning professional circuit. Professionalism spread from western Pennsylvania to eastern Ohio after the turn of the century. In 1904, Shelby, Ohio signed Charles Follis, previously a star black running back for the Wooster Athletic Association, to a contract for a full season and provided him with a job in the local hardware store. Such moves secured the loyalty of Follis through the 1906 season, for it was common practice for players to switch teams weekly, following the highest bidder for their services.[18]

Community pride and enormous bets required securing the best talent as professionalism spread to the East and westward, and African American players benefited. Akron signed Charles "Doc" Baker in 1906, and Henry McDonald began a long career among various New York teams in 1911. Gideon "Charlie" Smith played for Canton in 1915, and Bobby Marshall, the Minnesota All-American, was still playing professionally in 1927 at the age of forty-seven with the Duluth, Minnesota Eskimos in the National Football League. The emergence of Fritz Pollard on the professional scene in 1919 signaled the heyday of early black pros in the 1920s. Pollard enjoyed one of the highest salaries in the new professional league and a measure of prestige as the first African American to serve as a head coach. As player-coach Pollard led his team to the championship, and All-American Paul Robeson of Rutgers and Duke Slater of Iowa soon joined him in the pro games. More than a dozen black players appeared on six different teams before white owners followed the lead of baseball and banned them after 1933.[19]

For more than fifty years, while major league baseball excluded African Americans, football provided hope, opportunity, and a measure of recognition and esteem for black athletes. After Fritz Pollard helped a Pennsylvania coal town team defeat their rivals in 1923, the townspeople provided a Pullman berth for his train ride back to Chicago and threatened the crew lest they tried to invoke the color line restrictions. Pollard claimed that he was able to serve as the coach of the Hammond, Indiana Pros in

1923 to 1924 because "several of the players wanted me as coach," despite the presence of the Ku Klux Klan in the area.[20] Though more democratic, at least until 1934, black pioneers still faced racism from opponents, teammates, and fans. Racial slurs and intentional injuries were constant threats, but as African Americans prevailed they further damaged the restrictive barriers of Jim Crow and Social Darwinism. Black players demonstrated their power on the field, and both white owners and fans proved willing to pay for such prowess, allowing for greater inclusion in white popular culture. No longer could whites doubt black masculinity, as African American players won greater respect both on and off the field. Duke Slater became a municipal court judge in Chicago and Paul Robeson enjoyed national stardom in a theatrical career. Both had become "American" success stories before Robeson's social activism diminished white support. Whites gained greater appreciation and knowledge of black urban life as they flocked to black and tan cabarets throughout the 1920s, and by the 1930s scientists admitted to no proof of biological or mental differences between the races.[21]

Edward Henderson, a prominent black educator, stated that "athletics has done more to bring Negroes into the main stream of our American society than possibly any other medium."[22] Apparent harmony dissipated, however, as blacks achieved greater racial and class consciousness. Robeson questioned the capitalist system, and Joe Lillard, the last black pro player of the 1930s, questioned white leadership. Despite accolades from the white press, which acclaimed him as the team's star, the Chicago Cardinals suspended Lillard after a disagreement with his coach and fighting with white opponents. Like Jack Johnson, he had become the "bad nigger" who resisted white authority. Relegated to minor league play, blacks again forged their own destiny. Fritz Pollard coached the Brown Bombers which defeated white all-star teams during, the 1930s.[23]

A formidable black press and burgeoning black labor movement clamored for greater inclusion, and once again football provided an opportunity. A year before Jackie Robinson's debut in major league baseball, the Los Angeles Rams signed Kenny Washington and Woody Strode, and the Cleveland Browns of the All-America Football Conference hired Bill Willis and Marion Motley. Their success presaged the civil rights movement of the 1950s and the integration of southern colleges. By the 1970s even southern football had to integrate in the quest to maintain its regional pride.[24]

Football also highlighted the limited inclusion of Native Americans in white society. In 1879 the Carlisle Industrial School for Indians opened its doors in abandoned army barracks in Pennsylvania with the purpose of converting the Indians to white notions of civilization. The program of assimilation taught English, vocational skills, and the dominant white cultural values, but the football team represented its most visible success. Although beginning play in 1890, injuries, resulted in a two-year hiatus. Superintendent Richard Henry Pratt acceded to student requests to resurrect the game in 1893 because he perceived it as a means to instill teamwork, order, discipline, and obedience. Within two years the school embarked on a national schedule by challenging the eastern powers at their own game, as messianic movements and the Ghost Dance alarmed whites in the West through more traditional Indian rituals. At their first appearance in New York, patrons expected warpaint, tomahawks, and screeching and were disappointed to find that "They don't look any different than our boys." As Indians lost their traditional lifestyles, football may have served a surrogate function as a means to assert the skills and bravery previously displayed in war and the buffalo hunt. James Robertson has asserted that as a territorial game which required gaining ground or resisting such incursions, football replicated the frontier experience, and newspaper accounts of the era characterized it as such. As early as 1898 Dennis Wheelock, an Oneida Indian at Carlisle, stated that "the only way I see how he [the Indian] may reoccupy the lands that once were his, is through football, and as football takes brains, takes energy, proves whether civilization can be understood by the Indian or not, we are willing to perpetuate it."[25]

In 1898 quarterback Frank Hudson became the first of many Indian players to win All-American recognition, but Walter Camp, the selector, attributed his skills to coaching by a former Yale player. A.J. Standing, assistant superintendent at Carlisle, also acknowledged the team's success, but claimed the need for white coaching and management. Bemus Pierce, team captain, offered a rebuttal to that charge at the team banquet in 1898.[26]

Carlisle housed individuals from seventy different tribes, and the 1901 football team even included an Inuit, Nikifer Shouchuk. The school, and the team in particular, represented a showcase of government assimilation efforts masking Indian values in the process. With no home field the team traveled the length of the country, including West Coast tours in 1899 and 1903 to play against universities, middle-class athletic clubs, and other Indian schools. Such a nomadic existence may have replicated tribal life for some. In 1912 Carlisle even went to Canada to play a combined rugby-football game against Toronto University, in which Carlisle prevailed 49–1. Such exposure, and victories, garnered acclaim and power. Carlisle nearly defeated Harvard and Yale in the 1896 season, and beat Penn in 1899. Sportswriters ranked Carlisle among the best teams in the nation between 1904 and 1914. Its 1912 team, repre-

senting ten tribal groups, led the nation in scoring with 504 points. Jim Thorpe accounted for twenty-five of the team's sixty-six touchdowns. Combined with his feats as Olympic champion in both the 1912 pentathlon and decathlon, such performances shattered notions of white physical superiority, but white media inevitably characterized such victories as brawn over brain.[27]

Such a visible symbol of democracy and acculturation at work proved a commercial bonanza for opponents and provided a measure of power for the institution. As early as 1900, Coach Stagg at Chicago acknowledged the possibility of "a great financial success," but ultimately decided not to play the Indians because a loss might "jeopardize chances for (the) western championship."[28] Carlisle got a two-thousand-dollar guarantee from Michigan for a 1901 game in Detroit, and Chicago gave up seventeen thousand dollars for a 1907 contest, which Carlisle won 18–4.[29] Such enterprises drew the Indians into the mainstream urban, commercial culture, but did not ensure their full incorporation.

Winning at the box office and on the field may have gone a long way in resurrecting the image of Native Americans, except that "Pop" Warner, Carlisle's coach from 1899–1903 and again from 1907–1914, got most of the credit. The innovative formations and trick plays which the Indians featured were attributed to Warner's genius and only reinforced the Social Darwinian perception of the necessity for white leadership. When Carlisle hid the ball under a player's jersey and nearly defeated mighty Harvard in 1903, Warner reinforced the prevailing stereotypes by asserting, "The public expects the Indians to employ trickery and we try to oblige."[30] Warner likewise capitalized on the nativist sentiment that all Indians looked alike and that " 'Redskins' are hard to distinguish" by refusing to number players' jerseys.[31]

The white press continued to represent Indians as primitives or, at best, noble savages, despite the fact that the Indians' sportsmanship exceeded that of their white opponents. When kneed by an antagonist, Pete Hauser, a 1907 standout, retaliated with a simple question, "Who's the savage now?"[32] Often characterized as tricksters who won by deviousness or "massacre" if they scored a lot of points, such media descriptions reinforced white notions of Anglo moral superiority. One newspaper story stated:

[T]rue to his Indian origin, Thorpe had his occasional outbursts. After a 1912 scoreless tie . . . he went on a rampage. . . . Warner found him in a cafe . . . saturated in fire water . . . and beat his head up and down on the floor. This incident made Warner the only man whom Thorpe ever held in awe.[33]

Football taught Indians rules, discipline, and civilization, but ultimately they served as "good losers," as they had in the Anglo land quest for Manifest Destiny.

The game meant much more to the Indians, however, and provided them with a means to exhibit racial pride and a measure of vengeance. "Pop" Warner admitted approaching games as a frontier conflict and inciting his players in a continuation of the Indian wars. The Indians knew that such battles had been fought on unequal terms and proved anxious to show "what they could do when the odds were even." The importance of winning for the Indians can be deduced from Warner's remark that if the team lost more than one game in a season, "they felt like painting their faces black and throwing ashes over their head." When Dickinson's pre-game festivities included a cowboy scalping an Indian in 1905, Carlisle retaliated with a Dickinson dummy and proceeded to shoot arrows into its chest with each score in a 36–0 rout. In 1911 when Syracuse players smashed the nose of a Carlisle guard, they were amazed to witness his second-half return under a mask of tape. Only after the game did they realize that Carlisle's assistant coach, Emil Hauser (also known as Wauseka), had posed as an impostor to gain a measure of revenge.[34]

The Indians took particular pride in defeating Army more so than any other team, winning two of three games against the symbol of U.S. military might. A Carlisle historian noted that against the Army, "Redskins play football as if they were possessed."[35] Before the 1912 contest Warner allegedly told the Indians, "These are the long knives. You are Indians. Tonight we will know whether or not you are warriors."[36] When Jim Thorpe was ruled out of bounds on a kickoff that he presumably had returned for a touchdown, he avenged the decision by scoring another on the ensuing play. Carlisle won 27–6. Other Indians shared such sentiments. A player at the Haskell Indian Institute in Kansas wrote home in 1914, stating that he was at "hard practice for war . . . mobilizing our troops . . . trained and equipped for the coming campaign."[37]

Carlisle players also found particular joy in outsmarting the elite institutions with trick plays. The 1907 rules disallowed a pass completion out of bounds, so Albert Exendine ran around the Chicago bench before returning to the field to catch a touchdown pass in an 18–4 win. Trick plays were commonplace against Harvard, but unnecessary in 1911 when Thorpe scored a touchdown and four field goals in an 18–15 Carlisle win. After such games, players "had a lot of fun parodying the Cambridge accent, even those with very little English attempting the broad A." The pastime exemplified both the oral traditions of the Indians as well as their use of humor as a resistive device. After a win over Penn, one Carlisle player concluded, "Maybe white men better with cannon and guns, but Indian just as good in brains to think with," thus negating white claims and promoting racial pride and self-esteem.[38]

Football served the Native American players as a means both to resist and adapt the dominant culture that was imposed on them. Their entrance into the outlaw world of professional football continued that evolution into a gradual and limited adoption of commercialism that is still incomplete. As early as 1896, Green Bay reportedly paid Tom Skenandore, an Oneida Indian at Carlisle, and two players as well as coaches Warner and Pierce played in a New York tournament in 1902. John Mathews, a former Carlisle player, got paid by the Franklin, Pennsylvania team that same year. Carlisle players gained greater exposure to the renegade brand of football when it scheduled a Wednesday game against the Massillon, Ohio team in Cleveland in 1904. Despite the game being on a week day, they drew 3,600 patrons and thousands of dollars in bets, won by the Massillon pros 8–4.[39]

Forced to return his 1912 Olympic medals for violating the amateur ideal by playing professional baseball, Jim Thorpe openly adopted professional football in 1915, earning as much as 250 dollars a game from the Pine Village, Indiana and Canton, Ohio teams. Others soon found employment in the professional ranks after their college days. Joe Guyon, a member of the Chippewa tribe, starred at Carlisle before helping Georgia Tech to the national championship in 1917. Segregation policies proved less restrictive for Indians than blacks in the South. As an All-American, Guyon soon enjoyed a lucrative salary as a professional. Thorpe served, nominally, as the first president of the new professional league upon its founding in 1919. Both Thorpe and Guyon played for the all-Indian Oorang team on the professional circuit in 1922 and 1923, with Thorpe as player-manager of the twelve different tribes represented on the roster. The Oorang team served as a promotional gimmick for its white owner, but its composition also reflected a racial cohesiveness, a bond apparently lacking on mixed teams.[40]

Other Indians earned a measure of fame and status as football coaches and thereby gained greater inclusion in the dominant culture. Bemus Pierce, a Seneca Indian and a Carlisle star from 1894 to 1898, became Warner's assistant thereafter before assuming head coaching responsibilities at several schools. Albert Exendine, a member of the Delaware tribe, won All-America recognition in 1906 and 1907 before starting a long coaching career in 1908 that took him to both coasts and Oklahoma, where he retired to serve as a lawyer with the Bureau of Indian Affairs. Lone Star Dietz, a teammate of Thorpe's from 1907 to 1911, enjoyed an equally prestigious career as a coach, leading Washington state to an undefeated season and a 1916 Rose Bowl win. Dietz coached several collegiate squads before accepting the position of head coach of the professional Boston Braves in 1933 (later Washington Redskins). Dietz returned to the collegiate ranks in 1935 and a career as an artist. Indians thus proved to themselves and others that they could succeed both on and off the athletic field.[41]

The athletic tradition spawned by Carlisle ended in scandal when whites' financial mismanagement caused the school's closure in 1918. Indian players continued to earn acclaim and money in the National Football League for another decade, and Mayes McLain, of the Haskell Indian Institute, led the country in scoring with 253 points in 1926. Haskell garnered a 12-0-1 record that year, but the white media and NCAA record books subsequently diminished both team and individual achievements. Haskell had attempted to "attain a position among the foot ball teams of the west similar to that occupied by the Carlisle team among those of the east . . ." as early as 1900.[42] The most prominent teams, however, declined to schedule Haskell, thus limiting the Indian presence in the more elite circles. Despite Carlisle's success, the white media continued to reinforce old stereotypes a quarter of a century later. In the 1926 battle of unbeatens, Haskell and Boston College tied 21-21 in Boston. The *Boston Globe* declared the Indians "more powerful," but the Bostonians "smarter." When Haskell then defeated an unbeaten Xavier squad, the *Cincinnati Enquirer* called it "the modernized version of warfare of the Indian empire of the past." Perhaps it was such designation as "others," or perhaps the prowess of its players, that caused the Missouri Valley Conference to shun Haskell when scheduling, ensuring that there would be no more Carlisles.[43]

By 1932 even Jim Thorpe had to borrow a pass to get into the Los Angeles Olympics, a circumstance bemoaned by Vice President Charles Curtis, also of Indian descent. At a football banquet Thorpe had "received the greatest ovation ever given a football player on the coast," but went unrecognized as a man at the Olympics. Reduced to day labor and bit movie parts by 1933, Thorpe retained his pride, forcing movie executives to hire other Indians for Native American roles, but even he admitted that they would not be starring figures.[44]

Transformation of Identity

The perception of integration and assimilation fostered by the Carlisle teams masked the reality of limited inclusion in American society. Football allowed diverse tribes to obtain a sense of collective racial identity, combat Social Darwinian stereotypes, and develop pride in Indian athletic heroes. A select few gained socioeconomic status exemplifying the American dream. Whites, however, chose to arrest the development of full incorporation in American society by maintaining the separate and unequal reservation system that continues to plague Indian populations with poverty and the mixed blessing of limited autonomy.

Football enabled many blacks and Indians to redefine their own psychological identity. It brought a measure of self-respect, greater racial consciousness, and racial pride. Gus Welch, a Chippewa who had played for Warner at Carlisle, realized that he was morally superior to a white man that had "no principle." The coach, who swore at, kicked, and beat his players; gambled on games; and pocketed the receipts could hardly teach the virtuous life.[45] The minorities' athletic feats and successes destabilized norms, expectations, and stereotypes ascribed by whites, but socially they remained members of alternative cultures, marginalized with dual identities and limited inclusion, particularly off the field. But by the 1960s they had become part of several countercultures that changed the whole. Jim Brown personified the new assertive, proud black athlete with a greater sense of self. For African Americans, control of their own media had allowed for the promotion of inclusion and racial equality that served as a source of mobilization in the civil rights movement.[46]

Though race remained a social construct, both blacks and Indians redefined their self-conceptions. With the Indian Reorganization Act of 1934, more than one hundred tribes opted for their own constitutions, and a National Congress of American Indians appeared during the next decade, but a pan-Indian movement (the American Indian Movement) did not gain prominence until the 1970s. By that time both blacks and Indians had given new meaning to the separate-but-equal doctrine and reveled in their differences. Neither group needed nor wanted to become white, as they moved toward self-sufficiency. Football players such as Jim Brown, Gale Sayers, and others used their association with the game to combat racism. Brown certainly understood the historical importance of his predecessors in that process when he said, "I wonder if black stars ever study history. . . . Blacks who came before them paved the way."[47] Football helped many blacks and Indians lay the foundations for such identity formation by providing a collective memory of self-validation and the creation of kindred heroes as they successfully tested themselves against the beliefs of Social Darwinism and dispelled notions of white dominance. As Cornel West has more recently declared, the exposure and rejection of such white ideals was the first step in overcoming an imposed construction of racial identity and the affirmation of self-worth.[48] In that sense football proved to be not only an assimilative experience, but a resistive and liberating one as well.

Notes

1. The process of domination and negotiation of social power is part of Antonio Gramsci's hegemony theory. See Quintin Hoare and Geoffrey N. Smith, eds., *Selections from the Prison*

Notebooks (New York: International Pub., 1971); and Jeremy MacClancy, *Sport, Identity and Ethnicity* (Oxford: Berg, 1996), 3–7. For a comprehensive survey and analysis of African American studies, see Jeffrey T. Sammons, " 'Race' And Sport: A Critical Historical Examination," *Journal Of Sport History* 21:3 (Fall 1994):203–278.

2. Patricia Riley, ed., *Growing Up Native American: An Anthology* (New York: William Morrow & Co, 1993), 8; Fergus M. Bordewich, *Killing the White Man's Indian: Reinventing Native Americans at the End of the Twentieth Century* (New York: Doubleday, 1996), 343; Judith R. Kramer, *The American Minority Community* (New York: Thomas Y. Crowell, 1970), 192, 195, 203–206; Eugene D. Genovese, *Roll, Jordan, Roll: The World the Slaves Made* (New York: Pantheon Books, 1974); John D. Buenker and Norman A. Ratner, eds., *Multiculturalism in the United States: A Comparative Guide to Acculturation and Ethnicity* (Westport, Ct: Greenwood Press, 1992), 7–52; Gwendolyn Captain, "Enter Ladies and Gentlemen of Color; Gender, Sport, and the Ideal of African American Manhood and Womanhood During The Late Nineteenth and Early Twentieth Centuries," *Journal of Sport History* 18:1 (Spring 1991): 81–102.

3. Beth D. Kivel, "Adolescent Identity Formation and Leisure Contexts: A Selective Review of Literature," *Journal of Physical Education, Recreation and Dance* 69:1 (Jan. 1998): 36–38.

4. *Yale News*, Feb. 5, 1885, in Box 24, folder 1, Amos Alonzo Stagg Papers, University of Chicago, Special Collections.

5. J. Kinzer Shell, M.D., to Walter Camp, Apr. 21, 1894, Reel 15, Walter Camp Papers, Yale University. Social Darwinism applied Charles Darwin's evolutionary theory to social relations, with white assumptions of their own superiority in the survival of the fittest.

6. The jubilation in black communities around the country over Johnson's easy victory led to whites' retaliation and numerous altercations, dubbed riots by the press. Johnson's flaunting of racial mores of the time—including his marriage to and consorting with white women, some of whom were prostitutes—violated the Mann Act (transport of women across state lines for illegal purposes) and caused him to flee the country. See *New Orleans Times-Democrat* (Sept. 7, 1892, pp. 1, 4) for coverage of the Dixon-Skelly fight. See Randy Roberts, *Papa Jack: Jack Johnson and the Era of White Hopes* (Riverside, NY: The Free Press, 1983), on Johnson's eventful life.

7. John Hoberman, *Darwin's Athletes: How Sport Has Damaged Black America and Preserved the Myth of Race* (Boston: Houghton Mifflin, 1997), 61–75.

8. Ralph Stone to T. Hawley Tapping, Jan. 10, 1955; and Roger Sherman to T. Hawley Tapping, Jan. 19,1955, in Jewett file, Box 35, University of Michigan Archives, Bentley Historical Library.

9. Edna and Art Rust, Jr., *Art Rust's Illustrated History of the Black Athlete* (Garden City, NY: Doubleday & Co., 1985), 226; Morris A. Beale, *The History of Football at Harvard, 1874–1948* (Washington, D.C.: Columbia Pub. Co., 1948), 534–536.

10. Kim Townsend, *Manhood at Harvard: William James and Others* (New York: W. W. Norton & Co., 1996), 234, 247, W.E.B. DuBois, *The Souls of Black Folk* (New York: Penguin Books, 1989 reprint).

11. Michael Hurd, *Black College Football, 1892–1992: One Hundred Years of History, Education, and Pride* (Virginia Black, VA: Downing Co., 1993), 13, 28, 32; John Heisman, "Signals," *Collier's* (Oct. 6, 1928): 32.

12. Alexander M. Weyand, *The Saga of American Football* (New York: Macmillan, 1955), 78; John M. Carroll, *Fritz Pollard: Pioneer in Racial Advancement* (Urbana: University of Illinois Press, 1992), 18–20; *Chicago Tribune*, Nov. 24, 1902, 6; Dec. 7, 1902, 9 (quote).

13. W. J. Davis to Keene Fitzpatrick, Aug. 17, 1904, Box 1, Board in Control of Intercollegiate Athletics, University of Michigan, Bentley Historical Library.

14. Stagg-McGugin Correspondence, Nov. 16, 1916; Dec. 11, 1916, Dec. 14, 1916 (quote), in Box 42, folder 13, Stagg Papers.

15. Michael Oriard, *Reading Football: How the Popular Press Created an American Spectacle* (Chapel Hill: University of North Carolina Press, 1993), 232–233; Jack W. Berryman, "Early Black Leadership in Collegiate Football," *Historical Journal of Massachusetts* 9 (June 1981): 17–28, 85 fn. 51; Carroll, *Fritz Pollard*, 109–112; Bob Royce, "Bridge Builder," *College Football Historical Society* 5:2 (Feb. 1992): 5–6; Martin Bauml Duberman, *Paul Robeson* (New York: Alfred A. Knopf, 1988), 19–24.

16. *Chicago Defender*, Jan. 22, 1910, 1.

17. Arthur R. Ashe, Jr., *A Hard Road to Glory: Football* (New York: Amistad, 1988), 9; William Kenney, "Chicago's Black and Tans," *Chicago History* 27:3 (Fall 1997): 5–31, 22 on football game; Hurd, *Black College Football* 13, 163–165; Wanda Ellen Wakefield, *Playing to Win: Sports and the American Military, 1898–1945* (Albany: State University of New York Press, 1997), 126. So-called Jim Crow laws emanated from southern whites' attempts to reinforce traditional racial exclusionary practices during the post-Civil War Reconstruction period. The Supreme Court affirmed the separate-but-equal doctrine in the case of *Plessy v. Ferguson* in 1896.

17. Bob Braunwart and Bob Carroll, "The Ohio League," *Coffin Corner* 3:7 (July 1981): 1–3; Robert W. Peterson, *Pigskin: The Early Years of Pro Football* (New York: Oxford University Press, 1997), 173.

18. Peterson, *Pigskin*, 173–180; Carroll, *Fritz Pollard*, 81, 128–183; see Ocania Chalk, *Pioneers of Black Sport* (New York: Dodd, Mead & Co., 1975), 222–233, for the few African American players of the 1930s.

19. Peterson, *Pigskin*, 173–180; Carroll, *Fritz Pollard*, 81, 128–183; Ocania Chalk, *Pioneers of Black Sport* (New York: Dodd, Mead & Co., 1975), 222–233, for the few African American players of the 1930s.

20. Carroll, *Fritz Pollard*, 160, 155 (quote).

21. See Walter J. Lonner and John Berry, eds., *Field Methods in Cross-Cultural Research* (Beverly Hills, CA: Sage Pub., 1986), 293–302, on the process of acculturation via involvement in dominant group norms. Kenney, "Chicago's Black and Tans"; Otto Klineberg, *Race Differences* (New York: Harper & Bros., 1935), vii; David K. Wiggins, " 'Great Speed But Little Stamina:' The Historical Debate Over Black Athletic Superiority," *Journal of Sport History* 16:2 (Summer 1989): 158–185.

22. Henderson cited in Sammons, " 'Race' and Sport," 222.

23. *Chicago Defender*, Dec. 10, 1932, 10; *Chicago Tribune*, Nov. 10, 1932, pt. 2:4; Nov. 2, 1933, 23; Nov. 9, 1933; Nov. 15, 1933; *Boston Globe*, Nov. 17, 1932, 8, on Lillard. Aaron Baker and Todd Boyd, *Out of Bounds: Sports, Media, and the Politics of Identity* (Bloomington: Indiana University Press, 1997), 125–126; Carroll, *Fritz Pollard*, 198–206.

24. Thomas G. Smith, "Outside the Pale: The Exclusion of Blacks from the National Football League, 1934–1946," *Coffin Corner* 11:4 (Summer 1989): 4–4. See Charles H. Martin, "Racial Change and 'Big-Time' College Football in Georgia: The Age of Segregation, 1892–1957," *Georgia Historical Quarterly* 80:3 (Fall 1996): 532–562; Ronald E. Marcello, "The Integration of Intercollegiate Athletics in Texas: North Texas State College as a Test Case, 1956," *Journal of Sport History* 14:3 (Winter 1987): 286–316; and Andrew Doyle, "Bear Bryant: Symbol for an Embattled South," *Colby Quarterly* 2:1 (March 1996): 72–86, on football as an integrative force.

25. Frederic E. Hoxie, *A Final Promise: The Campaign to Assimilate the Indians, 1880–1920* (New York: Cambridge University Press,

1989); John S. Steckbeck, *Fabulous Redmen: The Carlisle Indians and Their Famous Football Teams* (Harrisburg, PA: J. Horace MacFarland Co., 1951), 3–17. For a more critical analysis of the Carlisle program, see Jack Newcombe, *The Best of the Athletic Boys: The White Man's Impact on Jim Thorpe* (Garden City, NY: Doubleday, 1975), and David Wallace Adams, *Education for Extinction: American Indians and the School Experience, 1875–1928* (Lawrence, KS: University Press of Kansas, 1995). See Luther Standing Bear, "At Last I Kill a Buffalo," in Riley, *Growing Up Native American,* 107–114, on the importance of the buffalo hunt. Robertson cited by Adams, *Education for Extinction,* 186–187; Wheelock quoted, 190.

26. *New York World* 1, Nov. 29, 1859, 9, cited Oriard, *Reading Football,* 236 (quote), 244, on Hudson. Adams, *Education for Extinction,* 189–190.

27. Glenn S. Warner, "The Indian Massacres," *Collier's,* Oct. 17, 1911, 8, 63; Steckbeck, *Fabulous Redman,* 31, 34, 45–47, 53, 57, 62, 96; Weyand, *Saga of American Football,* 124–125, Oriard, *Reading Football,* 237–247.

28. Glenn S. Warner to Amos Alonzo Stagg, Mar. 5, 1900; Stagg to Warner, Mar. 10, 1900, Stagg Papers, Box 41, folder 9.

29. Michigan-Carlisle game contract, Nov. 2, 1901, Board in Control of Intercollegiate Athletics, University of Michigan Archives; Warner, "Indian Massacres," 62.

30. Bealle, *The History of Football at Harvard,* 147.

31. K. E. Davis to Walter Camp, Feb. 16, 1914, Camp Papers, Reel 7.

32. Oriard, *Reading Football,* 233–247; Glenn S. Warner, "Heap Big Run-Most-Fast," *Colliers,* Oct. 24, 1931, 19 (quote).

33. Arch Ward, "The Red Terror," in undated newspaper reprint, *College Football Historical Society* 8:3, May 1995, 14. Jim Thorpe, a Sac and Fox Indian, winner of the Olympic pentathlon and decathlon in 1912, All-American football star, and a professional baseball and football player, is widely regarded as the greatest all-around athlete in American history.

34. Warner, "The Indian Massacres," 7, 8 (quote). Steckbeck, *Fabulous Redmen,* 54–55, 107.

35. Steckbeck, *Fabulous Redmen,* 61, 95 (quote). The only Carlisle loss came in 1917, a year before the school's closing when the football team was no longer prominent.

36. Weyand, *Saga of American Football,* 101.

37. Adams, *Education for Extinction,* 188–189.

38. Steckbeck, *Fabulous Redmen,* 110; Marc S. Maltby, *The Origins and Early Development of Professional Football* (New York: Garland Pub., 1997), 130; Warner, "Heap Big Run-Most-Fast," 19, 46 (quotes); Riley, *Growing Up Native American,* 9, 15.

39. Pro football was a renegade or outlaw form of the game because it violated the amateur standards of the colleges. Players who engaged in its practice usually played under aliases, or risked losing their amateur status and college eligibility. Pro football served as a working-class alternative to the whole concept of amateurism, which was rooted in British ideals of social class and gentility. Maltby, *The Origins and Early Development of Professional Football,* 60, 71–77, 90–92; Peterson, *Pigskin,* 38–39.

40. Peterson, *Pigskin,* 54–56; Maltby, *Origins and Early Development of Football,* 130–133; Bob Braunwart, Bob Carroll, and Joe Horrigan, "Oorang Indians," *Coffin Corner* 3:1 (Jan. 1981): 1–8.

41. David L. Porter, ed., *Biographical Dictionary of American Sports: 1989–1991 Supplement for Baseball, Football, Basketball, and Other Sports* (Westport, CT: Greenwood Press, 1992), 396–397, 469–470; John C. Hibner, "Lone Star Dietz," *College Football Historical Society* 1:5 (August 1988): 1–4.

42. Ray Schmidt, "Princes of the Prairies," *College Football Historical Society* 2:2 (Feb. 1989):1–8, on McClain and the 1926 Haskell team; William Peterson to Amos Alonzo Stagg, Dec. 6, 1900 (quote), Stagg Papers, Box 41, folder 9; University of Chicago, Special Collections; W. M. Peterson to Football team manager, Jan. 9, 1901, Board in Control of Intercollegiate Athletics, University of Michigan Archives.

43. Schmidt, "Princes of the Prairies," 5, 6 (quote), 8.

44. Arch Ward, "Red Terror."

45. Welsh's affidavit was offered during the investigation that eventually closed Carlisle. See Adams, *Education for Extinction,* 323–324.

46. Deborah E. S. Frable, "Gender, Racial, Ethnic, Sexual, and Class Identities," *Annual Review of Psychology* 48 (1997): 139–162; Karen A. Cerulo, "Identity Construction: New Issues, New Directions," *Annual Review of Sociology* 23 (1997): 385–409; Kramer, *American Minority Community,* 195; Joseph F. Healey, "An Exploration of the Relationship Between Memory and Sport," *Sociology of Sport Journal* 8:3 (Sept. 1991): 213–227.

47. Jim Brown with Steve Delsohn, *Out of Bounds* (New York: Zebra Books, 1980), 36–67, 51 (quote); Gale Sayers with Al Silverman, *I Am Third* (New York: Viking Press, 1970), 129–160.

48. Cornel West, *Race Matters* (New York: Vintage Books, 1993), 28–29.

Form at end of book

Issue 10: Is participation in sports the best avenue to minority success and acceptance?

Goal Discrepancy in African American Male Student-Athletes' Unrealistic Expectations for Careers in Professional Sports

Robert M. Sellers

University of Virginia

Gabriel P. Kuperminc

Yale University

The present study investigated whether African American male college student-athletes unrealistically focus their career goals on professional athletics to the detriment of their academic pursuits. The study considered the professional athletic aspirations of 702 African American male student-athletes from 42 NCAA Division I universities using the concept of goal discrepancy to identify individuals whose professional athletic aspirations were inconsistent with their current status as first team members of their football or basketball programs. The results found only 5% of the sample to be goal discrepant and that among goal discrepant student-athletes, the majority were underclassmen. Institutional characteristics, such as intensity of the athletic program and segregation of athletes from nonathletic students, were stronger predictors of goal discrepancy than personal characteristics, such as socioeconomic status or precollege academic preparation. The results are discussed in relation to social policy that influences access to educational opportunity for African Americans.

The perception that a large number of student-athletes are goal discrepant with respect to their expectations of a professional sport career has helped fuel the debate about re- cent policies by the National Collegiate Athletic Association (NCAA) that some critics have argued deny educational opportunities disproportionately to African Americans (e.g., Johnson, 1989; Sellers, 1993; Walter, Smith, Hoey, & Wilhelm, 1987). Investigating goal discrepancy within the context of the student-athletes' college life experiences provides a useful framework from which to study student-athletes' career expectations (Kuperminc, Sellers, & Thompson, 1996). The college life experience can be viewed from a social/ecological perspective that encompasses the interplay between personal factors and institutional factors that make up the student-athletes' phenomenological experiences. Such an approach also allows for the evaluation of the consequences of goal discrepancy with respect to both ecologically specific outcomes (academic performance) and general life outcomes (psychological well-being).

Historically, sport proficiency has been one of the few avenues of upward mobility in American society in which African Americans might hope to be judged on their ability instead of the color of their skin (Ashe, 1989; Edwards, 1979). Much of the progress with respect to race relations in the broader society has followed similar progress in the sports world (Tygiel, 1983). Today, some African Americans seem to view professional sports as a viable vocational option that is relatively free of racial barriers (Edwards, 1984). This perception is fueled in part by the reality that although African American men are underrepresented in just about every traditional avenue for upward socioeconomic mobility in our society (such as education), they are significantly overrepresented in professional sports such as football and basketball. African Americans constitute 12% of the United States population, and yet roughly 75% of National Basketball Association (NBA) players and 60% of National Football League (NFL) players are African American (Lapchick, 1991). African Americans are also overrepresented in the revenue-producing sports at the college level. Although African American males represent only about 8% of the male undergraduate population, approximately 51% of the football players and 65% of the male basketball players who participate in Division I college athletics are African Americans (NCAA, 1995).

Ironically, some community psychologists have hailed sports as an important activity that has the potential for preventing and/or reducing at-risk behavior and enhancing development in adolescents (e.g., Agnew & Peterson, 1989; Burling, Seidner, Robbins-Sisco, & Krinsky, 1992; Cusson, 1989). Reppucci (1987) has argued that youth sports is an underutilized prevention vehicle. Similarly, Danish (1983) has suggested that participation in sports can lead to the development of important competence skills. Midnight basketball has been used in a number of cities as a prevention tool against gang recruitment and crime. These programs have met with some success. For years, Boys Club of America has used baseball and basketball as a mechanism to teach young males the benefits of teamwork and cooperation. A disproportionate number of the youngsters participating in these programs are African Americans from economically disadvantaged inner-city environments.

However, there is some concern that too many African American young men are focusing too much on athletics and that this is manifesting into unrealistic aspirations for a professional sports career (Ashe, 1989; Edwards, 1979, 1984; Lapchick, 1991). Edwards (1984) argues that the broader society has capitalized on the past successes of African Americans in professional sports and has overpromoted athletic achievement as being a respectable career path for young African Americans. He further suggests that this overpromotion of athletics has been internalized by many African American families. As a result, he suggests that African American families are more likely than other ethnic groups in America to push their male children toward making a living as a professional athlete. Edwards argues that such a focus has dire consequences for the overwhelming majority of African American males in particular and the African American community in general. This viewpoint is consistent with Braddock's (1980) sport-as-impediment hypothesis. The sport-as-impediment hypothesis argues that sport involve-

ment negatively affects African American athletes' future career attainment. African American athletes are viewed as overinvesting themselves in athletics while neglecting other skills (such as academics) that are more likely to lead to upward social mobility (Harris & Hunt, 1982).

There is some empirical evidence to support the sport-as-impediment hypothesis. The Center for the Study of Athletics (1989) reported that African American football and male basketball players were more than twice as likely to expect professional sport careers than other athletes. In fact, 44% of these African American athletes suggested that they expected professional sport careers. Similarly, Kennedy and Dimick (1987) reported that 66% of the 38 African American athletes in their sample of college football and basketball players expected a professional sport career. In contrast, only 39% of the 84 White athletes in the sample expressed similar expectations for a professional sport career. Lapchick (1991) estimates that only about 4% of all African American college football players will make it into the NFL and roughly 6% of all African American college basketball players will have a career in the NBA.

The discrepancy between the number of African American athletes with expectations for professional sport careers and those who actually make it suggests that a large proportion of the student-athletes are goal discrepant. Goal discrepancy occurs when an individual's expectations are inconsistent with his or her current status with respect to the criteria associated with successful attainment of the individual's goals (Parker & Kleiner, 1966). However, it should be noted that the concept of goal discrepancy is based on each person's *unique chances* of succeeding given their current status. Thus a goal discrepant student-athlete would be someone who holds expectations of a professional sport career when his or her current athletic status does not warrant such a lofty goal.

The present study investigates goal discrepancy in the professional sport career expectations of African American Division I college basketball and football players. By examining goal discrepancy, the present study contributes to the current literature on student-athletes' professional sport expectations by looking at them within the context of the athlete's current status on the team. Specifically, we have three objectives. First, we will assess the prevalence of goal discrepancy in a national sample of African American male basketball and football players at a Division I institution. Next, we will investigate the relative influence of educational, socioeconomic, and athletic background, as well as institutional factors related to the college life experience, on whether student-athletes' discrepant expectations for a professional sport career exist. Finally, we explore the consequences of goal discrepancy with respect to psychological well-being, academic performance, and motivation.

The Importance of Studying Goal Discrepancy in African American Males

Some evidence suggests that institutional factors that influence the social ecology of the student-athletes' experiences on campus may also influence their professional sport aspirations. Student-athletes at institutions with more competitive athletic programs report feeling more pressure to emphasize athletics over academics (Sack & Thiel, 1985). Adler and Adler (1985) present a detailed description and analysis of the process by which the demands of participating in big time college basketball can influence student-athletes to narrow their career aspirations toward a professional sport career as a result of their increasingly difficult academic experiences. They suggest that some institutional policies such as segregating student-athletes from the rest of the campus population may also reinforce a myopic focus on athletics. Although historically Black universities and colleges (HBCUs) produce more than their share of professional football players, some have argued that HBCUs have been less exploitive of African American athletes (Johnson, 1989). They point to the overall mission of most HBCUs to educate all African American college students regardless of their academic background and their smaller athletic budget as reasons for their more supportive reputation.

Athletic goal discrepancy may be associated with poorer psychosocial adjustment once the student-athlete's career concludes. Some studies suggest that athletes whose athletic careers end unexpectedly suffer a number of psychosocial setbacks that spill into their later lives (Kleiber, Greendorfer, Blinde, & Samdahl, 1987; McPherson, 1978). The vast majority of African American student-athletes who expect to have a career in professional sports conclude their careers unexpectedly—after their last college game. According to some authors, an overemphasis on athletics is also a major factor in the relatively poorer academic performance of African American student-athletes (Ashe, 1989; Edwards, 1979, 1984). As a result, many African American student-athletes become less motivated to achieve academically.

The professional sport aspirations of African Americans are relevant to current social policy, which has profound implications for African American males' access to higher education. Approximately one out of every eight African American male students at the over 300 Division I universities is a scholarship athlete. The perception that a significant number of student-athletes only attend college because it is a necessary vehicle for a professional sport career has helped influence NCAA legislation that has raised the academic standards (SAT scores and high school grade point average) necessary for a potential student-athlete to receive an athletic scholarship. Meanwhile, growing evidence has emerged that African American student-athletes are disproportionately excluded as a result of the increased eligibility requirements (McArdle & Hamagami, 1994; NCAA, 1991). The NCAA reported that approximately 65% of the African American athletes who entered before Proposition 42 standards came into effect in 1990 would have been ineligible under those standards. Meanwhile, only 9% of the White male and female athletes would have suffered the same fate (NCAA, 1991). Other studies have reported evidence that suggests that many of the African American student-athletes who are excluded from full participation and scholarship opportunities by the initial eligibility requirements would actually graduate if they were given the chance (NCAA, 1984; Walter et al., 1987).

Sellers (1993) argues that African American student-athletes' relatively poorer academic performance is more a function of structural inequities in their precollege educational opportunities than their overemphasis on athletics. Thus he suggests that the NCAA would be better served to focus on the social ecology of the student-athletes' experiences once they are on campus, instead of its current focus on precollege factors as evidenced by the initial eligibility legislation. He further argues that such a change in focus by the NCAA could improve student-athletes' academic performances without the adverse side effects of denying educational opportunities for a number of potential African Americans.

The merit of such a focus has been supported by a growing body of literature that has documented the importance of examining both personal and institutional factors when investigating college students' academic attitudes and performance (e.g., Nettles & Johnson, 1987; Stage 1988, 1989; Stoecker, Pascarella, & Wolfle, 1988; Terenzini & Pascarella, 19178; Tracey & Sedlacek, 1984). Similarly, research on student-athletes suggests that both student-athletes' personal background influences as well as social ecological variables associated with the institution are predictors of such diverse phenomena as grades (Sellers, 1993), graduation (McArdle & Hamagami, 1994), and athletic-academic role conflict (Sack & Thiel, 1985; Sellers, 1993). For example, Sellers, Kuperminc, and Damas (1993) found in an investigation of academic athletic role conflict in college athletes that higher socioeconomic status, higher SAT scores, higher intensity of recruitment experiences, attendance at a predominantly White university, and living/dining conditions that segregated athletes from nonathletes were associated with higher levels of role conflict.

The previous findings in the literature suggest direction for the present study. With these findings in mind, we make the following predictions for this investigation. First, we predict that a significant number of African American student-athletes will be discrepant in their expectations to play professional sports. We also predict that poorer academic preparation and socioeconomic status, greater athletic potential, and lower class status will be associated with greater likelihood for goal discrepancy. Institutional characteristics are hypothesized to be related to goal discrepancy in such a way that predominantly White institutions, institutions with more intense athletic programs, and institutions that segregate their athletes from the rest of the student body should be more likely to have goal discrepant athletes. Also, goal discrepant individuals are predicted to report more symptoms of anxiety and depression and lower self-esteem and life satisfaction than nondiscrepant student-athletes. Finally, we predict that goal discrepancy will be negatively related to measures of academic motivation and academic performance.

Method

Sample and Procedure

The present study represents a secondary analysis of data collected by the American Institutes for Research during the spring of 1987. The research was commissioned by the President's Commission of the NCAA to provide empirical evidence for a national forum on the role of intercollegiate athletics in higher education. The data set consists of a nationally representative sample of student-athletes and other college students at 42 institutions that compete at the Division I level in men's basketball. The 42 institutions were randomly selected and stratified according to geographic region and athletic conference. Of the 42 institutions, 39 institutions are predominantly White and 3 are historically Black.

At each institution, a sample of student-athletes was randomly selected along with two comparison groups of students—students involved in extracurricular activities and African American students who were not athletes. (It should be noted that only student-athletes whose sport competed at the Division I level were included in the sample.) A total of 5,123 student-athletes were surveyed regarding their personal background and college life experiences. The student-athletes were administered the survey in groups and were offered the option of completing an interview. They were informed that their participation was voluntary and that their responses would remain confidential. A wealth of information was gathered, including (a) demographic, academic, and athletic background variables; (b) archival records from students' transcripts; (c) students' reports of current social and academic experiences on campus; and (d) self-description inventories relating to aspects of students' mental health (for more details on the data set, see Center for the Study of Athletics, 1988).

The present sample was a subset of the broader study. The sample ($N = 702$) consisted of only African American males who participated in the revenue-producing sports of men's basketball ($n = 267$) and football ($n = 435$). This sample comprised 188 freshmen, 189 sophomores, 189 juniors, 128 seniors, and 8 graduate students. Eighty-two percent ($n = 575$) of the student-athletes in the sample attended predominantly White universities, whereas the remainder ($n = 127$) attended the three predominantly Black universities. African Americans accounted for approximately 37% of the Division I football players and 56% of the Division I male basketball players in the primary study (Center for the Study of Athletics, 1989).

Measures

Goal Discrepancy

A measure of goal discrepancy was constructed by tabulating two indicators of student-athletes' abilities and professional athletic expectations. A dichotomous variable asking if the student-athlete expected to play professionally served as the basis for constructing a dichotomous measure of professional athletic expectations. This measure was adjusted using a continuous variable assessing how sure student-athletes were that they would play professionally (see Table 1). Student-athletes who answered "no" to the dichotomous question asking them whether they expected to play sports professionally were coded as a "No" response to the revised dichotomous measure of student-athletes' expectations of playing professional sports. Also, those student-athletes who responded "yes" to the original dichotomous variable and subsequently assessed their chances of playing sports professionally as "almost certainly will not" or "possibly" were coded as "No" in the revised dichotomous measure. This group made up approximately 77% of the sample. The remaining 23% of the sample responded that "they probably will" or that "they almost certainly will" play professionally, and were coded as "Yes" responses.

The student-athletes were also asked to respond to a question assessing their team position (e.g., redshirt, first team, second team, etc.). Ninety-two of the 702 African American male student-athletes in the sample were eliminated from the analyses because they were either classified as being ineligible or in the process of being redshirted, or had missing data. Thus the effective sample size was 610 African American male student-athletes.

Seventy-six percent ($n = 427$) of the effective sample responded that they were members of the first team or the traveling squad (see Table 2). Of those who were members of the second and third teams ($n = 184$), approximately 17% expect to play professionally ($n = 32$). These individ-

Table 1 — Construction of Dichotomous Variable for Expectation to Play Sports Professionally

	Continuous Variable				
	Definitely Not	Almost Certainly Not	Possibly	Probably Will	Almost Certainly Will
Dichotomous					
No					
Count	383	4	154		
Row %	70.8	.7	28.5		
Total %	54.6	.6	21.9		
Yes					
Count				111	30
Row %				68.9	31.1
Total %				15.8	7.1

Table 2 — Black Male Athletes' Expectations to Play Professional Sports by Playing Status

	Member of the Traveling Team	Not a Member of the Traveling Team
Does not expect to play professionally	313 (51.3%)	152 (18.5%)
Expects to play professionally	113 (24.9%)	32 (5.2%)

Note: Percentage of the entire sample of Black male athletes in revenue-producing sports is shown in parentheses.

uals were classified as goal discrepant because they reported high expectations despite contradictory information in their current status. A contingency table depicting this distribution is shown in Table 2.

Personal and Institutional Predictors of Goal Discrepancy

Academic and demographic background were measured using two indicators of student-athletes' academic preparation and a single composite indicator of socioeconomic status. High school grade point average was derived from a self-reported item regarding the student-athlete's grade average in high school. Student-athletes' composite SAT scores and equivalent ACT scores were obtained from their college transcripts. A socioeconomic status (SES) indicator was derived from family income, parents' occupational status, and parents' education levels. When available, father's occupation level was coded using prestige scores from U.S. census codes, otherwise, mother's occupation was used. Students reported their parents' education levels on a 6 point scale in which 1 represented

less than high school graduation and 6 represented having earned a post-baccalaureate degree (e.g., MA or PhD). Family income, occupational prestige, and parental education were standardized and averaged to construct a measure of SES.

The student-athletes' recruitment experience was measured using a composite indicator of the experiences the student-athletes' faced while being recruited (Cronbach's α = .60). A higher score on this variable represents being more heavily recruited. The rationale for constructing this indicator was that those student-athletes with the greatest athletic potential are also the ones who were the most heavily recruited. The composite indicator consisted of (a) the number of methods used by institutions to recruit a student (e.g., correspondence, visits to campus, special events, and media publicity), (b) the number of schools that recruited a student, and (c) the student-athletes' self-report of the pressure experienced during recruitment using a 4-point rating scale. The three items were standardized and then averaged.

Three institutional characteristics were assessed in the present study. Attending a predominantly White university was a dichotomous variable in which students attending the 39 predominantly White institutions were coded with a score of 1 and students attending the three predominantly African American institutions were coded with a score of 0. Another dichotomous variable was used to measure the intensity of the institutions' athletic program based on a measure of "successful competitiveness." Successful competitiveness is a derived measure based on the Sagarin formula for annually ranking all Division I men's football and basketball teams (Center for the Study of Athletics, 1988). The formula takes into account a team's win-loss record and strength of opponent. The formula also has a diminishing returns principle built in that rewards teams that do well against good opponents as well as preventing a team from building up its ranking by running up large margins of victory against weak teams. An unweighted average was constructed using the final men's basketball and football ratings for 1987–1988, the 1985–1986 final ratings for football, and the 1984–1985 final ratings for basketball for each institution. Programs rated at or above the median of the average in the present sample ($n = 42$) were coded as 1 and those below the median were coded as 0. A composite indicator reflecting athletic segregation represented the extent to which athletes are separated from other students. The composite indicator consisted of items measuring whether student-athletes are (a) required to live with teammates or other student-athletes, (b) required to eat most meals with teammates or other student-athletes, and (c) whether most students in an individual's dormitory or housing are athletes. A high score on this measure means that athletes at an institution are more likely to be segregated from other students at the institution.

Measures of Psychological Well-Being

Three self-description inventories and a single-item measure of life satisfaction were used to measure the student-athletes' psychological well-being. The Rosenberg Self-Esteem Scale includes 10 items measuring levels of self-acceptance and self-esteem. The Speilberger Trait Anxiety Inventory includes 20 items measuring the tendency to see stressful situations as dangerous and threatening and to respond with heightened anxiety. The Center for Epidemiological Studies Depression Scale (CES-D) measures the presence and frequency of 20 major clinical symptoms of depression. Student-athletes were also asked to rate on a 4-point scale (1 = *totally dissatisfied* to 4 = *totally satisfied*) how satisfied they were with their life in general. Previous research has found these measures to be reliable and valid for African Americans (Brown & Duren, 1988; Hoelter, 1983; Vernon & Roberts, 1981).

Measures of Academic Motivation and Performance

Three indicators of academic motivation and a single indicator of academic performance were utilized in the present study. The student-athletes were asked to rate on a 4-point scale (1 = *not important* to 4 = *highest importance*) at the present time how important it was to get a college degree. They were also asked whether they expected to get a college degree. A 4-point scale (1 = *totally dissatisfied* to 4 = *totally satisfied*) was used to rate student-athletes' satisfaction with their academic performance. Academic performance was measured using cumulative college grade

point averages (GPAs) obtained from college transcripts. All GPAs were converted to a 4-point scale where a 4.0 is equivalent to an A.

Results

An examination of Table 2 shows that only 32 of 610 African American male student-athletes were goal discrepant. Even within the subset of African American male student-athletes who were not members of the traveling team, only 17% of the student-athletes had professional athletic expectations that were inconsistent with their current status on the team. Further analysis examining the goal discrepant individuals by class shows a declining linear trend (c^2 [4 df] = 16.53; $p < .01$). The modal class of goal discrepant individuals was the freshman class ($n = 18$), followed by sophomores ($n = 8$), juniors ($n = 4$), and seniors ($n = 2$).

A logistic regression was performed on the professional sports expectations of the 184 student-athletes who were not members of the traveling squad in order to investigate whether personal characteristics and institutional characteristics help predict goal discrepancy in African American male student-athletes (see Table 3). The overall logistic regression model was significant ($c^2 = 33.18$; $p < .01$), and the independent variables explained approximately 20% of the variance in goal discrepancy. Significant predictors of goal discrepancy were class, type of institution, intensity of the athletic program, and whether the institution had policies that segregate athletes from the rest of the student population. Underclass student-athletes, student-athletes from predominantly African American institutions, student-athletes from more intense athletic programs, and student-athletes from institutions that segregate athletes were more likely to expect to be professional athletes despite not being members of the traveling squad. Student-athletes with higher SAT scores were slightly, but not significantly, less likely to be goal discrepant.

Next, a multivariate analysis of variance (MANOVA) was employed to test possible group differences in four indicators of psychological well-being of nonstarters by their expectations to play professional sports (see Table 4). The analysis yielded no significant differences between goal discrepant student-athletes and the other student-athletes who were not members of the traveling squad in the four indicators of psychological well-being (Hotelling's multivariate $F = .006$, ns). The goal discrepant student-athletes appear to suffer little in terms of their current psychological well-being as compared to student-athletes who are not goal discrepant.

Table 3 **Results of Logistic Regression of Background and Institutional Characteristics on Pro Sport Expectations for Nontraveling Team Members (*n* = 181)**

	B	SE	Partial *r*
Constant	.764	1.99	
Personal background variables			
High school GPA	−.059	.15	.00
SAT composite score	−.003	.00	−.09***
Socioeconomic status	.027	.03	.00
Recruitment experience	.002	.28	.00
College experience variables			
Class	−.660	.28	−.17*
Predominantly White	−1.758	.89	−.11**
Intensity of athletic program	1.657	.79	.12**
Athletic segregation	.448	.21	.12**

Note: 1 = Does not expect pro career. 2 = Expects pro career. Overall model χ^2 = 33.18*, pseudo R^2 = .20.

*$p < .01$. **$p < .05$. **$p < .10$.

Table 4 **Psychological Well-Being of Nontraveling Team Members by Expectations to Play Sports Professionally**

	Do Not Expect Pro Career (*n* = 152)		Expect Pro Career (*n* = 32)		
	Mean	SD	Mean	SD	F
Anxiety	39.19	10.17	39.94	8.84	1.36
Depression	14.34	9.35	13.40	7.82	.28
Self-esteem	24.18	5.44	24.06	4.61	.01
Life satisfaction[a]	3.07	.66	3.13	.71	.13

Note: The analysis yielded no significant differences.

a. 1 = *not satisfied at all.* 4 = *totally satisfied.*

Similarly, the MANOVA testing the effects of goal discrepancy on academic motivation and academic performance also found no group differences (Hotelling's multivariate *F* = .014, *ns*). Goal discrepant student-athletes placed similar levels of importance on getting a degree, have similarly high expectations of obtaining a degree, and are as satisfied as their other teammates who are not on the traveling team. Interestingly, both groups have cumulative GPSs that are relatively low (see Table 5).

Discussion

Contrary to our hypothesis, relatively few African American male student-athletes in our sample exhibit goal discrepant expectations with respect to a career in professional sports. On the contrary, our results suggest that a relatively small number of African American student-

athletes have an overly unrealistic expectation of playing professional sports. Only 5% of the sample were what we would consider goal discrepant. Of 32 individuals who were goal discrepant, 26 were either freshmen or sophomores. It is not too improbable for a person who is not a member of the traveling team as a freshman or a sophomore to go on and become a significant member of the team and even have a chance to play professionally. Thus it appears that the majority of African American student-athletes include their current status as a member of the traveling squad in assessing their probability for a professional sports career.

Institutional characteristics were better predictors of goal discrepancy than personal background characteristics. Intensity of program and athletic segregation was positively associated with goal discrepancy. Because more intense athletic programs produce more professional

Table 5 — Academic Motivation and Performance of Nontraveling Team Members by Expectations to Play Sports Professionally

	Do Not Expect Pro Career (n = 152)		Expect Pro Career (n = 32)		
	Mean	SD	Mean	SD	F
Importance of degree[a]	3.78	.52	3.78	.49	.00
Expect to get degree[b]	1.97	.18	1.97	.17	.00
Academic satisfaction[c]	2.84	.54	2.89	.49	.17
College GPA	2.09	.40	2.02	.56	.61

a. 1 = *not important.* 4 = *highest importance.*

b. 1 = *no.* 2 = *yes.*

c. 1 = *not at all satisfied.* 4 = *totally satisfied.*

athletes, student-athletes in these programs see a relatively larger proportion of their teammates going on to play professionally. As a result, student-athletes competing within more intensive athletic programs may be more willing to maintain high expectations in the face of their current status. Such student athletes are also more likely to have experienced individuals from their institution who overcame circumstances similarly to their own to make it into professional ranks. Such individuals serve as role models for those student-athletes who are not members of the starting or the traveling teams. At the same time, athletic segregation may also serve to enhance the effect of these role models and continue high expectations for a professional sports career in the face of contradictory evidence by limiting the student-athletes' opportunities for contact with other nonathletes' career expectations and aspirations. Adler and Adler (1985) note the impact of the student-athletes' constant interaction with their teammates on their developing common norms and values regarding the social, academic, and athletic realms.

Contrary to our original hypothesis, we found that historically Black institutions were more likely to produce goal discrepant student-athletes. This finding is troubling considering the historical role that predominantly African American college athletics has played in the development of the African American male athlete. Some have argued that predominantly African American institutions are less likely to exploit African American athletes than predominantly White universities (Johnson, 1989). However, the present findings along with recent graduation information challenges the validity of such an argument. Traditionally, most of the research on African American male student-athletes has focused on those at predominantly White institutions, whereas the African American male student-athletes at the historically Black institutions have been virtually ignored. Clearly, future research focusing specifically on the life experiences of African American

male student-athletes at historically Black institutions is needed to further explicate our findings.

None of the personal characteristic variables was a significant predictor of goal discrepancy. Neither academic preparation nor recruitment experience nor socioeconomic background was a significant predictor of goal discrepant student-athletes. These findings suggest that the ecological experiences of student-athletes on campus seems to be more important in predicting athletic goal discrepancy than the student-athletes' personal background.

Our analysis also found no relationship between unrealistic athletic expectations and academic motivation or academic performance. Goal discrepant student-athletes reported similarly high levels of academic motivation, as high as those who did not have unrealistic professional sport expectations. They also had achieved similarly low grade point averages. It appears that student-athletes are able to keep the athletic domain and the academic domain separate. Career motivation and aspirations do not appear to have a zero-sum relationship. High aspirations in one life domain (athletics) does not necessarily adversely impact aspirations or performance in another life domain (academics). It is possible for student-athletes to have unrealistically high athletic aspirations and still maintain high academic aspirations.

We also found no evidence that athletic goal discrepancy is associated with the student-athletes' psychological well-being. The goal discrepant student-athletes also appear to be oblivious to the incongruence between their expectations and their status on the team. If they were aware of their goal discrepancy, chances are that they would have changed their expectations to conform to their current status. Thus psychological consequences of the student-athletes' discrepancy may not occur until the student-athletes are forced to face possible failure to achieve their expected goal (Kleiber et al., 1987). It would be interesting to examine the student-athletes' mental well-being 5 or 10 years later when the vast majority of them have failed to have a professional career in sports. Future longitudinal research is warranted to more appropriately examine the possible long-term career attainment consequences of athletic goal discrepancy.

The present findings should be interpreted with some caution. We admit the operationalization of athletic goal discrepancy may have been somewhat arbitrary. The operational definition of goal discrepancy used in the present study was conservative in that many members of the traveling squad who expected to play professionally may also have unrealistic assessments. Clearly, the vast majority of the individuals who expect to play sports professionally will not, regardless of their current athletic status. However, because the concept of goal discrepancy is concerned with whether student-athletes' expectations for a career in professional sports is consistent with their current status, we argue that the present definition is an appropriate one. Nonetheless, it would be interesting to compare the present findings with other investigations that use a more liberal operationalization of athletic goal discrepancy. (However, it should be noted that the pattern of our results did not change when we used a more liberal operationalization of goal discrepancy that included those individuals who assessed their chances of having a professional career as being "possible.")

Policy Implications

One of the goals of the NCAA's move to increase initial academic standards is to weed out those athletes who only have athletic aspirations and expectations. The present findings contradict such a premise. Relatively few student-athletes had professional sport aspirations that were inconsistent with their athletic status. It should also be noted that academic background (high school GPA and SAT scores) was not a significant predictor of academic aspirations. The fact that institutional factors seem to have a greater influence on goal discrepancy is further evidence of the utility of examining the social ecology of the student-athletes' on-campus experience when developing academic policies (Sellers, 1993). Such a direction may lead to such desirable outcomes as a reasonable emphasis on athletics that may have a residual positive influence on student-athletes' academic performance without the undesirable side effects of denying a significant number of African American men an avenue to higher education.

In sum, the present study has found no support for the thesis that a significant number of African American male student-athletes have unrealistic aspirations for a professional sport career. Nor was there support for the thesis that unrealistic professional sport aspirations is associated with lower academic motivation and aspiration and poorer academic performance. In light of these findings and other studies of student-athletes' academic motivation (Center for the Study of Sport, 1988; Sellers, 1993), a modification of the sports-as-impediment hypothesis is suggested.

References

Adler, P., and Adler, P. A. (1985). From idealism to pragmatic detachment. The academic performance of college athletes. *Sociology of Education, 58,* 241–250.

Agnew, R., and Peterson, D. M. (1989). Leisure and delinquency. *Social Problems. 36*(4), 332–350.

Ashe, A. (1989). Is Proposition 42 racist? *Ebony, 44,* 131–140.

Braddock, J. H. (1980, Spring). Race, sports and social mobility: A critical review. *Sociological Symposium, 30,* 18–38.

Brown, M. T., and Duren, P. S. (1988). Construct validity for Blacks of the State-Trait Anxiety Inventory. *Measurement and Evaluation in Counseling and Development, 21,* 25–33.

Burling, T. A., Seidner, A. L, Robbins-Sisco, D., and Krinsky, A. (1992). Relapse prevention for homeless veteran substance abusers via softball team participation. *Journal of Substance Abuse, 4*(4), 407–413.

Center for the Study of Athletics. (1988). *Report No. 1: Summary results from the 1987–88 national study of intercollegiate athletics,* Palo Alto, CA: American Institutes for Research.

Center for the Study of Athletics. (1989). *Report No. 3: The experiences of Black intercollegiate athletes at NCAA Division I institutions.* Palo Alto, CA: American Institutes for Research.

Cusson, M. (1989). Disputes over honor and gang aggression. *Revue Internationale de Criminologie et de Police Technique, 42*(3), 290–297.

Danish, S. J. (1983). Musings about personal competence: The contributions of sport, health and fitness. *American Journal of Community Psychology, 11*(3), 221–240.

Edwards, H. (1979). Sport within the veil: The triumphs, tragedies and challenges of Afro-American involvement. *Annals, AAPSS, 445* 116–127.

Edwards, H. (1984). The Black "dumb jock": An American sports tragedy. *The College Board Review, 131,* 8–13.

Harris, O., and Hunt, L. (1982). Race and sports involvement: Some implications of athletics for Black and White youth. *Journal of Social and Behavioral Sciences, 28*(4), 95–103.

Hoelter, J. (1983). Factorial invariance and self-esteem: Reassessing race and sex differences. *Social Forces, 61,* 834–846.

Johnson, J. (1989). Is Proposition 42 racist? *Ebony, 44,* 138–140.

Kennedy, S. R., and Dimick, K. M. (1987). Career maturity and professional sports expectations of college football and basketball players. *Journal of College Student Personnel, 28,* 293–297.

Kleiber, D., Greendorfer, S., Blinde, E., and Samdahl, D. (1987). Quality of exit from university sports and life satisfaction in early adulthood. *Sociology of Sport Journal, 4,* 28–36.

Kuperminc, G. P., Sellers, R. M., and Thompson, W. (1996). Athletic ability, race, personal background, and institutional characteristics as factors in student-athletes' professional sport expectations. *Journal of Applied Psychology.* Manuscript submitted for publication.

Lapchick, R. (1991). *Five minutes to midnight. Race and sport in the 1990's.* Lanham, MD: Madison Books.

McArdle, J. J., and Hamagami, F. (1994). Logit and multilevel logit modeling of college graduation rates for 1984–85 freshman student-athletes. *Journal of the American Statistical Association, 89,* 1107–1123.

McPherson, B. D. (1978). The child in competitive sport: Influence on the social milieu. In R. A. Magill, M. J. Ash, and F. L. Smoll (Eds.), *Children in sport: A contemporary anthology.* Champaign, IL: Human Kinetics.

National Collegiate Athletic Association (NCAA). (1994). *Study of freshman eligibility standards: Executive summary.* Reston, VA: Social Sciences Division, Advanced Technology, Inc.

National Collegiate Athletic Association (NCAA). (1991). *NCAA Research Report #91–02: A statistical analysis of the predictions of graduation rates for college student-athletes.* Overland Park, KS: Author.

National Collegiate Athletic Association (NCAA). (1995). *1995 NCAA Division I graduation-rates report.* Overland Park, KS: Author.

Nettles, M. T., and Johnson, J. R. (1987). Race, sex and other factors as determinants of college students' socialization. *Journal of College Student Personnel, 28*(6), 512–524.

Parker, S., and Kleiner, R. J. (1966). *Mental illness in the urban Negro community.* New York: Free Press.

Reppucci, N. D. (1987). Teen-age pregnancy, child sexual abuse, and organized youth sports. *American Journal of Community Psychology, 15*(1), 1–22.

Sack, A. L., and Thiel, R. (1985). College basketball and role conflict: A national survey. *Sociology of Sport Journal, 2,* 195–209.

Sellers, R. M. (1993). Black student-athletes: Reaping the benefits or recovering from exploitation? In D. Brooks & R. Althouse (Eds.), *Racism in college athletics.* Morgantown, WV: Fitness Information Technology.

Sellers, R. M., Kuperminc, G. P., and Damas, A. (1993). *Background and institutional predictors of academic/athletic role conflict in student-athletes.* Unpublished manuscript.

Stage, F. K. (1988). Reciprocal effects between the academic and social integration of college students. *Research in Higher Education, 30*(5), 517–530.

Stage, F. K. (1989). Motivation, academic and social interaction, and the early dropout. *American Educational Research Journal, 26*(3), 385–402.

Stoecker, J., Pascarefla, E. T., and Wolfle, L. M. (1988). Persistence in higher education: A 9-year test of a theoretical model. *Journal of College Student Development, 29,* 126–209.

Terenzini, P. T., and Pascarella, E. T. (1978). The relation of students' precollege characteristics and freshman year experience to voluntary attrition. *Research in Higher Education, 9,* 347–366.

Tracey, T. J., and Sedlacek, W. E. (1984). Noncognitive variables in predicting academic success by race. *Measurement and Evaluation in Guidance, 16*(4), 171–178.

Tygiel, J. (1983). *Baseball's great experiment.* New York: Oxford University Press.

Vernon, S. W., and Roberts, R. E. (1981). Measuring nonspecific psychological distress and other dimensions of psychopathology: Further observations on the problem. *Archives of General Psychiatry, 38,* 1239–1247.

Walter, T., Smith, D.E.P., Hoey, G., and Wilhelm, R. (1987). Predicting the academic success of college athletes. *Reasearch Quarterly for Exercise and Sport, 58*(2), 273–279.

Form at end of book

WiseGuide Wrap-Up

The history of Carlisle Industrial School for Indians in Reading 22 illustrates some of the problems that minority athletes have faced—not only in getting opportunities to play but, more importantly, in the way the athletes' success was attributed to their coach, "Pop" Warner, over the efforts of the athletes themselves. At Carlisle, football was seen as a way to gain greater inclusion in American society. The Carlisle experience allowed diverse tribes to obtain a sense of collective racial identity, combat Social Darwinian stereotypes,

and develop pride in Indian athletic heroes, but it did not gain them greater acceptance into American culture. According to Gems, the continued maintenance of the reservation system arrested this acceptance.

Sellers and Kuperminc's research indicates that, while some student athletes are likely to have goal discrepancy in their expectations to play professional sports, this does not reflect the black community's selection of sports as a means of upward mobility. The institutional environment has a greater influence

on the student-athlete's view of professional career possibilities. The discrepancy is most likely to occur at predominantly white institutions, at institutions with more intense athletic programs, and at institutions that segregate their student athletes.

Limiting minorities to player positions and maintaining white dominance in the decision-making areas of sports will affect the future development of sports in American society. Having gained the right to play, minority athletes must focus on creating and controlling opportunities in professional sports.

R.E.A.L. Sites

This list provides a print preview of typical **Coursewise** R.E.A.L. sites. (There are over 100 such sites at the **Courselinks**™ site.) The danger in printing URLs is that web sites can change overnight. As we went to press, these sites were functional using the URLs provided. If you come across one that isn't, please let us know via email to: webmaster@coursewise.com. Use your Passport to access the most current list of R.E.A.L. sites at the **Courselinks** site.

Site name: National Association for the Advancement of Colored People

URL: http://www.naacp.org/

Why is it R.E.A.L.? The National Association for the Advancement of Colored People is one of the oldest organizations dedicated to the equal participation of black people in the United States. The web site offers information on current projects and on lobbying the U.S. Congress and other organizations. It has press releases on current cases and information on activists.

Key terms: equality, civil rights

Site name: Indians Are People, Not Mascots

URL: http://www.alphacdc.com/treaty/ nomascot.html

Why is it R.E.A.L.? The National Coalition on Racism in Sports in the Media is concerned with the use of Native Americans as mascots of school, university, and professional sports teams. Its web site provides information on the schools that use such names and on legal actions against the use of Native Americans as mascots. It also offers information on Native American history.

Key terms: racism, sports, mascots

section 11

Does Teaching Mathematics or Science in Traditional Ways Discriminate Against Minorities?

Take a Closer Look

1. Is there only one way to learn subjects like mathematics and science?

2. Why do we focus on the contributions made by Westerners and overlook those of other cultures? Does this affect the way we view who can be a mathematician or scientist?

3. Is scientific success due to the group or the individual? If science needs the work of many to increase knowledge, then why do we teach it in an isolated manner?

4. Are true answers and right answers the same?

5. Are science and mathematics the work of a specially selected elite, or can anyone become involved?

WiseGuide Intro

Once on an exam, a student informed me that Americans had made all the major discoveries in science and math. Surprised by the surety of the response, I looked at math and science texts and could see how the student arrived at that conclusion. Except for Europeans (who in the student's mind were precursors to U.S. culture), the texts gave few indications that mathematics and science were developed elsewhere. Are mathematics and science solely the invention of Western society, or has a systematic bias in attribution ignored the developments of other societies?

In a technological society such as the United States, mathematics and science should be accessible to everyone, but standardized tests at all levels show Americans consistently behind other countries in these areas. Are Americans less able to learn math and science, or is there a problem with how we teach? Learning math and science is sometimes seen as a mountain to climb. Have we made their study more of a chore than necessary by insisting that students study in isolation rather than in groups? Science builds on the work of others, but scientific reputations are built on the achievements of individuals, who are often recognized with prizes and honors.

In Reading 24, Dirk J. Struik looks at the history of how mathematics has been taught and discovers a Eurocentric bias that leads us to ignore, devalue, or distort contributions from outside Western culture. He sees recent attempts to include recent discoveries about the development of mathematics as improving mathematical education for everyone.

In Reading 25, Craig E. Nelson focuses on ways we can improve our teaching not only of the sciences and math but also of other disciplines by incorporating new techniques of teaching that do not include the middle-class bias. He suggests that changes in the classroom can lead to teaching success. Nelson believes that group study, preparation for meeting the demands of the discipline, and the use of study guides will improve success without decreasing standards or impeding the acquisition of professionalism.

Issue 11: Does teaching mathematics in traditional ways discriminate against minorities?

Everybody Counts

Dirk J. Struik

Dirk J. Struik, professor emeritus of mathematics at MIT, is the author of Yankee Science in the Making *(Dover, 1948).*

Abstract

Ethnomathematics, defined as the study of the elements that contributed to the growth of mathematics outside of the Western culture, is needed to effectively teach mathematics to people whose education are confined to Eurocentric concepts. It is important in improving the mathematical education of indigenous people and in increasing their understanding of their culture. The study and teaching of ethnomathematics also plays a major role in understanding and promoting multiculturalism.

Toward a Broader History of Mathematics

The customary way of presenting the history of mathematics has been to start with the so-called Greek miracle of insight, Euclid and Archimedes being the central figures, and then pass lightly over "the Arabs," whose task was supposedly to serve as a transmission belt between the Greeks and the European Renaissance, producing some elementary algebra in the process. Next we continue to Descartes and Newton, and finally arrive at the modern period and the computer. Along the way we usually add some kind words about the Babylonians and the Egyptians with their curious fractions, and the Hindus with their decimal position system (the one we still use).

The fact is, however, that research on mathematics in human society has been undermining this approach for years. For example, early this century, when Brown University historian of mathematics Otto Neugebauer and colleagues deciphered cuneiform mathematical clay tablets, they found that the scientific culture in ancient Sumeria and Babylonia was far more advanced than had been believed. The older mathematicians among us may

still remember our surprise when we learned that the theorem of Pythagoras was known in Babylon at least a millennium before the Greek sage gave his name to it.

Students of texts in ancient Indian languages have found that series with an infinite number of terms were studied, especially in the state of Kerala in southwest India, centuries before Western mathematicians such as Newton showed a lasting interest in them. And Cambridge University biologist Joseph Needham has shed considerable light on the character and methods of ancient Chinese mathematics, maintained and improved over millennia, in his tomes on Chinese science and civilization. Through its influence on Arabic and perhaps Indian mathematics, this Chinese science has contributed to the cultures of the world.

In addition to this research on ancient societies where reading and writing were well developed, recent studies indicate that people need not be highly literate to show mathematical achievement. Marcia and Robert Ascher of Ithaca College have documented that the Incas of the Andes region, who had little or no script, nonetheless possessed a bureaucracy based on considerable arithmetical and statistical ingenuity. They produced elaborate "quipus," assemblages of colored cotton cords with knots representing numbers in the decimal position system.

This raises the question of how much mathematical knowledge existed, or does exist, in the cultures of other nonliterate peoples, past and present. Seen in this way, the history of mathematics would go far back into the Stone Age. We might discover remnants of Stone Age mathematics in cave paintings and paleolithic and neolithic artifacts. And the search is on for the mathematical concepts and practices that still exist among indigenous tribes. Even accounts of missionaries and travelers in nonliterate cultures could tell us something about this early mathematics—call it "protomathematics," if you like.

Ethnomathematics—the general name mathematician Ubiratan D'Ambrosio of Brazil coined for this study of the concepts, practices, and artifacts through which we discover mathematical elements among peoples living outside or on the margins of Western culture—teaches us to look at "exotic" forms of mathematics as an intrinsic element of the civilizations in which they have flourished, well worth studying for their own sake. Naturally, such studies have to be seen as an example of the trend toward multiculturalism we hear so much about these days, but it may be more to the point to call them a protest against Eurocentrism—the bias that leads us to ignore, devalue, or distort intellectual contributions that come from outside Western culture. One important reason for defining ethnomathematics in this way has to do with the fact that the field's scope extends far beyond the ivory tower. Indeed, the goal of many ethnomathematicians is wholly practical: to facilitate the teaching of mathematics in countries where a Eurocentric focus has proven disastrous to education of any kind.

Math As Culture

Pioneering work in ethnomathematics has come from Claudia Zaslavsky, who has taught in the New York City high school system. Her book *Africa Counts* surveys mathematics and its history south of the Sahara, beginning with a bone dug up in Zaire, dated between 9000 and 6500 B.C. Notches carved into the bone in groups could be interpreted as tallying marks in a number system based on ten and referring to lunar phases, hunting records, or perhaps menstrual periods.

Zaslavsky goes on to show how mathematics was used in taboos, riddles, money, architecture, ornamentation, concepts of time, and weights and measures. She mentions magic squares. These are large squares divided up into smaller squares, each of which contains a specific number—the "magic" is that the sum of the numbers in all lines running vertically, horizontally, and diagonally is the same. Some of this may well be extremely ancient and traditional protomathematics, but there may have been Arabic influence as well. After all, there was a university at Timbuktu in what we Westerners call the Middle Ages.

Since the publication of Zaslavsky's book, new material has come to light every year. For instance, Paulus Gerdes of the Pedagogical Institute of Mozambique has found significant mathematical content in weaving patterns, describing in considerable detail how the construction of baskets and bags from reeds and other plant leaves might, in millennia of practice, have led to an understanding of abstract geometrical concepts—even the theorem of Pythagoras.

He and his students have also drawn attention to "sonas," or sand drawings, which belong to a tradition of proverbs, fables, myths, beliefs, and games. Detailing the construction of a standardized sona in Zambia, Gerdes says that a tribe's drawing experts first create a grid of equidistant points on the ground with their fingertips and then draw one or more lines around the points in a specific pattern. This method enables them to reproduce the whole drawing by remembering little more than two numbers (the dimensions of the grid) and a geometric algorithm (the rule that determines how to create the pattern). At least one sona, the pentagram, has been absorbed into Western civilization. Part of its magical and mythical character lies in the fact that it is "monolinear"—executed without ever lifting the drawing finger or stick from the surface.

Other outstanding research in ethnomathematics has come from Marcia Ascher, who, in addition to continuing her studies on the Incas, has focused on a wide range of different cultures. For example, she has pointed out that among some indigenous peoples kinship relations follow patterns that can be understood in remarkable diagrams. She has devoted special attention to the Warlpiri of Australia's Northern Territory, whose kinship structure has an interesting and complex mathematical structure.

Insight through Activity

Research in ethnomathematics has attained new importance as part of the campaign to preserve and revive the traditional cultures of those who have spent centuries under colonial rule. This campaign has been particularly intensive in the newly independent states of Africa, where educators hope to combine indigenous mathematics with instruction in modern ways of counting and measuring. Not only would the approach preserve students' native culture but it might improve their understanding of mathematical concepts. After all, ethnomathematics is largely the mathematics of everyday life—something students already know. It stands to reason that the more teachers can capitalize on such knowledge, the less fear mathematics will inspire, and the more effective teaching will be. Recognizing this, the African Mathematical Union and the Commission on the History of Mathematics in Africa publish a newsletter that helps educators stay abreast of studies in ethnomathematics.

Interestingly, the drive to improve mathematical education for indigenous peoples is merging with the drive to improve mathematical education for everyone. Teachers are taking problems from the history of Egyptian, Babylonian, and Chinese mathematics, stressing the multicultural character of the science. But in addition to drawing on the results of ethnomathematical research, teachers are also employing the general principle of building on the mathematical knowledge and skills students have acquired outside the classroom.

To put it another way, the methods used in teaching mathematics to children in African villages are being extended to American minorities, as well as whites in urban and rural ghettos—and even to students in middle-class suburbs. For example, the newsletter of the International Study Group on Ethnomathematics discusses a teaching strategy based on taking measurements for carpets to be laid in a home. Other lesson plans relate to food buying, employment and wage experience, and gambling.

With all the emphasis on creating a bridge between abstract and practical mathematics, let us hope that the beauty of the field is not obscured but enhanced. For as Gerdes has suggested in his writing on the nature and origin of mathematics, beauty and practicality need not be thought of as opposites.

Unlike those who imagine early humans acquiring mathematics through passive contemplation of objects in nature, he raises the possibility that people might have arrived at such insight through activity. The concept of numbers could have developed through hunting or otherwise tallying; geometrical concepts could have evolved from the making of artifacts.

Over generations of experience, these ideas would have been refined. Paraphrasing the Russian anthropologist Boris Frolov, Gerdes noted that even during the paleolithic era, "labor exercised a clearly observable influence on the development of the thinking process." For instance, the ax became smaller and more elegant, taking on a geometrically regular form that could not have been produced unless people developed higher intellectual functioning.

Since the most rational form of an artifact was often one exhibiting attributes such as symmetry, these objects may well have been seen as beautiful. In other words, it is possible that, at least to some extent, both mathematical concepts and aesthetic feelings found their origin in the experience of generations of craftspeople.

For Further Reading

"Ethnomathematics and Its Place in the History and Pedagogy of Mathematics" by Ubiratan D'Ambrosio, in *For the Learning of Mathematics: An International Journal of Mathematics Education* (February 1985).

The Code of the Quipu by Marcia and Robert Ascher (University of Michigan, 1981).

Ethnomathematics by Marcia Ascher (Brooks/Cole, 1991).

Ethnogeometrie by Paulus Gerdes (Franzbecker, 1990).

Africa Counts by Claudia Zaslavsky (Prindle, Weber & Schmidt, 1973).

Form at end of book

Issue 11: Does teaching mathematics in traditional ways discriminate against minorities?

Student Diversity Requires Different Approaches to College Teaching, Even in Math and Science

Craig E. Nelson

It now appears that all traditionally taught college courses are markedly (though unintentionally) biased against many non-traditional students, and, indeed, against most students who have not attended elite preparatory schools. Thus, when we teach merely in traditional ways we probably discriminate strongly on grounds quite different from those we intend (assuming that we intend only effort and merit). Easily accessible changes in how we teach have been shown repeatedly to foster dramatic changes in student performance with no change in standards—in some cases, no students now earn failing grades. Similarly dramatic improvements have been shown in the uniformity of outcomes. For example, the gap between Black performance and the performance of other groups can be entirely eliminated, even in "hard" courses such as calculus.

When I first encountered them, the arguments challenging professors to address diversity in our classrooms seemed to be largely specious and not likely to have any positive effect in most science courses, certainly not in those I taught in biology. Subsequently, I have come to understand that much of what I took as neutral teaching practice actually functions to keep our courses less accessible to students from non-traditional backgrounds. If my current understandings are a reasonable reflection of reality, then (almost) all traditionally taught courses are unintentionally but nevertheless deeply biased in ways that make substantial differences in performance for many students.

Treisman's Work and Its Implications

Let me start with an example. It once would have seemed to me that mathematics is so abstract and free of particular cultural constraints as to make it difficult to conceive how one might possibly teach it in a culturally biased way. Nevertheless, when Treisman (1992) began examining calculus at the University of California at Berkeley, he found that about 60% of the Blacks who had completed calculus there in the preceding decade received grades of D or F— grades so low that they could not proceed with a major in mathematics, science, or technology.

Treisman surveyed the faculty for possible explanations. All suggestions (save one) proposed that something was wrong with the students (a motivation gap, inadequate preparation, lack of family support, or just a function of income), thereby exonerating the faculty of culpability for the lower achievement by Blacks. Each suggestion failed to withstand scrutiny. Indeed, Treisman found that for Black students at Berkeley, math entry scores were negatively correlated with achievement in calculus—the more math the students already knew when they began, the worse they were likely to do! Similarly, for these students family income was negatively correlated with grades in calculus. The ones who did best came disproportionately from families of school and civil service employees. Of course, Blacks are not the only group that does poorly at Berkeley or elsewhere. Treisman also worked with Hispanics. And related studies (some discussed in Treisman, 1992) applying Treisman's approach have found that similar problems and similar remedies apply to Blacks, Hispanics, and rural Whites in a variety of other colleges and universities.

Students in the groups that did not do well in calculus at Berkeley, and in calculus and other science courses in related studies elsewhere, usually have had certain experiences in common. They have tended to come disproportionately from high schools that were not heavily oriented towards college preparation. They thus had few peers to study with in high school. Moreover, they often have been taught that only weak students study together (as in remedial study halls) or even (as I learned growing up in rural Kansas) that working together on homework was cheating. Finally, in their high schools studying and academic achievement have typically carried negative social prestige—they made you a nerd. Thus many of the students from these groups studied alone and in a "closet." Treisman (1992) found the greatest contrasts with students from some Asian American groups, many of whom formed study-squads to get through calculus, groups in which social status was increased by one's ability to help others.

Treisman's responses can be seen as taking control of the social system. He invited the students from the less successful groups into honors—not remedial, discussion sections. He told them that homework would be easy both because their math scores showed that they were ready for calculus and because the class would prepare them to do the homework before it was assigned. In some of the versions of his implementations, he told them that the homework had to be submitted on time. Further, to help the students get it right, they were required to do peer checking. With this required collaboration, the time required for in-class discussion of the homework dropped from all period to an average of three minutes a week. The students had mostly taught themselves the homework. However, the core of Treisman's success hinged on his use in-class of collaborative small groups—groups working on problems harder and different than the normal homework (Treisman, 1992). Note the use of a coaching approach. If you want students to run a 100 yard dash, you don't let them stop at 100 yards. If you want them to do well on an exam at the level of the homework, you must lead them beyond it.

Only about 4% of the Black students completing Treisman's "workshop" calculus made a D or F (versus the 60% earlier; see Fullilove and Treisman, 1990, for statistics). Moreover, the differences vanished between the average grades achieved by the Black students who did their workshop calculus and those achieved on the same exams by students in socially dominant groups, including Asian Americans. There thus were no differences in ability, industriousness, motivation, or background that were not totally nullified by making the social systems work more equitably for academic achievement. A key point is that the content of the course was not watered down— students from nondominant backgrounds were just taught better than before.

As a second example, Amendariz and McCaffrey (cited in Treisman, 1992) have developed a parallel program for Blacks and Hispanics at the University of Texas. There the grade point average for minority students is 3.53 whereas that for other students taught the regular way, but taking the same exams, is 1.67. Comparable success with similar approaches has been achieved at institutions very different from the University of California at Berkeley and in mathematics, physics, chemistry, and biology.

A key to achieving the gains towards uniformity of performance is a shift to structured, student-student group work. Such effective discussions must be distinguished from recitation. In recitation the teacher asks questions and the students respond one by one or, alternatively, the students ask questions and the teacher responds. Effective discussion, in contrast, requires that students work together in small groups (except, perhaps, for the small minority of faculty who can dependably conduct a good Socratic dialogue). To make discussions most effective, the teacher must make sure that the students are prepared for the discussion, that the students participate constructively and fairly evenly, and that the students are addressing questions that are sufficiently challenging. (For more on collaborative learning, see Johnson, Johnson, and Smith, 1991; Meyers and Jones, 1993; and Nelson, 1994.)

Disciplinary Discourse: Brighter and Harder Working Students

Different disciplines have very different standards for acceptable expression and adjudication (Bruffee, 1984, 1993). Rose (1989) provides eloquent examples of the barriers that result from implicitly assuming that the students have already mastered disciplinary discourse. In teaching teachers to teach writing across the curriculum, Colomb (1988) has found that the most difficult thing about writing is learning all of the reasonable things that one might say that are precluded by the literary conventions of the disciplines. For example, in English classes, a student who comments that the jewelled eyes of toads (upon which Shakespeare remarks) reflect a nocturnally adapted retina, although accurate, will usually not expedite the teacher's goals for the day. Similarly, in science the student is not supposed to remark that the color of the pH indicator is exquisite, nor that it matches exactly the central stone in the student's grandmother's garnet brooch.

If students go to a good, college preparatory, secondary school, they learn that expectations and literary conventions vary radically among disciplines. They also have had practice working in a dozen or so disciplines at levels that provide a good understanding of the expectations in freshman courses at colleges. In many cases where students have attended secondary schools that were not heavily college-oriented, the standards have been so basic that few differences between the disciplines were evident.

The prevalence of such basic standards among entering freshmen in most institutions makes it possible to produce brighter and harder-working students using only one hour of class time. Dr. Mitzi Streepey (personal communication), upon learning of the ideas connecting disciplinary discourse and bias, returned to her class and gave them an essay question over the material they had been studying. She included four or five answers that she had written to the question. The answers varied in quality in ways that illustrated the array she was used to getting on exams. She broke the class into small groups and had them decide which answers were better in what ways, doing a whole group synthesis at the end in which she further clarified her expectations. She then gave the students a second question to work on and had them compare their draft answers with the criteria they had developed. Her students suddenly became brighter and harder-working, as evidenced by their success on the next exam (the way we always tell when students are bright and hard working). Several students reported that they were now doing better than ever before in their other classes too.

My own experience also illustrates the idea that students are often bright enough and hard-working enough to do well in class, but lack a clear understanding of what it is we want them to do. Thus, like Dr. Streepey, I find that many freshmen are not accustomed to checking to see whether they have explicitly addressed each segment of a complex essay question. Strangely enough, a similar problem exists for multiple-choice questions. When my biology classes are too large for exclusive use of essay questions, I often put on the overhead projector a multiple-choice question covering the material that I have just taught in the preceding 10- or 15-minute segment of lecture. I include a dozen answers, some of which are factually wrong, some of which are factually true but irrelevant to the question, and at least two of which are true. I find that students often think initially that any true answer is a right answer, so that judging the acceptability of the answer in combination with the stem of the question is a new skill. Many are also surprised to see that right answers can be expressed in several ways and that one question might have several strikingly different right answers. (This, of course, is what allows multiple-choice questions to be used to test student comprehension. And it is one reason that students must understand the material, and not just memorize it, even for multiple-choice exams.)

Expectations differ among courses in ways that extend well beyond answering questions. For example, in many high schools, most of the effort in reading a book goes into understanding what it says. In college, what a book means reflects the questions that one brings to it as much as what the author says. The same novel used in courses in economics, psychology, women's studies, and literature means different things in each course because we focus different questions upon it. Thus we need to provide explicit guidance to our students in reading and thinking about texts as well as in assessments. I typically give out a study guide with each reading assignment, at least early in the course. The study guide indicates specific questions that the students should be able to answer from that particular reading assignment.

When we assume that students must come to us already knowing how to read a text in our field and how to respond to questions on our exams, we are in essence assuming that the students have gone to a good, college preparatory, secondary school and that they have paid attention. A small amount of effort showing the students what we want them to do can pay large dividends in terms of increased performance by students who have not previously learned how to proceed in our subjects.

One-Shot Grading and Social Background

I first began to think seriously about how my teaching might be needlessly perpetuating social class differences when I read an article by Bowles and Gintis (1973). They suggested that currently the major function of higher education was to sort the children of the upper classes into positions in which they would remain well off while convincing most of the children of the poor classes, first, that they were either unable or unwilling to do what it took to obtain a professional job and, second, that the system was fair and unbiased. They also suggested that teachers did this by basing their evaluations heavily on social class behaviors, such as the ability to complete assignments on time, rather than on the ability to understand and apply the content.

If we are sorting on social class behavior, it would make relatively little difference what major a student chose, so long as the conventions for evaluation were sufficiently social-class biased in every major. My concern for these issues has been deepened by several other readings, most powerfully by Rose (1989). Further support for the basic theses comes from my own experiences in high school in rural Kansas and from the reactions of many of the faculty from nontraditional backgrounds with whom I have discussed these issues. The presumption that students must come to us having already learned the disciplinary standards for reading, writing, and evaluation, as discussed in the last section, would of course be an example of how we assume that the students should have had a fairly upper middle-class background. This presumption is often heightened by the deadlines we use in grading.

When we assign a fixed, one-shot deadline for grading we typically assume, first, that the student can tell when she has adequately mastered the content with little or no feedback. Secondly, we assume not only does she come to us knowing how to master the material but also knowing how long that it will take to master the material—so students often become fully aware before an exam that their mastery is short of their own standards but find that they have misjudged the time it takes to master the material. Our grades for them will then reflect neither ability nor willingness to learn.

Further, with one-shot grading we assume that students are largely isolated from worldly concerns. Thus, a student may have learned to recognize A-level mastery, have a very good idea of how long it will take to achieve it, and have allowed an adequate time to do the work but still have these plans interrupted by externally imposed changes in work schedules, by sick children (especially in single parent households), or other nonacademic factors. Clearly, these constraints are least severe for upper middle-class students who have at best marginal jobs and have no children. These constraints are much greater for the non-traditional students who now form the new majority in higher education. All of these issues are intensified by the habit of teachers at most institutions of assigning deadlines independently. It is not unusual for a student to have exams or major papers due the same week in three of the four courses she is taking.

Considerations such as these have led me to write two versions of each exam (finals excluded for logistic reasons). Students who don't like their grade on the first one can take the second exam two weeks after the first. They then get the higher grade of the two. Students can also opt to skip the first exam, do the work for their other courses, and then take the second exam. Practical considerations clearly affect the attractiveness of such changes. One issue to consider with such a scheme is the amount of grading. I have found that writing an exam that is about 70% as long as I used to use will keep me from doing much extra grading, because several students will elect to only take one of the two exams.

A second issue that arises when I discuss this extra-exams approach with other faculty is the loss of "coverage" entailed by using a second class period for an exam. Initially, I scheduled make-up exams in the evening at a time convenient to all of the students who wanted to take it. This is still a fine solution in modest sized classes but can be nearly impossible in larger classes. Eventually, I re-

alized that the second exam caused most students to study many extra hours. Hence, I was teaching substantially more biology by giving the second exam than I could with any other use of class time. The increase in grades that approach produces represents, of course, a corresponding increase in my success in fostering student mastery of the material.

A third issue is that of appropriate professional conduct. Like most faculty, I want our graduates to be able to meet deadlines and otherwise perform in a professional manner. The question, however, is whether we assess in ways that eliminate as freshmen or sophomores most of those who come to us without these upper-middle-class skills in place or whether we should teach them the skills during the time they are in our programs, fostering them in freshmen and assessing them in seniors.

In this article I have advocated the use of structured, small-group discussions, the explicit teaching of disciplinary discourse, and flexibility with respect to time deadlines. There are many other layers of bias built into our teaching, even in science (starting outline in Nelson, 1993). For example, deep changes are needed in what we teach (e.g., Beldacos, 1988; Harding, 1986; Rosser, 1985) as well as in how we teach (the subject of this article). Indeed, I became convinced some time ago that the only effective way to teach science is a set of processes in which we look for the presently better alternative rather than suggesting that we have found certain truth (Nelson, 1986, 1989, 1997). This comparative approach fosters a deeper understanding of science as a set processes for critical thinking, and thus as a concrete example of critical thinking. It is also both more representative of the real nature of science and much less threatening to the students when controversial issues arise.

However, I have concentrated in this article on changes in how we teach rather than what we teach. These may or may not be less satisfying philosophically than changing the basic way we structure the content. But they are the ones for which I know the strongest evidence that they make a real difference in student achievement.

Fundamental Changes in Pedagogical Paradigms

The first conclusion I want to draw from my experience and from these examples is that several alternatives to our traditional ways of teaching have been shown to lead to stunning improvements in student achievement. Angelo and Cross (1993) present many examples showing how to diagnose what changes are needed (a process they call classroom assessment) and how to assess the effects of those changes ("classroom research").

One of the examples from Angelo and Cross (1993, pp. 69–72) shows especially clearly that massive improvements are fairly easy to attain, even if one does not directly deal with diversity. A calculus instructor, frustrated with student performance, changed from five homework problems per period to four but added the requirement that the students take one of the four and explain in English sentences how they solved it (this counting as 20% of the day's homework grade). He then built upon these explanations during the in-class discussion of homework and related problems (i.e., he used what I above called structured discussions). To the teacher's surprise, not only were midterm and final exam scores much higher than usual, but "for the first time in nearly thirty years of teaching calculus, he did not fail a single student" (Angelo and Cross, 1993, p. 72).

Similarly, an economics professor who tried some of the ideas suggested here reported that he had created a major problem for his department (personal communication). He taught one of 10 sections of introductory economics, all having a common midterm and common final. Scores on the common exams were assigned grades by a formula that gave a fixed percentage of the class each grade from A through F. He reported that in three years of using these approaches, none of his students had received an F. Consequently, his colleagues were all eating extra Fs. However, they were quite unprepared for the question: How do you grade if some or all of you can teach in ways in which no students make marks as low as those that you used to call F?

There is thus no doubt that we know how to make massive differences in overall student achievement. And, again, gains are not just on comprehension, but also on application, synthesis, retention, enthusiasm, and more (McKeachie, 1994).

My second conclusion is that these nontraditional approaches usually produce large gains by the groups of students who have been hardest to reach with standard pedagogy. This conclusion is supported not just by the studies such as Treisman's (1992) that have addressed the issue directly, but also by those that have looked just at overall classroom performance. Clearly, if no one is making an F, then no one from the hard to reach groups can be making an F either.

These two conclusions together make it hard to justify offering any course that uses largely passive pedagogies. Specifically, a straight lecture course is quite unlikely to be as effective overall as one making extensive use of structured discussion. And studies like Treisman's (1992) have made it clear that a failure to make effective use of these techniques is also (unintentionally) discriminatory against Blacks and other traditionally under-represented groups.

This raises the question of whether it has already become immoral to teach without extensive use of the active learning techniques that so enhance performance. Please note that I did not say that lecture and other traditional techniques have no place in a well-taught course. And let me stress that questions of morality must be carefully evaluated in the overall context of faculty teaching "loads" and support for innovation and for more time-intensive methods. Yet, major effects can be achieved with effort no greater than that required to offer a new course, a task we each undertake occasionally.

The evidence that these alternative pedagogies are more effective and equitable is now so strong that it seems to me that the burden of proof has shifted. As a consequence, I would suggest that any faculty member offering (and any administrator supporting) a straight lecture course might be required to show that it is at least as effective in producing student learning as it would be if enriched with a generous admixture of these nontraditional approaches.

In so saying, I do not wish to understate the extent of change that is required. Two fundamental changes in paradigm must underlie any major requirements in higher education and, especially, in our prospects of success with under-represented groups. The first is the change from measuring teaching by what is taught (or other teacher behaviors) to measuring it by what is learned. Bart and Tagg (1995) eloquently discuss the need to shift from a teaching-focused paradigm to a learning-centered paradigm. The second major change I see needed is a switch from seeing our roles as sorting out the unfit to seeing our roles primarily as coaches striving to maximize the success of all students in mastering our disciplines and attaining the a truly liberal education.

To achieve such shifts, we as individual teachers and administrators will have to seek out and take seriously the literature on the improvement of college teaching (e.g., Feldman and Paulsen, 1994; Halpern and Associates, 1994; Menges and Mathis, 1988) and will also need to use classroom assessment and research systematically in our own classes (Angelo & Cross, 1993). We will also need to pay special attention to the burgeoning literature on diversity and college teaching (e.g., Adams, 1992; Border & Van Note Chism, 1992; Turner, Garcia, Nora, & Reardon, 1996).

However, as Treisman (1992) emphasizes, the deeper issue is one of institutional reform—how institutions might make it possible and attractive for faculty members to work on course and curriculum reconstruction and how they might provide resources and rewards that encourage departments to pursue such changes. Thus individual faculty responsibility is joined to institutional responsibility.

Meanwhile, it has become clear that we each could fairly easily make large differences in student achievement and in the extent to which our courses and institutions are fair. As Treisman (1992) says,

Ultimately, one must realize that the Black and Latino students who do make it into higher education are national treasures and must be treated as such . . . their success will have important ramifications not only for the academic disciplines and professions they pursue, but for the very fabric of American society. (p. 371)

It is clear that we already know what to do first. And it is clear that much of it is doable without further delay—each of our classes can change in important and effective ways as soon as tomorrow morning. There are no risks and minimal costs in getting started. And much more than individual lives (as if that were not enough) hangs in the balance. On what grounds can we possibly justify further delay?

For Further Information

Angelo, T. A., and Cross, K. P. (1993). *Classroom Assessment Techniques.* Great tools for improving teaching.

Border, L. L. B., and Van Note Chism, N. (Eds.) (1992). *Teaching for Diversity.* Diversity and college teaching.

Johnson, D. W., Johnson, R. T., and Smith, K. A. (1991). *Cooperative Learning.* An overview.

Rose, M. (1989). *Lives on the Boundary.* Traditional teaching and under-represented groups. Chapters 7 and 8 are essential.

References

Adams, M. (Ed.) (1992). *Promoting Diversity in College Classrooms: Innovative Responses for the Curriculum, Faculty and Institutions* (New Directions for Teaching and Learning, No. 52). San Francisco: Jossey-Bass.

Angelo, T. A., and Cross, K. P. (1993). *Classroom Assessment Techniques* (2nd ed.). San Francisco: Jossey-Bass.

Barr, R. B., and Tagg, J. (1995). From teaching to learning. *Change,* 27(6), 13–25.

Beldacos, A. et al. [as Biology and Gender Study Group] (1988). The importance of a feminist critique for contemporary cell biology. *Hypatia,* 3(1), 61–76.

Border, L. L. B., and Van Note Chism, N. (Eds.) (1992). *Teaching for Diversity* (New Directions for Teaching and Learning, No. 49). San Francisco: Jossey-Bass.

Bowles, S., and Gintis, J. (1973). I.Q. in the United States class structure. *Social Policy,* 3, 4–5. Reprinted in A. Gartner, C. Greer, and F. Riessman (Eds.) (1974), *The New Assault on Equality: I.Q. and Social Stratification* (pp. 7–84). New York: Harper and Row.

Bruffee, K. (1984). Collaborative learning and the "conversation of mankind." *College English,* 46(7), 635–652.

———. (1993). *Collaborative Learning: Higher Education, Interdependence, and the Authority of Knowledge.* Baltimore: Johns Hopkins University Press.

Colomb, G. G. (1988). *Disciplinary Secrets and the Apprentice Writer.* Upper Montclair, NY: Institute for Critical Thinking, Montclair State College.

Feldman, K. A., and Paulsen, M. B. (Eds.) (1994). *Teaching and Learning in the College Classroom* (Association for the Study of Higher Education Reader). Needham Heights, MA: Ginn Press.

Fullilove, R. E., and Treisman, P. U. (1990). Mathematics achievement among African American undergraduates of the University of California, Berkeley: An evaluation of the Mathematics Workshop Program. *Journal of Negro Education,* 59(3), 463–478.

Halpern, D. F. and Associates (Eds.) (1994). *Changing College Classrooms: New Teaching and Learning Strategies for an Increasingly Complex World.* San Francisco: Jossey-Bass.

Harding, S. (1986). *The Science Question in Feminism.* Ithaca, NY: Cornell University Press.

Johnson, D. W., Johnson, R. T., and Smith, K. A. (1991). *Cooperative Learning: Increasing College Faculty Instructional Productivity.* ASHE-ERIC Higher Education Report 1991(4). Washington, DC: George Washington University.

McKeachie, W. (1994). *Teaching Tips: A Guidebook for the Beginning College Teacher* (9th ed.). Lexington, MA: Heath.

Menges, R. J., and Mathis, B. C. (1988). *Key Resources on Teaching, Learning, Curriculum, and Faculty Development.* San Francisco: Jossey-Bass.

Meyers, C., and Jones, T. B. (1993). *Promoting Active Learning.* San Francisco: Jossey-Bass.

Nelson, C. E. (1986). Creation, evolution or both? A multiple model approach. In R. W. Hanson (Ed.), *Science and Creation: Geological, Theological and Educational Perspectives* (pp. 128–159). New York: Macmillan.

———. (1989). Skewered on the unicorn's horn: The illusion of [a] tragic tradeoff between content and critical thinking in the teaching of science. In L. W. Crowe (Ed.), *Enhancing Critical Thinking in the Sciences* (pp. 17–27). Washington: Society of College Science Teachers (National Science Teachers Association).

———. (1993). Every course differently: Diversity and college teaching: an outline. In *National Science Foundation Publication 93–108, The role of faculty from the scientific disciplines in the education of future science and mathematics teachers* (pp. 94–100). Washington, DC: National Science Foundation.

———. (1997). Collaborative learning and critical thinking. In K. Bosworth, and S. Hamilton (Eds.), *Collaborative Learning and College Teaching* (New Directions for Teaching and Learning, No. 59) (pp. 45–58). San Francisco: Jossey-Bass.

———. (1997). Tools for tampering with teaching's taboos. In W. Campbell and K. A. Smith (Eds.), *New Paradigms for College Teaching.* Edina, MN: Interaction.

Rose, M. (1989). *Lives on the Boundary: A Moving Account of the Struggles and Achievements of America's Underclass.* New York: Penguin Books.

Rosser, S. V. (1986). *Teaching Science and Health from a Feminist Perspective.* New York: Pergamon Press.

Treisman, U. (1992). Studying students studying calculus: A look at the lives of minority mathematics students in college. *The College Mathematics Journal,* 23(5), 362–372.

Turner, C., Garcia, M., Nora, M., and Reardon, L. I. (Eds.) (1996). *Racial and Ethnic Diversity in Higher Education* (Association for the Study of Higher Education Reader). Needham Heights, MA: Simon & Schuster.

Form at end of book

WiseGuide Wrap-Up

Science and mathematics have been presented as unbiased ways of understanding both the physical and social world. We look to mathematical models and statistics to explain who does what and why, and we look to science and theory to explain human as well as physical phenomena. But are these areas of academic inquiry any less culturally biased in their approach than any other discipline? The methods may be free of bias, but the topics chosen for study may not be as value free. There is always a selection process in deciding what questions should be pursued, which projects should be funded, and whose research is meaningful. Since the 1960s, women and minorities have criticized not only the questions and approaches of science, but also the selectivity in presenting the history of science and mathematics. As Struik notes in Reading 24, everyone counts, but in a social context that is not true.

This critical approach is also applicable to the way in which science and math are taught. There, too, cultural values reflect assumptions of how the class should be conducted, what examples should be used, and how students should work and demonstrate their mastery of the material. Is it cheating if you study with others? Must we carefully weigh the contribution of individuals in all group projects to see who really gets the *A*? Is effective teaching the same as effective learning? Traditional ways of teaching may not be as productive as the interactive techniques currently being introduced. We should all be comfortable with the language of science and mathematics. We should all be able to think critically and to apply what we have learned to our everyday lives. Ability and hard work—not minority group membership—should be factors in learning.

R.E.A.L. Sites

This list provides a print preview of typical **Coursewise** R.E.A.L. sites. (There are over 100 such sites at the **Courselinks**™ site.) The danger in printing URLs is that web sites can change overnight. As we went to press, these sites were functional using the URLs provided. If you come across one that isn't, please let us know via email to: webmaster@coursewise.com. Use your Passport to access the most current list of R.E.A.L. sites at the **Courselinks** site.

Site name: Eisenhower National Clearinghouse for Mathematics and Science Education

URL: http://www.enc.org/

Why is it R.E.A.L.? This web site contains a variety of materials to promote the teaching of mathematics and science. One of the web pages specifically focuses (ENC Focus) on multicultural approaches to teaching these subjects. The Clearinghouse also offers programs, pedagogical ideas for reform, resources, essays, and products.

Key terms: mathematics, multicultural teaching

Site name: Center for Science and Mathematics Teaching

URL: http://ase.tufts.edu/csmt/

Why is it R.E.A.L.? This web site has a variety of resources for teachers, including teacher training programs and discussion sites on student-centered teaching of mathematics and science.

Key terms: mathematics, science, teaching

section 12 | What Is American Identity?

Take a Closer Look

1. Who is an American?

2. Is a common culture necessary to define our society?

3. Is diversity a threat to cohesiveness?

4. What do we need to share to have a functioning society?

5. Who would you select to represent the United States at an intergalactic meeting? Why?

WiseGuide Intro

Which image describes Americans best? Are we a "melting pot," "salad bowl," "mosaic," or jigsaw puzzle? Are we a society of individuals or groups? Do we owe our loyalty to the language we speak, the family we are born into, the religion we preach, the state or region we are from, the flag we salute? How do we define ourselves as Americans? For many people, individualism best defines who we are. We are people who live under the Constitution, where we are free to pursue happiness without governmental interference in our religious, political, or economic beliefs and choices. However, underneath this "We, the people" has always been the understanding that this refers to a particular group of people who share fundamental cultural and social identities. This permits a degree of individual variation but not the acceptance of practices that vary too much from a cultural norm. Who are "We, the people," and what makes us American? Is it necessary to define our national identity to be a successful society?

Does a common culture mean that we are all the same? Does equality mean that we are all clones and therefore equal? Historically, the groups covered under the Constitution and the Bill of Rights have been extended. The small group of elite white males who penned these documents are no longer the only ones protected. The ideal of social and political equality is based on respect for the individual. But when individuals who do not feel they are being accorded that respect seek a reason, it is often their group membership that accounts for their exclusion and negative treatment. Sometimes, we are dealt with as individuals, but sometimes, our group identity determines how we are treated. The sacredness of the individual must be balanced with a concern for the common good. We are individuals, but we are also members of a larger community.

In Reading 26, Jerry Adler discusses the emergence of class identity as a new factor in the definition of what it is to be an American. Going beyond the past divisions based on religion and ethnicity, Adler explores the importance of economic and lifestyle issues in defining who is an American. He also asks: Why should America admit almost a million immigrants a year, merely for them to re-create self-sufficient national enclaves on our shores?

In Reading 27, Robert Bellah focuses on the relationship between culture and institutions. Our institutional order creates the cultural order. Bellah demonstrates this with a look at the roles of education and the media in creating a dominant culture in the United States. The state-funded educational system and the media and market economic system socialize all of us to the same degree, regardless of ethnic, religious, or class background. Bellah discusses the "sacredness of the individual conscience, the individual person" in religious, political, and social matters as one of the core values of the society.

Issue 12: What is American identity?

Sweet Land of Liberties

If everyone has his own niche, what do we have in common anymore?

Jerry Adler

with Steven Waldman

Like millions of Mexican-American teenage girls, I still remember where I was when I learned that Selena had been shot. I was on my way to work, and I saw the story in the *Times,* and I said, Gee, never heard of her, and turned the page.

And then I thought: Wait a minute, this happened in America, not Bangledesh! She was the biggest star in tejano music, and I'd never heard of that either! And after reading a description of it as "a fast-paced mix of accordion, guitars and lyrics . . . with roots both in the oom-pah music of European settlers in Texas and in Mexican ballads," I still don't know what the hell it is, except that millions of other Americans were practically throwing themselves out of windows because the queen of it was dead. If it was this big, why hadn't I heard about it on National Public Radio?

Perhaps we're just too big, too diverse to hold together. Thomas Jefferson surely would think so, although he probably would have thought so a hundred years ago, too. The great centrifugal engine of American culture turns faster and faster, spinning off fashions, slogans, ideologies, religions, artistic movements, economic theories, therapeutic disciplines, cults and dogmas in fabulous profusion. In America even fringe movements seem to number their adherents in the millions. Everyone's identity is politicized—not just in terms of race, ethnicity, religion and language (as in the nation formerly known as Yugoslavia, say) but also gender, sexual behavior, age, clothing, diet and personal habits. To smoke in public is a political act; to consume as much as a leaf of arugula is to make a potential statement of one's class and outlook.

Is our national identity really threatened by this? A substantial minority of Americans seem to think so, predicting that the United States will cease to exist in recog-

nizable form sometime in the next century (*Newsweek* Poll, page 26)* If so, 1995 may turn out to be a turning point—not because of Selena, but owing to the other big news that also broke last spring, that right-wing militias were arming themselves against federal law-enforcement officials. America will survive tejano just as it endured zydeco and klezmer, and it will work its way into the mainstream in the form, most likely of a jingle for Taco Bell. But it remains to be seen whether any society can endure if even a fraction of its people believe that their own government was capable of planting the Oklahoma City bomb.

Eugene Richards, *Magnum:* These parents were very caring yet they're what a lot of people fear.

Not that fanaticism is a new development in American politics. If someone accused Bill Clinton of personally driving the bomb to Oklahoma, it wouldn't be much worse than what was said about Franklin Roosevelt, Harry Truman, Lyndon Johnson, Richard Nixon—or George Washington. Our standard for civic comity remains the placid 1950s, the decade most commonly cited by Americans, especially white Americans, as a time when "people in this country felt they had more in common . . . than Americans do today" (poll).* But the three-and-a-half decades of chaos that followed should have given Americans the idea that upheaval and turmoil is in fact their country's normal condition. Nor was the 1950s as empty of conflict as we like to recall. This year's rebels—Western ranchers who aren't about to let government bureaucrats tell them where their cattle can step—had their counterparts 45 years ago in a Montana draft board that took it upon itself to withhold inductions unless Gen. Douglas MacArthur was given *nuclear weapons* to use against North Korea. Later in the decade, America didn't seem like an especially harmonious place to black children who needed federal troops to protect them on their way to elementary schools in the South. Perhaps unsurprisingly, a plurality of blacks in the *Newsweek* Poll chose the 1960s as

*Does not appear in this publication.

the nation's halcyon era. But both groups—as well as Hispanics—agreed by wide margins that the American "national character" has gotten worse since 20 years ago (poll, p. 186).

Over the centuries, various institutions have held America together against the centrifugal tug of its sheer size and diversity. In successive generations these have been the Protestant religion, the English language, the Constitution, the shared experience of war, the three television networks and Disney World, of which only the last remains a universal, unchallenged touchstone of national identity. The Constitution is still in effect, naturally. But in the May decision striking down term limits a forceful minority on the Supreme Court seemed intent on radically reinterpreting it as a compact among sovereign states rather than the people—an inherently separatist view that has been out of favor at least since the Union won the Civil War.

From the 1950s to the 1970s, the belief in shared prosperity was a powerful, if not exactly inspirational, unifying force in American society. But more recent economic trends have called even that basic tenet of Americanism into question. Housing data analyzed by Paul A. Jargowsky, an economist at the University of Texas at Dallas, show what he calls "a pronounced trend toward increasing economic segregation" since 1970. It was in those years that millions of people left their homes in cities—notorious for letting poor people poach on the same census tracts as rich ones—for suburban developments whose walls and gates enclose a population self-selected for income compatibility. Many people, although not economists, were shocked to discover a few months ago that the United States now has the least equitable income distribution among all developed countries, including those, like England, with a hereditary aristocracy.

As common purpose and shared interests have declined, national unity has increasingly become a matter of symbols. We have symbolic enemies—Japanese auto manufacturers, invoked by President Clinton to represent the global economic forces behind the stagnation in real American wages. And symbolic heroes—Scott O'Grady, whose success in hiding in the woods for six days stood in for the war we didn't fight against Serbian genocide. We even have symbolic symbolism, in the form of a proposed amendment that would unleash the awesome power of the United States Constitution against "desecration" of the American flag, which has been occurring at the epidemic rate of around 10 times a year. This retroactive slap at the 1960s doesn't get at the contemporary problem of emigration by rich Americans (still a trickle, but an increasing one) who decide they'd rather salute the flags of nations with lower income taxes.

Many of the issues that divide Americans are familiar ones. One of the most widely discussed books of 1995 has been *Alien Nation,* in which journalist Peter Brimelow sounds the alarm that if present trends in birth and immigration continue, some time in the next century white Americans will be outnumbered by those of black, Hispanic and Asian descent. Brimelow acknowledges that even to raise the subject is to risk condemnation as a racist, but he's willing to take the chance. A naturalized American of English birth, he evidently holds a fairly narrow view of who qualifies as white, leading him to the ludicrous observation that "when you leave Park Avenue and descend into the subway . . . you find yourself in an underworld that is not just teeming but is also almost entirely colored . . . where do all these people get off and come to the surface?" Leaving aside the fact that he's wrong (according to the Metropolitan Transportation Authority, whites make up roughly 45 percent of New York's subway riders), it is hard to think of another time in the last 25 years when a white writer would have felt free to make such a dismissive generalization about the "colored."

Herb Ritts: Being an American is about having the right to be who you are. Sometimes that doesn't happen. The flag, even the flag, can be a gag.

But in fact immigration seems to be making one of its periodic resurgences as a divisive political issue. In part this is driven by economics. Brimelow's book conclusively demonstrates that contrary to myth, not all immigrants win the Nobel Prize after they get here; some drive cabs their whole lives, and quite a few wind up on welfare. Many Americans seem to have figured out the same thing for themselves. By a small but significant margin (52 percent to 40 percent), Americans in the *Newsweek* Poll* were more likely to agree that "immigrants are a burden on our country because they take jobs, housing and health care" than with the view that "immigrants strengthen our country because of their hard work and talents." Psychologically, "multiculturalism" has also changed the terms of the debate, by dropping the presumption that immigrants come here in order to assimilate. The sentimental argument for immigration has been that newcomers "enrich" American society. But how can they do that, if they never even join it? If Selena was so great, why should Mexican-Americans (and, apparently, mostly just those who had settled in southwestern Texas, not the ones in California) have had her all to themselves? Brimelow is not the only one to ask why America should admit almost a million immigrants a year merely for them to re-create self-sufficient national enclaves on our shores.

*Not included in this publication.

William Albert Allard, National Geographic Society: In the 1800s, many cowboys were even younger than T. J., 17. But regardless of age, what could be more American than the American cowboy?

But this is a variation on an old debate. The 1990s has been marked by the unpleasant discovery of a whole new set of fault lines running through American society, superimposed on the familiar ones of race, religion and ethnicity. Gun control and grazing rights are not unimportant issues, but no one 20 years ago could have predicted that they would become rallying cries for a militant right-wing separatist movement, fueled by the class resentments of the one group that wasn't supposed to have any, white men. Nor did most people expect the relation of intelligence to race to surface suddenly as a divisive issue in American society. Educated people who suspected that whites were smarter than blacks, or vice versa, kept it to themselves; the unspoken consensus was that television was reducing us all to morons at about the same rate anyway.

The common thread here is *class,* another issue that supposedly was put to rest in America two generations ago. The upper class, which no one expected to recover from its betrayal by Franklin Roosevelt, has risen again, but in a different form consisting of a self-perpetuating elite of managers, professionals and marginal hangers-on such as journalists and artists. Two influential new books—*The Next American Nation* by Michael Lind, and *The Revolt of the Elites* by the late Christopher Lasch—describe this group, which seems to include many of the same people who decade ago were semi-affectionately known as Yuppies. Lind goes out of his way to make the generally unacknowledged point that Americans have sorted themselves out partly on religious lines. He writes: "If you are Episcopalian or Jewish, have a graduate or professional degree from an expensive university . . . watch MacNeil Lehrer on PBS and are saving for a vacation in London or Paris, you are a card-carrying member of the white overclass . . . If you are Methodist, Baptist or Catholic, have a B.A. from a state university, work in or for a small business or for a career government service, watch the Nashville Network on cable and are saving for a vacation in Las Vegas . . . you are probably not a member of the white overclass, no matter how much money you make."

The creation of such a class must constitute a significant development. Obviously there have always been subcultures in America, and rich people were more likely to vacation in Europe than poor ones. But until fairly recently most "managers" and "professionals" probably thought of themselves as part of a broad middle class, together with civil servants and the owners of small businesses, with shared aspirations and tastes. Some people

Newsweek Poll

Has the American national character changed in the last 20 years?

Changed for the Better

Blacks	Whites	Hispanics
19%	12%	9%

Changed for the Worse

Blacks	Whites	Hispanics
41%	63%	51%

Stayed the Same

Blacks	Whites	Hispanics
34%	23%	32%

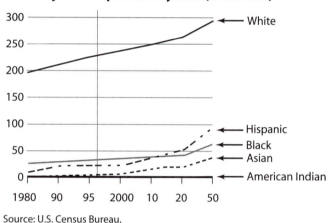

Projected Population by Race (in Millions)

Source: U.S. Census Bureau.

Income Distribution (Percent of Population, 1993)

Under $5,000	4.5%
$5,000–9,999	9.7%
$10,000–14,999	9.2%
$15,000–24,999	16.9%
$25,000–34,999	14.7%
$35,000–49,999	16.3%
$50,000–74,999	16.1%
$75,000–99,999	6.7%
$100,000 and over	5.8%

Source: Department of Commerce.

smoked and others didn't, but the choice didn't signify anything about one's social status, as it does today; in 1990 people earning between $10,000 and $20,000 were 50 percent more likely to smoke than those making $50,000 or more. In William Manchester's compendious history of mid-20th-century America, *The Glory and the Dream,* he reports a 1954 survey that found that the overwhelming choice of most Americans for dinner, cost no object, would be fruit cup, vegetable soup, steak, french fries and apple pie à la mode. What's interesting is not the absence of arugula from this menu, but the very assumption that a meaningful consensus could be arrived at. A comparable exercise today would undoubtedly result in what statisticians call a bipolar distribution, defined by the presence or absence of truffle oil as an ingredient. Conversely, the phrase "à la mode" can stand in for all the other tests by which Lind distinguishes the "white overclass"; it's virtually vanished from their vocabulary.

The larger point Lind and Lasch make is that white wine and aerobics aren't just neutral choices about lifestyles, but essential badges of privilege in contemporary America. And, according to these authors, the widespread suspicion on the part of middle- and working-class white American that the overclass condescends to them is absolutely correct. Having arranged society for their own convenience, the privileged class is now busily siphoning off an increasing share of the national wealth. They use it not to advance the general welfare, but to erect ever more barriers between them and the kind of people for whom "oil" brings to mind "Quaker State" rather than "extra-virgin olive." They "have made themselves independent not only of crumbling industrial cities but of public services [schools, transit, hospitals . . .] in general," Lasch wrote. "In effect, they have removed themselves from common life . . . Many of them have ceased to think of themselves as Americans in any important sense . . . Their ties to an international culture of work and leisure . . . make many of them deeply indifferent to the prospect of American national decline."

This is a pretty serious indictment. Americans of this class are presumably not about to express their disaffection by building bombs (and if they did, they would be more likely to blow up a Kentucky Fried Chicken or a Dairy Queen than a federal office building). But their alienation is in some ways even more dangerous. It's hard to imagine a real scenario in which the "Aryans" of the Northwest actually secede from the Union, but the investors of Wall Street and the screen-writers of Brentwood can secede just by getting on a plane. It would be ironical if America survived civil war, black separatism, white separatism, international terrorism and domestic terrorism only to become the first nation to fall victim to a revolt by its Yuppies.

Henri Cartier-Bresson, *Magnum:* I would have preferred a square with a question mark. Readers would have used their imagination.

For that matter, we can't really afford to lose anyone. For the social contract to work, it must bind us all, irrespective of skin color, native language, I.Q. or the percentage of fat in our diet. The forces of separatism are on the rise in many parts of the world, and it would be naive to think we are beyond their reach. Right now, before setting off for London, Paris or Las Vegas, would be a good time for all Americans to rededicate themselves to the proposition that we are all in this nation together. Or else Selena will have died in vain.

Form at end of book

Issue 12: What is American identity?

Is There a Common American Culture?

Robert N. Bellah

Robert N. Bellah is Elliott Professor of Sociology, Emeritus, at the University of California, Berkeley, CA 94720–1980

I might begin my talk this morning somewhat facetiously by asking the question, not whether there is a common American culture, but how is it that a plenary session of the American Academy of Religion is devoted to this question in a society with so powerful and monolithic a common culture as ours? The answer, however, is obvious: it has become part of the common culture to ask whether there is a common culture in America.

K. Anthony Appiah, Professor of Afro-American Studies and Philosophy at Harvard, in a review of Nathan Glazer's recent book *We Are All Multiculturalists Now* (whose very title makes the point) quotes the book as saying "The Nexis data base of major newspapers shows no reference to multiculturalism as late as 1988, a mere 33 items in 1989, and only after that a rapid rise—more than 100 items in 1990, more than 600 in 1991, almost 900 in 1992, 1200 in 1993, and 1500 in 1994 . . ." (7). Appiah adds, "When it comes to diversity it seems we all march to the beat of a single drummer" (32). There is something very congenial to multiculturalism in common American culture, but such congeniality is not to be assumed as natural or shared in all societies today. It is worth looking at the contrast case of France. Rodney Benson, a graduate student in my department, is writing a most interesting dissertation, which, among other things compares the fate of multiculturalism in France and the U.S. Benson describes a nascent French multiculturalism of the late 1970s and early 1980s as ultimately being rejected by virtually the entire ideological spectrum in favor of a universalistic republicanism in the late 1980s, just when multiculturalism in the U.S. was taking off. Why American culture has been so singularly receptive to multiculturalism as an ideology is a point to which I will return.

But, first, a sociological point about why there not only is but has to be a common culture in America: cul-ture does not float free from institutions. A powerful institutional order will carry a powerful common culture. An example of just how important this relation between culture and institutions is comes from the recent reunification of Germany. In the last days of the German Democratic Republic the protesters chanted "*Wir sind ein Volk,*" and the chant stirred euphoria among West Germans as well. But the painful and unexpected experience of living together, as made vivid to me by an outstanding Harvard doctoral dissertation filed earlier this year by Andreas Glaeser, using the integration of East and West German police officers into a unified police force in Berlin as a microcosm, showed that they were not, after all "*ein Volk,*" but indeed "*zwei.*" It wasn't just that the "*ossies*" and the "*Wessies*" ("Easterners" and "Westerners") had different views on common problems, they had different and to some degree mutually unintelligible ways of thinking about the world altogether. Forty-five years of radically different institutional orders had created two cultures which to this day are very far from united, although the experience of a unified institutional order will, almost certainly, though not without time and pain, ultimately re-unite them.

The United States, surely, has an exceptionally powerful institutional order. The state in America, even though it is multi-leveled and, to a degree, decentralized, has an enormous impact on all our lives. For example, the shift in marriage law in the late sixties and early seventies toward "no-fault divorce" was a response to but also an impetus for the emergence of "divorce culture" in America as a serious competitor to "marriage culture." The state is even responsible to a degree for the construction of multiculturalism through the little boxes that must be checked on a myriad of forms. Haven't you ever been tempted to check them all or to leave them all empty? If the state intrudes in our lives in a thousand ways, the market is even more intrusive. There is very little that Americans need that we can produce for ourselves any more. We are dependent on the market not only for goods but for many kinds of service. Our cultural understanding of the world is shaped every time we enter a supermarket or a mall. I taught a senior seminar of about twenty students this spring, roughly divided into one-fourth Asian-American, one-fourth Hispanic, one-fourth African-American, and one-forth Anglo. What was remarkable was how easily they talked because of how much they shared. Beyond the ever-present state and market, they shared the immediate experience of coping with a vast state university, with its demands and its incoherence.

Education, which is linked largely though not exclusively to the state, and television (and increasingly the Internet) linked to the market are enormously powerful purveyors of common culture, socializers not only of children but of all of us most of our lives. Not only are we exposed from infancy to a monoculture, we are exposed to it monolingually. The cultural power of American English is overwhelming, and no language, except under the most unusual circumstances, has ever been able to withstand it, which is what makes the English Only movement such a joke. As Appiah notes, 90 percent of California-born Hispanic children of immigrant parents have native fluency in English and in the next generation only 50 per cent of them still speak Spanish. One more generation and you can forget about Spanish. When third generation Asian-Americans come to college, they have to learn Chinese or Japanese in language classes just like anyone else—they don't bring those languages with them. Appiah contrasts our society with his own experience growing up in Ghana where there were three languages spoken in the household: English, Twi, and Navrongo. "Ghana," he writes, "with a population smaller than that of New York State, has several dozen languages in active daily use and no one language that is spoken at home—or even fluently understood—by a majority of the population" (31). Ghana is multilingual and therefore multicultural, in a way that we, except for first generation immigrants, have never been. When language, which is the heart of culture, goes, then so, in any deep sense, does cultural difference. I don't say identity, which is something I will come back to, but culture. Serious multicultural education would begin by teaching native English speakers a second language, but that, unlike most of the rest of the world, almost never happens in the United States. The half-hearted effort to teach Spanish in California public schools results in very few native English speakers with a secondary fluency in Spanish. Why don't most Americans speak another language? Because we don't have to—everyone in the world speaks English—or so we think. Tell me about multiculturalism. (The truth is that American culture and American English are putting their stamp on every other culture in the world today.)

There are exceptions, though they are statistically small, but I had better talk about them. Enclaves of genuine cultural difference, centered on a language different from English, can persist, or even emerge, under special conditions: where socio-economic status is low and residential segregation is effective. A particularly poignant example is the emergence among one of the oldest groups of English speakers in America, African-Americans, of enclaves of Black English dialects in a few inner cities in the northeastern U.S. that are mutually unintelligible with standard American English. This can happen under conditions of hyper-segregation where opportunities to participate in the larger society are almost completely denied. Native American languages survive on a few reservations, though many are dying out, even with strenuous efforts to maintain them. Since there is much less hypersegregation of Hispanics or Asians than of Blacks, enclaves of Spanish or Korean, or other Asian languages, have the generational transience of, say, Polish or Italian a hundred years ago.

If I am right, there is an enormously powerful common culture in America, and it is carried predominantly by the market and the state and by their agencies of socialization: television and education. What institutions might withstand that pressure and sustain genuine cultural difference? In simpler societies kinship and religious communities might do so, but in our society families and churches or synagogues are too colonized by the market and the state to provide much of a buffer. They may give a nuance, an inflection, to the common culture, but families and even religious communities are almost always too fragile to provide a radical alternative. Nevertheless, such nuances and inflections are important, not only in their own right, but because they can provide the wedge through which criticism of the common culture, and the possibility of altering it, can occur.

What, then, is the content of this common culture? If we realize that the market and the state in America are not and have never been antithetical, and that the state has had the primary function, for conservatives and liberals alike, of maximizing market opportunities, I believe I can safely borrow terminology from *Habits of the Heart* and say that a dominant element of the common culture is what we called utilitarian individualism. In terms of historical roots this orientation can be traced to a powerful Anglo-American utilitarian tradition going back at least as far as Hobbes and Locke, although it operates today quite autonomously, without any necessary reference to intellectual history. Utilitarian individualism has always been moderated by what we called expressive individualism, which has its roots in Anglo-American Romanticism, but which has picked up many influences along the way from European ethnic, African-American, Hispanic, and Asian influences. Here, too, the bland presentism of contemporary American culture obliterates its own history. Our Anglo students do not come to college with a deep knowledge of Jane Austen or Nathaniel Hawthorne any more than our Japanese-American students bring a knowledge of Lady Murasaki or Natsume Soseki. What they bring, they bring in common: Oprah Winfrey, ER, Seinfeld, Nike, Microsoft, the NBA and the NFL. If the common culture is predominantly Euro-American, or, more accurately, Anglo-American, in its roots, the enormous pressure of the market economy, and the mass media and mass education oriented to it, obliterate the genuine heritage of Anglo-American, European, African, and Asian culture with equal thoroughness.

And yet, and yet . . . nestled in the very core of utilitarian and expressive individualism is something very deep, very genuine, very old, very American, something we did not quite see or say in *Habits*. Here I come to something that will be of especial interest to this audience, for that core is religious. In *Habits* we quoted a famous passage in Toqueville's *Democracy in America*: "I think I can see the whole destiny of America contained in the first Puritan who landed on those shores" (279). Then we went on to name John Winthrop, following Tocqueville's own predilection, as the likeliest candidate for being that first Puritan. Now I am ready to admit, although regretfully, that we, and Tocqueville, were probably wrong. That first Puritan who contained our whole destiny might have been, as we also half intimated in *Habits,* Anne Hutchinson, but the stronger candidate, because we know so much more about him, is Roger Williams.

Roger Williams, banished from the Massachusetts Bay Colony by John Winthrop, founder of Providence and of the Rhode Island Colony, was, as everyone knows, a Baptist. The Baptists in seventeenth-century New England were a distinct minority, but they went on to become, together with other sectarian Protestants, a majority in American religious culture from the early nineteenth century. As Seymour Martin Lipset has recently pointed out, we are the only North Atlantic society whose predominant religious tradition is sectarian rather than an established church (1996:19–20; for a detailed contrast of the influence of church and sect religion in America, see Baltzell). I think this is something enormously important about our culture and that it has, believe it or not, a great deal to do with why our society is so hospitable to the ideology, if not the reality, of multiculturalism.

What was so important about the Baptists, and other sectarians such as the Quakers, was the absolute centrality of religious freedom, of the sacredness of individual conscience in matters of religious belief. We generally think of religious freedom as one of many kinds of freedom, many kinds of human rights, first voiced in the European Enlightenment, and echoing around the world ever since. But Georg Jellinek, Max Weber's friend, and, on these matters, his teacher, published a book in 1895 called *Die Erklärung der Menschen- und Bügerrechte.* translated into English in 1901 as *The Declaration of the Rights of Man and of Citizens,* which argued that the ultimate source of all modern notions of human rights is to be found in the radical sects of the Protestant Reformation, particularly the Quakers and Baptists. Of this development Weber writes, "Thus the consistent sect gives rise to an inalienable personal right of the governed as against any power, whether political, hierocratic or patriarchal. Such freedom of conscience may be the oldest Right of Man—as Jellinek has argued convincingly, at any rate it is the most basic Right of Man because it comprises all ethically conditioned action and guarantees freedom from compulsion, especially from the power of the state. In this sense the concept was an unknown to antiquity and the Middle Ages as it was to Rousseau . . ." Weber then goes on to say that the other Rights of Man were later joined to this basic right, "especially the right to pursue one's own economic interests, which includes the inviolability of individual property, the freedom of contract, and vocational choice" (1209). I will have to return to the link to economic freedom, but first I want to talk about the relation between the sectarian notion of the sacredness of conscience and what we mean by multiculturalism today, starting with the Baptist Roger Williams.

It is worth remembering that one of the sources of Williams's problems was his unhappiness with John Winthrop's assertion that the Massachusetts Bay Colonists were building "a city upon a hill," because, in Williams's view, it was *somebody else's hill!* The hill belonged to the native Americans, and if the other Puritans were inclined to overlook that, Roger Williams wasn't.

When Williams was banished from Massachusetts Bay in January of 1636, he probably would not have survived the winter in Rhode Island without the "courtesy" of the Indians, with whom he had, not surprisingly, an excellent relationship. Of this courtesy he wrote, in his charming doggerel:

The courteous pagan shall condemn
   Uncourteous Englishmen,
Who live like foxes, bears and wolves,
   Or lion in his den.

Let none sing blessings to their souls,
   For that they courteous are:
The wild barbarians with no more
   Than nature go so far.

If nature's sons both wild and tame
   Humane and courteous be,
How ill becomes it sons of God
   To want humanity. (Miller:61–62).

Williams would have nothing to do with the idea that Europeans were superior to Indians. He wrote, "Nature knows no difference between Europe and Americans [that is, Native Americans] in blood, birth, bodies, God having of one blood made all mankind (Acts 17) and all by nature being children of wrath (Ephesians 2)." (Miller:64) And he admonished his fellow Englishmen:

Boast not, proud English, of thy birth and blood,
  Thy brother Indian is by birth as good.
Of one blood God made him and thee and all,
  As wise, as fair, as strong, as personal.

By nature, wrath's his portion, thine no more,
  Till grace his soul and thine restore.
Make sure thy second birth, else thou shalt see
  Heaven ope to Indians wild, but shut to thee. (Miller:64)

We know that the passage of the Virginia act for religious freedom and of the First Amendment to the Constitution (and it was no accident, following Jellinek and Weber, that it was indeed the *First* Amendment), of which I will have more to say in a moment, depended on an alliance of enlightenment Deists like Jefferson and Madison, and sectarians, largely Baptists. The fundamental Baptist position on the sacredness of conscience relative to government action is brought out in a passage discovered by Lipset in *The First New Nation*. The idea must seem quaint to us today, but in 1810 Congress passed a law decreeing that mail should be delivered on Sundays. In 1830 a Senate committee reported negatively on a bill to abolish Sunday mail delivery. The report, written by Richard Johnson, a Kentucky senator and an active Baptist leader, argued that laws prohibiting the government from providing service on Sunday would be an injustice to irreligious people or non-Christians and would constitute a special favor to Christians. The report spelled out these principles:

The constitution regards the conscious of the Jew as sacred as that of the Christian, and gives no more authority to adopt a measure affecting the conscience of a solitary individual than that of a whole community . . . If Congress shall declare the first day of the week holy, it will not satisfy the Jew nor the Sabbatarian. It will dissatisfy both and, consequently, convert neither . . . It must be recollected that, in the earliest settlement of this country, the spirit of persecution, which drove the pilgrims from their native homes, was brought with them to their new habitations; and that some Christians were scourged and others put to death for no other crime than dissenting from the dogmas of their rulers . . .

If a solemn act of legislation shall in *one* point define the God or point out to the citizen one religious duty, it may with equal propriety define *every* part of divine revelation and enforce *every* religious obligation, even to the forms and ceremonies of worship, the endowment of the church, and the support of the clergy . . .

It is the duty of this government to affirm to *all*—to the Jew or Gentile, Pagan, or Christian—the protection and advantages of our benignant institutions on *Sunday*, as well as every day of the week. (Lipset 1963:164–165)

My fellow sociologist of religion, Phillip E. Hammond, has written a remarkable book, *With Liberty for All: Freedom of Religion in the United States,* which I have been privileged to see in manuscript, detailing the vicissitudes of this sectarian Protestant concern for the sacredness of the individual conscience as it got embodied in the First Amendment to the Constitution and has been given ever wider meaning by the judicial system, especially the Supreme Court, ever since. For Hammond, the key move was to extend the sacredness of conscience from religious belief to any seriously held conviction whatever. A key moment in this transformation was the Court's decision to extend the right of conscientious objection to military service to those whose beliefs were not in any traditional sense religious, but were fervently held nonetheless. Individual conviction and conscience have become the standards relative to which even long-established practices can be overturned. Hammond argues that *Roe v. Wade* is an example of the extension of this principle, and that its logic will ultimately lead to the legitimization of gay marriage. In the course of the extension of the sacredness of individual conscience from religion to the entire range of belief, Hammond argues, the sacred core of the *conscience collective,* the very sacred center of our society, what might even be called our civil religion, has moved from the churches to the judiciary. Whether we need to go that far with Hammond could be argued, but he has surely uncovered something very important about our society, something deeper than utilitarian or expressive individualism, the sacredness of the individual conscience, the individual person. And, I might add as an aside, here, in the city of San Francisco, where you can probably do almost anything within reason and still not raise an eyebrow, it is all ultimately thanks to the Baptists, even though some Baptists today find it rather upsetting!

It is with this background in mind that I think we can understand why multiculturalism as an ideology is so appealing to Americans today, but why the emphasis on culture is so misleading. A common culture does not mean that we are all the same. Common cultures are normally riven with argument, controversy, and conflict. Those who imagine that in *Habits of the Heart* we were arguing for homogeneous "communities" languishing in bland consensus could hardly have gotten us more wrong. Difference between communities (and we must also remember that there are differences within communities, starting with the family, which someone recently defined as "the place we go to fight"), even when the cultural differences between them are remarkably thin, such differences can give rise to significant differences in identity. Identity is not the same thing as culture, but it can be just as important. Remember Bosnia, where Serbs, Croats, and Muslims share a common language and probably 99 per cent of their culture, but where the memory of ancestral religion, in a highly secularized society, has led to murderous conflicts of quite recently constructed political identities.[1]

And yet in America the rise of identity politics on a local or a national scale probably signifies something else, something much closer to the core of our common culture. Again, Anthony Appiah has put it well:

But if we explore these moments of tension [between groups in contemporary America] we discover an interesting paradox. The growing salience of race and gender as social irritants, which may seem to reflect the call of collective identities, is a reflection, as much as anything else, of the individual's concern for dignity and respect. As our society slouches on toward a fuller realization of its ideal of social equality, everyone wants to be taken seriously—to be respected, not "dissed." Because on many occasions disrespect still flows from racism, sexism, and homophobia, we respond, in the name of all black people, all women, all gays, as the case may be . . . But the truth is that what mostly irritates us in these moments is that we, as individuals, feel diminished.

And the trouble with appeal to cultural difference is that it obscures rather than diminishes this situation. It is not black culture that the racist disdains, but blacks. There is no conflict of visions between black and white cultures that is the source of racial discord. No amount of knowledge of the architectural achievements of Nubia or Kush guarantees respect for African-Americans. No African American is entitled to greater concern because he is descended from a people who created jazz or produced Toni Morrison. Culture is not the problem, and it is not the solution. (35–36)

If the problem is disrespect for the dignity of the person, then the solution is to go back to that deepest core of our tradition, the sacredness of the conscience and person of every individual. And that is what a great deal of the ideology of multiculturalism is really saying: We are all different; we are all unique. Respect that.

But there is another problem, a very big problem, and its solution is hard to envision. Just when we are moving to an ever greater validation of the sacredness of the individual person, our capacity to imagine a social fabric that would hold individuals together is vanishing. This is in part because of the fact that the religious individualism that I have been describing is linked to an economic individualism which, ironically, knows nothing of the sacredness of the individual. Its only standard is money, and the only thing more sacred than money is more money. What economic individualism destroys, and what our kind of religious individualism cannot restore, is solidarity, a sense of being members of the same body. In most other North

Atlantic societies a tradition of an established church, however, secularized, provides some notion that we are in this thing together, that we need each other, that our precious and unique selves aren't going to make it all alone. That is a tradition singularly weak in our country, though Catholics and some high church Protestants have tried to provide it. The trouble is, as Chesterton put it, in America even the Catholics are Protestants. And we also lack a tradition of Social Democracy such as most European nations possess, not unrelated to the established church tradition, in which there is some notion of a government that bears responsibility for its people. But here it was not Washington and Hamilton who won but Jefferson and Madison, with their rabid hatred of the state, who carried the day.

Roger Williams was a moral genius but he was a sociological catastrophe. After he founded the First Baptist church, he left it for a smaller and purer one. That, too, he found inadequate, so he founded a church that consisted only of himself, his wife, and one other person. One wonders how he stood even those two. Since Williams ignored secular society, money took over in Rhode Island in a way that would not be true in Massachusetts or Connecticut for a long time. Rhode Island under Williams gives us an early and local example of what happens when the sacredness of the individual is not balanced by any sense of the whole or concern for the common good. In *Habits of the Heart* we spoke of the second languages that must complement our language of individualism if we are not to slip into total incoherence. I was not very optimistic then; I am even less so today. Almost the only time this society has ever gotten itself together has been in time of war, and I am sure that my understanding of America is deeply formed by experiencing the depression as a child and the Second World War as an adolescent. It is not easy to hear those second languages today, and some of those who are too young to have shared my experiences seem hardly able to recognize them even when they hear them. But the poignant reality is that, without a minimal degree of solidarity, the project of ever greater recognition of individual dignity will collapse in on itself. Under the ideological facade of individual freedom, the reality will be, is already becoming, a society in which wealth, ever more concentrated in a small minority, is the only access to real freedom. "The market" will determine the lives of everyone else. So, much as we owe the Baptists, and I would be the first to affirm it, we cannot look to them for a way out. All you have to do is look at the two Baptists in the White House to see that. And yes, I know Hillary is a Methodist—I meant Clinton and Gore.

But, if I can pull myself back from the abyss, which sometimes in my Jeremiah mood is almost the only thing I can see, I can describe even now resources and possibilities for a different outcome than the one toward which we seem to be heading. By the time we came to publish the 1996 edition of *Habits of the Heart* we realized that even the biblical and civic republican traditions, which we had called "second languages," had made their own contribution to the kind of individualism that we had largely blamed on utilitarianism and expressivism in the first edition. This does not mean, however, that the second languages haven't still much to teach us, even if what we have to learn from them must pass through the fires of self-criticism from within these traditions themselves. Our situation is curiously similar to that of post-Communist Eastern Europe in at least one respect. Vaclav Havel and others have opposed an effort to distinguish too sharply between the guilty and the innocent in the former Communist regimes, since it was the very nature of those regimes to draw almost everyone into some kind of complicity. The line between guilt and innocence ran through rather than between individuals, it was argued. I think of the banner in an East German church shortly after the fall of the Berlin wall which read: "We are Cain *and* Abel." With respect to our American individualism, even in its most destructive forms, it is useless to try to sort out the good guys from the bad guys. We are all complicit, yet change is never impossible.

Here I would like to return to the reference to nuances and inflections in our common culture that I made early in this essay. Recognizing that we are all, of whatever race and gender, tempted to exalt our own imperial egos above all else, we can still find those social contexts and those traditions of interpretation which can moderate that egoism and offer a different understanding of personal fulfillment. Every church and synagogue that reminds us that it is through love of God and neighbor that we will find ourselves helps to mitigate our isolation. Every time we engage in activities that help to feed the hungry, clothe the naked, give shelter to the homeless, we are becoming more connected to the world. Every time we act politically to keep the profit principle out of spheres where it ought not to set the norms of action we help to preserve what Jürgen Habermas calls the lifeworld (1987), and, incidentally, to prevent the market from destroying the moral foundations which make itself possible. It must be obvious from the example of recent history that without the legal and ethical culture of public morality a market economy turns into Mafia gangsterism. We will have more of what has come to be called "social capital" than many other nations, but it cannot be taken for granted. It survives only when we in our religious and civic groups work strenuously to conserve and increase it.

It is the special responsibility of those of us who are intellectuals to appropriate and develop our cultural resources, even while criticizing them. William Dean in his *The Religious Critic in American Culture* has given us a splendid example of the work that needs to be done. He draws heavily from the tradition of American Pragmatism, especially William James, and from contemporary thinkers as diverse as George Lindbeck and Cornel West, to argue for the necessity of conventions, and indeed sacred conventions, for a viable culture. He speaks of the "religious critic" as a public intellectual, situated not just in the university but in third sector institutions, including churches, working to criticize, but also to reclaim a viable myth of America.

Thus, I still believe that there are places in the churches, and other religious and civic organizations, and even nooks and crannies in the universities, to which we might look. But the hour is late and the problems mount. In this hour of need in our strange republic, it is up to us to teach the truth as we discern it.

Note

1. William Finnegan in a fascinating article (1997) describes the hunger for identity but the shallowness of cultural resources for it in Antelope Valley, a recently developed suburb of Los Angeles. For example, he mentions a girl named Mindy who became a Mormon but before that she had "wanted to become Jewish. But that had turned out to be too much work. Becoming a Mormon was relatively easy. All this was before Mindy got addicted to crystal methamphetamine and became a Nazi, in the ninth grade." (62–63). Finnegan's article concludes: "Martha Wengert, a sociologist at Antelope Valley College, said, 'This area has grown so fast that neighborhoods are not yet communities. Kids are left with this intense longing for identification.' Gangs, race nationalism, and all manner of 'beliefs' arise from this longing. I thought of Debbie Turner's inability to comprehend Mindy's enthusiasm for the likes of Charles Manson and Adolf Hitler. 'The Kids reach out to these historical figures,' Dr. Wengert said, 'But it's through TV, through comic books, through word-of-mouth. There are no books at home, no ideas, no sense of history" (78). These identities that lack any cultural depth are nonetheless powerful enough to be literally matters of life and death for the young people involved.

References

Appiah, K. Anthony. 1997. "The Multiculturalist Misunderstanding." *The New York Review of Books* 44/15, October 9: 30–36.

Baltzell, E. Digby. 1979. *Puritan Boston and Quaker Philadelphia.* New York: Free Press.

Bellah, Robert N., Richard Madsen, William M. Sullivan, Ann Swidler, and Steven M. Tipton. 1985. *Habits of the Heart: Individualism and Commitment in American Life.* Berkeley: University of California Press.

Benson, Rodney D. 1997. "Constructing and Dismantling a French 'Right to Difference': A Social Constructionist Re-interpretation." Paper presented at the Harvard University Conference on Politics and Identity Formation in Contemporary Europe. April 12, 1997.

Dean, William. 1994. *The Religious Critic in American Culture.* Albany, NY: State University of New York Press.

Finnegan, William. 1997. "The Unwanted." *The New Yorker* 73/37, December 1: 60–78.

Glaeser, Andreas. 1997. "Divided in Unity: The Hermeneutics of Self and Other in the Postunification Berlin Police." Doctoral Dissertation, Department of Sociology, Harvard University.

Glazer, Nathan. 1997. *We Are All Multiculturalists Now.* Cambridge, MA: Harvard University Press.

Habermas, Jürgen. 1987. *The Theory of Communicative Action.* Vol. II: *Lifeworld and System: A Critique of Functionalist Reason.* Boston: Beacon Press.

Hammond, Phillip E. 1998. *With Liberty for All: Freedom of Religion in the United States.* Louisville, KY: Westminster John Knox Press.

Jellinek, George. 1901. *The Declaration of the Rights of Man and of Citizens [Die Erklärung der Menschen- und Bürgerrechtel].* New York: Holt.

Lipset, Seymour Martin. 1963. *The First New Nation: The United States in Historical and Comparative Perspective.* New York: Basic Books.

———. 1996. *American Exceptionalism: A Double-Edged Sword.* New York: Norton.

Miller, Perry. 1953. *Roger Williams: His Contribution to the American Tradition.* Indianapolis: Bobbs-Merrill.

Tocqueville, Alexis de. 1969 [1835, 1840]. *Democracy in America.* Trans. By George Lawrence and ed., by J. P. Meyer. Garden City, NY: Doubleday.

Weber, Max. 1978[1921–1922]. *Economy and Society.* Ed. By Guenther Roth and Claus Wittich. Berkeley: University of California Press.

Form at end of book

WiseGuide Wrap-Up

Who am I? As children, we are sometimes asked to list the words that identify us. Do we list gender, age, occupation, religion, and family membership? Do we identify ourselves by the groups we belong to, or do we list personal attributes? Do we say: I am an honest person; I am a good person; I am a moral person. Do we identify ourselves by cultural or occupational appellations? Do we

say: I am a Navajo; I am a German-American; I am Asian/Chinese; I am a doctor, lawyer, teacher, butcher, baker. What do we mean when we answer, "I am an American"?

The question "Who am I?" has no right or wrong answers. What defines us as a society is not our uniformity but our consensus on the type of society we want to live in and our willingness to create that society. It is

a dynamic process that is not free of conflict. Diversity can be our strength and our weakness. Conformity is not necessarily the value that will enable us to endure as a society. Respect for the individual and a willingness to ensure a common good are how we will be able to provide real freedom to fulfill the promise of the Declaration of Independence and the Bill of Rights.

R.E.A.L. Sites

This list provides a print preview of typical **Coursewise** R.E.A.L. sites. (There are over 100 such sites at the **Courselinks**™ site.) The danger in printing URLs is that web sites can change overnight. As we went to press, these sites were functional using the URLs provided. If you come across one that isn't, please let us know via email to: webmaster@coursewise.com. Use your Passport to access the most current list of R.E.A.L. sites at the **Courselinks** site.

Site name: People for the American Way

URL: http://www.pfaw.org/

Why is it R.E.A.L.? People for the American Way is a nongovernmental organization that defines itself as a defender of American values. It is concerned with violations of basic American rights and supports public education. Its web site reports and comments on right-wing speakers in the media and identifies its activities and support for other such organizations.

Key terms: pluralism; individuality; freedom of thought, expression, and religion

Site name: Center for the American Founding

URL: http://www.founding.org/

Why is it R.E.A.L.? The Center for the American Founding is a nongovernmental organization that seeks support in restoring America's sense of direction regarding the rule of law and individual rights. It is an advocate for action, and invites involvement in its various activities. The organization's web site provides discussion of various issues relating to American identity.

Key terms: rule of law, individual rights

Index

Names and page numbers in **bold** type indicate authors and their articles; page numbers followed by *f* indicate figures; page numbers followed by *n* indicate numbered notes.

T

Tajima, Renee, 103
talent development in sports, 151
Tanton, John, 34
Tawney, R.H., 119–20
Tchen, John, 94
teaching, improvement of, 20, 172, 176–81
Teahouse of the August Moon (film), 97
teamwork and societal operation, 151
Tebet, David, 101
Technology Review, 173n
Tedeschi, J.T., 50
television, stereotype enhancement, 103
tension-reduction and humor, 54–55
Terman, Lewis, 26
test bias, evidence of, 127–28
testing, I.Q. (Intelligence Quotient), 115, 117–20, 121–24, 125–36, 137–38
Thirty Seconds over Tokyo (film), 97
Thomas, Wayne P., 20, 21–24
Thompson, G.G., 26
Thomson, Godfrey, 119
Thorpe, Jim, 156, 157, 158
three races, American perception of, 145–46
Thurstone, L. L., 119
Time/CNN poll, 3–4
Title I of Elementary and Secondary Education Act, 132–33
Title VII of Civil Rights Act (1964), 9, 10–11, 15, 16
tolerance, 72, 90
Toquerville, Alexis de, 190
Tora! Tora! Tora! (film), 97
Tower, John, 11, 12
transcontinental railroad contruction, 94
Treisman, U., 176, 177, 180, 181
Trotter, Monroe, 153
true answers *vs.* right answers, 172
TV Guide, 100
TV programs and series, Asian stereotypes, 96, 97, 98
Twentieth Century Fund, 10
two-way bilingual model, 22–23

U

U.C.L.A Law Review, 69
Umeki, Miyoshi, 95
underacheivement and bilingual education, 21–22
unemployment rate of Blacks *vs.* Whites, 3, 4f
UNESCO Courier, 140n
Unfinished Business (film), 103
unions, 12, 15
United Nations, Universal Declaration of Human Rights, 72–73, 74–76

United Nations: Human Rights (R.E.A.L. site), 90
United Steelworkers of America, 15
United Steelworkers v. Weber, 15
Universal Declaration of Human Rights, 72–73, 74–76, 77–82
University of California Medical School, 14–15
University of Texas Law School, *Hopwood v. State of Texas,* 8
University of Washington Law School, 14
U.S. Census Bureau, 137
U.S. Commission on Civil Rights, 100
U.S. Court of Appeals, Fifth Circuit, 13
U.S. Court of Appeals, Third Circuit, 14
U.S. Department of Commerce, 4
U.S. Department of Health, Education and Welfare (HEW), 14
U.S. Department of Justice, 62
U.S. Department of Labor, 3
U.S. Justice Department, 100
U.S. News & World Report, 98
U.S. Office of Personnel Management, 109
U.S. Supreme Court rulings
    abortion rights *vs.* Human Rights, 80
    anti-miscegenation laws, 101
    bilingual education policy, 28–29
    employment testing, 11–13
    hate crimes, 62–63, 67
    sterilization of feebleminded, 148

V

validity of *Bell Curve* research, 115
Van Dame, Jean-Claude, 100
Veltman, Calvin, 36
victimization and hate crime legislation, 64–65
Vienna Declaration (1993), 72, 77–81
Vietnam War, 107
Vygotsky, Lev, 123

W

Wake Island (film), 96
The Wall Street Journal, 8
Wang, Wayne, 103
Wards Cove v. Atonio, 16
Warner, "Pop," 156, 157, 171
Warren, Earl, 11
wars and Human Rights Declaration, 73, 85
Washington, Booker T., 153
Washington, Kenny, 155
WASP jokes, 56
Waters, Maxine, 99
Watson, James, 148
Wayans, Damon, 55
We Are All Multiculturalists Now (Glazer), 188

Weber, Brian, 15
Weber, Max, 190
Wechsler Intelligence Scale for Children, 124, 128, 130
Welbourne, Edward, 120
Welch, Gus, 158
West, Cornel, 158, 193
Western contributions to science and math, 172
What is History? (Carr), 103
Wheelock, Dennis, 156
White, Byron, 16
White, Theodore H., 100
White House Conference on Equal Employment Opportunity, 9–10
whites
    discrimination against, 2, 4, 7, 14–17
    I.Q. scores v. Asians, Blacks, 126–27
Who Killed Vincent Chen? (film), 103
Wilkins, Roger, 4–5
William Mitchell College of Law, 13
Williams, Clayton, 50
Williams, Raymond, 39
Williams, Roger, 190–91, 192
Willig, A., 28
Willis, Bill, 155
Wilson, Woodrow, 38
Winthrop, John, 190
Wirtz, Willard, 13
With Liberty for All: Freedom of Religion in the United States (Hammond), 191
women. *See* gender issues
Wong, Anna May, 95
Wong, Eugene Franklin, 96, 97
Wood, Thomas, 7
"world civilization," 141
World Conference on Human Rights (1993), 72, 77–81
The Worm of Suzie Wong (film), 96
Wyant, David, 61

X

xenophobia, 91, 94, 99

Y

Year of the Dragon (film), 96, 100
Yellow Peril, 94–95
"yellowfacing," 91–92, 100–101
Yost, Fielding, 154
Young, Roy, 154
Yuppies, 186

Z

Zaslavsky, Claudia, 174
Zucker, David and Jerry, 54

Frame the Debate
Review Form

Name _____ **Date** _____

Issue _____

1. Prior to reading about and discussing this issue, my personal beliefs were:

_____

_____

_____

_____

2. Describe the credentials and/or credibility of experts cited in each of the readings for this issue.

_____

_____

_____

_____

3. Summarize the main idea presented in each of the readings for this issue.

_____

_____

_____

_____

4. Summarize the facts that support each main idea.

_____

_____

_____

_____

5. Identify any opinions expressed.

_____

_____

_____

_____

_____

6. List any examples of bias or faulty reasoning.

_____

_____

_____

_____

_____

7. How does this issue correlate with material presented in class and/or in your textbook?

_____

_____

_____

_____

_____

8. Based on further consideration of this issue, my personal beliefs are now/still:

_____

_____

_____

_____

_____

COPY ME! Copy this form as needed. This form is also available at http://www.coursewise.com
Click on STAND!